THE ELECTORAL IMAGINATION

What happens when we vote? What are we counting when we count ballots? Who decides what an election should look like and what it should mean? And why do so many people believe that some or all elections are rigged? Moving between intellectual history, literary criticism, and political theory, *The Electoral Imagination* offers a critical account of the decisions before the decision, of the aesthetic and imaginative choices that inform and, in some cases, determine the nature and course of democratic elections. Drawing on original interpretations of George Eliot and Ralph Ellison, Lewis Carroll and Kenneth Arrow, Anthony Trollope and Arthur Koestler, Richard Nixon and Jean-Jacques Rousseau, the Palm Beach Butterfly Ballot and the Single Transferable Vote, *The Electoral Imagination* works both to understand the systems we use to move between the one and the many and to offer an alternative to the "myth of rigging."

KENT PUCKETT is the author of *Bad Form: Social Mistakes and the Nineteenth-Century Novel* (2008), *War Pictures: Cinema, Violence, and Style in Britain, 1939–1945* (2017), and *Narrative Theory: A Critical Introduction* (2016), winner of the 2018 Barbara Perkins and George Perkins Prize of the International Society for the Study of Narrative. His essays have appeared in *Critical Inquiry*, *Representations*, *MLQ*, *Novel*, *Victorian Literature and Culture*, *Public Books*, and other journals.

THE ELECTORAL IMAGINATION

Literature, Legitimacy, and Other Rigged Systems

KENT PUCKETT

University of California–Berkeley

CAMBRIDGE
UNIVERSITY PRESS

CAMBRIDGE
UNIVERSITY PRESS

University Printing House, Cambridge CB2 8BS, United Kingdom

One Liberty Plaza, 20th Floor, New York, NY 10006, USA

477 Williamstown Road, Port Melbourne, VIC 3207, Australia

314–321, 3rd Floor, Plot 3, Splendor Forum, Jasola District Centre, New Delhi – 110025, India

103 Penang Road, #05–06/07, Visioncrest Commercial, Singapore 238467

Cambridge University Press is part of the University of Cambridge.

It furthers the University's mission by disseminating knowledge in the pursuit of education, learning, and research at the highest international levels of excellence.

www.cambridge.org
Information on this title: www.cambridge.org/9781009206655
DOI: 10.1017/9781009206686

© Kent Puckett 2022

First published 2022

Printed in the United Kingdom by TJ Books Ltd, Padstow Cornwall

A catalogue record for this publication is available from the British Library.

Library of Congress Cataloging-in-Publication Data
NAMES: Puckett, Kent, author.
TITLE: The electoral imagination : literature, legitimacy, and other rigged systems / Kent Puckett.
DESCRIPTION: Cambridge, United Kingdom ; New York : Cambridge University Press, 2022. | Includes bibliographical references and index.
IDENTIFIERS: LCCN 2022007084 (print) | LCCN 2022007085 (ebook) | ISBN 9781009206655 (hardback) | ISBN 9781009206662 (paperback) | ISBN 9781009206686 (epub)
SUBJECTS: LCSH: Voting–Philosophy. | Elections–Philosophy. | Democracy–Philosophy. | Politics, Practical. | Literature–Philosophy.
CLASSIFICATION: LCC JF1001 .P83 2022 (print) | LCC JF1001 (ebook) | DDC 324.6–dc23/eng/2022-02-17
LC record available at https://lccn.loc.gov/2022007084
LC ebook record available at https://lccn.loc.gov/2022007085

ISBN 978-1-009-20665-5 Hardback

Our habit of treating the voice of a majority as equivalent to the voice of all is so deeply engrained that we hardly think it has a history.

—F. W. Maitland, *Township and Borough*

All my ideas hold together, but I cannot elaborate them all at once.

—Jean-Jacques Rousseau, *The Social Contract*

Contents

Acknowledgments

I began, although I did not finish, working on this book a long time ago. On the one hand, this meant I had to write through unexpected and unwelcome periods of political upset and uncertainty. When I started thinking about Lewis Carroll and voting more than a decade ago, the problems felt arcane, peculiar, and fun; after the helter-skelter, sideshow elections of 2016 and 2020 and after all the real violence and horror that came before, during, and after, those same problems felt a lot more urgent and more and more grim. I've tried to register that difference in the pages that follow. On the other hand, a long time writing meant that I have had a lot of time to ask for help. That was and is only a good thing. I'd like to thank friends and colleagues who read or heard or talked with me about some or all of *The Electoral Imagination*. As always, Ray Ryan did treble duty as a crack editor, a critical interlocutor, and an unabashed enthusiast. Without early invitations to speak or to publish from Rachel Ablow, Danny Hack, and Nancy Ruttenburg, the book would never have gotten off the ground. Katie Hobbs read one of the last drafts of the book, not only catching my many mistakes but also offering brilliant suggestions about what I could do to make my arguments better, stronger, more persuasive. As I was working on this book, I often felt something like the Ancient Mariner, fixing friends and colleagues with a "glittering eye," and going on and on about cyclical majorities and the independence of irrelevant alternatives. I am very grateful for the patience and, dare I say, the interest of Ayelet Ben-Yishai, Dan Blanton, Sanders Creasy, Eliot D'Silva, Emma Eisenberg, Imogen Forbes-Macphail, Catherine Gallagher, Josh Gang, Mehak Khan, Celeste Langan, Grace Lavery, D. A. Miller, Garreth O'Brien, Laura Ritland, Hilary Schor, Sydney To, Robin Varghese, Alex Woloch, and Rudi Yniguez. I am especially grateful to those who read some and, in a few heroic cases, read all of *The Electoral Imagination*. Uncountable thanks go to Nancy Armstrong, Sukanya Banerjee, Eric Bulson, Ian Duncan, Mark Dzula, Matt Garrett, Amanda

Jo Goldstein, Yoon Sun Lee, John Plotz, Scott Saul, and James Vernon. My parents, Kent Puckett and Franceen Puckett, remain my favorite political analysts. I've discussed and discussed every page of this book with Kara Wittman, my best critic and friend. The book is all the better for her skepticism, forbearance, attention, and care. At the start of the third grade, my son Harry had to make a list of things he wanted to learn or to learn about in the coming year. Below "playing guitar like Jimi Hendrix" and above "rocks and gems," he wrote "politics." I couldn't have been more proud.

Introduction
Rigging the System

> In elections the fiction of popular sovereignty makes its strongest
> approach to reality, as actual people ostensibly go about selecting
> from among themselves the few to whose government they consent.
> In many elections the ostensible comes close to the actual, the fiction
> momentarily approaches the fact, and our belief in the sovereignty of
> the people – or our willingness to suspend disbelief – is heightened.
> But not always.
>
> —Edmund Morgan, *Inventing the People*

> "Rigged system" – you've heard that word before.
>
> —Donald Trump, July 24, 2020

Anyone even indifferently tuned in to the political news of the last few
years will recognize that the term "rigged" – as in a rigged game, a rigged
election, or a rigged system – has been used and reused to the point of near
inanity. A cursory search of book titles, newspaper headlines, blog posts,
and political speeches turns up endless variations on the phrase: *Rigged:
America, Russia, and One Hundred Years of Covert Electoral Interference*;
The System: Who Rigged It How We Fix It; *Rigged: Unlearning Financial
Propaganda and Building Your Personal Fortune*; *Ball of Collusion: The Plot
to Rig and Destroy a Presidency*; "The Oscars Are Still Rigged in Favor of
Whites;" "Rigged Rates, Rigged Markets;" "*Survivor*'s Stacey Sues CBS:
Claims Show Was Rigged;" "Elizabeth Warren, Speaking to Black
Graduates, Warns 'the Rules Are Rigged';" "Rigging the System for
GOP Control;" "'Rigging the Game': Stacey Abrams Kicks Off
Campaign to Fight Voter Suppression;" "A Good Jobs Report Does Not
Mean a Rigged Jobs Report;" "Trump Goes All in on Rigging the System
to Advance White Rural Political Power;" "Texas Officials Have Already
Rigged the 2020 Election;" "Trump's 'Rigged Election' Talk Sparks Fear
of Post-Election Chaos;" "The Cynicism of 'Everything Is Rigged.'" In a
2019 *New York Times* op-ed appearing under that last title, the political
scientist Greg Weiner begins, "President Trump wants his supporters to

know that he is still draining the swamp over which he has presided for nearly three years. One of his Democratic rivals, Senator Elizabeth Warren, says Americans are trapped in a 'rigged system that props up the rich and powerful and kicks dirt on everyone else.'"[1] Catching at the increasingly catholic absurdity of the term, the satirist Andy Borowitz joked in the late summer of 2020 that "Trump said that eliminating November from the calendar was 'long overdue,' calling it 'a rigged month.'"[2] In each case, the term "rigged" suggests, however obscurely, that someone or something has interfered unfairly with the design, the functioning, or the outcomes of a system, institution, or event and, implicitly, that those institutions or events would or could have been legitimate if only someone or something hadn't gone and done that. In other words, the idea of the rigged system almost always implies and relies on – even if it can't really identify or describe – the promise, dream, or lie of an *unrigged* system, some prior and unsullied condition ruined by the meddling, intentional, and specific interference of some very bad actors.

I Know You Are, but What Am I

In part, the current ubiquity of "rigged" feels like another tired artifact of our degraded, oh-yeah-well-what-about-you moment, where deliberative engagement often gives way to someone answering serious allegations of corruption, incompetence, or racism simply by saying that someone else is corrupt, incompetent, or racist. Like the phrase "fake news," which (as if anyone can remember) began its life as a pointed criticism of the Trump campaign's misrepresentations before almost immediately becoming Trump's preferred cudgel, "rigged" appears everywhere today because it can be not only a real, if limited, term of historical or political analysis but also an absurd and even nihilist rejection of analysis as such. Indeed, one of the sobering discoveries of the last several years has been that one or another version of the idiot expression, "I know you are, but what am I," is apparently almost all that a successful, if morally grotesque, politician

[1] Greg Weiner, "The Shallow Cynicism of 'Everything Is Rigged,'" *The New York Times*, August 25, 2019, www.nytimes.com/2019/08/25/opinion/trump-warren-sanders-corruption.html.
[2] Andy Borowitz, "Trump Signs Executive Order Banning Month of November," *New Yorker*, July 31, 2020, www.newyorker.com/humor/borowitz-report/trump-signs-executive-order-banning-month-of-november.

requires.[3] "This isn't a new phenomenon," observes Philip Bump in *The Washington Post*: "When segregationist Alabama Gov. George Wallace was asked if he considered himself to be a racist during a 1968 interview, he offered a similar deflection. 'No sir, I don't regard myself as a racist,' Wallace said, 'and I think the biggest racists in the world are those who call other folks racist. I think the biggest bigots in the world are those who call other folks bigots.'"[4]

To recognize something as empty, idiotic, or puerile is not, however, necessarily to deny that it has power. On the contrary, what makes "I know you are, but what am I" both dumb and brutally efficient is the fact that, although it lacks all content, its palindromic form is a nearly perfect and thus perfectly seductive thing. Without saying anything at all, it breathlessly apes the beginning, middle, and end of real argumentation. A kind of Keatsian caricature, it is beautiful because stupid and stupid because beautiful; and, as poets, bosses, and bureaucrats like to remind us, that is sometimes "all ye need to know." One might think here of Roman Jakobson's famous analysis of the campaign slogan, "I like Ike," a phrase that tells you next to nothing about Dwight D. Eisenhower or his politics but, because "both cola of the trisyllabic formula 'I like / Ike' rhyme with each other, and the second of the two rhyming words is fully included in the first one (echo rhyme), /layk/ — /ayk/," it produces "a paronomastic image of a feeling which totally envelops its object."[5] The slogan's cradling stupidity doesn't, in other words, get in the way of its "poetic" efficacy; rather, because it is stupid, which is to say because it does not *refer*, its form stands almost totally free to do its comforting, juvenile work. Similarly, the cheap chiastic balance of "I know you are, but what am I" seems to bring thought – always hard – to a comfortable if unearned conclusion before

---

[3] "Inevitably, after Barack Obama called Trump a demagogue in a speech," recalls Eric Posner, "a commentator said no, it was Obama who was the demagogue." Eric A. Posner, *The Demagogue's Playbook: The Battle for American Democracy from the Founders to Trump* (New York: St. Martin's Publishing Group, 2020), 5. And, when asked about Michelle Obama's DNC observation that "he is clearly in over his head," Trump responded, "Well, she's in over her head!"

[4] Philip Bump, "Trump Embraces the 'Reverse Racism' Feared by His Supporters in a New 'Squad' Attack," *Washington Post*, July 22, 2019, www.washingtonpost.com/politics/2019/07/22/trump-embraces-reverse-racism-feared-by-his-supporters-new-squad-attack/.

[5] Roman Jakobson, "Linguistics and Poetics," in *Language in Literature*, eds. Krysyna Pomorska and Stephen Rudy (Cambridge, MA: Harvard University Press, 1987), 70. It is striking, by the way, that Jakobson begins his great essay, which appeared in print the same year Kennedy beat Nixon, with an oblique reference to the institutions and mechanisms that underwrite political decisions: "Fortunately, scholarly and political conferences have nothing in common. The success of a political convention depends on the general agreement of the majority or totality of its participants. The use of votes and vetoes, however, is alien to scholarly discussion … " (62).

thinking really begins. A travestied dialectic, the syntactical form of "I know you are, but what am I" pretends to take us away from and then bring us back to the "I" in a mode dimly reminiscent of what Geoffrey Hartman saw as essential to the structure of the Romantic lyric: "For the Romantic 'I' emerges nostalgically only when certainty and simplicity of self are lost. In a lyric poem it is clearly not the first-person form that moves us ... but rather the 'I' toward which that 'I' reaches."[6] Where, however, the lyric at least pretends to move from callow certainty to real understanding, "I know you are, but what am I" collapses "I" and "I" in order to celebrate callowness for its own sake.

The semantic poverty of the phrase, "I know you are, but what am I," is thus no impediment to its tested schoolyard power. Even when or, rather, precisely when an argument is empty, unfounded, or simply wrong, it can rely on its shape, its simplicity, and its form rather than on the risible content of its claim. Albert Hirschman's *The Rhetoric of Reaction* captures this productive mix of base political strategy and heady aesthetic pleasure when he writes about the "obvious relish" some reactionaries take when they argue that the policies of their progressive counterparts don't just fail but fail *perfectly* because they produce consequences that are not merely unintended but rather the topsy-turvy antithesis of what the progressive had wanted: "Here the failure of foresight of ordinary human actors is well-nigh total as their actions are shown to produce precisely the opposite of what was intended; the social scientists analyzing the perverse effect ... revel in it. Maistre naively said as much when he exclaimed in his gruesome chapter on the prevalence of war in human history: 'It is sweet [*doux*] to fathom the design of the Godhead in the midst of general cataclysm.'"[7] Richard Hofstadter relies on a similarly epicurean play

---

[6] Geoffrey Hartman, "Romanticism and Anti-Self-Consciousness," in *Romanticism and Consciousness: Essays in Criticism*, ed. Harold Bloom (New York: Norton, 1970), 52.

[7] Albert O. Hirschman, *The Rhetoric of Reaction: Perversity, Futility, Jeopardy* (Cambridge, MA: Harvard University Press, 1991), 36. One finds a beautiful version of Hirschman's argument at work in Dwight Macdonald's "Beat Me, Daddy," a 1945 response to James Burnham's curiously excited treatment of Stalin not only as a "great man" but also as socialism's inevitable and logical conclusion; paraphrasing Burnham, he writes, "Even if the 'revolutionary regime' had been able to spread to Germany in 1922–33 ... even this would have changed nothing. To state that the extension of communism in the early years of the Russian revolution to the most powerful and industrially advanced nation in Europe would not have altered the later course of that revolution 'except in lesser details' – here is an almost theological determinism. Revolutions *must* always turn into their opposite, regardless of any temporal, earthly or merely historical circumstances. Why must they? The only answer is that human nature is intrinsically evil. . . and the only ultimate basis for a concept of human nature as having innate and unchanging qualities apart from all historical and social conditioning is . . . the theological concept of Original Sin." Macdonald, "Beat Me, Daddy." *Partisan Review* 12(2) (Spring 1945), 186.

between politics and aesthetics when he writes in "The Paranoid Style in American Politics" that, "When I speak of the paranoid style [of the American right-wing], I use the term much as a historian of art might speak of the baroque or the mannerist style."[8] Although "I know you are, but what am I" is undeniably dumb, the cut-rate and yet nervy elegance of its style offers an aesthetic pleasure that might dispose one to choose what is lovely or lovable over what is right.

A Night in Which All Cows Are Black

I want to argue that there is something similarly at stake rhetorically, logically, and historically with the distinctively modern ubiquity of "rigged." Although the use of the term as a synonym for "manipulated or managed in a fraudulent or underhand manner" (*OED*) has its origins in world of Victorian stock-jobbing, it has come fully into its own only in the last decade or so. In the case of the phrase, "rigged election," a Google Ngram search shows that the phrase starts to climb in 1950 and then more or less follows an American or, rather, a Nixonian electoral schedule, peaking in 1968; it then burbles consistently along for a few decades until it hits a very sharp peak in 2016. The situation is even more striking with "rigged system," which, over most of this same period, is used consistently less than "rigged election" until it is – again in 2016 – suddenly and strikingly used all the more.

As a pervasive, amorphous, and thus emotionally satisfying feeling that "they" have stacked the deck against "us," rigging is, in its least defined but maybe most powerful sense, thus part of the longer history that Hofstadter identified in his great 1964 essay:

> The central image [of the paranoid style] is that of a vast and sinister conspiracy, a gigantic and yet subtle machinery of influence set in motion to undermine and destroy a way of life. One may object that there *are* conspiratorial acts in history, and there is nothing paranoid about taking note of them. This is true. . . . The distinguishing thing about the paranoid style is not that its exponents see conspiracies or plots here and there in history, but that they regard a "vast" or "gigantic" conspiracy as *the motive force* in historical events. History *is* a conspiracy.[9]

---

[8] Richard Hofstadter, *The Paranoid Style in American Politics* (New York: Knopf Doubleday, 2008), 4. Elsewhere he says: "A distorted style is, then, a possible signal that may alert us to a distorted judgment, just as in art an ugly style is a cue to fundamental defects of taste" (6).

[9] Hofstadter, *Paranoid Style*, 29.

The claim or belief or faith that the systems that govern our lives are *rigged* is powerful not just because it is sometimes concretely and sometimes disastrously true but because it is also an abstract, fluid, totalizing, and emotionally satisfying way to undermine the ideas, choices, or the very value of those with whom we disagree.

Lorraine Minnite argues in her book on *The Myth of Voter Fraud* that the long-running and largely groundless story (which is to say, the lie) of an American democracy threatened relentlessly by unscrupulous fraudsters

> sifts, rearranges, condenses, and omits our actual, complex, and heterogeneous experience, weaving the sweep of history into a simple tapestry of good and evil, the pure and the corrupt. ... And in so doing, it imposes order on some of the most fundamental contradictions of American democracy, a constitutional democracy forged through the conquest and genocide of native peoples, the contradictions of freedom and slavery sanctioned by the Constitution and chiseled into the tablets of U.S. law, and the contradictions of equality and a continuing disfiguring racism.[10]

Rigging works – both practically and rhetorically – because its vast, totalizing, willfully amorphous, and quasi-sacred narrative potential seems always to anticipate and thus always to undermine real differences between freedom and slavery, equality and inequality, winning and losing, and so on.[11] Rigging works because, if everything is rigged, nothing matters; and, if nothing matters, all is permitted.

This is why in 2016, when it still seemed likely that he would lose, Trump sought proleptically to muddy the waters:

> throughout the 2016 campaign, Trump insisted that millions of illegal immigrants and dead people on the voting rolls would be mobilized to vote for Clinton. For months, his campaign website declared "Help Me Stop Crooked Hillary from Rigging This Election!" In August, Trump told Sean Hannity, "We'd better be careful, because that election is going to be rigged ... "[12]

---

[10] Lorraine C. Minnite, *The Myth of Voter Fraud* (Ithaca, NY: Cornell University Press, 2010), 91.

[11] "It is nothing if not coherent – in fact, the paranoid mentality is far more coherent than the real world, since it leaves no room for mistakes, failures, or ambiguities." Hofstadter, *Paranoid Style*, 36. In a June 4, 2021, piece on the flurry of new and restrictive voting laws advanced by Republican state legislatures after the 2020 election, *The New York Times* referred with neat economy to "the standard phantasm of voter fraud," a figure that gets at the haunting and atmospheric power of rigging. Editorial Board, "Congress Needs to Defend Vote Counting, Not Just Vote Casting," *The New York Times*, June 4, 2021, www.nytimes.com/2021/06/04/opinion/voting-law-rights-congress .html?action=click&module=Opinion&pgtype=Homepage.

[12] Steven Levitsky and Daniel Ziblatt, *How Democracies Die* (New York: Crown, 2018), 61.

And this is also why, months before the 2020 election, Trump was again tweeting out, "RIGGED 2020 ELECTION... IT WILL BE THE SCANDAL OF OUR TIMES!"[13] A few weeks later, he made the same point again when, asked by Chris Wallace if he would accept the results of the 2020 election if he lost, he responded, "You don't know until you see. It depends. I think mail-in voting is going to rig the election. I really do. ... No, I'm not going to just say yes. I'm not going to say no, and I didn't last time either."[14] When CNN's Jake Tapper later confronted Mark Meadows, Trump's chief of staff, with the fact that there is "no widespread evidence of voter fraud," Meadows offered an idiotic undenial unworthy of the Mad Hatter: "There's no evidence that there's not either. That's the definition of fraud, Jake."[15] Winning is losing, yes is no, A is not A: "This," as Hegel says, "is cognition naively reduced to vacuity."[16] When one allows that a system and its rules might be rigged in this scattershot, paranoid sense, otherwise fundamental distinctions begin to lose all meaning. "Few things," writes Richard Hasen, "are more important to democratic legitimacy than the losers' acceptance of the results of elections, yet this new rhetoric shows that the country's faith in elections, which we have long taken for granted, may be fraying."[17] The rigged system: a "night in which all cows are black."[18]

---

[13] Donald J. Trump, quoted in Barton Gellman, "The Election That Could Break America," *The Atlantic*, November 2020, www.theatlantic.com/magazine/archive/2020/11/what-if-trump-refuses-concede/616424/.

[14] Of course, it turned out that Trump would not accept his election loss. Grasping at more and more farfetched theories and telling more and more outright lies, Trump and his followers filed dozens of obviously spurious lawsuits, bullied election officials, and worked to undermine democratic institutions at every turn. All of this, of course, culminated in the January 6th attack on the Capitol. Although the mob did a lot of things – it stole, defaced, and destroyed private and government property, attacked, wounded, and killed members of the Capitol police, built a gallows, waved Confederate flags, and called for the summary execution of the vice president – what's most pertinent, if not most spectacular, here is that it managed to delay (if not entirely to thwart) an event that is usually significant *only* for the symbolic legitimacy it lends to election results: the congressional counting of electoral votes. The attack was, in other words, an attack on rules *qua* rules; it was an attack on legitimacy as such. How successful that attack was or ultimately will be remains to be seen.

[15] Quoted in James Downie, "Even Trump's Most Die-Hard Minions Struggle to Defend Him Anymore," *Washington Post*, August 16, 2020, www.washingtonpost.com/opinions/2020/08/16/even-trumps-most-die-hard-minions-struggle-defend-him-anymore/.

[16] G. W. F. Hegel, *Hegel's Phenomenology of Spirit*, trans. A. V. Miller (Oxford: Oxford University Press, 1977), 9.

[17] Richard L. Hasen, *Election Meltdown: Dirty Tricks, Distrust, and the Threat to American Democracy* (New Haven, CT: Yale University Press, 2020), 10.

[18] Hegel, *Phenomenology of Spirit*, 9.

The Liar's Dividend

To call a system "rigged" can stand as a strategic expression of what Peter Sloterdijk famously termed "cynical reason": "It is the universally widespread way in which enlightened people see to it that they are not taken in for suckers. There even seems to be something healthy in this attitude, which, after all, the will to self-preservation generally supports."[19] To see or to claim to see that a system is or has been or will be rigged is, in one way, to refuse to be a jerk or a fool or a sap; in another and more corrosive way, it is to undermine confidence in systems to the point where they will lack the legitimacy and thus the authority to enforce their rules or, in the case of elections, their results.[20] "Like the fish rotting from the head," writes Pippa Norris, "any corrosion of public confidence in elections can gradually spread to weaken trust in the core representative intuitions of political parties, parliaments, and governments, to erode civic engagement and voting turnout, and to encourage losers to reject the fairness and legitimacy of the outcome."[21] Bobby Chesney and Danielle Citron have recently argued for the ways in which the spread of "deep fakes" and "fake news" has produced effects of "truth decay." Referring to this byproduct of lying (lies not only falsify matters on their own but also diminish the fragile standing of whatever other truths might remain) as a "liar's dividend," they write, "a skeptical public will be primed to doubt the authenticity of real audio and video evidence. This skepticism can be invoked just as well against authentic as against adulterated content."[22] This generalized skepticism, this liar's dividend, is, of course, especially powerful in politics, where it has become common to overlook an individual politician's

---

[19] Peter Sloterdijk, *Critique of Cynical Reason*, trans. Andreas Huyssen (Minneapolis, MN: University of Minnesota, 1987), 5.

[20] Months before the election, William A. Galston, chair of the Brookings Institution's Governance Studies Program, said: "What the president is doing is willfully and wantonly undermining confidence in the most basic democratic process we have. Words almost fail me – it's so deeply irresponsible. He's arousing his core supporters for a truly damaging crisis in the days and weeks after the November election." Quoted in Elise Viebeck and Robert Costa, "Trump's Assault on Election Integrity Forces Question: What Would Happen if He Refused to Accept A Loss?," *Washington Post*, July 22, 2020, www.washingtonpost.com/politics/trumps-assault-on-election-integrity-forces-question-what-would-happen-if-he-refused-to-accept-a-loss/2020/07/22/d2477150-caae-11ea-b0e3-d55bda07d66a_story.html.

[21] Pippa Norris, *Strengthening Electoral Integrity* (Cambridge: Cambridge University Press, 2017), 3–4.

[22] Bobby Chesney and Danielle Citron, "Deep Fakes: A Looming Challenge for Privacy, Democracy, and National Security," *California Law Review* 107(6) (December 2019), 1785.

unethical or criminal acts because, what did you expect, they're all crooks, right?

If this type of cynical reason is generally powerful in politics, its effect on the particular business of designing, holding, and settling elections is especially pronounced; this is, in part, because the logistical challenges that all elections face can foreground, heighten, and sometimes support broader attacks on the legitimacy of political systems. "Since," writes Jill Lepore, "the election of 2000, with its precariously hanging chad, many people worry that voting in America is a shambles and even a sham, that the machinery of our democracy is broken, crippled by confusing, illegible, and deceptive ballots."[23] Seeing elections either as in-and-of-themselves rigged or as local indices or expressions of what's rigged about the larger systems they support relies on and encourages a figural collapse of the particular and the general necessary to the larger logic of cynical reason. On the one hand, inevitable and usually accidental errors (what Hasen refers to as "pockets of electoral incompetence") can feed easily if irrationally into one's already half-baked sense that the whole thing is rigged, anyway.[24] On the other hand, if one has already accepted and even taken a perverse, jaded pleasure in knowing that everything's rigged and that nothing really matters, any individual act of rigging becomes what Freud might have called ego-syntonic proof of the existence of "a vast and sinister conspiracy" as opposed to a real, practical, and mitigable problem.

Myth Today

To put this in different terms, one might think of rigging in general and election rigging in particular as *myths* in the technical terms Roland Barthes laid out long ago in *Mythologies*. Writing in a midcentury style that steers a knowing course between structural analysis and *l'engagement à la Rive Gauche*, Barthes understood myth not simply as what is fake or false (as in the false consciousness of vulgar Marxism) but rather as a structurally distinct mode of signification that negotiates a relation between reality and fiction, between what I know to be true and what I want to believe,

---

[23] Jill Lepore, "Rock, Paper, Scissors: How We Used to Vote," *New Yorker*, October 6, 2008, www.newyorker.com/magazine/2008/10/13/rock-paper-scissors.

[24] "Pockets of incompetence in election administration have enabled both Democrats and Republicans to raise cries of rigged or stolen elections that appear increasingly credible to hardcore partisans. Even though most election administrators are doing an admirable and professional job, often under serious resource constraints, in close elections it is the weakest link among those who run elections that matters most. The problem happens with some frequency in large American cities, which are often controlled by Democrats." Hasen, *Election Meltdown*, 7.

between historical experience and ideological fantasy. Drawing on Saussure's fundamental understanding of the linguistic *sign* as the livewire play between a *signifier* or "sound pattern" and a *signified* or "concept," Barthes understands the myth as a mode of "second-order signification," where a historically embedded and thus richly meaningful sign (a both arbitrary and historically situated relation between a signified and a signifier) is repurposed and, as it were, emptied out in order to float an unhistorical, impoverished, and yet still-potent myth (a *motivated* – as opposed to an *arbitrary* – relation between a sign and the subsequent and specific ideological use to which that sign is put).

"It is time," as Barthes says in "Myth Today," his volume's densely methodological conclusion, "to give one or two examples":

> I shall borrow the first from an observation by Valéry. I am a pupil in the second form in a French *lycée*. I open my Latin grammar, and I read a sentence, borrowed from Aesop or Phaedrus: *quia ego nominor leo*. I stop and think. There is something ambiguous about this statement: on the one hand, the words in it do have a simple meaning: *because my name is lion*. And on the other hand, the sentence is evidently there in order to signify something else to me. Inasmuch as it is addressed to me, a pupil in the second form, it tells me clearly: I am a grammatical example meant to illustrate the rule about the agreement of the predicate. I am even forced to realize that the sentence in no way *signifies* its meaning to me, that it tries very little to tell me something about the lion and what sort of name he has; its true and fundamental signification is to impose itself on me as the presence of a certain agreement of the predicate. I conclude that I am faced with a particular, greater, semiological system, since it is co-extensive with the language: there is, indeed, a signifier, but this signifier is itself formed by a sum of signs, it is in itself a first semiological system (*my name is lion*). Thereafter, the formal pattern is correctly unfolded: there is a signified (*I am a grammatical example*) and there is a global signification, which is none other than the correlation of the signifier and the signified; for neither the naming of the lion nor the grammatical example are given separately.[25]

In this first, anodyne example, Barthes shows how a first-order *meaning*, which tells or could tell us something about one or another lion ("I am an animal, a lion, I live in a certain country, I have just been hunting, they would have me share my prey with a heifer, a cow and a goat," etc.) loses its "fullness," its "richness," and its "history" when it assumes the motivated, second-order *form* of a grammatical example, which says simply as it

---

[25] Roland Barthes, *Mythologies*, trans. Annette Lavers (New York: Farrar, Straus, and Giroux, 1972), 116.

expressly hails the student, "I am a grammatical example."[26] Barthes uses the term *meaning* to refer to the thick, historically situated, and "full" semiotic relation between signifier and signified. He uses the term *form* to refer to its thin, abstract, and "empty" – but nonetheless effective – second-order equivalent. Crucially, the move from first-order to second-order signification is not a matter of simple substitution or loss. It is, rather, a kind of sustained oscillation (Barthes compares it to a "constantly moving turnstile"), a motivated and mobile arrangement that preserves the richness of *meaning* in a "stunned," attenuated, and purely potential condition so that an otherwise wraithlike and ideological *form* can batten on the reality of that potential and invoke its historical presence as kind of "perpetual alibi." "The meaning," says Barthes, "will be for the form like an instantaneous reserve of history, a tamed richness, which it is possible to call and dismiss in a sort of rapid alternation: the form must constantly be able to be rooted again in the meaning and to get there what nature it needs for its nutriment; above all, it must be able to hide there."[27]

To think of rigging as myth in this Barthesian sense is not for a moment to doubt the reality or the meaning of election rigging as a historical phenomenon. It is not to doubt that a kind of rigging sometimes really happens: it does and, as I will show, looking back over the history of elections and thinking about elections in Britain, the USA, and elsewhere offers ample evidence of how rules can be written, bent, or broken in order to sustain or to add to the power of the powerful at the expense of everyone else; what's more, when elections have in fact been rigged, those rigging them have tended to invoke the largely phantasmatic threat of *other people* rigging them first as their reason for doing so: I know you are, but what am I? To understand rigging *as myth* is, instead, to notice how the particular and the general aspects – the form – of that myth (its suspended status as both manifest and latent, meaning and form, *langue* and *parole*) come together into an ideological whole greater than or at least different from the apparent sum of its parts. It is, in fact, to see how the *myth* of election rigging from below has been imaginatively deployed to authorize and to direct the *reality* of election rigging from above.

People Believe that People Don't Believe What They Say They Believe

Think, for example, of the repeated and unfounded claim that mail-in ballots lead to election rigging. At the level of meaning, the claim is risible:

[26] Barthes, *Mythologies*, 118.   [27] Barthes, *Mythologies*, 118.

one knows not only that mail-in ballots are not especially susceptible to manipulation, but also that they tend – when not manipulated – not even to benefit one or the other party. "There is," writes Amber Phillips, "no evidence of widespread fraud, in either regular voting or mail voting. It's true that in voting by mail, the ballot is filled out in private, which opens up more potential avenues of fraud. But there is not any evidence of routine or even statistically significant fraud in the five states that do all-mail elections, election experts say."[28] This failure at the level of *meaning*, at the level of the particular substantive allegation, does little to offset and may even contribute to the claim's undeniable success at the level of *form*: a Gallup poll released in May 2020 that half of "All Americans" and 76 percent of Republicans believed that there would be "more fraud if all voters cast their votes by mail."[29] Of course, unfounded claims that bad actors (often and absurdly hiding behind the antic unreality of cats, dogs, and the voting dead) were going to rig the election draws on a long and sustained American effort to disenfranchise voters – often Black voters – that reaches back from the dog-whistle race-baiting of Mark "Thor" Hearne, Karl Rove, Cleeta Mitchell, John Fund, and Hans von Sapkovsky all the way back to Jim Crow registration laws (poll taxes, literacy tests, understanding clauses, newfangled voter registration rules, and "good character" clauses) that sought to institutionalize racial discrimination as a grotesque solution to nonexistent problems: the "repeat voting, voter impersonation, and voting the graveyards" that those in power have long imagined as the inevitable result of any expanded franchise.[30] That is,

[28] Amber Phillips, "Examining the Arguments against Voting by Mail: Does It Really Lead to Fraud or Benefit Only Democrats?," *Washington Post*, May 20, 2020, www.washingtonpost.com/politics/2020/05/20/what-are-arguments-against-voting-by-mail/.

[29] Mohamed Younis, "Most Americans Favor Voting by Mail as Option in November," *Gallup*, May 12, 2020, https://news.gallup.com/poll/310586/americans-favor-voting-mail-option-november.aspx.

[30] Carol Anderson, *One Person, No Vote: How Voter Suppression Is Destroying Our Democracy* (New York: Bloomsbury, 2019), 3. In a "Statement of Concern" signed and circulated by dozens of prominent scholars of government and democracy on June 1, 2021, the history and the legacy of the myth of rigging had – unfortunately – to be evoked yet again: "Statutory changes in large key electoral battleground states are dangerously politicizing the process of electoral administration, with Republican-controlled legislatures giving themselves the power to override electoral outcomes on unproven allegations should Democrats win more votes. They are seeking to restrict access to the ballot, the most basic principle underlying the right of all adult American citizens to participate in our democracy. They are also putting in place criminal sentences and fines meant to intimidate and scare away poll workers and nonpartisan administrators. State legislatures have advanced initiatives that curtail voting methods now preferred by Democratic-leaning constituencies, such as early voting and mail voting. Republican lawmakers have openly talked about ensuring the 'purity' and 'quality' of the vote, echoing arguments widely used across the Jim Crow South as reasons for restricting the Black vote." "Statement of Concern: The Threats to American Democracy and the

even if people cannot prove or even really articulate what's wrong with mail-in ballots (which, of course, is because *there is nothing wrong with mail-in ballots*), they can undermine confidence in the use of mail-in ballots, confidence in elections in general and, more to the point, confidence in *some voters* in particular. "Today there was a big problem," Trump dog-whistled at the end of his first presidential debate with Joe Biden. "In Philadelphia they went in to watch. They're called poll watchers. A very safe, very nice thing. They were thrown out. They weren't allowed to watch. You know why? Because bad things happen in Philadelphia, bad things."[31] Just as the particular and false charge against mail-in ballots feeds the general sense that the system is rigged, the general sense that the system is rigged makes it easier to believe that those ballots – any ballots, but especially *those* ballots – could be or will be manipulated: "The meaning," says Barthes, "is always there to *present* the form; the form is always there to *outdistance* the meaning."[32]

To take another, maybe hazier example: in a recent Monmouth University poll, participants were asked, "Do you think there are so-called secret voters in your community who support Donald Trump but won't tell anyone about it, or not really?" It turned out that 57 percent of those polled "believe there are a number of so-called secret voters in their communities who support Trump but won't tell anyone about it."[33] On its own, the "secret voter" or the "hidden voter" isn't a myth. One can easily imagine real people who, in order to avoid conflict at work, shame at home, or awkward holidays visiting with the family, would say they weren't going to vote for someone when in fact they were: "'There are many people who are voting for Trump who are in environments where it's politically untenable to admit it because he's become so toxic,' said Whit Ayres, a Republican pollster."[34] (We should think of the "secret voter" phenomenon alongside its close conceptual cousins, the "Bradley effect" and the "shy Tory.") Since the 2020 election, the "secret voter"

Need for National Voting and Election Administration Standards," *New America*, June 1, 2021, www.newamerica.org/political-reform/statements/statement-of-concern/.

[31] Quoted in Ellie Rushing, Chris Brennan, and Jonathan Lai, "'Bad Things Happen in Philadelphia,' Trump Says at Debate, Renewing False Claim About Poll Watchers," *Philadelphia Inquirer*, September 29, 2020, www.inquirer.com/politics/election/trump-poll-watchers-philadelphia-early-voting-20200929.html.

[32] Barthes, *Mythologies*, 118.

[33] Monmouth University Polling Institute, "Biden Leads but Many Anticipate Secret Trump Vote," July 15, 2020, www.monmouth.edu/polling-institute/reports/monmouthpoll_pa_071520/.

[34] Jeremy W. Peters, "'Hidden' Trump Voters Exist. But How Much Impact Will They Have?," *The New York Times*, August 16, 2020, www.nytimes.com/2020/08/16/us/politics/trump-polls.html.

theory has been invoked alongside a number of other factors to account for the undercounting of Trump voters in polls leading up to the election itself.[35] That, however, is not exactly what the poll asked. Instead of asking whether one is a secret voter or whether one knows a secret voter (in which case, of course, the voter's secret would no longer be a secret), the poll asked whether the people polled doubted the results of other polls because they believed that *other* people were saying something other than what they believed.[36] On the one hand, this gets at a problem essential to the history of electoral theory – what to do with the possible difference between what a voter means or believes and what that voter says or does. I'll come back to the question of secret or strategic or sophisticated or bad-faith voters later. Lewis Carroll, for instance, saw addressing this potential difference as crucial to the design of sound voting procedures, a fact that contributed to his and others' support for the Ballot Act of 1872; William Morris lost faith in parliamentary politics when it was revealed that some socialist candidates were being floated as "spoilers" with the help of "Tory Gold"; and Richard Nixon's electoral success was partly built on his ability to identify or imagine or, in fact, invent a "silent majority" of putatively secret voters. On the other hand, the question is finally less about the real existence of secret voters than about our belief in the secrecy and thus the bad faith of other people. What, in other words, looks at first like a question about other voters, is really a question about *you*: what do *you* believe about the beliefs of others, and what, implicitly, does that belief say about *you*? Polls show that polls don't show anything. People say they believe that people don't believe what they say they believe. The system is rigged.

It is in these terms that the secret voter is a myth: A secret voter is potentially a real and particular person who will for some reason not say out loud what they really believe; the secret voter is also, as an ostensibly living proof of my own paradoxical belief about the meaninglessness of

---

[35] The myth of the secret or the "silent" voter is an old one, particularly in conservative circles: "The phrase," notes William Safire (who would know), "is most often used today by apologists for candidates who are far behind in the public opinion polls; workers for Goldwater in 1964 cheered themselves up with the assurance that an enormous 'silent vote' would appear on Election Day." Safire, *Safire's Political Dictionary* (New York: Random House, 1978), 651.

[36] "'The idea that people lie, it's an interesting theory, and it's not like it's completely off-the-wall,' said David Winston, a pollster who works with congressional Republicans. 'But it's obviously a very complicated thing to try to prove because what do you do? Ask them, "Are you lying?"'" Peters, "'Hidden' Trump Voters."

belief, a figure for a generalized or paranoid theory or feeling or explanatory fiction about how things *really* are. Claude Lefort refers to something
like the same forked structure of myth in his definition of the political:

> The political is thus revealed, not in what we call political activity, but in
> the double movement whereby the mode of institution of society appears
> and is obscured. It appears in the sense that the process whereby society is
> ordered and unified across its divisions becomes visible. It is obscured in the
> sense that the locus of politics (the locus in which parties compete and in
> which a general agency of power takes shape and is reproduced) becomes
> defined as particular, while the principle which generates the overall con-
> figuration is concealed.[37]

The secret voter is thus an embodied and real person *and* yet also a
phantasmatic or bad-faith argument for and against the kinds of beliefs
or intentions on which modern elections in general rely. It is in this
doubled sense that the secret voter is both meaning and form. The secret
voter is a myth.

The Rhetoric of Reaction

If the idea of so rhetorical or aesthetic or abstract a threat to representative
democracy seems arcane or willfully obtuse at a time of immediate and
pressing social crises, one should note that antidemocratic thinkers have
long relied on the rhetorical forms of generalized cynicism and, even more,
the imagined, almost perfectly paradoxical collapse of democracy into its
ostensible opposite – tyranny.[38] Putting aside the antidemocratic Plato,
one might think of Alexis de Tocqueville's early encounter with the
tyranny of the American majority:

> What I most reproach in democratic government, as it has been organized
> in the United States, is not, as many people in Europe claim, its weakness,
> but on the contrary, its irresistible force. And what is most repugnant to me
> in America is not the extreme freedom that reigns there, it is the lack of a
> guarantee against tyranny.[39]

---

[37] Claude Lefort, *Democracy and Political Theory* (Minneapolis, MN: University of Minnesota, 1988), 11.
[38] For a quick and useful digest of democratic skeptics, see the opening pages of Gerry Mackie's *Democracy Defended* (Cambridge: Cambridge University Press, 2003).
[39] Alexis de Tocqueville. *Democracy in America*, trans. Harvey C. Mansfield and Delba Winthrop (Chicago: University of Chicago Press, 2002), 241.

We might think, too, of Gustave Flaubert or Jacob Burckhardt declaring with equal parts reactionary aversion and aesthetic gusto that, thanks to the essential stupidity of "the people," universal suffrage was not only not a self-evident good but also *perfectly* equivalent to its apparent opposite. Flaubert to George Sand in 1869: "Every flag has been so drenched in blood and shit that it is time to do without them altogether. Down with words! No more symbols! No more fetishes! The great moral lesson of this reign will be to prove that universal suffrage is as stupid as divine right, though a little less odious."[40] Burckhardt said to a friend in 1845: "The word freedom sounds rich and beautiful, but no one should talk about it who has not seen and experienced slavery under the loud-mouthed masses, called the 'people,' seen it with his own eyes, and endured civil unrest ... I know too much history to expect anything from the despotism of the masses but a future tyranny, which will mean the end of history."[41] Displaying a similar faith in and, perhaps, love for the cleft structure of paradox, H. L. Mencken writes in his *Notes on Democracy* that, "Our laws are made, in the main, by men who have sold their honor for their jobs, and they are executed by men who put their jobs above justice and common sense. The occasional cynics leaven the mass. We are dependent for whatever good flows out of democracy upon men who do not believe in democracy."[42] And, later: "Whenever democracy, by an accident, produces a genuine statesman, he is found to be proceeding on the assumption that it [democracy] is not true."[43]

Mencken's younger contemporary, Walter Lippman, less an antidemocrat than a democratic skeptic, sees a necessary if not necessarily willing suspension of disbelief as essential to democratic processes:

> For when public opinion attempts to govern directly it is either a failure or a tyranny. It is not able to master the problem intellectually, nor to deal with it except by wholesale impact. The theory of democracy has not recognized this truth because it has identified the functioning of government with the will of the people. This is a fiction.[44]

---

[40] Gustave Flaubert, *Selected Letters*, trans. Geoffrey Wall (London: Penguin Classics, 1998), 339.

[41] Quoted in Hayden White, *Metahistory: The Historical Imagination in Nineteenth-Century Europe* (Baltimore: Johns Hopkins University Press, 2014), 235.

[42] H. L. Mencken, *Notes on Democracy* (New York: Dissident Books, 2008), 98.

[43] Mencken, *Notes on Democracy*, 100.

[44] Walter Lippman, *The Phantom Public* (New York: Transaction Publishers, 1993), 61. Robert A. Dahl makes a useful distinction between the "adversarial" and the "sympathetic" critics of democracy in *Democracy and Its Critics*. Where Flaubert and Burckhardt are undoubtedly adversaries, Lippman is, I think, skeptical but ultimately sympathetic. Dahl, *Democracy and Its Critics* (New Haven, CT: Yale University Press, 1989).

Lippman suggests here that the paradoxes of democracy and, more to the point, the paradoxes of representative democracy are tied up with what we have come also to understand as the paradoxes of fiction and fictionality; the relation between elections and what Catherine Gallagher and Stephen Greenblatt have identified as "the novel and other discourses of suspended disbelief" is both rich and deep.[45] Democratic elections rely, as the historian Edmund S. Morgan has shown in the related cases of England in the seventeenth century and America in the eighteenth, not only on fictions, on "propositions" that "were fictional, requiring suspension of disbelief, defying demonstration," but also on a conceptual milieu that includes and relies on analogous and intertwined modes of belief and disbelief that literary fiction did much both to embody and to refine.[46]

As opposed to taking seriously the vituperative intellectual *content* of these cynical attacks on "the people," I want rather to gesture toward their reliance on insistently elegant *forms* of aesthetic antithesis, paradox, and radical skepticism to produce a *feeling* of rightness, what the archconservative Maistre experienced as reaction's fundamental "sweetness." As Hirschman argues about reactionary rhetoric in general, the antidemocrat's delight in the shapeliness of "the famous Hubris-Nemesis sequence" contributes to "a certain elementary sophistication and paradoxical quality that carry conviction for those who are in search of instant insights and utter certainties."[47] This paradoxical delight is, appropriately enough, a close cousin to a pleasure that, according to Tocqueville, the jaded and secular historian of "democratic times" takes in the "blind fatality" of things: "It is not enough," he says, "for them to show how the facts have come about; they also take pleasure in making one see that it could not have happened otherwise."[48] I want to argue that the myth of rigging (as opposed, that is, to its undeniably real and local occurrences within particular contexts and its sometimes definitive influence on particular elections) can be seen as part of the longer and somewhat louche tradition of antidemocratic thought; and that, if one is to understand the fragility and the aspirational reality both of particular elections and of democracy in general, one needs to understand and criticize both the myth and the rhetoric of rigging (as well, frankly, as some myths of representative

---

[45] Gallagher, Catherine, and Stephen Greenblatt, *Practicing New Historicism* (Chicago: University of Chicago Press, 2001), 163–211.

[46] Edmund S. Morgan, *Inventing the People: The Rise of Popular Sovereignty in England and America* (New York: W. W. Norton, 1989), 15.

[47] Hirschman, *Rhetoric of Reaction*, 37, 43.   [48] de Tocqueville, *Democracy in America*, 472.

democracy itself). To see the reality of rigging behind the myth of rigging, we need to adopt the guise of what Barthes calls the *mythologist*.

To Speak Excessively about Reality

As opposed to the "producer of myths" (the politician, press secretary, the Svengali) or the "reader of myths" (the consumer, the voter, the believer, and – all too often – the sucker or the sap), the *mythologist* focuses on the "full signifier, in which [one can] clearly distinguish the meaning and the form, and consequently the distortion which the one imposes on the other."[49] Where the producer sets spinning and the consumer gets dizzily lost within the mystifying oscillation between historical reality and ideological fantasy, the mythologist "must voluntarily interrupt this turnstile of form and meaning" and "focus on each separately, and apply to myth a static method of deciphering."[50] If, that is, the interminable spin of myth turns "reality inside out" and empties "it of history," if, in other words, it blurs and thus conceals the historical particularity and thus the meaning of things behind or within a hectic relation to the seductive regularity of forms, the mythologist has to undo that false and mobile synthesis to give us at least a chance of appreciating what's real, historical, and urgent about a given situation. Of course, working to see critically past the apparently given surface of things, to refuse the agreeable lull of common sense, to counter mystification with interpretation has recently and somewhat inexplicably fallen into a mild kind of disciplinary disrepute. As opposed to seeing this kind of criticism as a pressing mode of intellectual or political resistance, it has been cast instead as a too-cool-for-school (and thus hopelessly uncool) "mood" that does more to satisfy the pride of the disaffected critic *manqué* than it does to reveal the nature of its ostensible objects. Whatever the fate of the postcritical mood, it doesn't, at least, have much to say about what Barthes acknowledges as the necessary and dear toll that critical work must take on the mythologist:

> The fact that we cannot manage to achieve more than an unstable grasp of reality doubtless gives the measure of our present alienation: we constantly drift between the object and its demystification, powerless to render its wholeness. For if we penetrate the object, we liberate it, but we destroy it; and if we acknowledge its full weight, we respect it, but we restore it to a state which is still mystified. It would seem that we are condemned for some time yet always to speak *excessively* about reality.[51]

[49] Barthes, *Mythologies*, 128.   [50] Barthes, *Mythologies*, 124.   [51] Barthes, *Mythologies*, 159.

The mythologist doesn't overcome illusion in order to master reality; the mythologist agrees rather to come off as kind of awkward, "a little stiff and painstaking" in order simply to say *more* about the world and its objects than the world often wants really to hear. "The truth," says Rousseau, "brings no man a fortune ... "[52] And why not? Because: whatever the critics of critique might say, the mythologist doesn't aim to reveal the one true thing hiding behind this or that symptom or surface; the mythologist has, rather, to speak "excessively" and to say *more and more* about the things, contexts, forms, feelings, and histories that both make and obscure the reality of our shared experience. Because myth works by reducing the immanent complexity of its concepts, the mythologist must say at least more than a little and, probably, a lot more than most would really like: "To parody a well-known saying," says Barthes at a well-known moment in *Mythologies*, "I shall say that a little formalism turns one away from History, but that a lot brings one back to it."[53] In what follows, I will often verge on saying *too much* about things: too much about people and their stories, too much about practices and their sometimes unexpected derivations, too much about procedures and the paradoxes they both generate and obscure. In doing so, I hope to defamiliarize some electoral forms and thus to make them freshly available to criticism as well as to historical analysis.

The Tacit Dimension

What, though, should the aspiring mythologist of rigging do? What would it mean to interrupt this "turnstile of form and meaning" when this turnstile turns so fundamentally on and around many deeply held beliefs about elections and their legitimacy, on the many ways those elections can be really flawed or intentionally undermined, and on their relation to both the high ideals and the nitty-gritty details of actually existing democracy? And how, in turn, might seeing that relation between fact and feeling allow for a franker and more productive, a more critical way of thinking about elections as they seem, are, and might someday be?

I am not a politician or a political scientist; I am a literary critic, and what I have to offer to this discussion might seem excessive, odd, or oblique. Because I come to these questions from, at best, a peripheral background and with a probably skewed sense of what's most interesting

---

[52] Jean-Jacques Rousseau, *The Social Contract*, trans. Maurice Cranston (London: Penguin, 1968), 72.
[53] Barthes, *Mythologies*, 112.

or important about the history and practice of modern voting, my methods and examples may sometimes seem, at best, eccentric and, at worst, irrelevant. Does it make sense, or is it perverse to organize a book ostensibly about the nuts, bolts, limits, potential, and formal paradoxes of electoral design around linked analyses of Lewis Carroll, Reinhold Niebuhr, and Richard Nixon; Ralph Ellison, George Eliot, and Kenneth Arrow; William Morris, Arthur Koestler, and Amartya Sen; Pippa Norris, Anthony Trollope, and *Robert's Rules of Order*? The immediate answer is *both*: It is somewhat perverse, *and* it makes perfect sense to approach this topic in these ample terms. My sense is that understanding the mix of practice and belief, aspiration and exhaustion, due diligence and pure imagination that underwrites modern voting demands both an openness to imaginative eccentricity and a complementary commitment to good analytic sense.

This is in part because, although they are an essential, apparently ordinary, and nearly ubiquitous aspect of modern life, elections tend nonetheless to proceed without our noticing or taking much stock of the conceptually significant rules, assumptions, and formal mechanisms that underwrite them. We don't notice, that is, until those rules go wrong. As Jon Elster argues, the analytic resistance of electoral rules is both a logical and a historical problem. It is a logical problem because of the existential status of the decisions we make when we make electoral rules; they are "second-order decisions – decisions about how to decide."[54] As a result, "the question raises the specter of an infinite regress . . . since it invites us to ask about the third-order decision by which the assembly adopts the second-order rule, and so on."[55] While democratic elections depend on the idea that *the people* are making the decisions, in order for the people to do that, someone else will have already had to lay claim to the constituent authority necessary to have made another, prior decision, a decision before and about the subsequent democratic decision – the decision that allows the people later to decide. As Rousseau puts it, "The law of majority-voting itself rests on an agreement, and implies that there has been on at least one occasion unanimity."[56] Because democracy depends on rules, and because those rules need to exist before democracy, those rules – or the rules before *those* rules – cannot themselves be democratic, which is to say they cannot be the result of any prior democratic process. "The paradox," writes Astra

---

[54] Jon Elster, *Securities Against Misrule: Juries, Assemblies, Elections* (Cambridge: Cambridge University Press, 2013), 21.
[55] Elster, *Securities*, 22.   [56] Rousseau, *Social Contract*, 59.

Taylor, "is that democracy appears to require, in advance, the very structures and sensibilities on which it needs to rely in order to emerge, persist, and thrive."[57] One might try to imagine a situation in which a group votes about the rules of a subsequent vote before that second vote occurs, but that will, as Elster acknowledges, beg the question of who gets to vote on the rules of the vote before the vote and how. At some point a functioning society will have to accept as an enabling fiction legitimate rules, practices, and procedures that cannot be the authentic result of some prior democratic decision: "It brings out the important conceptual point that the self-government of collective bodies may have an inevitable component of arbitrariness."[58] The political philosopher Charles Larmore associates this "inevitable component of arbitrariness" with what, after Bernard Williams, he calls "legitimation stories," the stories we tell ourselves when we can "see no better way available by which [a] common life can be secured."[59]

This logical problem, the legitimating disavowal of the arbitrary, violent, or fictive origin of the decisions that let us decide, can have complicated historical or, rather, historiographical results.[60] Although there is rarely a shortage of narrative or commentary or information about modern democratic elections, their rules and the conditions under which those rules were made tend—*unless there is a problem*—to fall into the category of what Michael Polanyi refers to as "tacit knowledge" or the "tacit dimension." At some level one must know without actively knowing that someone designed and produced this ballot or this voting booth or set this electoral schedule in this way as opposed to another, but unless something goes wrong or someone *says* something has gone wrong, one ignores or forgets that tacit knowledge in order to focus on the event of the election and that event's consequences; in Polanyi's terms, we *attend from* the rules and procedures that structure the election in order better to *attend to* the

---

[57] Astra Taylor, *Democracy May Not Exist but We'll Miss It When It's Gone* (New York: Henry Holt, 2019), 11.

[58] Elster, *Securities*, 23. I'll come back to this anxiety about the presence of an antidemocratic core, remainder, or paradox within democracy in Chapter 4.

[59] Charles Larmore, *What Is Political Philosophy?* (Princeton, NJ: Princeton University Press, 2020), 42.

[60] Andrew Reynolds, Ben Reilly, and Andrew Ellis, *Electoral System Design: The New International IDEA Handbook* (Stockholm: International Institute for Democracy and Electoral Assistance, 2005): "... while conscious design has become far more prevalent recently, traditionally it has been rare for electoral systems to be consciously and deliberately selected. Often the choice was essentially accidental, the result of an unusual combination of circumstances, of a passing trend, or of a quirk of history, with the impact of colonialism and the effects of influential neighbours often being especially strong" (1).

Figure I.1   "Who breaks a butterfly upon a wheel?"

election itself.[61] This is one reason why, despite the rich professional and popular literature on the history of votes and elections, writing about electoral rules, procedures, and theories tends to remain a specialist's endeavor.[62] If, however, something does go wrong, or if someone claims that something has gone wrong, what was tacit becomes suddenly and sometimes disastrously extant.

One need think only of Theresa Lepore's infamous Palm Beach Butterfly Ballot, the double-column design that was supposed to allow for larger print and thus greater legibility, but that in fact confused voters, leading many of them inadvertently to cast votes for Pat Buchanan instead of Al Gore (Figure I.1). It was partly because of that confusion that Palm Beach produced a measurable "overvote" for Buchanan, helping George W. Bush win the 2000 US Presidential election. What's more, over a period of weeks, Americans not only watched what was to have been a day's election play out in slow motion, but also learned more than they knew there was to know about the subtleties and the downstream effects of

---

[61] Michael Polanyi, *The Tacit Dimension* (Chicago: University of Chicago Press, 2009), 10.

[62] David M. Farrell begins his *Electoral Systems: A Comparative Introduction* with this teacher's lament: "For people who do not specialize in this area, electoral systems are usually seen as a big 'turn-off.' It can be difficult to instill much interest in the subject of counting rules; to enthuse about the details of how one electoral system varies from another. . . . Pity the student on a hot Friday afternoon who has to struggle through the niceties of the 'Droop quota.'" Farrell, *Electoral Systems* (London: Palgrave, 2011), 1.

good and bad ballot design. It was a moment at which the lived relation – the *gestalt* – between exception and rule, between figure and ground, between what we *attend from* and what we *attend to* shifted suddenly and with strange consequence. Onlookers not only learned something about elections, but also learned that there had been something there in the first place to learn; a submerged but real tacit knowledge became suddenly explicit, agonizing, and inescapable all at once. To use Bonnie Honig's evocative phrase, Florida 2000 was a moment when many were forced to confront the resistant and, in its way, mordantly funny "*political thingness*" of the otherwise ordinary ballot.[63] According to Richard Hasen, the 2000 Florida recount also initiated a historical shift in how politicians, parties, and voters *thought* about what counts as and in an election: "bad machinery, partisan hacks turning up on cable news, turf wars among election officials, dueling courts and judges, and spurious allegations of fraud – has its origins in Florida."[64] If Florida didn't make the rules and the meaning of the rules equally visible to everyone, it did render those rules differently and virulently available to hyperpartisan manipulation in government, the courts, and public opinion; it also made elections and the apparatuses that surround and support them differently available to the *imagination*.

It is, as I will argue throughout this book, no coincidence that this moment of realization or, rather, materialization, had not only a crassly political but also a curiously imaginative or aesthetic character. The sudden and somewhat absurd emergence of "hanging chads, pregnant chads, dimpled chads, tri-chads, swinging-door chads, and pierced chads" as both wholly trivial and yet also enormously significant was an oddly gritty expression of what Naomi Schor once saw as "the ongoing valorization of the detail" in critical theory. The many images of exhausted officials examining ballots with the assiduous attention of a Renaissance antiquary simultaneously evoked the dedication of the public servant, the sophistication of the connoisseur, and the ruthlessness of the political hack.[65]

---

[63] Bonnie Honig, *Public Things: Democracy in Disrepair* (New York: Fordham University Press, 2017), 30.
[64] Richard L. Hasen, *The Voting Wars: From Florida 2000 to the Next Election Meltdown* (New Haven, CT: Yale University Press, 2013), 5.
[65] Naomi Schor, *Reading in Detail: Aesthetics and the Feminine* (London: Routledge, 2006), xlii. In the spring of 2021, excessive attention to the materiality of the ballot made an absurd, racist, and frankly insane return as activists in the bogus Arizona recount subjected ballots to a slapdash "forensic" analysis in order find bamboo in some votes. Asserting, without any evidence, that the Chinese government had managed to smuggle 40,000 votes for Biden into Maricopa County, half-baked conspiracy theorists like Jovan Pulitzer claimed that the so-called "China Ballots" would wear

When officials looked at the chad, they saw it not only as the enigmatic index of an intention but also as the even less determinate index of an intention to intend: "you looked," said David Boies in his argument before the Supreme Court, "at the entire ballot...if you found something that was punched all the way through in many races, but just indented in one race, you didn't count that indentation, because you saw that the voter could punch it through when the voter wanted to. On the other hand, if you found a ballot that was indented all the way through, you counted that as the intent of the voter."[66] The chad was, in other words, the enigmatic index of an intent to indent, and indenting was, in its turn, the equally enigmatic effort to index *another* intent. David Estlund usefully distinguishes between votes understood as "desires, interests, and dispositions to choose" and votes understood as "desire *reports*, interest *reports*, and disposition-to-choose *reports*," a distinction that gets at all that was unreasonably expected from the humble chad.[67] Whatever it was, in the context of the 2000 recount, a chad was not just a chad; it was empirical if inexplicable proof of a voter's intention and thus also a material point at which things, ideas, individuals, groups, intentions, and desires came together to imply a weird theory of actually existing democracy. It is as if the chad, little on the outside and big on the inside, came imbued with the totemic power to revive as farce what Michel Foucault once saw as essential to the grammar of the classical episteme, "a meticulous observation of detail, and at the same time a political awareness of ... small things." In Palm Beach as well as in Napoleonic France, "Discipline is a political anatomy of detail."[68]

To make matters more complicated, and to move more firmly from the *form* to the *meaning* of the event, while observers were, both at the time and ever since, focused on the legal and material details of the recount,

---

their otherness all the way down: "China does not have the tree and lumber population we have because it got deforested primarily a long time ago. They use bamboo – and they do use wood pulps – they use bamboo in their paper and they use about 27 different mixes of grasses that we don't have here in the United States. And even though you can't look at it and see it, it's very detectable." Jeremy Stahl, "Arizona's Republican-Run Election Audit Is Now Looking for Bamboo-Laced 'China Ballots,'" *Slate*, May 5, 2021, https://slate.com/news-and-politics/2021/05/arizona-republican-audit-bamboo-ballots-china.html.

[66] Victoria Bassetti, "New Anxieties and Old Friends," in Alicia Yin Cheng, *This Is What Democracy Looked Like: A Visual History of the Printed Ballot* (New York: Princeton Architectural Press, 2020), 169; Hasen, *Voting Wars*, 13.

[67] David M. Estlund, "Democracy without Preference," *The Philosophical Review*, 99(3) (July 1990), 411.

[68] Michel Foucault, *Discipline and Punish: The Birth of the Prison* (New York: Vintage Books, 1995), 141, 139.

they tend mostly to ignore the fact that the chad *mattered* not only because it registered the paradox of the actor's strangled intention but also because it operated within the larger effort to disenfranchise Black and Latino voters. "Florida," writes Carol Anderson,

> was a festering election cesspool – as racially backward as it was bureaucratically inept. Secretary of State Katherine Harris had used faulty data to purge approximately twenty thousand names, mostly of Blacks and Hispanics, from the voter rolls. In polling stations in Jacksonville's Black neighborhoods, police officers stationed themselves conspicuously around the buildings and at entry points as if this were Mississippi in the 1950s all over again. In other cases, voters who knew they were registered learned on Election Day that their names were nowhere to be found on the registrar's list. Poll workers could not get in touch with election officials to do any kind of verification because the phone lines were jammed. There was a more effective method via laptop computers; however, those were placed in predominantly white, Republican precincts. There was also a limited number of working voting machines in polling stations that had sizable minority populations. In some areas, none of the machines tallied even one vote for a presidential candidate. Not one. And then there were the hanging chads.[69]

Understanding this as the ugly context in which the chads were so examined with such gratuitous and, as it turns out, such *distracting* care, one can see that the scene relied on the motivating and obfuscating overlap between three distinct but, in this case, mutually reliant senses of the term, "rigged."

The first, **rigged₁**, refers to real, mostly minor, sometimes intentional, sometimes unintentional, and sometimes half-intended screw-ups, accidents, and dirty tricks that call unwonted attention to the fragility and artificiality of elections; they are those mostly hapless and practically rare "pockets of electoral incompetence" that remind us of the necessary distance between our idea of elections and what real elections must inevitably be. The second, **rigged₂**, refers to rigging not as the odd, erratic, or hairbrained real *and* fictional failures of elections (hanging chads, misspelled names, or ballots ostensibly but never really sent to cats, dogs, and the dead) but rather as the systemic and often legal efforts on the part of those in power to tilt the scales in their favor. Here we need to think of the systematic disenfranchisement of voters of color, gerrymandering, unlimited campaign contributions, agenda-setting, and so on; again, as opposed to the stray and sometimes bathetic events or things associated

---

[69] Anderson, *One Person, No Vote*, 35–36.

with **rigged₁**, these entirely effective efforts to predetermine the results of putatively democratic elections are often legal if also wholly unjust. The third, **rigged₃**, refers to a big lie about elections that draws, albeit in bad faith, on the stuff of **rigged₁** for its evidence in order to give cover to the coordinated legal, quasilegal, and extralegal efforts associated with **rigged₂**; it is a myth that uses the real stuff of history in order to underwrite elections that work for only some of the people only some of the time. The hanging chad, as a material representative of a local, maybe faulty, maybe **rigged₁** election, was a problem *because* it "made sense" as a part of a prior and systematic effort to disenfranchise Black and Latino voters; and that longstanding effort to hold a really **rigged₂** election by suppressing and undercounting votes was, as similar efforts had been since the days of Jim Crow, dependent on creating rules that were themselves based on false claims about the threat of election fraud, claims that an election had been or would be **rigged₃**. The election seemed **rigged₁** because it was **rigged₂** because of people saying, without evidence, that it would be **rigged₃**. In a short piece touching on the long history of this big lie, Anderson writes, "Rampant voter fraud does not exist. There is no epidemic of illegal voting. But the lie is so mesmerizing, it takes off like a wildfire so that the irrational fear that someone might vote who shouldn't means that hundreds of thousands who should can't cast ballots . . . ."[70] Rigging isn't a myth because it is false; it is a myth because it is true *and* false, real *and* imaginary; it is meaning *and* form, history *and* ideology. And, it is because it is all these things that it has worked and continues to work so well.

To take an earlier, establishing case: Consider when, under the mounting economic and political pressures of 1789, Louis XVI reconvened the French Estates-General for the first time in nearly two centuries. Although Louis made this move to get ahead of a looming crisis, the effort led to practical problems of its own: "Because," writes John Dunn, "it had not

---

[70] Carol Anderson, "The Republican Approach to Voter Fraud: Lie," *The New York Times*, September 8, 2018, www.nytimes.com/2018/09/08/opinion/sunday/voter-fraud-lie-missouri .html. In a circular pattern that occurred again and again in the wake of the 2020 election, GOP state legislators across the country cast doubt on election results or entertained outright lies about elections in order to justify new restrictions on voting. The resulting "perpetual motion machine" is a distilled and insane expression of what I have called the "myth of rigging": "The bills," writes Maggie Astor, "demonstrate how disinformation can take on a life of its own, forming a feedback loop that shapes policy for years to come. When promoted with sufficient intensity, falsehoods – whether about election security or the coronavirus or other topics – can shape voters' attitudes toward policies, and lawmakers can cite those attitudes as the basis for major changes." Maggie Astor, "'A Perpetual Motion Machine': How Disinformation Drives Voting Laws," *The New York Times*, May 13, 2021, www.nytimes.com/2021/05/13/us/politics/ disinformation-voting-laws.html.

met for such an immense span of time, no one knew quite how to summon the Estates General, even once the decision had been taken; and no one could be certain quite how its members were to be selected, let alone what they would be commissioned to concede or demand. No one even knew what forms it would meet in once its members did duly assemble."[71] On the one hand, this was a logistical issue: "Throughout France, in the months from July onwards, busy archival research in one place after another probed into the question of how things had been done back in the distant days of 1614, with varying and confusing results."[72] On the other hand, the technical incoherence of the archival record was arguably an index of contradictions immanent and essential to both constitutive and legislative authority, the emergence of which gave intellectual momentum to the coming revolution: "How can it be imagined," asked the Abbé Sieyès in "What Is the Third Estate?," "that a constituted body can decide upon its constitution?"[73] An early anticipation of Elster's anxiety about "the specter of an infinite regress," Sieyès's question leads him to the crucial and, arguably, revolutionary point where real logistical issues and the political imaginary meet:

> It is time to go back to the title of this chapter: *What should have been done* amidst the confusion and disputes over the forthcoming Estates-General? Summon the Notables? No. Allow the Nation and its affairs to languish? No. Negotiate with interested parties to get them all to give some ground? No. There should have been recourse to the great means of an extraordinary representation. It is the Nation that should have been consulted.[74]

Forced by events to recognize that the idea of sovereignty relied on a legitimizing fiction, Sieyès argued that a specifically *representative* democracy both allowed and demanded one to understand the essential difference between constituent and constituted powers, and yet also to act *as if* that difference did not matter and, thus, *as if* the constituted authority of the state were an adequate representation of the legitimizing and constituent power of the people. As Morgan writes, "the impossibility of empirical demonstration is a necessary characteristic of political fictions."[75] This sense of a necessary settlement between practical politics and imaginative fiction may be one reason why Sieyès understood his larger project not

---

[71] John Dunn, *Democracy: A History* (New York: Atlantic Monthly Press, 2005), 99.

[72] Dunn, *Democracy*, 99.

[73] Emmanuel Joseph Sieyes, *Political Writings*, trans. Michael Sonenscher (Indianapolis, IN: Hackett, 2003), 138.

[74] Sieyes, *Political Writings*, 140.   [75] Morgan, *Inventing the People*, 59.

simply as a social science but rather as a "science of the social art." Although it might seem trivial when measured against subsequent events, the sudden and simple realization that political legitimacy relies on the prior existence of coherent rules and procedures, and that those rules and procedures had to be either unearthed or invented in order to secure a state's authority, was not only a practical effect of an immediate political crisis, but also a conceptual and historical cause that contributed in turn to the intellectual foundations of the French Revolution and, thus, to modern democratic procedure as a whole.

This is why I focus throughout on the origin, nature, and paradoxes of electoral procedure as opposed to elections in general. I've taken this approach for two related reasons. First, although they are often apparently minor, sometimes incoherent, or awkwardly ad hoc, the many procedures that precede and govern actually existing elections are enormously, if sometimes cryptically, powerful. Choosing between one ballot and another, one way to count votes and another, one presentation of candidates and another can determine not only how an election is won, but also who will *in fact* win that election. Second, because of this mix of apparent insignificance and real power, the history and character of electoral procedures have tended to elude close critical attention. Attending freshly to procedure is, I argue, necessary to any full understanding of the history, politics, and limits of democracy. Second, because electoral procedure exists at a middle and often tacit level of abstraction, it has been hard not only to tell its story but also to see that it even has a story to tell. In other words, because the history of elections has tended to focus on campaign crises and charismatic candidates, it has been harder to see that electoral procedure has any history at all. Attending to electoral procedure is, in that case, an effort to understand both the importance and the character of a relatively unacknowledged but hugely consequential aspect of the political imagination.

This is not, however, the same thing as *proceduralism*. I don't believe that procedure is somehow different or separate from or more important or autonomous than other aspects of social life. On the contrary, my larger effort throughout is to show how the apparent abstractions of ballot designs, voting schemes, and ranked choices are resolutely historical and, what's more, always complicit in the push and pull of conflict, power, and privilege. This was true in Britain in 1832 and 1867, Australia in 1856 and 1902, and the United States in 1865 and 1965. It has been true wherever and whenever elections are held. So, while I will need from time to time to make deep dives into the procedural arcana of electoral theory, I ask my reader to remember that I do it not for its own sake, but rather to make even the most abstract abstractions differently available to critical reckoning. What's more, if it can seem that proceduralism exists as a false and brittle alternative to the everyday vehemence of class conflict, sexual violence, and white supremacy, I want to argue instead for the *worldliness* of procedure, for its motivated and motivating place, as Bernard Williams puts it, in the rough scrum of things as they are "now and around here."

Elections and Other Discourses of Suspended Disbelief

In one sense, this is all to follow Edmund Morgan who offers in *Inventing the People* a detailed account of how the related hopes for popular representation in Britain and the United States rely not only on a number of discrete and more and less debatable fictions (about the divine right of kings, the voice of the people and the "People's Two Bodies," the essential nature and sources of liberty, etc.) but also on a wider and fundamentally modern commitment to what we now recognize as the logic of fictionality. In a chapter on the intellectual heavy lifting and conceptual tightrope walking that characterized political theory before and after the English Civil War, Morgan writes that:

> popular sovereignty, like divine right, had a life and logic of its own that made demands on those who used it. As a fiction it required the *willing* suspension of disbelief, which meant that perceived reality must not depart so far from the fiction to break the suspension. As the king must not behave in a way that would betray his claim to be God's lieutenant, a Parliament (or new-style king) must not become so isolated from the people as to render absurd the claim to speak for them. On the other hand, a fiction taken too literally could destroy the government it was intended to support. A government that surrendered to direct popular action would cease to govern. The fiction must approach the fact but never reach it.[76]

Although it was evident that there was necessary contradiction between the logistical need to appoint or to elect representatives to speak on our behalf and the urgent political fantasy that a people could or should simply speak for itself, the ideological composure of popular sovereignty required that one act *as if* there weren't a contradiction between those two positions even when one couldn't help but know exactly that.[77]

---

[76] Morgan, *Inventing the People*, 90–91.

[77] One is reminded of the astonishing moment when, during the Putney Debates over what a post-revolutionary English constitution ought to look like, Oliver Cromwell wondered aloud: "How do we know if, whilst we are disputing these things, another company of men shall not gather together,

Morgan's account of the logic of popular sovereignty relies on two senses of the fictional. First, he offers an argument about the nature of early modern political representation that resembles contemporary and later questions about mimesis and the intentional structure of aesthetic representations. As Robert Kaufman puts it in an essay on the relation between aura and "auratic distance" in Adorno and Benjamin, aesthetic mimesis can be understood as "a mode of thought-representation that does not in the first instance operate via conceptuality and argumentation but through an experience of affinity and difference."[78] Because mimesis serves both to nourish a representation's affinity with the represented object while also reminding us of its distance from that object, it acts as what Kaufman refers to as a "felt-as-necessary (but notoriously difficult to account for) 'bridge' between nature and freedom, cognition and morality, theoretical and practical reason, fact and value."[79] And so, although both aesthetic and political representations seem to promise an ultimate diminution of the distance between a thing or a people and a representation of a thing or a people, they must also *preserve* that distance both as a kind of security against perplexity and as a sustained occasion for what Sir Philip Sidney might have called a "profitable" – because always unfulfilled – desire. Indeed, not long before some seventeenth-century advocates for the power of the English Parliament would argue that direct democracy would result in what Hobbes cast as a state of mute and undifferentiated ungovernance, Sidney was arguing in similarly Aristotelian terms for the importance of distance between a fictional representation and its putative objects:

> What child is there, that coming to a play and seeing "Thebes" written in great letters upon an old door doth believe that it is Thebes? If then a man can arrive at that child's age to know that the poet's persons and doings are but pictures what should be and not stories what have been, they will never give the lie to things not affirmatively but allegorically and figuratively written; and therefore, as in history, looking for truth, they may go away full fraught with falsehood, so in poesy, looking but for fiction, they shall

and put out a paper as plausible perhaps as this? I do not know why it might not be done by that time you have agreed upon this, or got hands to it if that be the way. And not only another, but many of this kind. And if so, what do you think the consequence of that would be? Would it not be confusion? Would it not be utter confusion?" It is as if, under the conceptual pressure of making a constitution, Cromwell had to imagine *another* Cromwell making *another* constitution in order both to reckon with and to deny what was fictional about his own hugely audacious effort. *The Putney Debates*, ed. Philip Baker (London: Verso Books, 2007), 64.

[78] Robert Kaufman, "Aura, Still." *October,* 99(Winter 2002), 77.   [79] Kaufman, "Aura, Still," 76.

use the narration but as an imaginative ground-plot of a profitable invention.[80]

In both cases, mimetic distance is understood not as a fall from some earlier state of nature but rather as a pragmatic means of benefitting from an imaginative engagement with things as they could be while remaining nonetheless critically cognizant of things as they are; they are in both cases related but different "experiences of a provisional, enabling distance from the reigning concepts of presently existing society."[81]

The second and related aspect of literary fictionality at work in Morgan's account is a ductile play of belief and disbelief that defines both the production and the consumption of something like the classic realist novel. What seems most to strike Morgan about modern thinking about popular sovereignty is its Humean – which is to say its blithely and yet corrosively skeptical – character: "Nothing," writes Hume in a passage of which Morgan approves,

> appears more surprising to those who consider human affairs with a philosophical eye, than the easiness with which the many are governed by the few; and the implicit submission, with which men resign their own sentiments and passions to those of their rulers. When we enquire by what means this wonder is effected, we shall find, that, as Force is always on the side of the governed, the governors have nothing to support them but opinion. It is, therefore, on opinion only that government is founded; and this maxim extends to the most despotic and most military governments, as well as to the most free and most popular.[82]

Hume's sense of the light touch of opinion as opposed to the coercive push or pull of faith, his sense that kings and congressmen rely less on a people's falling for the real presence of an original contract and more on that people's willingness to act knowingly *as if* such a contract existed when they know that it doesn't, aligns both his and Morgan's attitudes toward modern political legitimacy with Gallagher and Greenblatt's account of that *other* discourse of suspended disbelief, the novel: "Novels may therefore be said to activate a fundamental practice of modern ideology – acquiescence without belief, crediting without credulousness – while significantly altering its disposition, transforming the usually guarded

---

[80] Sir Philip Sidney, *Sidney's "The Defence of Poesy" and Selected Renaissance Literary Criticism*, ed. Gavin Alexander (London: Penguin, 2004), 36.

[81] Kaufman, "Aura, Still," 66.

[82] David Hume, *Selected Essays*, ed. Stephen Copley and Andrew Edgar (Oxford: Oxford University Press, 1998), 24.

wariness into pleasurable expectations."[83] All of this is to say, simply
enough, that, alongside the historical relation between credit and novelistic
fiction as contemporary discourses of suspended disbelief, we might also
include the institutional discourse of modern representative democracy
and the periodic elections on which it relies. It is a political system that
relies on people acting (1) *as if* the majority is right simply because it is the
majority; (2) *as if* elected representatives really represent their interests; (3)
as if voters can know enough to decide on complex matters of governance;
and (4) *as if* one vote out of a million votes might be the decisive or even,
somehow, the last vote, a vote that would tip the scales. Democracy works,
and it only works – this is one of its foundational paradoxes – when
enough people participate and act *as if* they believe even when they do not
believe or, perhaps, when they believe just a little bit. Democracy requires –
and this is, perhaps, its hidden genius – that people believe enough and no
more than enough. If, in that case, one wants to better understand
elections as both historical and conceptual phenomena, one had also better
understand imaginative fiction.

Skepticism without Despair

All of which brings me back to the myth of rigging. I don't take myth here
as a simple illusion or trick or lie, as a bad idea that can be easily revealed
and then replaced with a better and truer idea; instead, I follow Barthes in
understanding myth as a "sustained oscillation" between the specificity and
historicity of first-order significations and the abstract, ideological force of
second-order significations (Barthes refers, you'll remember, to the former
as *meaning* and the latter as *form*). As we saw with the myths of the mail-in
ballot, the secret voter, and the hanging chad, rigging works as an especially potent expression of cynical reason because it holds us suspended
between the rich, if indeterminate, particularity of real events and the
abstract and corrosive appeal of an indiscriminate skepticism. As Omar
H. Ali says, "When Trump says the elections are rigged, there's actually
something to what he's saying, but not in the way he's talking about."[84] As
everyone knows (and as I will discuss), even ostensibly successful democratic elections have been routinely, sometimes illegally, and sometimes
legally undermined by more and less organized efforts to disenfranchise
voters on the basis of gender, class, ethnicity, religious belief, and – above

[83] Gallagher and Greenblatt, *Practicing New Historicism*, 169.
[84] Quoted in Taylor, *Democracy*, 60.

all in the US context – race. As Adam Przeworski recognizes, "Repression, intimidation, manipulation of rules, abuse of state apparatus, and fraud are standard instruments of electoral technology."[85] The question, as I began to detail in relation to the Florida recount (to which, like migratory birds, we will make a brief return), is how to demystify the general and politically motivated and morally enervating myth of rigging without denying the practical and often grotesque reality of rigging. How can one recognize both the urgent value and the susceptible fragility of democratic procedures, processes, and norms? How, against the nihilism of cynical reason, can one cultivate a vigilant, directed, and critical attention to the specific and complex reality of elections and the political systems they support? How can one cultivate what Amanda Anderson calls "commitment amid bleak conditions"?[86] How might one cultivate *skepticism without despair*?

To begin, I want to offer yet another and more properly dialectical definition of rigging, one that might escape the myth's sterile oscillation between meaning and form. Instead of understanding rigging simply as the underhanded manipulation of an already existing system, one should also consider the word in its earlier nautical sense, "to prepare or make," "to assemble and adjust." At the same time that rigging can refer to the intentional and usually treacherous corruption of an already existing system, so can it refer to an act of arranging or making, an act that implicitly connects the idea of a rigged system with what Gallagher and Greenblatt take as the novel's characteristically modern "readiness to disclose the open secret of its fictionality," which is in turn part of a "dominant nineteenth-century 'ideological' tendency toward epistemological flexibility." "We've argued," they write, "that . . . ideology has required a mode of supplementing disbelief with a willingness to enter into known illusions, a disposition to take obvious inventions of the human hand and brain for independently living entities under certain conditions and for certain purposes."[87] Although one needs often to act *as if* elections and the systems they support are given, natural, and "independently living," one also knows at one or another level that they are, in fact, made. Seen in the terms of this modern compromise, calling a system "rigged" need not stand as a disqualifying pejorative; it can rather serve as a neutral description that acknowledges that elections and the systems they support may look given, natural, or perfect when in fact they are the contingent products of

[85] Adam Przeworski, *Why Bother with Elections?* (New York: Wiley, 2018), 50.
[86] Amanda Anderson, *Bleak Liberalism* (Chicago: University of Chicago Press, 2016), 11.
[87] Gallagher and Greenblatt, *Practicing New Historicism*, 188.

"human hand and brain." Elections, says Przeworski, "are inextricably manipulated. 'Manipulated' because rules are promulgated by incumbent majorities in their own interest, but these rules are legally adopted and some rules must be adopted if elections are to be a determinate procedure."[88] It is with something like this in mind that, in an essay on the historicity of political philosophy, Bernard Williams writes,

> once the resultant picture of ethical thought without foundationalism is made historically and socially realistic, in particular by registering in it the categories of modernity, it provides a possibility of deploying some parts of it against others, and of reinterpreting what is ethically significant, so as to give a critique of existing institutions, conceptions, prejudices, and powers.[89]

Or, to paraphrase Marx: "Men rig their own history, but they do not rig it as they please."

The homonymic confusion between the tripartite myth of rigging I laid out above and rigging understood as the essentially *made* quality of any human system – the legitimacy of which is not externally guaranteed by divine right, natural law, or any other transcendental norm (what Max Weber calls "the validity of the ever-existing") – is not a category mistake but rather an error characteristic of certain rearguard tendencies within modernity.[90] If the unmystified, earthy, and realist contingency of rigging as an act of making is, for some, a source of anxiety, resentment, or fear, the threefold myth's founding assumption – that before there was rigging, there was a prior and then lost existence of a natural, unsullied, and *unrigged* system – can be illogically invoked in order to counter a real fact about history with a bogus and ideologically motivated legend of the fall. It is with something like this in mind that Williams writes,

> All that ethical nostalgia can generate from its own resources is, literally, reaction. Reactionary aspirations necessarily share the mythological aspects of the nostalgia; just as nostalgia looks back to an indeterminate or fictional place, so what it yearns for is an impossible journey. Unfortunately, this does not mean that there is no such thing as reactionary politics, or that reactionary thoughts leave everybody as stationary as they would be if they were sitting in something they imagined to be a time machine. What it does mean is that reactionary politics cannot be what it pretends to be, namely a

---

[88] Przeworski, *Why Bother,* 55.

[89] Bernard Williams, *In the Beginning Was the Deed: Realism and Moralism in Political Argument* (Princeton, NJ: Princeton University Press, 2009), 37.

[90] Max Weber, *Economy and Society,* trans. Keith Tribe (Cambridge, MA: Harvard University Press, 2019), 115.

practice which may indeed need to deploy coercive force, but only in order to turn the ship around. It proposes, rather, an ongoing ship the direction of which is concealed by a regime of coercive force.[91]

The idea that democratic elections, rules, and procedures are not and cannot be taken as natural or given can seem to lead to the reactionary's conviction that those elections, rules, and procedures should not be trusted even when they cannot be reasonably replaced with some other system. Uncertainty begets fear, and fear begets reaction.

I want to suggest something else, something closer to Przeworski's argument in favor of countering electoral despair not with a disavowal, but rather with a clear-eyed reckoning with the limits of politics, elections, and democracy:

> Politics in any form or fashion has limits in shaping and transforming societies. This is just a fact of life. I believe that it is important to know these limits, so as not to criticize elections for not achieving what no political arrangements can achieve. But this is not a call for complacency. Recognizing limits serves to direct our efforts toward these limits, elucidates directions for reforms that are feasible. Although I am far from certain to have correctly identified what the limits are and although I realize that many reforms are not undertaken because they threaten interests, I believe that knowing both the limits and the possibilities is a useful guide to political action.[92]

I'll have more to say about the details of Przeworski's arguments later. For now I want to recognize his analytic focus on the *limits* of elections as an invitation to think about elections and our indistinct, anxious, aspirational, right *and* wrong sense that they might be rigged; I want to take rigging as a myth that conceals while appearing to reshape and to reveal a set of immanent contradictions that, in turn, condition our expectations for and our experience of democratic elections. I understand limits here in both practical and analytic senses. Elections are *practically* limited both because they can never be perfect, can never anticipate nor overcome the problems that will inevitably bedevil them, and because even successful elections can only do so much to represent the distress, needs, and experiences of real people. Elections are *analytically* limited because attending closely to them and their attendant procedures requires that we attend *from* other kinds of experience, levels of social abstraction or mediation that would precede or supersede the election and its rules. I hope to remain cognizant of both kinds of limit throughout this volume. Approaching

---

[91] Williams, *Realism and Moralism*, 43–44. [92] Przeworski, *Why Bother*, 5.

electoral logics from the perspective of the mythologist is thus not a simple matter of discrediting ideals or losing illusions; it is rather a mode of reckoning with a necessarily incomplete form of thought and thus a necessarily unfinished form of society upon which the theory and practice of modern democracy depends.

"I can," wrote Walt Whitman, "conceive of no better service … by democrats of thorough and heart-felt faith, than boldly exposing the weakness, liabilities, and infinite corruptions of democracy."[93] The more downbeat Joseph Schumpeter put it in starker, more skeptical and less savory terms: "For it has nothing to do with the fervor or dignity of democratic conviction in any given situation. To realize the relative validity of one's convictions and yet stand for them unflinchingly is what distinguishes a civilized man from a barbarian."[94] Or, take Reinhold Neibuhr, writing in the immediate wake of the World War II: "But in this latter day, when it has become important to save what is valuable in democratic life from the destruction of what is false in bourgeois civiliza-tion, it has also become necessary to distinguish what is false in democratic theory from what is true in democratic life."[95] More recently, Jeffrey Edward Green has written that

> what is needed, and what in large part has yet to be attempted, is … a democratic theory that can maneuver between the twin pitfalls of relying on perfect ideals (like undominated discourse, pluralist equilibrium, or one-person-one-vote) that mask the way disappointment has become a part of the phenomenology of democratic experience and, from the other side, becoming so committed to exposing dysfunction within today's democratic systems that all ideals, and with them all political hope, are seen as illusory.[96]

Looking, however, for the political *real* of elections and election-rigging cannot be the end of this project; to imagine a democratic skepticism without despair, it can be only a beginning.

---

[93] Walt Whitman, *Democratic Vistas and Other Papers* (London: Walter Scott, 1888), 162.
[94] Joseph A. Schumpeter, *Capitalism, Socialism, and Democracy* (New York: Harper Perennial, 2008), 243.
[95] Reinhold Niebuhr, *Major Works on Religion and Politics* (New York: Library of America, 2015), 512.
[96] Jeffrey Edward Green, *The Eyes of the People: Democracy in an Age of Spectatorship* (Oxford: Oxford University Press, 2009), 6–7.

CHAPTER I

Seeing Aspects
Considering Some Kinds of Electoral Realism

The question now arises: could there be human beings lacking in the capacity to see something *as something* – and what would that be like? What sort of consequences would it have? – Would this defect be comparable to colour-blindness or to not having absolute pitch? – We will call it "aspect-blindness"– and will next consider what might be meant by this. (A conceptual investigation.)
—Ludwig Wittgenstein, *Philosophical Investigations*

I want now to look at three ways to think past, against, and sometimes with the myth of rigging and thus toward both the political possibilities and limits of actually existing democracy. And, in thinking toward and hopefully past those limits, I want also to think about the relation between democracy understood as a set of real and sometimes incommensurate historical facts and democracy understood as a set of variously wrought and deployed conceptual forms – forms that must, after all, limit and shape what will seem real to us about our political lives. Insofar as democracy exists not only in its practical instantiations but also within the imaginative frames or ideological horizons on which it at different moments depends (and which it, in turn, helps to shape), thinking about democracy also means thinking *about thinking*, which is to say, thinking about all the ways in which we think and struggle to think about the meaning of lives lived with other people while also living exactly the lives we're thinking about. The need to *think* about the possibilities and limits of a system while dwelling within that same system makes any serious effort to understand democracy also a *critical* effort; and, at a moment when most societies identify themselves as democratic even – or even especially – when they are *not* democratic, the effort to identify a standpoint from whence we might perceive, understand, and perhaps think beyond our conceptual limits – to think otherwise about our democratic norms and expectations – is important.[1]

One needs, in other words, to imagine some real or imaginary standpoint from which to perceive and thus to get at a problem. "The Here and Now," says Ernst Bloch, "lacks the distance which does indeed alienate us, but makes things distinct and surveyable."[2] You can't see your microscope with your microscope; or, if you want to get a good look at your eyes, you need something more or other than your eyes. Georg Lukács considers just this question in *History and Class Consciousness*. Given that both the bourgeoisie and the proletariat exist *within* the totality that is capitalist or bourgeois modernity, they can neither see nor understand the meaning of or their position in that world: "To judge or even investigate the validity of these values is not possible *within that* framework . . . ."[3] As a result, meaningful qualities of that world will seem meaningless, chaotic, or irrational. For Lukács (like Hegel and Marx before him), the goal of historical, political, and critical inquiry is thus to make one's way from the incomprehensible immediacy of life in history toward an understanding or view of things that is at once more concrete, more particular, more real, and yet also capable of grasping the historical world conceptually as a whole:

> If change is to be understood at all it is necessary to abandon the view that objects are rigidly opposed to each other, it is necessary to elevate their interrelatedness and the interaction between these "relations" and the "objects" to the same plane of reality. The greater the distance from pure immediacy the larger the net encompassing the "relations," and the more complete the integration of the "objects" within the system of relations, the sooner change will cease to be impenetrable and catastrophic, the sooner it will become comprehensible.[4]

Readers of Lukács's great essay will remember that his solution to the problem of "irrationality" and its resistance to understanding was the

---

[1] Antidemocratic politicians tend to like the word democracy, suggests Joseph Schumpeter, because they "appreciate a phraseology that flatters the masses and offers an excellent opportunity not only for evading responsibility but also for crushing opponents in the name of the people." Schumpeter, *Capitalism, Socialism, and Democracy* (New York: Harper Perennial, 2008), 268.

[2] Ernst Bloch, *The Principle of Hope*, trans. Neville Plaice, Stephen Plaice, and Paul Knight (Cambridge: Massachusetts Institute of Technology Press, 1986), 180.

[3] Georg Lukács, *History and Class Consciousness: Studies in Marxist Dialectics* (Cambridge: Massachusetts Institute of Technology Press, 1972), 151.

[4] Lukács, *History and Class Consciousness*, 154.

proletariat's emergence into an aspirational and revolutionary consciousness:

> It is the proletariat that embodies this process of consciousness. Since its consciousness appears as the immanent product of the historical dialectic, it likewise appears to be dialectical. That is to say, this consciousness is nothing but the expression of historical necessity. The proletariat "has no ideals to realize."[5]

Lukács's claim here is that, although no one can see the whole of a world from within that same world, the perfectly antithetical because perfectly oppositional nature of the proletariat's structural relation to bourgeois capitalism means that, even if the proletariat can't see everything, what it *can* see will really count. The proletariat thus occupies a unique standpoint in relation to the class struggle, to the history of the class struggle, and thus – for both Marx and Lukács – to the significant reality of history itself. The proletariat's seeing is thus a process of seeing what's real and, as a result, the proletariat can realize the ends not only of the class struggle but also of a representational imperative – an aspiration toward totality – that Lukács, writing later and again as a literary critic, will associate with the classic realist novel. As a result of claiming the lived standpoint of an authentic and dialectical realism, the proletariat will at last see things as they are and reshape them into what they ought to be.

Our problem is, I think, *a version* of Lukács's problem. That is, to see through the myth of rigging, to see the real possibilities and limits of democratic elections without falling prey to the distortions of dumb naiveté or unreasonable expectations, we will have to look for *another standpoint* from which to look at those possibilities and limits. If, however, Lukács's problem is our problem, his solution isn't ours or, at least, not exactly. Although democracy, parliamentary democracy, and ostensibly democratic elections all (as I will discuss particularly in relation to William Morris) have apparently insoluble structural and historical relations to class struggle and the logic of private property, there is no *single* other standpoint or process from which to look at something as definitionally inchoate and institutionally multifarious as modern democracy. For reasons I will detail in what follows, both the theory and the practice of democratic relations are, as it turns out, essentially resistant to any attempt at explanation that relies on even the most scrupulously imagined end of history.

[5] Lukács, *History and Class Consciousness*, 177.

Instead of looking for a preferred standpoint, I want, as it were, to hold Lukács's imperative suspended within Wittgenstein's solution. I want, that is, to treat the relation between democracy and democratic elections as a complex historical and ideological reality that is best seen in the mobile play between its more and less commensurate *aspects*. As Linda M. G. Zerilli has recently written: "Whatever distortions arise from viewing the object from one perspective can be corrected by viewing the same object from other perspectives."[6] After sharing the famous gestalt image of the duck-rabbit in the *Philosophical Investigations*, Wittgenstein reflects on what it feels like to shift from one of the picture's aspects (the rabbit-aspect) to another of its aspects (the duck-aspect):

> The change of aspect. "But surely you would say that the picture is altogether different now!"
> But what is different: my impression? my point of view? – Can I say? I *describe* the alteration like a perception; quite as if the object had altered before my eyes.
> "Now I am seeing *this*," I might say (pointing to another picture, for example). This has the form of a report of a new perception.
> The expression of a change of aspect is the expression of a *new* perception and at the same time of the perceptions' being unchanged.[7]

As we will see, one of the essential truths of democracy and elections as political and historical phenomena is that they mean different things to different and – sometimes – to the same people. Rather than taking this nagging complexity as evidence of incoherence, I want to see incoherence as evidence of what's both bewildering and real about the play between social promise and structural limit, utopian aspiration and lost illusions, honest anticipation and crass calculation that characterizes democracy and the elections that support, represent, and sometimes threaten it.[8] I want, simply put, to identify not one but three different and related aspects in order, first, to introduce some key methods and concepts that I'll draw on in what follows and, second, to model something necessary about the aspectual density of a perplexing historical fact. These three ways of seeing what's *real* about modern democratic elections, these three ways of

---

[6] Linda M. G. Zerilli, *A Democratic Theory of Judgment* (Chicago: University of Chicago Press, 2016), 5.

[7] Ludwig Wittgenstein, *Philosophical Investigations*, trans. G. E. M. Anscombe (Oxford: Blackwell, 1958), 195–196.

[8] "Democracy," writes Robert Dahl, "has been discussed off and on for about twenty-five hundred years, enough time to provide a tidy set of ideas about democracy on which everyone, or nearly everyone, could agree. For better or worse, that is not the case." Dahl, *On Democracy* (New Haven, CT: Yale University Press, 2008), 2–3.

thinking toward what's at stake in their design, their execution, their effects, and their contradictions, will represent three aspects of the critical method I hope to bring to the case studies that follow. Because I need to clear a lot of conceptual ground here, some of what follows in this chapter will have a decidedly introductory flavor. Readers already familiar with these debates within democratic theory and political philosophy may prefer to skim or to skip ahead.

A. Unfinished Business

Perhaps the most immediate way to counter the myth of rigging is to look carefully at the many mundane but hugely consequential legal and logistical details that shape and sometimes distort democratic elections. This is, one might say, the realism of *getting real*. Despite the once widely held and apparently self-evident conviction that world-historical events had ushered in an unstoppable and global wave of liberal or, at least, neoliberal democratization, recent history has pointed instead to the unnerving doggedness of autocracy, the return or rise of old and new nationalisms, the persistence of racism and ethnic antagonism, the enormously determinate political power of economic inequality, the raw tenacity of electoral bad faith, as well as the more innocent but no less consequential logistical problems – the unforced errors – that will confound and compromise any and all elections. "According to one well-respected annual report," notes Astra Taylor, "seventy-one countries suffered net declines in political rights and civil liberties in 2017, leading to an overall decrease in global freedom."[9] "And," writes James Miller, "the United States ... was ranked twenty-first" in that same report, appearing as "a 'flawed democracy' for the first time in the history of the index."[10] "Overall," writes political scientist Pippa Norris, "the mood of the international community towards opportunities for democracy promotion shifted from the predominantly sunny optimism that prevailed in the late 1980s and early 1990s (around the time of the fall of the Berlin Wall) to reflect more pessimistic expectations in an increasingly chilly climate."[11]

[9] Astra Taylor, *Democracy May Not Exist but We'll Miss It When It's Gone* (New York: Henry Holt, 2019), 6.
[10] James Miller, *Can Democracy Work? A Short History of a Radical Idea, from Ancient Athens to Our World* (New York: Picador, 2019), 239.
[11] Pippa Norris, *Strengthening Electoral Integrity* (Cambridge: Cambridge University Press, 2017), 5. A more recent "Statement of Concern," signed by Norris and dozens of other experts in the field, makes the case in even starker terms: "We, the undersigned, are scholars of democracy who have

In response to that widening gap between dreams of more and more democracy and the discouraging and often crude experience of elections as they in fact occur, writers have looked increasingly to address how democracies can or do disappoint. Norris lists just some of them at the start of *Why Elections Fail*:

> Numerous types of flaws and failures undermine elections. In some, opponents are disqualified. District boundaries are gerrymandered. Campaigns provide a skewed playing field for parties. Independent media are muzzled. Citizens are ill-informed about choices. Balloting is disrupted by bloodshed. Ballot boxes are stuffed. Vote counts are fiddled. Opposition parties withdraw. Contenders refuse to accept the people's choice. Protests disrupt polling. Officials abuse state resources. Electoral registers are out of date. Candidates distribute largesse. Votes are bought. Airwaves favor incumbents. Campaigns are awash with hidden cash. Political finance rules are lax. Incompetent local officials run out of paper ballots. Incumbents are immune from effective challengers. Rallies trigger riots. Women candidates face discrimination. Ethnic minorities are persecuted. Voting machines jam. Lines lengthen. Ballot box seals break. Citizens cast more than one ballot. Laws suppress voting rights. Polling stations are inaccessible. Software crashes. "Secure" ink washes off fingers. Courts fail to resolve complaints impartially.[12]

The passage is striking, and, indeed, nearly identical versions of it appear on the first pages of each of the three volumes that make up Norris's essential trilogy on electoral integrity, *Why Electoral Integrity Matters*, *Why Elections Fail*, and *Strengthening Electoral Integrity*.[13] In its effort to account empirically for the myriad ways in which elections break down, the passage relies on a familiar rhetorical strategy, a *paratactic* style that allows Norris to invoke and thus perhaps to address the concrete particularity of these different issues while tacitly acknowledging the half-digested role they play

---

watched the recent deterioration of U.S. elections and liberal democracy with growing alarm. Specifically, we have watched with deep concern as Republican-led state legislatures across the country have in recent months proposed or implemented what we consider radical changes to core electoral procedures in response to unproven and intentionally destructive allegations of a stolen election. Collectively, these initiatives are transforming several states into political systems that no longer meet the minimum conditions for free and fair elections. Hence, our entire democracy is now at risk." (Statement of Concern: The Threats to American Democracy and the Need for National Voting and Election Administration Standards, *New America*, June 1, 2021, www .newamerica.org/political-reform/statements/statement-of-concern/.)

[12] Pippa Norris, *Why Elections Fail* (Cambridge: Cambridge University Press, 2015), 3.

[13] *Why Electoral Integrity Matters* (Cambridge: Cambridge University Press, 2014), *Why Elections Fail* (Cambridge: Cambridge University Press, 2015), and *Strengthening Electoral Integrity* (Cambridge: Cambridge University Press, 2017)

in a larger, more general, and, unhappily, a potentially inexhaustible field of possible electoral lapses, accidents, and abuses.

What distinguishes parataxis from other modes is its avowedly *inorganic* quality, its reluctance to look for the meaning of or the solution to the problematic part in its ultimate subordination to one or another whole.[14] As opposed to a sonnet or a syllogism, a list can get longer and longer and longer. This essentially unfinishable quality is why Aristotle cast the paratactic or "loose" style as inferior to what he saw as a more modern emphasis on organic or hypotactic unity:

> The language of a prose work is necessarily either loose and unified by connectives, like the preludes of dithyrambs, or structures, like the anti-strophic songs of the old poets. The loose style . . . is the original one, in the sense that, while it is not in common use nowadays, in the past everyone was using it. By "loose" I mean that it possesses no stopping point in itself, except in so far as the matter being talked about comes to an end. It is too indefinite a style of speech to be pleasing, because everyone likes to have an end in sight. It is at the finishing-line that runners expel air and relax; they maintain their efforts as long as the end is in sight ahead of them.[15]

In the case of Norris's "loose" catalogue of democratic faults, parataxis serves a similar function as it gives conceptual shape to different aspects of a difficult and urgent phenomenon while also recognizing that phenomenon's indefinitely large and frankly exhausting scale. If "strengthening electoral integrity" is imagined as a race, it must be one run without "end in sight." As opposed, in that case, to a "periodic" view of elections and their problems, the passage evokes a "looser" view of things, one that accepts in advance both the necessity and the impossibility of seeing all sides of a problem or the whole of a world all at once. "Lists of details," observes Elaine Freedgood, "become a kind of paradoxically dilatory shorthand for big cultural formations."[16]

This tactical looseness is not only a rhetorical quality of this passage; it is also a structuring aspect of Norris's whole political and therapeutic project. As she argues toward the end of the trilogy, her work should be seen as a *pragmatic* (as opposed to normative) alternative to popular accounts of elections and democratic procedures that would subordinate each and

---

[14] James A. Notopoulos, "Parataxis in Homer: A New Approach to Homeric Literary Criticism," *Transactions and Proceedings of the American Philological Association* 80 (1949), 1–23.

[15] Aristotle, *The Art of Rhetoric*, trans. Robin Waterfield (Oxford: Oxford University Press, 2018), 133.

[16] Elaine Freedgood, *The Ideas in Things: Fugitive Meaning in the Victorian Novel* (Chicago: University of Chicago Press, 2006), 14.

every one of their aspects to some larger, progressive narrative: "The collapse of the Soviet Union in the late 1980s and early 1990s catalyzed heady optimism about the 'end of history' and the triumph of liberal democracy, globalization, and free markets."[17] The allusion here is, of course, to Francis Fukuyama's consummately "periodic" or hypotactic account of liberal democracy's place as the narrative culmination of a single Universal History in 1989's *The End of History and the Last Man*. Notorious for its embrace of a blunt version of Hegel to account for the end of communism and the triumph of a free market version of liberal democracy – what we would now call neoliberalism – Fukuyama's book enacts at the level of both its content and its form Aristotle's commitment to an organic or "periodic" relation between the beginning, middle, and end of political and human history.

At the level of content, Fukuyama is explicit about his reliance on a wholly plotted theory of what happens. He writes in his preface that, "what I suggested had come to an end was not [history understood as] the occurrence of events, even large and grave events, but History: that is, history understood as a single, coherent, evolutionary process . . . "[18] Like the plot of the successful tragic drama, Fukuyama's history is, to use Aristotle's definition, "an action that is complete, and whole, and of a certain magnitude." At the level of form, the book's 2019 edition, for example, pushes its commitment to plot toward an absurd and almost cheeky threshold. This *End* begins with its original 1989 preface, "By Way of an Introduction," a tacit nod to one of Fukuyama's key influences, Alexandre Kojève, whose own *Introduction to the Reading of Hegel* begins with "In Place of an Introduction," a self-consciously excessive introduction to an introduction to a reading of Hegel. Fukuyama's book then ends with an "Afterword to the 2006 Afterword," either a neatly periodic or a warily parodic by-the-way answer to his impish introduction to the introduction. He thus uses the occasion of the reissue's paratextual apparatus to call ironic, belated, and, as it were, contrapuntal attention both to the resistant shape and to the demonstrable failures of his 1989 volume. It begins with beginning that isn't a beginning and ends, similarly, with an ending that isn't one. As a result, this self-consciously *late* version of Fukuyama's book seems to fetishize, to defamiliarize, and maybe even to satirize its earlier reliance on the same narrative coordinates – beginning

[17] Norris, *Strengthening Electoral Integrity*, 259.
[18] Francis Fukuyama, *The End of History and the Last Man* (New York: Free Press, 2006), xii.

and end, introduction and afterword – on which its narrative account of Universal History almost entirely depends:

> From the beginning, the most serious and systematic attempts to write Universal Histories saw the central issue in history as the development of Freedom. History was not a blind concatenation of events, but a meaningful whole in which human ideas concerning the nature of a just political and social order developed and played themselves out. And if we are now at a point where we cannot imagine a world substantially different from our own, in which there is no apparent or obvious way in which the future will represent a fundamental improvement over our current order, then we must also take into consideration the possibility that History itself might be at an end.[19]

To paraphrase: History is not a coherently periodic narrative because we can see that it is one; History is a coherently periodic narrative because *we can't see that it isn't*.

As opposed, then, to the "periodic" and hollow elegance of a Universal History that *is* simply because it *isn't not*, Norris offers a realist program that, with its open-ended and pragmatic style, sees democratic reform and what she calls "electoral assistance" not as a whole story, but rather as an indefinitely large number of procedural solutions to an indefinitely large number of contingent problems:

> Given that broader processes of democratization are closely linked with the spread of multiparty elections, intellectual frameworks derived from democratic theory can be ransacked as the steel girders and concrete foundations to construct plausible explanations and empirically testable propositions as to why elections may be flawed or failed.[20]

When, at the end of her trilogy, she offers a list of potential fixes, it repurposes and adapts the rhetorical style of the epic catalogue of faults with which she began:

> Electoral assistance covers a multitude of agencies, policies, and programs, whether providing support to legislators about the design, drafting, and revision of new electoral and quota laws; helping EMBs with the process of recruiting and training poll workers and their manages, implementing more convenient facilities for voter registration and balloting, and using digital technologies for tabulating results; strengthening the capacity of the independent judiciary to mediate in electoral disputes and prevent electoral malpractices; advising political parties about the rules used for the recruitment of nomination of candidates, the organization of campaigns, and the

---

[19] Fukuyama, *End of History*, 51.   [20] Norris, *Why Elections Fail*, 14.

regulation of political funding and working with multiple civil society organizations including supporting education for news workers in the independent media, civic education for citizens, and election watch activities by domestic observer NGOs.[21]

Although these remedies come indefinitely together under the blanket term, "electoral assistance," the mix of institutional, legal, and community practices for which Norris advocates don't add up to a single narrative, ideological, or "periodic" program; they rather represent an open and unfinished field of *ad hoc* or "loose" practices and procedures that might sometimes be successfully (because tactically) implemented in particular cases, while still being read against the more general backdrop of an internationally shared set of unfinished political and social norms. In a sense, the paratactic and pragmatic realism that runs across Norris's rhetoric and method recalls some of what Erich Auerbach saw as the paratactic style's stoutly vernacular capacity to capture "a certain motley variegation in external phenomena," and thus something real about a complex, heterogenous, and unofficial social world: "That," he writes, "is the way it is – a paratactic situation made up of theses which, extremely narrow as they are, are yet full of contradictions."[22]

With this understanding of elections as a loose field of discrete problems and solutions, Norris's books and her work with the Electoral Integrity Project represent a larger trend within recent writing about elections and democracy, a number of more or less popular works written mostly after 2016 that accept as given different degrees of democratic crisis and seek to offer pragmatic, local, or targeted fixes.[23] For instance: Steven Levitsky and Daniel Ziblatt's *How Democracies Die* offers a detailed account of how, in the US and elsewhere, the weakening of shared political norms (what they call the "guardrails of democracy") has led to the rise of new forms of autocratic overreach. Levitsky and Ziblatt advocate a general return to norms of "mutual toleration" and "institutional forbearance" and, more particularly and tendentiously, a rebuilding and revision of the political party's traditional role as gatekeeper and custodian. As opposed to seeing

---

[21] Norris, *Strengthening Electoral Integrity*, 259.

[22] Erich Auerbach, *Mimesis: The Representation of Reality in Western Literature* (Princeton, NJ: Princeton University Press, 2013), 110, 102. I'll return to this idea of voting rules as a variegated and inconsistent lattice in Chapter 4, where we'll see how the looseness of electoral logics abetted efforts to disenfranchise Black voters under Jim Crow.

[23] For more on the rhetoric and reality of our democratic crisis, see Hélène Landemore, *Open Democracy: Reinventing Popular Rule for the Twenty-First Century* (Princeton, NJ: Princeton University Press, 2020), 25–52.

political parties as the Capraesque habitat of sweaty, cigar-chomping power brokers, Levitsky and Ziblatt take them, *when they work*, as upholders of what is not necessarily right or good but legitimate. This kind of legitimacy – what Max Weber understood to as "formal" as opposed to "traditional" or "natural law" legitimacy – relies not on some prior or absolute or external guarantee, but rather on the situational agreement of winners and losers about the rules the game. Because you can't have a game if you and your opponents don't play by the same rules, it is in the interest of *healthy* political parties to protect the game and to keep the spoilsports, fanatics, and ruiners at bay. In the US and elsewhere, major political parties have given up on that custodial task.[24]

Stacey Abrams's *Our Time Is Now* draws on her own concrete experience as an organizer and political candidate in Georgia to offer practical responses to bad acts that underwrite systemic voter suppression: unnecessary obstacles to registration, limited access to the ballot, the poor quality of voting equipment, the uneven nature of the rules governing the counting of ballots, and so on. She writes that "the disenfranchisement of individuals and entire populations from democracy through the booby traps of registration, access to the ballot, and ballot counting works to divide groups, often leaving the privileged unscathed by the process but hurt by the outcomes. Representative democracy is a brute force exercise, where who counts *matters*."[25] The book's analysis of how registering to vote, casting votes, and counting votes represent distinct pressure points within democratic systems supports Abrams's political action committee, *Fair Fight*, "a twenty-state strategy to finance the infrastructure of voter protection": "In our target states," she writes, "we fund voter protection directors, deputies, and hotline managers to answer voter concerns, as well as organizers dedicated to voter protection to recruit and support volunteers across each state."[26] Emerging from the everyday experience of political organization, Abrams's book represents a kind of tactical realism:

[24] For an influential account of the waning of party power in America, see Austin Ranney, *Curing the Mischiefs of Faction: Party Reform in America* (Berkeley: University of California Press, 1975); for an alternate and critical account of that same history, see Alan Ware, *The American Direct Primary: Party Institutionalization and Transformation in the North* (Cambridge: Cambridge University Press, 2002).

[25] Stacey Abrams, *Our Time Is Now: Power, Purpose, and the Fight for a Fair America* (New York: Henry Holt & Company, 2020), 122.

[26] Abrams, *Our Time Is Now*, 214; alongside *Fair Fight*, one should also take a look at Marc Elias's *Democracy Docket*, which warehouses information about voter suppression and chronicles Elias's many efforts to fight that suppression in court: www.democracydocket.com.

it is both a reckoning with what is and a modest and pragmatic primer on how to usher in what should be instead.

In *The Voting Wars* (2012) and *Election Meltdown* (2019), Richard L. Hansen offers short-, medium-, and long-term fixes for what he identifies as the four main sources of Americans' diminished confidence in their electoral system: voter suppression, pockets of electoral incompetence, dirty tricks, and incendiary rhetoric:

> The longest-term project is civics education for children and adults on the importance of the rule of law, democratic legitimacy, and peaceful transitions to power following fair elections. Political and civic leaders, teachers, and others in the public sphere must foster discussions across platforms and venues about these subjects. This includes discussions about the specific danger of loose talk about "stolen" or "rigged" elections without any proof or even basis in reality.[27]

As Hasen has described in real time in a series of quickly but sharply written press pieces, the electoral events of late 2020 and early 2021 – the risible, the terrible, and the grotesque – affirmed the urgent need not only for civic education but also for immediate legislation and a number of specific political reforms.[28] And, indeed, widespread efforts at the level of state legislatures to use the linked myths of election rigging and "the purity of the vote" as an excuse to make voting harder, more intimidating, and more exclusive have made both Hasen's legal and his journalistic analysis all the more urgent.

Carol Anderson's *One Person, No Vote* situates current US politics within the long history of efforts, legal, quasi-legal, and extralegal, to disenfranchise Black voters. Tracing a more or less unbroken line from the egregious poll taxes and impossible literacy tests of the Jim Crow South to more recent (and yet all too familiar) efforts to suppress votes, purge voter rolls, and lose, miscount, or invalidate ballots, she writes,

---

[27] Richard L. Hasen, *Election Meltdown: Dirty Tricks, Distrust, and the Threat to American Democracy* (New Haven, CT: Yale University Press, 2020), 137–138.

[28] See for instance, "I've Never Been More Worried about American Democracy than I Am Right Now," *Slate*, September 23, 2020, https://slate.com/news-and-politics/2020/09/trump-plan-supreme-court-stop-election-vote-count.html; "Trump's Legal Farce Is Having Tragic Results," *The New York Times*, November 23, 2020, www.nytimes.com/2020/11/23/opinion/trump-election-courts.html?searchResultPosition=1; "We Can't Let Our Elections Be This Vulnerable Again," *The Atlantic*, January 4, 2021, www.theatlantic.com/ideas/archive/2021/01/we-cant-let-our-elections-be-vulnerable-again/617542/; "The Only Way to Save American Democracy Now," *Slate*, January 11, 2021 https://slate.com/news-and-politics/2021/01/biden-pelosi-schumer-john-lewis-save-democracy.html.

Whether it was reconfiguring congressional district boundaries, removing polling stations from minority neighborhoods, reducing the dates for early voting, or ratcheting up the standards for those conducting voter registration drives, all those little, virtually unnoticeable-until-it's-too-late bureaucratic tricks had major consequences ... [T]hey created "a sense that something has gone amiss with American democracy, that there is this effort to rig the rules of the game."[29]

As we shall see, what can be most striking about all these dirty little tricks is, firstly, that they are rarely illegal; working within the letter of the law after Reconstruction, southern state legislatures used the legal system and, more to the point, the technical minutiae of electoral procedure not merely to suppress but, for a time, nearly to eliminate the Black vote. Secondly, these tricks are multifarious; they work according to a nagging, exhausting logic of overlap and accretion. For Anderson, understanding the long tail of Jim Crow is crucial to confronting what faces us today. I'll come back to her work in Chapter 4.

Nic Cheeseman and Brian Klass's *How to Rig an Election* focuses on a series of discrete and increasingly costly electoral abuses, from gerrymandering and vote buying to hacking an election, stuffing the ballot box, and outright physical violence. For them, improving the quality of elections turns on "preventing governments with authoritarian instincts from illegitimately passing themselves off as democracies," a task that "will involve closing off one avenue of rigging after another until counterfeit democrats have nowhere left to turn."[30] This emphasis on the importance of *watching* elections, politicians, and putative democracies appears in more abstract and more radical modes in the work of a few other recent writers. For instance, John Keane argues that the decline of moribund representative, parliamentary, or party democracies should give way to the restless and reactive potential of "monitory democracy," which

> means something much richer: the ongoing struggle by citizens and their representatives, in a multiplicity of settings, to humble the high and mighty. Democracy is the unending, never-finished public business of scrutinizing and restraining their power. It is the struggle against arbitrary power and the hubris it breeds by people and institutions skilled at using

[29] Carol Anderson, *One Person, No Vote: How Voter Suppression Is Destroying Our Democracy* (New York: Bloomsbury, 2019), 96–97.

[30] Nic Cheeseman and Brian Klass, *How to Rig an Election* (New Haven, CT: Yale University Press, 2018), 226, 228.

both the weapon of periodic elections and various monitory mechanisms positioned beneath and beyond parliamentary and state institutions.[31]

For Keane, the work of safeguarding and improving democratic elections is a matter of really and continually *seeing* democracy clearly: to act proactively as a citizen in large and unwieldy societies is, in other words, a matter of bearing witness.[32]

As will already be clear, this book isn't really one of those books. Although the stakes of these efforts couldn't be any higher, *The Electoral Imagination* is a different but, I hope usefully related kind of work. On the one hand, I will try in each chapter to consider my different cases from a discrete and, as it were, pragmatic perspective. What were the problems that the introduction of the secret ballot in Britain or America was meant to solve, and how did those problems and solutions both draw on and shape other, contemporary, and aesthetic forms that similarly relied on some real or imagined relation between representation and the secret? What potentials were imagined and yet unrealized as the Victorians imagined and reimagined new and increasingly involved ways to cast, count, and understand the meaning of votes? And what might that imaginative excess have to do with the representative ambitions of, for instance, the realist novel? How should we understand the weirdly detailed and almost prosaic utopianism of William Morris's *News from Nowhere*, first, in relation to the competing discourse of the realist novel and, second, as a specific contribution to thinking about the nature and limits of parliamentary democracy at century's end? How should we understand the relation between Ralph Ellison's long commitment to the novel as an

---

[31] John Keane, *Power and Humility: The Future of Monitory Democracy* (Cambridge: Cambridge University Press, 2018), 14–15; see also Jeffrey Edward Green, *The Eyes of the People: Democracy in an Age of Spectatorship* (Oxford: Oxford University Press, 2010).

[32] See also John P. McCormick's *Machiavellian Democracy*, which offers a more radically monitory proposal, the establishment of an annual "college of tribunes," made up of "fifty-one private citizens, selected by private lottery"; these "non-elite" citizens, selected at random from a national pool of individuals who have never held municipal, state, or federal office and whose household income falls beneath $345,000, would "contribute substantively to ... public affairs" and, even more, offset a tendency toward an entrenched and corrosive elitism that, following Machiavelli, McCormick takes as endemic to representative or "republican" government. David Van Reybrouck makes a similar case for government by sortition in *Against Elections*: "a randomly composed parliament could make democracy more legitimate and efficient, more legitimate because it would revive the ideal of the equitable distribution of political opportunities and more efficient because the new representatives of the people would not lose themselves in party-political tugs of war, electoral games, media battles or legislative haggling." John P. McCormick, *Machiavellian Democracy* (Cambridge: Cambridge University Press, 2011), 183; David Van Reybrouck, *Against Elections*, trans. Liz Waters (New York: Seven Stories Press, 2018), 132–133.

especially democratic form and the spectacularly and procedurally anti-democratic nature of the Jim Crow South?

On the other hand, I first started thinking about this book more than a decade ago when I naïvely thought overt threats to American electoral processes were a thing of the past and when paying attention to the technical minutiae of voting theory seemed still like an arcane if surprisingly, or even secretly, significant task. Since then, I have watched with some discomfort as what had been a source of personal and scholarly appeal has become a matter of shared political urgency. I find that a book that was to have been solidly – if eccentrically – about the past has been pulled again and again into rough and reluctant contact with the present.

This came into vivid and wholly unwelcome focus on January 6, 2021, when the arcane, procedural, and usually *pro forma* business of tallying electoral votes gave way to propaganda, pepper spray, broken glass, zip-ties, gunfire, face paint, animal pelts, and a gallows set on the steps of the US Capitol. To my growing and horrified disbelief and against all my inclinations, my writing became differently relevant. I want this book both to attend to and to resist the pull of relevance and the present *in a certain way*. That is, while I cannot deny the present's sometimes hopeful, sometimes deadly, but always indisputable refusal to leave the past well-enough alone, I want to understand the past *in spite* of the present, *in spite* of its immediacy, brutality, folly, and tendency to treat bad, ignorant, irrational, or self-serving descriptions of problems as if they were solutions. I also write knowing that, whatever I might want, the present will have its way. It will, whatever we might wish, leave none of us alone.

I hope, in what follows, to take a longish view of the fraught history, theory, and rhetoric of elections and their limits so that when I do come back to the present – and when the present all-too-certainly comes back at me – it will be neither in the service of a wish nor for the cultivation of my own despair; it will be in an effort to understand both the relations and the differences between, on the one hand, what elections have been and have meant at the levels of the detail, the event, and the concept and, on the other hand, what they seem to mean to us now when it's hard to see beyond the bad horizon of the present. If this book is not pragmatic in the way Pippa Norris's book is, it does embrace a pragmatism that both recognizes the contextual, contingent, but nonetheless *real* meaning of past events and tries to put that meaning to work – however obscurely – in and for the present. Which brings me to my second of three aspects: political realism.

B.   A Reduced Sense of Reality

Alongside a paratactic realism of discrete details, the next methodological
aspect I want to explore stems from what might be called the realism of lost
illusions. Instead of looking for the nature and consequence of democratic
elections in a pragmatic or *ad hoc* analysis of individual cases, the writers
I'll consider next are committed to the analysis of how available models,
assumptions, or ideals *fail* to reckon fully with whatever democracy is or
should be. These writers assume that people get democracy wrong and
that – if one is ever to imagine authentically democratic norms, rules, and
procedures – one better begin to get it right; and, because it is hard to
know what democracy really is, it is probably best to try to think first
about what it *isn't*. Where, in other words, many imagine democracy as
identical to one of its salutary ethical byproducts (justice, virtue, the good),
the *political realist* takes democracy as a legitimate and good-enough way to
confront the inevitability of social conflict. This brings me back to an
earlier distinction between two big ideas I claimed were implied by and
stood unresolved within the term "rigging": Rigging as the human, historical, and thus the necessarily limited character of any given election; and
rigging as the "myth of rigging," an ideologically motivated legend of the
fall that pushes an unreasonable but compelling fantasy of what democracy
should be in order to further the interests and authority of some voters
over the interests and authority of others. A tension between reality and
fantasy, between history and illusion, is thus not only built into rigging's
etymology but also becomes a source of ideological strength for those who
would use it not to identify mitigable problems, but rather to undermine
the political autonomy of others. It is both that tension and its practical
dissolution that motivates the ideas I consider in this section.

   To see the relation and the difference between the *paratactic* models
I discussed in the previous section and the *critical* or *minimalist* models
which I will address in this one, let's take a detour and remember a telling
sequence in that greatest and most detailed novel of disenchantment,
Balzac's *Illusions Perdues*. When he first arrives at Paris, Lucien de
Rubempré spends close to his last sous outfitting himself in a get-up he
thinks appropriate to the dog-eat-dog world of Parisian society, a process
that Balzac lays out with a characteristically fine eye for detail: "Lucien left,
the possessor of a green coat, white trousers, and a fancy waistcoat, all for
the sum of two hundred francs. He next found a pair of very elegant ready-
made boots. Then, having bought everything he needed, he sent for a
hairdresser at his hotel, to which his various purchases were also

delivered."[33] Preparing for his society debut is an accretive process for Lucien, a matter of many actions, arrangements, and parts. Left there, fashion and fashionable Paris appear to be ordinal systems, paratactic assemblages of different persons, events, and things. As it turns out, we have misread the situation, and, taking Paris as an ordinal system, we have made a cardinal error. (As we shall see, the difference between ordinality and cardinality will prove central to the theory and practice of modern elections.) Appearing at the opera in his new suit of exquisite shreds and patches, Lucien's paratactic illusion crumbles *all at once* when, in a stage whisper, one dandy asks another, "who is this extraordinary young man who looks like a tailor's dummy?"[34] Up to that point, Balzac has lulled us into thinking that what's real about the Parisian world works according to one logic – an ordinal logic – and that, if you have the money to meet the right number of needs with the right number of things, you will surely succeed.

What we learn instead is that there is something *more real* than that piecemeal, accretive reality, a whole, negative, and precipitate truth that can be revealed only in (and might exist only as) a threshold moment of disillusionment:

> The principal merit of beautiful manners and the tone of high society is that it presents a harmonious whole, in which everything is so subtly blended that nothing jars. Even those who do not, either from ignorance or because they are carried away by some impulse, observe the laws of this science will understand that a single false note is, as in music, a complete negation of the art itself, all of whose conditions must be observed down to the smallest details, or that art cannot even exist.[35]

This moment is not merely one of galling personal failure; rather, because Balzac lulls not only Lucien but also the reader into believing in the security of a whole discursive logic, the sudden revelation of that logic *as an illusion* is a shattering blow not only to the character, but also to readers who thought they, too, had understood the rules of the game. More than something specific about the situational reality – the verisimilitude – of clothes, people, books, or, for that matter, competing political systems, Balzac forces one to confront the limits of and to imagine the *really real reality* of what lies behind the rigged heuristics one uses to "know" the world. As it turns out, what is really real is only what is *not* unreal, what

[33] Honoré de Balzac, *Lost Illusions* (New York: Modern Library, 2001), 171.
[34] Balzac, *Lost Illusions*, 180.   [35] Balzac, *Lost Illusions*, 174–175.

escapes the partial expectations, impositions, and illusions we project onto a world that will, at last, do just what it will.

Of course, similar efforts to reveal or, indeed, to shatter the partial errors and dreams – the illusions – behind the idea of *democracy* are as old as the idea itself. Consider the Old Oligarch. Against the stirring and halcyon backdrop of Periclean democracy – "we are," said Pericles in his famous funeral oration, "free to live exactly as we please, and yet we are always ready to face any danger," "we believe that happiness is the fruit of freedom and freedom that of valor" – the Pseudo-Xenophon or the "Old Oligarch," produced a document, the *Constitution of Athens*, which cast Athenian democracy (in John Dunn's paraphrase) as "a robust but flagrantly unedifying system of power," one that grudgingly ceded authority to "the poor, the popular, and the base" not because the Athenian rich really believed everyone to be equal but rather because, without the poor, there would be no one to pull at the oars that drove the Athenian navy.[36] Karl Popper, who takes the Old Oligarch as one of the open society's original enemies, writes that the "ingenious" *Constitution of Athens* "is a ruthless attack written no doubt by one of its best brains. Its central idea, an idea which became an article of faith with Thucydides and Plato, is the close connection between naval imperialism and democracy."[37] Says the Old Oligarch:

> First of all, I will say this, that the poor and the *demos* are justified there in having more than the well-born and the rich, because of the fact that it is the demos who operate the ships and confer its strength on the city; the steersmen, the boatswains, the lieutenants, the look-outs and the naval engineers—these are the people who confer its strength on the city, much more than the hoplites and the well-born and the valuable. Since this is the case, it seems right that everyone should share in the holding of public office, both the allotted and the elective offices, and that any citizen who wishes should be allowed to have his say.[38]

For the Old Oligarch, there was, hiding just behind Pericles's pleasing illusion of everyone "living as we please," the bad faith and bitter truth of political compromises grudgingly tolerated in the service of sustained military and commercial expansion: "For where there is a naval power,

---

[36] Pericles, quoted in Karl Popper, *The Open Society and Its Enemies* (Princeton, NJ: Princeton University Press, 2013), 177; John Dunn, *Democracy: A History* (New York: Atlantic Monthly Press, 2005), 28.

[37] Popper, *Open Society*, 177–178.

[38] The "Old Oligarch," *The Constitution of the Athenians Attributed to Xenophon*, ed. J. L. Marr and P. J. Rhodes (Liverpool: Liverpool University Press, 2008), 37.

economic reasons make it necessary for us to be slaves to our slaves ... ."[39]
The Old Oligarch thus gives early expression not only to democratic
skepticism but also to an elitist fear of the "tyranny of the majority" that
is an important and sustained strain within anti-democratic traditions:
once they get political power and realize themselves as a majority, the
slaves will make slaves of us.

Coming soon after the Old Oligarch, Plato, certainly the most influential theorist of democracy's illusions, imagined it not as a lucrative bad faith
compromise, but rather as a commodity dangerously seductive instead of
justly wise, as a treacherous bauble or, maybe, as something like Lucien's
doomed but nonetheless "fancy" waistcoat: democracy, says Plato, is "like
a coat embroidered with every kind of ornament."[40] Fed, perhaps, by that
"primal stain on democracy's honor," the terrible but nonetheless procedurally legitimate vote that resulted in Socrates's death, Plato's argument
against democracy is equal parts political and aesthetic: "He sees it," writes
Dunn, "in essence as an all but demented solvent of value, decency and
good judgment, as the rule of the foolish, vicious, and always potentially
brutal, and a frontal assault on the possibility of a good life."[41] Indeed,
Plato says with a sneer that, "these and others like them are the characteristics of democracy. And it would seem to be a pleasant constitution,
which lacks rulers but not variety and which distributes a sort of equality to
both equals and unequals alike."[42] For Plato, democracy was not, however,
simply a beguiling illusion, shiny and bright. Rather, because its version of
equality relied on a structural rejection of difference and because serious
thought relies exactly on the kinds of comparison that difference allows,
democracy was a threat to the kind of *thinking* required to distinguish
illusion from reality: "And in the absence of these guardians, false and
boastful words and beliefs rush up and occupy this part of him. ... Won't
he then return to these lotus-eaters and live with them openly?"[43] Because,
in other words, democracy assumes that thinking based in the drawing of
distinctions is meaningless or at least unappealing, it also precludes the
very possibility of disillusionment, that quintessentially Platonic escape
from dusky lull of fantasy into the harsher, but truer, light of the real.
Without difference, illusion not only conceals reality; without difference,
illusion *becomes* reality. And that, of course, is anathema to Plato.

---

[39] *Constitution of the Athenians*, 41; for more on "the myth of classical Athens as a direct democracy,"
see Landemore, *Open Democracy*, 66–74.
[40] Plato, *Republic*, trans. G. M. A. Grube (Hackett Publishing Company, 1992), 227.
[41] Dunn, *Democracy*, 45.   [42] Plato, *Republic*, 228.   [43] Plato, *Republic*, 230–231.

Democracy is a problem for Plato not only because it is untrue; it is a problem because it makes truth impossible.

To take a more recent and less dogmatic example, Alexis de Tocqueville is explicit about his understanding of criticism as the analytic refusal of illusions: It was, for instance, the first-hand experience of a "sentiment of envy" characteristic of American democracy that, he writes, "demonstrated to me that those who regard universal suffrage as a guarantee of the goodness of choices make a complete illusion for themselves. Universal suffrage has other advantages, but not that one."[44] Refusing the fantasy of democracy's essential "goodness," Tocqueville argues instead that its appeal was a matter more of belief, faith, or fiction than of consistent or good governance; "The government of the Union rests," he says, "almost wholly on legal fictions. The Union is an ideal nation that exists so to speak only in minds, and whose extent and bounds intelligence alone discovers."[45] That said, Tocqueville isn't really against democracy in *Democracy in America*; the same things that make democracy sloppy, ignorant, and violent also make it dynamic, improvisational, inspiring:

> Democracy does not give the most skillful government to the people, but it does what the most skillful government is often powerless to create; it spreads a restive activity through the whole social body, a superabundant force, an energy that never exists without it, and which, however little circumstances may be favorable, can bring forth marvels.[46]

Indeed, closer to the canny pragmatism of the Old Oligarch than to Plato's patrician rage, Tocqueville believes that what lay behind the bright-colored thing is *conflict*, an interminable play of forces necessary to the structure of people, societies, and history. Says Hayden White:

> The forces at play in history, which make it an arena of irremissible conflict, are not reconcilable, either in society or in the heart of man himself. Man remains, as Tocqueville put it, "on the verge between two abysses," the one comprised of that social order without which he cannot be a man, the other comprised of that demonic nature within him which prevents his ever becoming fully human.[47]

---

[44] Alexis de Tocqueville. *Democracy in America*, trans. Harvey C. Mansfield and Delba Winthrop (Chicago: University of Chicago Press, 2002), 190.
[45] Tocqueville, *Democracy in America*, 155.   [46] Tocqueville, *Democracy in America*, 234.
[47] Hayden White, *Metahistory: The Historical Imagination in Nineteenth-Century Europe* (Baltimore: Johns Hopkins University Press, 2014), 193. See also Corey Robin, who writes of Tocqueville's *need* for conflict that: "The politics of moderation and compromise produced moderation and compromise; it did not produce politics, at least not as Tocqueville understood the term. During the 1830s and 1840s, 'what was most wanting . . . was political life itself.' There was 'no battlefield

This ironic faith in the obduracy of conflict is why White identifies Tocqueville not simply as a realist but rather as a *tragic* realist, as a critic committed to a realism of enigmatic but still dominant and determining *relations* instead of a realism of discrete and empirically given *things*. "We seem," writes A. C. Bradley in some lines on Shakespeare that could have come from one of the purpler passages of *Democracy in America*:

> ... to have before us a type of the mystery of the whole world, the tragic fact which extends far beyond the limits of tragedy. Everywhere, from the crushed rocks beneath our feet to the soul of man, we see power, intelligence, life and glory, which astound us and seem to call for our worship. And everywhere we see them perishing, devouring one another and destroying themselves, often with dreadful pain, as though they came into being for no other end. Tragedy is the typical form of this mystery, because that greatness of soul which it exhibits oppressed, conflicting and destroyed, is the highest existence in our view. It forces the mystery upon us, and it makes us realize so vividly the worth of that which is wasted that we cannot possibly seek comfort in the reflection that all is vanity.[48]

For Bradley, tragedy is defined by its frank encounter with a waste that is both a result of and figure for the conflicts that define human beings and human societies.

The question of whether democratic elections or their equivalents exist *to overcome* conflict in the service of deliberation, ethical comity, or organic community or, rather, *to preserve* conflict as a necessary aspect of an unfinished, pluralistic, and sometimes fractious society has been essential to the field of democratic theory. Democracy, likewise, exists in a state of irresolvable and paradoxical structural tension in Tocqueville; like myth in Barthes, democracy is a whirligig, good and bad, fast and slow, old and new, clever and vulgar. Writes David Runciman:

> The things that democracies are good at (commerce, comfort) are bad for democracy, because they breed narrow-mindedness and complacency; the things that democracies are bad at (crisis management, international confrontation) are good for democracy, because they might broaden its horizons and shake that sense of complacence. There is no easy way out of this

for contending parties to meet upon.' Politics had been 'deprived' of 'all originality, of all reality, and therefore of all genuine passions.'" Robin, *The Reactionary Mind: Conservatism from Edmund Burke to Donald Trump* (Oxford: Oxford University Press, 2018), 78. See also McCormick's effort to follow "Machiavelli's injunction to make class conflict central to republican discourse and democratic practice." McCormick, *Machiavellian Democracy*, 12.

48 A. C. Bradley, *Shakespearean Tragedy* (London: Penguin Books Limited, 1991), 38.

dilemma...because in a crisis there are always two sides to a democracy –
good and bad – and it can be very hard to reconcile them.[49]

That Bradley's late Victorian negotiation of mystery, possibility, intelligence, adamant conflict, and inevitable loss could have come from
Tocqueville points not only to a common cultural inheritance and a shared
critical disposition; it points to the persistence of a realist *style* of thinking
about democracy and its limits I want to explore further and – with
important caveats – to understand as another aspect of the method I hope
to pursue in the chapters that follow. This style is at work in the many
extraordinary machines that appeared in the midst of both Victorian realism
and Victorian reform; in the play between dreamworlds, democratic theory,
and political violence in *Alice's Adventures in Wonderland*; in the relation
between William Morris's strategic resistance to democratic socialism and
the fraught negotiation between realism and utopia that defines works like
News From Nowhere, A Dream of John Ball, and *The House of the Wolfings*; in
an anxious and aesthetic overinvestment in models and modeling that
characterized the intellectual culture in and around the RAND
Corporation; in the Janus-faced character of the rules of order in *Invisible
Man*; and in a characterological nihilism that defined the Nixonian milieu
and helped to exalt the crank, the hack, and the ratfucker.

This sense of a critical method built on the rejection or refusal of ideology
or myth is also characteristic of group of recent writers associated with what
has been loosely called "political realism." In his introduction to an edited
volume on "the revival of realism in contemporary political theory," Matt
Sleat acknowledges that, as opposed to any single argument, political realism
represents a methodological disposition or an intellectual style:

> The now familiar realist charge against much contemporary political theory
> is that through inappropriate idealizations, abstraction, and moralization it
> presents a misleading, if not outright false, account of politics that sits at too
> great a distance from reality to offer us much that can help us to compre-
> hend or get any meaningful intellectual grasp of our political lives.[50]

As I've begun to suggest, something like this realist's refusal of political
illusion goes back to variously disposed skeptics like Plato, Tocqueville,
Weber, Mencken, Lippman, Schumpeter, and Neibuhr, who wrote in
1944:

[49] David Runciman, *The Confidence Trap: A History of Democracy in Crisis from World War I to the
Present* (Princeton, NJ: Princeton University Press, 2017), 28.
[50] Matt Sleat, "Introduction," in *Politics Recovered: Realist Thought in Theory and Practice*, ed. Matt
Sleat (New York: Columbia University Press, 2018), 3.

The consistent optimism of our liberal culture has prevented modern democratic societies both from gauging the perils of freedom accurately and from appreciating democracy fully as the only alternative to injustice and oppression. When this optimism is not qualified to accord with the real and complex facts of human nature and history, there is always a danger that sentimentality will give way to despair and that a too consistent optimism will alternate with a too consistent pessimism.[51]

For Neibuhr, realism is necessary to democratic thinking because it allows the critic and the politician to break free from a sterile oscillation between the imaginary extremes of "consistent optimism" and "consistent pessimism." A realism of the affectively excluded middle, Neibuhr's approach casts "the real and complex facts of human nature and history" as a significant basis for analysis and action that tends to get lost behind or within the turnstile of democratic myth; and, although "real and complex facts" might seem anemic when compared to the ideological purity of one or another democratic ideal, they are not only what might make a really existing democracy possible, but also what makes that more avowedly limited democracy "the *only* alternative to injustice and oppression."

The philosopher Bernard Williams is a figure central to this realist turn. Williams's fundamental concern is with what he takes as an error pervasive in political philosophy since the publication of John Rawls's *A Theory of Justice* in 1971: its reduction of politics to what Williams calls "something like applied morality."[52] Williams (like the subsequent and variously vituperative realists Raymond Guess, John Gray, and Charles Larmore) tends to characterize the Rawlsian and adjacent positions as "Kantian" because of their emphasis on ostensibly universal norms of justice, deliberation, epistemic agreement, and so on; and, because Rawlsian liberalism takes justice as essential and prior to any definition or situated assessment of politics, it fails, in Williams's view, to account both for what is necessary to politics as opposed to ethics and for the reality and historicity of real-world political beliefs. Gray is characteristically severe

---

[51] Niebuhr, *Major Works*, 484. Similarly, Christopher Achen and Larry Bartels argue in *Democracy for Realists* that broad acceptance of what they take as an unreasonable because unreasonably idealized "folk theory" of democracy has not only led analysts, activists, and ordinary people to want things from democracy that it cannot give but also prevented us from achieving a functional and at least potentially just democracy: "One of the most deleterious consequences of adherence to unrealistic ideas about democracy is that it keeps us from seeing what a truer and deeper democracy would be like." Larry M. Bartels and Christopher H. Achen, *Democracy for Realists: Why Elections Do Not Produce Responsive Government* (Princeton, NJ: Princeton University Press, 2016), 325.

[52] Bernard Williams, *In the Beginning Was the Deed: Realism and Moralism in Political Argument* (Princeton, NJ: Princeton University Press, 2005), 2.

on this point: "The oddity," says he, "and indeed the absurdity, of this new Kantian liberalism – one that has cut itself loose from the traditional concerns of philosophy so as to pursue the political objective of practical agreement – is that it is at the same time elaborated at a vast distance from political life in the real world."[53] As a result, political philosophy after Rawls makes, say the realists, the category mistake of taking a concept – liberalism – that works well in some historical and social circumstances but not necessarily in others as a universal norm. With this mistake, political philosophy becomes confused about its means and ends, and, as a result, politics becomes an effect, reflection, or practical instantiation of a prior ethical claim; a political philosophy tipsy with ethics will thus fail, in Hans Morganthau's phrase, to reckon with "the autonomy of the political sphere."

For Williams, the return to politics *as* politics starts with a return to Thomas Hobbes (as well as to Machiavelli and Max Weber) and to what Williams calls "the first political question," that is, "the securing of order, protection, safety, trust, and the conditions of cooperation."[54] Although returns to Hobbes sometimes carry with them dismal delight in the apparent originality of sin, for Williams it leads less to an assumption simply that life is "nasty brutish and short" and more to an understanding that any and all definably political systems will share two related characteristics. First, as opposed to models that imagine disagreement or deliberation as the means necessary to the end of eventual comity, Williams sees *conflict* as inevitable and necessary to every society. Conflict is, in itself, neither a means nor an end: it is a social fact.[55] More than that, he takes the political recognition of political conflict as a way to forestall other, more egregious or violent *because* ethical varieties of conflict:

> [W]e should not think that what we have to do is simply to argue with those who disagree: treating them as *opponents* can, oddly enough, show

[53] John Gray, *Enlightenment's Wake: Politics and Culture at the Close of the Modern Age* (London: Taylor & Francis, 2007), 4.

[54] Williams, *In the Beginning Was the Deed*, 3.

[55] "No one," notes Larmore, "has laid out so succinctly as Williams the substance of the realist position, even though there are many today … who similarly invoke the name of 'realism' in rejecting much of contemporary, particularly liberal, political philosophy as a flight from the reality of politics, which they regard as the omnipresence of conflict and the need for authority." Similarly, Gray writes that, "This insight – whose applications in ethics have been best explored in the work of Bernard Williams – has the inestimable value of returning us to the realities of political life, which have to do with balancing competing claims of similar validity, finding a *modus vivendi* among forms of life that are irreconcilable, and mediating conflicts that can never be resolved." Charles Larmore, *What Is Political Philosophy?* (Princeton, NJ: Princeton University Press, 2020), 23; Gray, *Enlightenment's Wake*, 13.

more respect for them as political actors than treating them simply as arguers – whether as arguers who are simply mistaken, or as fellow seekers after truth. A very important reason for thinking in terms of the political is that a political decision – the conclusion of a political deliberation which brings all sorts of considerations, considerations of principle along with others, to one focus of decision – is that such a decision does not in itself announce that the other party was morally wrong or, indeed, wrong at all. What it immediately announces is that *they have lost.*[56]

Unlike moral or ethical questions, which assume the existence of one right, good, or true answer to a question, political questions are *political* precisely because they accept that individuals or groups will disagree about answers while nonetheless meeting minimal criteria of rationality and good faith. As Joseph Schumpeter put it in 1942, there is "no such thing as a uniquely determined common good that all people could agree on" because "to different individuals and groups the common good is bound to mean different things."[57]

Although the absence of ethical norms and the inevitability of conflict might seem like a terrible thing, accepting those as facts does make it harder to think of one's political opponent as essentially, morally flawed and thus as someone you might be right to exile, imprison, or kill. You won't – or at least you shouldn't – hate your opponent because they win or lose a game, particularly when, as is the case with regular, periodic, and transparent elections, you can always look forward to a rematch. This is where, as he acknowledged with appropriate apprehension, Williams shares something with Carl Schmitt, whose famous friend-enemy distinction was, at least in its first iteration, meant not to authorize but rather to forestall excessive or even genocidal violence: As opposed to its *ethical* counterpart, "the political enemy need not be morally evil or aesthetically ugly."[58] What's more, because all political systems are defined by the

---

[56] Williams, *In the Beginning Was the Deed*, 13.

[57] Schumpeter, *Capitalism, Socialism, and Democracy*, 251. As we will see in Chapter 4, the question of whether it is possible or even advisable to posit the existence of a common good against which we might compare the status or the satisfaction of different individuals will appear at the heart of democratic theory after Kenneth Arrow; what's more and as I will show, the problem of the "interpersonal comparison of utilities" offers another surprising point of only apparently arcane contact between the economic theory of democracy and the rise of the novel.

[58] Carl Schmitt, *The Concept of the Political*, trans. George Schwab (Chicago: University of Chicago Press, 1996), 27. Williams: "Carl Schmitt famously said that the fundamental political relation was that of friend and enemy. This is an ambiguous remark, and it can take on a rather sinister tone granted the history of Schmitt's own relations to the Weimar Republic and eventually to the Third Reich. But it is basically true in at least this sense, that political difference is of the essence of politics, and political difference is a relation of political opposition, rather than, in itself, a relation of intellectual or interpretative disagreement." Williams, *In the Beginning Was the Deed*, 78.

inevitability of conflict, they must aim to be *legitimate* in a specific and limited sense. By "legitimate" (LEG), Williams means that the members of a state must believe or at least must act *as if* they believe that the state has the authority to enforce its laws, decisions, rules, etc., which means in turn that they must believe or at least must act *as if* they believe that the state has the authority to impose the will of a person or group onto other persons or groups even though those persons or groups disagree with – and may indeed even suffer from – the imposition of that will.

Williams refers to this condition as the "Basic Legitimation Demand" or BLD. Writes Williams:

> The situation of one lot of people terrorizing another lot of people is not *per se* a political situation: it is, rather, the situation which the existence of the political is in the first place supposed to alleviate. . . . If the power of one lot of people over another is to represent a solution to the first political question, and not itself be part of the problem, something has to be said to explain (to the less empowered, to concerned bystanders, to children being educated in this structure, etc.) what the difference is between the solution and the problem, and that cannot simply be an account of successful domination.[59]

Of course, when one reads this and thinks, *as one must*, of tyrants, strong men, and bullies, Williams's sense of the ethical neutrality of power *qua* power is disturbing, to say the least; any account of things that would use LEG to give intellectual cover to the domination of the strong over the weak is morally repellant. If, however, one thinks about this not in terms of the powerful exploiting the powerless but rather in terms of a free and fair majority election where 50.1 percent of the people vote one way and 49.9 percent vote the other way, then the state's use of its authority to enforce the will of the 50.1 percent over the others is understood often to be not only LEG, but also wholly just. "Voting," says Przeworski, "is an imposition of a will over a will. When a decision is reached by voting, some people must submit to an opinion different from theirs or to a decision contrary to their interest."[60] Seen in these terms, the imposition of one will over the will of another is not or at least it is not inevitably repellant. It's democracy!

That said, even though both tyranny and democracy can meet the BLD in theory, that does not make them ethically, practically, or, most crucially for Williams, historically equivalent. While almost any form of

[59] Williams, *Realism and Moralism*, 63.
[60] Adam Przeworski, *Why Bother with Elections?* (New York: Wiley, 2018), 14.

government can count as politically legitimate in Williams's rigorously restricted sense of the term, what will in fact count as legitimate will vary – sometimes absolutely – depending on particular historical and social conditions. While, in other words, one cannot – as Williams says Rawls tries to do – endorse liberalism as a political system on the grounds that it is more essentially good than other possible systems, one can say that liberalism is better for us, if "us" is understood as some people living in a modern society "conceived of as technically advanced, democratic, and, above all, pluralistic."[61] Or, in the terms of Williams's simple equation: "LEG + Modernity = Liberalism."[62] The point is that, while any number of systems can meet the BLD at a minimum, only some will Make Sense (MS) in particular places at particular times (a state that Williams helpfully codifies with the deictic "now and around here"):

> "MS" is a category of historical understanding – which we can call, if we like, a hermeneutical category. There are many difficulties of interpretation associated with it, for example whether there are not some historical constellations of belief which altogether fail to MS. ... But when we get to our own case, the notion "MS" does become normative, because what (most) MS to us is a structure of authority which we think we should accept. We do not have to say that these previous societies were wrong about all these things, though we may indeed think, in the light of our *entzaubert* state, that some of what MS to them does not MS to us because we take it to be false, in a sense that represents a cognitive advance – a claim which carries its own responsibilities, in the form of a theory of error,

---

[61] This is, of course, a deliberately limited use of "us," and tracing the story of how some members of "technically advanced, democratic, and, above all, pluralistic" societies became ideologically identical to the first-person plural of history is to confront one of liberalism's – indeed, one of capitalism's – founding myths. The ready move from "some people" to "us" is, in other words, an expression of the "ex-nominating operation" that Barthes takes as characteristic of the bourgeoisie; converting itself at the level of ideology from a real social class to a kind of natural phenomenon, the bourgeoisie thrives on the tactical play between ubiquity, invisibility, and privilege. Although Williams seems prepared to accept a rightness-of-relation between a certain way of thinking and a certain moment in time, he nonetheless insists throughout on the historicity of any given political arrangement. Even if it seems to "us" that liberalism is the best of all possible systems, that seeming must be understood as the result of real and often bloody conflict. "Let's not," says Chantalle Mouffe, "forget that, while we tend today to take the link between liberalism and democracy for granted, their union, far from being a smooth process, was the result of bitter struggles." Barthes, *Mythologies*, 137–141; Mouffe, *The Democratic Paradox* (London: Verso, 2009), 3.

[62] Williams, *In the Beginning Was the Deed*, 9. With this and much else, Williams recalls Schumpeter's minimal account of democracy in *Capitalism, Socialism, and Democracy*: "Democracy is a political *method*, that is to say, a certain type of institutional arrangement for arriving at political – legislative and administrative – decisions and hence incapable of being an end in itself, irrespective of what decisions it will produce under given historical conditions. And this must be the starting point of any attempt at defining it" (242).

something which [liberalism] in its current forms has spectacularly tended to lack.[63]

Williams's modestly historicist defense of liberalism recalls Niebuhr's odd but compelling sense that the best argument for democracy isn't the universality of any particular ideal, but the intractable, material, and perfectly historical limits of human experience and knowledge that he comes close to calling original sin:

> The reason this final democratic freedom is right, though the reasons given for it in the modern period are wrong, is that there is no historical reality, whether it be church or government, whether it be the reason of wise men or specialists, which is not involved in the flux and relativity of human existence; which is not subject to error and sin, and which is not tempted to exaggerate its errors and sins when they are made immune to criticism.[64]

This critical realism might also give us a better sense of what it means to say that a political system is *rigged*. When one takes successful political systems and the institutions that support them as valuable because they are legitimate instead of "good," the idea of rigging takes on a historical or political as opposed to an ethical character. It can serve as the basis for a productive analysis of the conditions necessary to real political legitimacy rather than an excuse preemptively to demonize and disenfranchise those seen as one's opponents. And while the air around philosophical or "first" questions about legitimacy, authority, and conflict can get pretty thin, thinking about these same ideas in relation to the practical business of running elections is illuminating to say the least. That is, while the philosophers are arguing about what democracy is or what it ought to be, someone else sits in an office, making apparently minor, potentially devastating, and, in their way, oddly exquisite design decisions about how many names can fit legibly on one side of a ballot; about what color the ballot or the ballot's ink should be; about where to put poll workers, voting machines, pens, pencils, and signs; and about how many "I Voted!" stickers to order; about who will carry the ballots from one place to another; and about who will count the votes and how they will do it. Elections allow us to see otherwise abstract relations between rules, institutions, and events in strikingly concrete and historical terms. Where, in other words, it can be difficult to imagine where an idea about democracy and the quotidian experience of democratic society meet, it is all-too-easy to imagine and to see how both benign and malign electoral rules – ballot

---

[63] Williams, *In the Beginning Was the Deed*, 11.   [64] Niebuhr, *Major Works*, 535.

design, electoral logistics, literacy tests, poll taxes, agenda-setting – can have profound effects on the outcome of elections and, thus, on the shape of whole societies.

While it can seem equally unreal to ask if a whole and complex society is just or legitimate, the question of electoral legitimacy is, as we saw in the previous section, fundamental to the everyday work of designing, conducting, and adjudicating elections. Put differently, if a government is to have authority – which is to say, if it will be able to enforce a state's rules even when those rules go against the avowed interests or preferences of some of its citizens – that government will have to be first recognized as legitimate; and, in a representative democracy, that means that the processes that both led to and followed from a vote will also have to be recognized as legitimate by of those affected by that election's results. And, what's more, where it can seem abstract to the point of absurdity deciding whether something as complex and multifarious as a political system is or isn't "good," it can, at least in some cases, be quite easy to say whether an election was legitimate. Does the election have rules? Do its rules make sense? Are they consistent? Do the candidates and the officials involved in the election understand and observe those rules? Will the candidates and their followers respect the legitimate outcome of an election once it legitimately happens?

That it is possible to ask and answer these questions doesn't mean they will lead to satisfactory or reasonable answers; that the questions can be asked and answered does not mean elections will never be rigged or that the results of even legitimate elections will be happy, equitable, or just. It does not mean even wholly legitimate elections won't be undermined, called into question, or thwarted. We know that. What it does mean is it is possible, practical, and necessary to ask and answer these questions in relation to elections in a way that it is not necessarily possible in relation to the political systems, political choices, and social and political values that those elections support. That, in turn, means that thinking critically about elections, their limits, and the illusions they engender can offer a solid and surprisingly strong basis from which to move with greater confidence back up into the headier regions of political philosophy. Karl Popper writes in *The Open Society & Its Enemies,*

> He who accepts the principle of democracy in this sense is therefore not bound to look upon the result of a democratic vote as an authoritative expression of what is right. Although he will accept a decision of the majority, for the sake of making the democratic institutions work, he will feel free to combat it by democratic means, and to work for its revision. And should he live to see the day when the majority vote destroys the democratic

institutions, then this sad experience will tell him only that there does not exist a foolproof method of avoiding tyranny. But it need not weaken his decision to fight tyranny, nor will it expose his theory as inconsistent.[65]

This minimalist emphasis on the "rules of the game" as opposed to the ethical content of particular electoral outcomes is, as we have all seen, more urgent than one might have imagined only a few years ago; as elections are decided more and more frequently in the protracted and picayune litigation that follows the vote and the tally, the coherence and clarity of rules, processes, and procedures become more and more important.

As Adam Przeworski says in *Why Bother with Elections?*, a book that combines the conceptual minimalism of Williams's BLD with practical attention to the details of electoral design,

> some popular criticisms of elections – specifically that they offer no choice and that individual electoral participation is ineffective – are mistaken, based on an incorrect understanding of elections as a mechanism by which people decide together as a collectivity. I contend that, in societies in which people have different interests and divergent values, looking for rationality (or 'justice') is futile, but that elections provide an instruction to governments to minimize the dissatisfaction with how we are governed. ... The greatest value of elections, for me by itself sufficient to cherish them, is that at least under some conditions they allow us to process in relative liberty and civic peace whatever conflicts arise in society, that they prevent violence.[66]

He goes on: "Politics, in any form or fashion, has limits in shaping and transforming societies. This is just a fact of life. I believe that it is important to know these limits, so as not to criticize elections for not achieving what no political arrangements can achieve."[67] Przeworski's argument about elections shares a number of qualities with what Williams and other realists say about politics in general: (1) a political disposition needs realistically to accept disagreement, conflict, and even violence as necessary to human societies, and (2) political realism has what Wittgenstein might have recognized as a *therapeutic* value because it does not ask from political systems what they cannot give: "democracy," Przeworski says elsewhere, "has become an altar on which everyone hangs his or her favorite *ex voto*. Almost all normatively desirable aspects of political, and sometimes even social and economic, life are credited as

[65] Popper, *The Open Society*, 119.   [66] Przeworski, *Why Bother*, 4.
[67] Przeworski, *Why Bother*, 5.

intrinsic to democracy ... ";[68] and (3) the basis for the evaluation of political systems cannot be the question of whether they are "good" and must rather be the question of whether they meet conditions that would allow both us and those with whom we will disagree to agree *at least* that those conditions have been met and that a given election and its results thus legitimate in those and only those terms: "if," he says, "the point of departure is that in any society there are conflicts, of values and of interests, electing rulers appears nothing short of miraculous."[69]

A negative or minimalist conception of democracy "does not," says Przeworski, "alleviate the need for thinking about institutional design. In the end, the 'quality of democracy,' to use the currently fashionable phrase, does matter for its very survival. But my point is not that democracy can be, needs to be, improved, but that it would be worth defending even if it could not be."[70] As I'll discuss in the next section, although I find this realist account of the normative limits of elections persuasive, it is not necessarily self-evident. Other accounts of collective decision making, such as deliberative, epistemic, monitory, or "liquid" models, which are based on different ethical or cognitive assumptions, argue that it is possible either to create processes that can produce the normatively best or at least measurably better outcomes or to imagine those processes as having sufficient value in and of themselves to stand as ethical ends as opposed to merely procedural means. That said, a realist or minimalist approach to elections is useful to me, "now and around here," for a few reasons. First, when we manage our expectations about elections and resist the impulse to imagine them as designed either to produce reliably good outcomes or to make us better people, it becomes possible not only to see how we can make them better *in that sense* but also to understand what it really means to rig an election. While someone might *feel* that elections are rigged when they lead to outcomes that someone doesn't like, that feeling has less to do with an election and more to do with what the realist would recognize as either inflated expectations or bad faith. Writes Ian Shapiro,

> What should be as clear to us today ... is that democratic competition under conditions of majority rule remains the bedrock of democratic accountability. Its alleged pathologies have often been oversold, and the alternatives to it have often been overhyped. It is, to be sure, a minimal

---

[68] Adam Przeworski, "Minimalist Conception of Democracy," in *The Democracy Sourcebook*, ed. Ian Shapiro, Jose Antonio Cheibub, and Robert Dahl (Cambridge: Massachusetts Institute of Technology Press, 2003), 12.

[69] Przeworski, "Minimalist Conception," 12.   [70] Przeworski, "Minimalist Conception," 16.

democratic requirement. But minimal is not negligible, as the billions who continue to be governed without it know all too well.[71]

To know if an election succeeds or fails or if it has been rigged, we need a clearer sense both of what really counts as an election and of how our hopes for and fears about democracy can support or distort our sense of what ought to count.

C.   To Find a Form of Association

In the last section I looked at democratic elections from the perspective of political realism, which is to say at elections as events that can be defined as *political* because of their coherent relation to what Bernard Williams calls the BLD. That is, where many see democracy as identical to one of its salutary ethical byproducts (justice, virtue, the good), the political realist understands democracy as a legitimate means of managing rational disagreements between members of a society. Something like this realist or minimalist view of democracy as a procedure or method as opposed to an end or norm appears, as I said, in Schumpeter's influential account: "Democracy is a political *method*, that is to say, a certain type of institution arrangement for arriving at political – legislative and administrative – decisions and hence incapable of being an end in itself, irrespective of what decisions it will produce under given historical conditions."[72] In order, that is, for a political system to have and to maintain the authority necessary to enforce its rules, those living – and, both inevitably and reasonably for the minority, living reluctantly – within and under that system must recognize its basic procedural legitimacy as real and, crucially, as distinct from the contestable quality of its outcomes. It's easy to believe in democracy when it gives us what we want; its limits are only revealed when it requires some of us to accept what we don't want and maybe can't stand.

Defined in these minimal terms, the BLD becomes for Williams a stable point against which to engage in the comparative historical analysis of political systems; because historical and social conditions change, the terms of what could satisfy the BLD will change even if the BLD itself does not. While it doesn't make sense to say that liberal democracy is and always will be good, it can make reasonable if distinctly limited sense to say that it might be good *for us*. That is, because it meets the basic demand for

[71] Ian Shapiro, *The Real World of Democratic Theory* (Princeton, NJ: Princeton University Press, 2010), 79.
[72] Schumpeter, *Capitalism, Socialism, and Democracy*, 242.

legitimacy as that demand is experienced by some in pluralistic, technologically advanced, and largely secular societies, it can make sense for some to embrace it as a good political system "now and around here." The realist's work, at least as Williams understands it, is thus not simply to deny the value of liberalism or liberal democracy or, in fact, any other system outright; it is to caution us against mistaking what works "now and around here" for what will work for everyone, always and everywhere. Because even realist arguments about legitimacy, authority, and historicity can feel pretty abstract when pursued at that level of generality, it makes sense to look not only at democracy as such but also at the elections on which democracy ostensibly depends. The countless little (but practically immense) logistical details that can determine the course and outcome of an election make palpable both the relation between the logic of elections and the logic of democracy and the real value of legitimacy *qua* legitimacy as a way potentially to understand political authority or at least to mitigate political violence.

In this section, I want to turn to a different but related aspect of the question, to an aspect of democratic elections that stands as a necessary precondition to all those little but immense details: what do we expect elections to do, and how we should go about helping them do it? If the previous sections focused on the realist's account of what *democracy* is and how the example of elections might help us to think about it, in this section I want to consider the election itself – as an imaginative technology, a shared event, a set of beliefs, a heuristic problem, a form of life. I want to consider a line of political thinking that runs from Jean-Jacques Rousseau to the present and focuses on the figural logics that get one from the real or imaginary preferences, interests, beliefs, or desires of individuals to those of a group. Thinking about elections in terms of their outcomes tends to obscure the problems, contradictions, and paradoxes that arise when we design procedures that could take us from the one to the many. That is why I'll focus here on the imaginative character and figurative force of that process. And, although interest in these procedures and paradoxes can seem like the exclusive province of consultants, specialists, and trainspotters, they have enormous consequences for the actual outcomes of real elections and carry a formal or conceptual or even aesthetic impulse that suggests the excessive presence of something awkward, strange, or even sometimes beautiful within the humdrum details of even the most ordinary election. Although elections are imagined as almost purely political events, the contingent imaginative work necessary, first, to make them legitimate and, second, to make people agree to act *as if* they believe they are legitimate will always rely on a set of rhetorical, figural, or formal moves that will turn thinking about elections into a matter of aesthetic and rhetorical, as well as strictly political, analysis.

Where, in other words, literary and cultural critics interested in democracy have tended to look to novels, plays, and films that represent real or imagined elections, I want to consider what it means that those real or imagined elections are themselves already representations of some other, earlier form of representation. Because elections exist not simply to register or produce unanimity but rather to make provisional and yet operable sense out of otherwise insuperable conflicts that exist between reasonable people, elections are always figural – always, as it were, metaphorical or maybe even allegorical: they represent conflict *as if* it were consensus, the many *as if* they were one and the one *as if* it were many, the impoverished information conveyed by a ballot *as if* it were a full statement of one's desires or beliefs. Because we use elections to represent and thus to process inevitable conflicts between reasonable people in the form of a majority decision (the first figural transformation), and then take that majority decision as the singular expression or intention of a society, a people, or what Rousseau called the *general will* (the second figural transformation), elections are never a mirror held up to nature; they are, instead, a difficult and mysterious kind of creative, refractive, imaginative act, a frankly poetic act that asks one willingly to suspend one's disbelief and to treat one thing *as if* it were another.[73] It is with something like this layered figural transformation in mind that Rousseau writes, "if there were no different interests, we should hardly be conscious of a common interest, as there would be no resistance to it; everything would run easily of its own accord, and politics would cease to be an art."[74] It is this *art* of politics that gets us from "different interests" to the "common interest" of the general will. So, it may be that we need to think about the aesthetic or the figural as coming both before and after the election – *before* in the form of paradoxes and conflicts no design can fully represent or overcome and *after* in the form of mimetic efforts to reckon with what happens whenever someone tries.

---

[73] Josiah Ober argues that as opposed to *embodiment* or *manifestation*, the classical Athenian concept of political representation is probably best understood as a form of *synecdoche*, "a figure of speech in which a part stands for and refers to a whole, or vice versa. Each of the various institutional 'parts' of the citizen body . . . could stand for and refer to the whole citizen body. . . . Synecdoche takes us from the vocabulary of constitution to that of signification, but this should cause difficulties only for those who assume that the Athenians were concerned more with legal definition than with symbolic reference." Ober, "Review Article: The Nature of Athenian Democracy," *Classical Philology*, 84(4) (October 1989), 330–331.

[74] Jean-Jacques Rousseau, *The Social Contract*, trans. Maurice Cranston (London: Penguin, 1968), 73.

And, if this all seems like a needlessly convoluted way of thinking about the everyday fact of democratic elections, I hope to show that something like this question (i.e., how does one represent history when history is itself the lived representation of a problem) is essential to some works fundamental to the history of democratic theory.

Before moving on, I should say a word or two about some of my assumptions in *The Electoral Imagination*, especially as they relate to the idea of the individual as person, value, or argumentative given. My ideas about the individual as an object or a problem are likely to fall between two stools and to displease readers of nearly opposite ideological dispositions. On the one side, some Marxists and others who treat bourgeois individualism as a sin nearly as original as primitive accumulation might say that my attention to the effort to aggregate individual decisions, desires, and interests into a single and operable social choice – a general will – is evidence of an unreconstructed liberalism. In other words, because belief in the aggregation of individual wills depends on a prior and often untested belief in the existence of individuals and wills as always already imagined by bourgeois ideology, to worry about aggregation is, in some sense, to accept bourgeois ideology as a tacit and transhistorical horizon. One of my more severe readers (who naturally was also one of my best readers) suggested that worrying so much about why and how *individuals* think what they think and do what they do risked turning *The Electoral Imagination* into a late-style Robinsonade. On the other side, some readers invested in the explanatory power of economic models might feel that, rather than being a creature of unearned and, for that reason, mythic authority, the individual as pictured in my book is instead all too anemic. As opposed to identifying one or another metric along which the rational acts of rational and self-interested individuals could be understood, compared, and, at last, added up, I come back again and again to what seems to me both entirely real and wholly incoherent about individuals not only as they are represented but also as they in fact are. It is, as I argue throughout, hard to know the difference between a wish, a desire, an interest, and a belief, and, as a result, one can believe in the social meaning of the individual in terms that exceed and fall short of either the intellectual demands of either rational choice modeling or the ideological demands of bourgeois individualism. Simply put, while the idea of the individual *qua* individual can't explain much on its own, neither will the individual simply go away; if the individual isn't a solution, it remains nonetheless an interesting and recalcitrant problem.

This is why I rely in my title and throughout on the hoary concept of the *imagination*. One of the most striking things about the many more or less elaborate electoral procedures I describe throughout this book is that, while they are always meant to do a kind of work and always exist within a crowded field of social determinates, they are also the peculiar products of peculiar imaginations. Although the details electoral procedure and electoral modeling can seem like pretty dry stuff, the field – in both its practical and theoretical modes – tends to attract enthusiasts, eccentrics, oddballs, and loners. What figures like Rousseau, Bentham, George Grote, Thomas Hare, Lewis Carroll, William Morris, Duncan Black, and Robin Farquharson share beyond politics, ideology, or social position is a kind of imaginative or even visionary intensity. Although the imagination understood in these generative, unruly, and idiosyncratic terms is undoubtedly individual, it does not lend itself easily to either ideological or methodological individualism. Closer to the feral character of the Freudian and post-Freudian unconscious, this version of the individual requires one not to fall between two stools, but rather to push them aside, recognizing the imagination as too much for either the myth of the multitude or the fable of the bees.

So: is it possible to imagine a political system that could ensure the freedom of each of its citizens and yet still make and enforce laws, interact with other states, and operate as a single, coherent, and intentional political body? This is the question Rousseau asks in what remains both one of the most influential and yet also one of the most resistant or, to use Louis Althusser's phrase, most *discrepant* accounts of electoral procedure: *The Social Contract*. How can we recognize everyone as distinct and yet also act together as one? "Since," says Rousseau, "men cannot create new forces, but merely combine and control those which already exist, the only way in which they can preserve themselves is by uniting their separate powers in a combination strong enough to overcome any resistance, uniting them so that their powers are directed by a single motive and act in concert."[75] How, though, can individuals remain individuals, preserving their different passions and desires, and yet come authentically together as equal parts of an intentional and significant "combination"? What aggregative or imaginative process can take us from the pathological specificity of the individual will to the enlightened rationality of the general will? "How," he asks at a crucial moment, "to find a form of association which will defend the person and goods of each member with the collective force

---

[75] Rousseau, *Social Contract*, 59.

of all, and under which each individual, while uniting himself with the others, obeys no one but himself, and remains as free as before. . . . This is the fundamental problem to which the social contract holds the solution."[76]

And what is Rousseau's solution to this fundamental problem? What is the "general will"? How can it be both the sum of and yet also something greater than the sum of the wills of all the people? How will we know the general will when we see it? And how did Rousseau manage not only to bring an abstraction as strange, new, and "artificial" as the general will to life but also to persuade so many after him that such an invention could serve as the practical and legitimizing basis for a democratic state? It is important to see from the outset that Rousseau's own handling of this problem is pulled in two apparently incompatible directions. As David Lay Williams points out, much of the confusion around *The Social Contract* comes from the "considerable debate on whether or not the general will is largely a formal or procedural concept on the one hand, or a substantive one on the other."[77] On one of those hands, Rousseau's work is a nuts-and-bolts procedural exercise, a merely but powerfully consistent technical blueprint for getting from the one to the many and back again. For Joshua Cohen, while Rousseau might *dream* about the dissolution of the self into the ecstatic unity of the state, he *argues* for a complex but practical political system that can balance what Cohen – with almost extravagant sanity – calls the Particular Interest Condition and the Common Good Condition: "Citizens *share* and it is *common knowledge* that they share a conception of their 'common good,' although they may have – and indeed can in general be expected to have – different beliefs about what will advance that good." In these terms, Rousseau's text ought to be understood, for all its apparent obscurity, as a procedural argument about inputs, outputs, conflict, deliberation, consensus, and good institutional design. It's a blueprint, a guide.

On the other hand, *The Social Contract* has seemed to many an essentially imaginative or literary performance: we need to *imagine* individuals, groups, acts, and intentions in a fundamentally new way if we are to square the democratic circle of freedom and equality. Hegel suggests in *The Philosophy of Right* that what makes Rousseau both powerful and limited is the fact that, for him, the state was at last *only* a way of thinking:

---

[76] Rousseau, *Social Contract*, 60.
[77] David Lay Williams, "The Substantive Elements of Rousseau's General Will," in *The General Will: The Evolution of a Concept*, ed. David Lay Williams and James Farr (Cambridge: Cambridge University Press, 2015), 222.

"it was," he says, "the achievement of Rousseau to put forward the *will* as the principle of the state, a principle which has *thought* not only as its form ... but also as its content, and which is in fact *thinking* itself."[78] And, while this act of *thinking* a state into existence represented a truly extraordinary moment in intellectual history, it became something both wonderful and terrible when perversely realized in the later days of the French Revolution: "when these abstractions were invested with power, they afforded the tremendous spectacle, for the first time we know of in human history, of the overthrow of all existing and given conditions within an actual major state and the revision of its constitution from first principles and purely in terms of *thought*."[79] Similarly, in his essay on *The Social Contract*, Louis Althusser takes the text not as a coherent argument but rather as figural or rhetorical response to a real but repressed state of affairs, as an intricate and even exquisite play of discrepancies, disavowals, and masks: "The 'solution' of the political 'problem' by the 'social contract' is only possible because of the theoretical 'play' of this Discrepancy. However, the 'Social Contract' has the immediate function of masking the play of the Discrepancy which alone enables it to function. To mask means to denegate and reject."[80] Whatever *The Social Contract* is, it isn't what it says it is, which makes it more a rhetorical or poetic performance than a political argument or, certainly, any kind of practicable plan. And, finally, Paul de Man is explicit in *Allegories of Reading* about what he takes to be the figural character of *The Social Contract*. As opposed to a specific procedure that might provide a political foundation for a real society, de Man sees Rousseau as tacking endlessly between the tropic poles of metaphor and metonymy: "The distinction between metonymic aggregates and metaphorical totalities, based on the presence, within the latter, of a 'necessary link' that is lacking in the former, is characteristic of all metaphorical systems ... " and especially, he says, *The Social Contract*.[81]

So, which is it? Is *The Social Contract* a blueprint or a poem, an algorithm or an imaginative leap? It is odd, to say the least, that so famous, so essential a text would be understood not merely in different ways but in ways that are fundamentally incommensurate. In what follows, I want to consider the aggregative and ecstatic versions of *The Social Contract*. I'll

[78] G. W. F. Hegel, *Elements of the Philosophy of Right*, trans. H. B. Nisbet (Cambridge: Cambridge University Press, 1991), 277.
[79] Hegel, *Philosophy of Right*, 277.
[80] Louis Althusser, *Politics and History: Montesquieu, Rousseau, Marx* (London: Verso, 2007), 114.
[81] Paul de Man, *Allegories of Reading: Figural Language in Rousseau, Nietzsche, Rilke, and Proust* (New Haven, CT: Yale University Press, 1982), 259.

begin by looking more closely at figural logic of Rousseau's text before suggesting that his great innovation is his understanding that logic and rhetoric, proceduralism and poetry, the metonymic and the metaphorical are in fact two aspects necessary to the same general will. What Rousseau prepares us to see is that even the driest and most familiar of electoral procedures must at some level rely on a more or less unsupported act of the imagination.

Given its obvious and overriding interest in the reciprocal relation between parts and wholes, its investment the significant difference between merely mechanical or metonymical aggregates (the will of all) and natural or metaphorical totalities (the general will), and its sustained effort to manage the unlikely passage from quantity to quality, it does make sense to approach *The Social Contract* from an aesthetic perspective. Although Rousseau's book is an argument for the organic coherence of the general will, *The Social Contract* is also an argument about the problems and tensions that might prevent that coherence from coming fully into being: the tension between the political imperatives of freedom and equality, the tension between the centripetal force of a healthy state and the centrifugal force of the population growth that that health encourages, the tension between the *amour-propre* of the individual and the *amour de soi* of the citizen, and so on. It isn't hard to see where the unruly textual or rhetorical energies of *The Social Contract* threaten to overwhelm or at least to leaven its urge toward coherence and thus to demand rhetorical as opposed to logical modes of analysis.

Take for example the several times Rousseau compares the state to a body. By and large, he relies on the metaphor as a way of thinking through the relation between the state, its different members, and the executive intention that could somehow move those different members *as if* they were joint parts of a single living organism. He says:

> If the state, or the nation, is nothing other than an artificial person the life of which consists in the union of its members and if the most important of its cares is its preservation, it needs to have a universal and compelling power to move and dispose of each part in whatever manner is beneficial to the whole.[82]

Here, Rousseau assumes the existence of some natural relation between body and mind or body and soul to envision a similarly reciprocal *political* relation between the different parts of the state. "The body politic," says

---

[82] Rousseau, *Social Contract*, 74.

Judith Shklar, "has to be integrated and it needs a 'force' in order to move and act."[83] Where, however, these lines assume that relation as a given, an earlier use of nearly the same figure emphasizes instead that relation's more difficult historical dimension: "this act of association," says Rousseau, "creates an artificial and corporate body composed of as many members as there are voters in the assembly, and by this same act that body acquires its unity, its common *ego*, its life and its will."[84] Where, in other words, the first lines I quoted simply assume the existence of this "compelling power," these lines imply the before-and-after of a constructive and maybe fictional act, one that could "infuse a spark of being" into a body that would otherwise lack both life and will. What was taken as natural reappears as something instead forged by "human hand and brain."

My reference to *Frankenstein* and the "spark of being" that brought the creature to life is intentional here. It seems clear that Mary Shelley had "J.-J. Rousseau, Citizen of Geneva" in mind when she decided to set her tale in that same city, and, while critics have tended to focus on the influence of certain biographical details from *The Confessions*, the several corporate bodies in *The Social Contract* offer, I think, a more interesting point of comparison. The reappearance of Rousseau's "compelling power" literalized as Shelley's "spark of being" helps to account for the mix of the natural and the artificial, the human and the divine, on which Rousseau also depends; whether understood as science or magic, "the act by which people become *a* people" is undoubtedly rare and enigmatic. This makes this next appearance of the corporate body in *The Social Contract* even more suggestive:

> Sometimes our theorists . . . make the sovereign a creature of fantasy, a patchwork of separate pieces, rather as if they were to construct a man of several bodies – one with eyes, one with legs, the other with feet and nothing else. It is said that Japanese mountebanks can cut up a child under the eyes of spectators, throw the different parts up into the air, and then make the child come down, alive and all of a piece. This is more or less the trick that our political theorists perform – after dismembering the social body with a sleight of hand worthy of the fairground, they put the pieces together again anyhow.[85]

In one instance, Rousseau simply assumes the relation between the body and the soul of the state as a given; in the next, he acknowledges the

[83] Judith Shklar, *Men and Citizens: A Study of Rousseau's Social Theory* (Cambridge: Cambridge University Press, 1985), 209.
[84] Rousseau, *Social Contract*, 61.   [85] Rousseau, *Social Contract*, 71.

appearance of the state's "life and will" as a wonderful invention, as "an act of association" that marks out a historical before and after; here he suggests that, at least in the hands of other theorists, what seems to animate the body isn't nature, magic, or even science. It is, rather, "a sleight of hand worthy of the fairground," a cheap trick that Poe might have seen as the "cock's feathers, . . . red paint and . . . black patches" of political philosophy.[86] As Emily Steinlight says of the creature's similarly corporate body in *Frankenstein*, "that great multitude, in becoming one, becomes one too many."[87] Although Rousseau invokes this strange image to dismiss what *other* theorists do, even invoking the possibility that the state's motive power could be a trick, a con, a fiction discloses a difficult and textual complexity immanent to Rousseau's great work. "Legislator and charlatan," writes Geoffrey Bennington, "remain radically undecidable" in Rousseau.[88] As we'll soon see, something like this image returns not only with the distended and disembodied figures that populate Lewis Carroll's imagination but also at the start of Ellison's *Invisible Man*: "Like the bodiless heads you see sometimes in circus sideshows, it is as though I have been surrounded by mirrors of hard, distorting glass."[89] For reasons I'll discuss, the possible impossibility of the invisible man's body forces us to reconsider both Rousseau's "creature of fantasy" and the logical torsions of Arrow's impossibility theorem in relation to the dismembering and yet grotesquely "law-preserving" violence of institutional racism.[90] Coming back to *The Social Contract*: between his three references to the body

---

[86] Edgar Allan Poe, *Selected Poetry and Tales*, ed. James Hutchisson (Guelph, Ontario: Broadview Press, 2012), 504.

[87] Emily Steinlight, *Populating the Novel: Literary Form and the Politics of Surplus Life* (Ithaca, NY: Cornell University Press, 2018) 49.

[88] Quoted in Honig, *Emergency Politics: Paradox, Law, Democracy* (Princeton, NJ: Princeton University Press), 22.

[89] Ralph Ellison, *Invisible Man* (New York: Vintage, 1995), 3.

[90] Also consider the brief and maybe disingenuous foreword with which Rousseau begins *The Social Contract*: "This little treatise is part of a larger work which I undertook many years ago without thinking of the limitations of my powers, and have long since abandoned. Of the various fragments that might have been taken from what I wrote, this is the most considerable, and the one I think the least unworthy of being offered to the public. The rest," he concludes, "no longer exists." As opposed to advertising his book as a finished and systematic treatise, Rousseau casts his great work of political theory instead as a "unfinished" fragment, as a part without a whole, as a sort of inadvertent precursor to other romantic fragments and, especially to that other great and unfinished essay on the formal limits of sovereignty, Coleridge's "Kubla Khan." Just as the cracked dream of Coleridge's preface to that poem seems to anticipate or to reflect or even to image forth that "miracle of rare device, / A sunny pleasure-dome with caves of ice," so does Rousseau's foreword – with its odd acknowledgment that what follows is, after everything, only a fragment – bring out an irony dangerously and maybe necessarily latent in a project invested wholly in the resolution of many discrete fragments into a political entity singular, intentional, and whole.

politic, the act of making a state or identifying the general will in Rousseau drifts between postulate, aspiration, and farce; it is, at the very least, a problem.

Left there, we would probably want simply to side with the readers of Rousseau who see his work as unruly, problematic, or ecstatic. As opposed to figures like Cohen or Richard Boyd who work to place Rousseau "squarely in the camp of modern procedural justice," we might thus feel with Althusser, de Man, Judith Shklar, and others that the romantic ironies, logical paradoxes, and sharply critical commitments of *The Social Contract* are, finally, too many to overcome, and that, even if Rousseau *had* wanted to prepare a roadmap to the general will, he ended up with something very different: a thought experiment, political fiction, maybe a kind of dream, but not, to be sure, a workable political program.[91] He was, writes Shklar, "a social critic, the most devastating of all, and not a designer of plans for political reform."[92] It wouldn't make sense, then, to look to Rousseau for an idea of *how* practically to bridge the gap between the one and the many and thus *how* to imagine an electoral process that could produce a result while also meeting certain conditions related to our ordinary understanding of and expectations for the meaning of individuals, groups, and political legitimacy. In order, however, to make that choice and to prefer one Rousseau over the other, we would need first to accept as apposite that choice's terms. We would need, in other words, to accept that we *should* think about Rousseau as a creature caught between the various oppositions that have tended to structure the field: head or heart, classic or romantic, dreamer or schemer, idealist or realist, liberal or communitarian, democrat or totalitarian, and so on.

I think forcing a choice between the imaginative and the institutional in Rousseau misses the point. Indeed, the brilliance of Rousseau's performance lies in his understanding that all procedures are imaginative, that the act of deciding apart and, thus, the act of making a state together will always depend on a leap into the dark. Consider one of the most gratuitously procedural moments in *The Social Contract*. There is, says Rousseau,

> a great difference between the will of all and the general will: the general will studies only the common interest while the will of all studies private

---

[91] Richard Boyd, "Justice, Beneficence, and Boundaries," in *The General Will: The Evolution of a Concept*, ed. James Farr and David Lay Williams (Cambridge: Cambridge University Press, 2015), 249.
[92] Shklar, *Men and Citizens*, vii.

intertest, and is indeed no more than the sum of individual desires. But if we take away from these same wills, the pluses and minuses which cancel each other out, the balance which remains is the general will.[93]

Like a good social scientist, policy wonk, or quant, Rousseau identifies apparently measurable aspects of different actors and social states and uses a mathematical model to imagine a process that could take us responsibly from one to the other. Feed the relevant information (wills, desires, etc.) into the algorithm and see what comes out. Crunch the numbers. Do the math. Add it up. That said, it is hard to take Rousseau's numbers all that seriously. Seyla Benhabib writes that, "Rousseau's 'arithmetic' solution does not satisfy, because it is not at all clear what the language of 'taking away the pluses and minuses of the individual wills' could mean concretely or institutionally."[94] Hélène Landemore agrees that "it is not clear that Rousseau used mathematical concepts as more than rhetorical tools. Rousseau was trying to dress up his theory in the scientific clothes of his time . . . without necessarily being fully successful at the task."[95] Elsewhere Rousseau seems to acknowledge as much:

> If anyone, wishing to ridicule this system . . . I should reply that I am here using numbers only as an example; and the ratios of which I speak are not measured merely by the number of men but more generally by the amount of activity, which results from the concurrence of innumerable causes; I should add that although I have borrowed momentarily for the sake of expressing myself in fewer words, the language of mathematics, I am still well aware that mathematical precision has no place in moral calculations.[96]

It's not math; it's mathy!

Instead, though, of simply dismissing Rousseau's "moral calculations," we should pause to consider what they might mean and where they might get us. Although his scheme is obscure, its obscurity is perhaps less an issue with his thinking or writing than with his precocity; Rousseau is, I think, reaching toward a mode of expression that, while unfinished and thus ambiguous, will prove essential to subsequent electoral theories. As we will see, *all* efforts to move from individual preferences to the preference of the group – no matter how empirical or economic – must depend on some prior idea of or assertion about what people really are and what it would take to represent them as comparable. To move from what a lot of

[93] Rousseau, *Social Contract*, 73.   [94] Quoted in Honig, *Emergency Politics*, 18.
[95] Hélène Landemore, *Democratic Reason: Politics, Collective Intelligence, and the Rule of the Many* (Princeton, NJ: Princeton University Press, 2017), 74.
[96] Rousseau, *Social Contract*, 105.

individuals believe or think or want to what a whole society should do, one needs first to discover or invent a means of capturing and then quantifying desire. This isn't true only of something as ambitious as the general will; it is, as we shall see, true of every election. Every election relies on some formula, some alchemical process that would transmute desires into votes and votes into leaders and laws. Because, however, every such formula must rely on an idea or belief about what people and desires really are, our elections are built on more or less conscious postulates that, because they are at least somewhat arbitrary, must rely on taste, inclination, imagination, fiction, or faith. Whenever anyone tries to reckon rightly with the "pluses and minuses" of an electoral process, they will have already *imagined* something about what people and groups are.

In *Emile*, published in the same year as *The Social Contract*, Rousseau returns to the numerical relation between citizen and the state: "Natural man is entirely for himself. He is numerical unity, the absolute whole which is relative only to itself or its kind. Civil man is only a fractional unity dependent on the denominator; his value is determined by his relation to the whole, which is the social body."[97] On the one hand, the passage is about contrasts, the difference between the "natural man" and the citizen, between the naïve and the sentimental, between the ancients and the moderns. On the other hand, it is about the citizen's quantitative relation to other citizens, the state, and the general will. While representing citizen and social body as quantities falling above and below the fraction line seems at first to accentuate the existential distance between them, the point of a fractional representation is rather to acknowledge that an apparent or aspectual difference is in fact the index of a larger unity. Because, in other words, both sides of a fraction depend on the assumption of some other prior and shared field of comparison or measurement, it allows us to enjoy the *feel* of local difference against the tacit backdrop of a larger harmony; writes Ernst Cassirer,

> the ordinary system of fractional numbers is obviously an intellectual instrument adequate in every respect to accomplish all the tasks that can arise [in relation to the measurement of concrete things]. For within this system there is no smallest difference, for between any two elements, however near, there can always be given a new element belonging to the system; thus a conceptual differentiation is offered here, which is never

---

[97] Jean-Jacques Rousseau, *Emile: or, On Education*, trans. Allan Bloom (New York: Basic Books, 1979), 39–40.

reached in the observable relations of things, to say nothing of being surpassed.[98]

When, in that case, Rousseau opts to represent the difference between the individual and the group as a fraction, he takes difference as paradoxical proof of identity. That they are different makes us want to compare them; that they are also the same allows us to do so. In the fraction, difference is proof of equivalence and equivalence is what motivates difference. The point is that, in imagining or inventing the citizen as part of a fraction, Rousseau is imagining a form of real and measurable difference that is *also* a similarity amenable to numerical aggregation. He is doing the thinking – the imagining – that will let later theorists do the math. He shows that there is no real difference between procedure and pure imagination.

Rousseau fine-tunes some of this pseudo-mathematical work in his late chapter on "The Suffrage." It is a strange chapter because, after so much difficult and abstract thinking and writing about sovereign authority, private interests, and the general will, it all comes back to people voting and majorities winning:

> When a law is proposed in the people's assembly, what is asked of them is not precisely whether they will approve of the proposition or reject it, but whether it is in conformity with the general will which is theirs; each by giving his vote gives his opinion on this question, and the counting of votes yields a declaration of the general will.[99]

And, after so many pages, that's that: The general will is what we get when we have a vote and let the majority decide. Rousseau then gets uncharacteristically officious about the details. Reflecting, for instance, on what proportion of the people ought to constitute a real majority and thus stand as a representative of the general will, he says that,

> Two general maxims may serve to determine these ratios: the first, that the more important and serious the matter to be decided, the closer should the opinion which is to prevail approach unanimity; the second, the swifter the decision the question demands, the smaller the prescribed majority may be allowed to become; and in decisions which have to be given immediately, a majority of one must suffice.[100]

---

[98] Ernst Cassirer, *Substance and Function and Einstein's Theory of Relativity* (Chicago: Open Court Publishing Company, 1923), 57.
[99] Rousseau, *Social Contract*, 153.   [100] Rousseau, *Social Contract*, 154.

These maxims will, of course, make familiar sense; for instance, *Robert's Rules of Order* agrees when it tells us that,

> Some motions require a majority vote, a number greater than half the votes cast, others a two-thirds vote. One of the fundamental principles of parliamentary law requires a two-thirds vote for every motion that suppresses a main question without free debate. Sometimes a vote is unanimous. A plurality vote – the most votes cast for a candidate – is used only in elections when authorized by bylaws.[101]

Now, taken by itself, the logic in both *Robert* and Rousseau is straightforward enough: Different motions should require different majorities to pass. What's hard is thinking about the *general will* as differently equivalent to these different majorities. If there are 100 people in an assembly or a community, and they hold a vote to express the general will, the essential *quality* of the general will would somehow be equal to entirely different *quantities* depending on the importance and the timing of the question. For a "more important and serious" matter, the general will is equal to 67 votes; for a matter requiring "swifter" attention, the general will is equal to 60 votes; and "in decisions which have to be given immediately, a majority of one must suffice," the general will is equal to 51 votes. If, however, the general will can be expressed by and thus be equal to each of these numbers, what does that mean? Does it mean that 67 equals 60 equals 51? That a majority is sometimes not a majority and that the general will is sometimes not general enough?

If, however, the math gets complicated, we should see what's at stake here. What, after all, does Rousseau want? His use of the fraction as a figure for the relation between the will of the individual and the will of the group served as a tacit acknowledgement that, in order to design procedures that could compare and connect voter with voter and voters with the general will, one needs first to identify, invent, or imagine a common denominator that individuals and groups might share. For Rousseau, that common denominator is what he refers to as the state of nature, a nebulous set of qualities or characteristics that are basic, universal, and that would be leftover if we were able to take away the social "pluses and minuses" of selfish or private interest that prevent us from seeing the content of the nonpathological and, thus, the general will; that common denominator is what we would know if, as Rousseau writes in the *Second Discourse*, we could separate "the unshakeable base" of natural man out from the

---

[101] Henry M. Robert, *Robert's Rules of Order*, ed. Rachel Vixman (New York: Jove Books, 1977), 145.

contingent "successive developments" that come with history, culture, and, above all, the invention of private property.[102] The point is that, while imagining what persons were like in the state of nature is a speculative and historical project in the *Second Discourse*, in *The Social Contract* it is also a procedural necessity. Knowing what people are and, even more, what it is that all people share over and above or before the appearance of pathological passions and desires is a necessary and, as it were, methodologically modest precondition for doing the kind of aggregative, apples-to-apples work required to convert an indefinitely large number of differences of interest, intention, and understanding into something as coherent, effective, and intentional as the general will. The imaginative project *is* the procedural project.

Rousseau's investment in the state of nature not only as a good but also as a transitive and common denominator thus anticipates what economists and social choice theorists understand as the problem of *the interpersonal comparison of utilities*. Mid-century economists and political theorists like Lionel Robbins, J. R. Hicks, Paul Samuelson, and Kenneth Arrow argued that earlier utilitarian or socialist efforts to translate the good of many ones into the one good of the many came to grief when confronted with the complexity, epistemic richness, and, as it were, the *market freedom* of individual preferences. When, that is, one starts to supplement the utilitarian relationship between preference and pleasure with increasingly thick kinds of information about the effects of timing, intensity, uncertainty, mutual dependency, bad faith, sour grapes, etc., it becomes less and less possible to imagine a scheme that could compare and thus aggregate those complex states into a single expression of a group's shared experience and sense of welfare. This is why Vilfredo Pareto, another figure crucial to the history of electoral theory, moved at the beginning of the twentieth century away from efforts to represent utilities as independent, content-rich, *cardinal* values and opted instead to represent them as schedules of *ordinally* ranked preferences (this was the start of the "ordinal revolution"). Where a cardinal representation of a utility would say something about why and how much I want a thing *qua* thing, an ordinal ranking tells me only that I prefer one thing to another; it doesn't say why I want it, how much I want it, or even how much *more* I want it than another thing.[103] Pareto takes this ordinal flattening to suggestive and strange extremes:

---

[102] Jean-Jacques Rousseau, *The First and Second Discourses*, trans. Roger Masters and Judith Masters (New York: St. Martin's Press, 1964), 97.

[103] John W. Thompson, "Coombs' Theory of Data," *Philosophy of Science* 33(4) (December 1966), 367. "Where there are cabbages and kings and everything between, or when the characteristics to be measured are intangible, it may be possible to prefer A to B and B to C, but not be possible to say which of the two preferences (for A rather than B, or B rather than C) is the greater."

> A man faced with the choice between ten strokes of the cudgel and a good
> dinner will choose the dinner. We then say that this man, at least at the
> moment when he is being observed, prefers the good dinner to the ten
> strokes. Another man, say an ascetic, prefers ten strokes to the good dinner.
> We are not examining whether these men find pleasure in their choices; we
> are not at all seeking to ascertain the motives which impel them to perform
> the action; we need merely note the fact.[104]

Although, as Pareto clearly understands, the difference between the "good
dinner" and the "ten strokes of the cudgel" is real, rich, and we might even
say *novelistic*, and although one could write hundreds of pages about why
the choice really matters and what it really means, one needs, in order to
understand that choice as part of a general system of countless other
choices, to reduce its multifarious complexity to the common denominator
of ordinally ranked preference. And, although Freud, Nietzsche, and
Dostoevsky would and did have much to say about the thick distinction
between the man who chooses the good dinner (GD) and the man who
chooses the ten strokes (TS), there is for Pareto's system only and somewhat perversely the simple but undeniable difference between the ordering
GD > TS and the ordering TS > GD. If, in other words, the enigmatic
and, as it were, historical texture of cardinal values is what made those
values *meaningful*, that same quality is what made them difficult or
impossible to compare or to aggregate.

As a result, Pareto recommended their *methodological reduction*, strip-
ping away that detail to arrive at a pure and purely relative representation
of preference; and he did so not because he believed that that was how
people really lived or felt, but rather because how people really lived or felt
made aggregation and, thus, *one kind* of knowing impossible.

> An individual purchases a bottle of wine and puts it in his cellar; at this
> point, the economic phenomenon may end. Our individual will, at some
> later point, drink the bottle as and when it pleases him, alone or with
> friends, on a working day or on a holiday, at lunch or in the evening over a
> game of cards, taking deep draughts or sipping it. In short, he can consume
> it in an infinity of ways. Admittedly there's many a slip 'twixt the cup and
> lip, but we need not concern ourselves with this.[105]

We need not, in other words, concern ourselves with when the drinker
drinks, why the drinker drinks, where, how, or with whom the drinker

---

[104] Vilfredo Pareto, "Summary of Some Chapters of a New Treatise on Pure Economics by Professor
Pareto," *Giornale degli Economisti e Annali di Economia* 67(3) (December 2008), 457.
[105] Pareto, "Summary," 476.

drinks; if, that is, these are exactly the kind of details that would fascinate the philosopher or the novelist, they must mean nothing to the economist *qua* economist who would seek not to know the drinker but rather to know how the drinker adds to or takes away from a state of general equilibrium. There is a reason why Pareto's favorite term for bad economists was *les économistes littéraires*; they were, to him, writing novels or doing philosophy when they should have been doing economics.

The loss registered in the move from a cardinal or *thick* description of values – with their timing, tastes, compulsions, pleasures, memories, rhetoric, and regrets – to the ordinal or thin ranking of preferences is nonetheless palpable in Pareto: "the economic theories which will prove extremely instructive as regards the conditions governing the production of wheat, iron, and cotton will not provide any important information on the production of masterpieces such as those of Michelangelo or Moliere."[106] Pareto's system could, in that case, be taken as a secular or as a cynical or even as a resignedly melancholy response to the fundamental problem that Rousseau attempted to confront; instead, though of hoping for or regretting the absence of either pure reason or the state of nature, Pareto simply and pragmatically accepts the partial and deracinated methodological fiction of ordinally ranked and thus aggregable preferences. This is also why Arrow, in his classic work on social choice, begins with the assumption "that interpersonal comparison of utilities has no meaning and, in fact, that there is no meaning relevant to welfare comparisons in the measurability of individual utility."[107] I'll have a lot more to say about Pareto and Arrow as we go. For now, however, I want simply to note that what Pareto and Arrow accept as an intractable problem is one impetus behind Rousseau's desire to imagine the state of nature as a common denominator that would allow for the interpersonal comparison of utilities and thus the expression of an authentically general will. As Rousseau understood, to get to the necessary procedures, to do the math, one needs first to take an imaginative leap. To see the real of elections, one needs, in fact, to reckon with the electoral imagination.

D. *Un Abécédaire électoral*

In the three previous sections, I looked somewhat laboriously at three different aspects of electoral thinking. In Section A, I considered the

---

[106] Pareto, "Summary," 460.
[107] Kenneth J. Arrow, *Social Choice and Individual Values* (New Haven, CT: Yale University Press, 2012), 9.

practical and immediate engagement with electoral things. On the one hand, this meant looking at the historical and social particularity of particular elections, their rules, and the materials on which they rely. On the other, it meant thinking about different ways of reforming or engaging politically or procedurally with elections as they exist here and now. Section B thought through "political realism," an old but recently rejuvenated line of minimalist or skeptical thought that tries to distinguish between the real and the ideal of democracy and what is necessary to or in excess of a reasonably democratic life. In addition to casting this line of thought as an extension of the literature of lost illusions, I focused on the equally philosophical and historical question of *legitimacy*, especially as it is imagined in the work of Bernard Williams. In Section C, I turned to what was procedurally and rhetorically necessary to move coherently from the one to the many. I focused there on Rousseau's *The Social Contract* in order to track some of the risks and rewards that come with *imagining* schemes and procedures that might take us from the one of the individual, through the many of the group or the crowd, on to the one of a community, state, or general will. As I showed with Rousseau's great work, the conceptual requirements of modern elections demand that we think beyond the apparent difference between institutionalism and pure imagination. How to manage the fraught relation between the wish, belief, preference, or the liberty of the one and the disposition, obligations, and fate of the many is, we know, a problem that modern democracies and modern novels share. Before we can arrive at even the most mundane of rules, we must first have taken a leap into the dark.

In what follows, I want to draw on each of these aspects – A, B, and C – in order to understand both the political and aesthetic particularity of and the historical relations between my different cases: the weird suppositional intensity of Victorian efforts to imagine a workable ballot; the imaginative energy that William Morris and Lewis Carroll drew from the limits of parliamentary democracy; an encounter with the idea of impossibility that formed an unexpected link between the abstractions of social choice and the violence of white supremacy; and the dismal art that underwrote Nixon's invention of the silent majority. Seeing how some elections and some representations of elections exist at once as objects of practical, procedural, philosophical, and even visionary significance will not only demand that we think in terms of aspectual density, but that we also understand how and why the electoral imagination might serve as an index of problems and possibilities that go far beyond the apparent minutiae of Droop quotas, butterfly ballots, and first-past-the-post primaries. To recognize that the truth or the meaning of elections lies somewhere in the overlap between these and other aspects is to see, once again, "that we are condemned for some time yet ... to speak *excessively* about reality."[108]

[108] Roland Barthes, *Mythologies*, trans. Annette Lavers (New York: Farrar, Straus, & Giroux, 1972), 159.

CHAPTER 2

Electoral Things
Realism, Representation, and the Victorian Ballot

> Well, if things could talk, then I'm sure you'd hear/ A lot of things to make you cry, my dear. /Ain't you glad?/ Oh, ain't you glad?/ Ain't you glad, glad that things don't talk?
> —Ry Cooder, "If Walls Could Talk" (1974)

> Officer, Organist, Sweep, Weaver, Waterman, Gravedigger.
> —Occupations Listed in the Bristol Election Pollbook (1841)

In the last chapter I suggested that, following Bonnie Honig, we might think about the details of elections and electoral systems as "public things," as objects and events (or aspects of objects and events) that hover somewhere between the officious invisibility of equipment and the stubborn opacity and recalcitrant agency of the thing. They are, as Elaine Freedgood says of "novelistic things," "at once material and figural, fetishized and fugitive, here and gone."[1] "Objects of both facticity and fantasy," the material and procedural paraphernalia of elections are intentional, highly designed, and, we might say, aesthetically charged, and yet they tend all the same to elude our notice and to settle – like hidden pictures – into the otherwise ordinary and undifferentiated field of dentist appointments, telemarketers, and trips to the DMV.[2] And there they will remain; or, rather, there they will remain until something goes wrong. And, as I've already said, something going wrong is exactly what happened in Florida in 2000. Victoria Bassetti writes:

---

[1] Bonnie Honig, *Public Things: Democracy in Disrepair* (New York: Fordham University Press, 2017), 2; Elaine Freedgood, *The Ideas in Things: Fugitive Meaning in the Victorian Novel* (Chicago: University of Chicago Press, 2006), 29.

[2] Honig, *Public Things,* 38. D. A. Miller writes that "the force of the hidden picture does not lie in whatever glib meanings its *content* may be hosting, but in its *form* as an enactment – latent if you don't see it, overwhelming if you do – of a semiotic stoppage productive only of nonsense." Miller, *Hidden Hitchcock* (Chicago: University of Chicago Press, 2016), 8.

In the long days following that general election when the system failed to produce a president, Americans slowly came to discover a dirty little secret: in many places, the system was rickety, error prone, and sloppy. When people started examining the process, the results were not pretty. All those mechanisms – the lever machines, the punch-card systems, the paper scanners – suffered from a constellation of maladies with mundane names: High residual vote. Poor ballot design. Poor tabulation systems. Florida's election system showed evidence of all of them.[3]

If the election hadn't been all that close, people would have used but not really noticed all the broken or half-broken things that would nonetheless have made that election possible; the booths, ballots, buttons, and bunting would have fallen away, ending up in storage lockers, donation bins, or in the hands of collectors of presidential memorabilia.[4] Because, however, the election *was* close, they found themselves instead staring with strange intensity not only at the simultaneously sober and sensational layout of the Palm Beach Butterfly Ballot but also at that "rice-grain-size bit of paper produced when a voter pushes a hole through a punch card": the chad.[5]

For a few weeks in late 2000, the humble chad became a public thing. Compared to the ruthless utility of the ballot from whence it came, the chad should have held on to its almost purely thingly character. Where a whole election ballot is a textbook example of what Heidegger refers to as "a piece of equipment," that which is "produced expressly for employment and use," the chad is, on the contrary, a "mere thing," which "means, first, the pure thing, which is simply a thing and nothing more; but then, at the same time, it means that which is only a thing, in an almost pejorative sense."[6] Because, in other words, it is only the hole left in the ballot that stands as a proper index of an intention, the essentially meaningless – the "mere" – chad is an undifferentiated material residue that the dream of pure intention or perfect efficiency must repress or deny. The chad is junk thought wants to forget. It is almost as if Heidegger had the chad in mind when he defined the "thing" as "whatever is not simply nothing."[7] A chad is not nothing, but only just. When, however, national attention turned to

---

[3] Victoria Bassetti, "New Anxieties and Old Friends," in Alicia Yin Cheng, *This Is What Democracy Looked Like: A Visual History of the Printed Ballot* (New York: Princeton Architectural Press, 2020), 169.

[4] Mihir Zaveri and Alan Yuhas, "Where Does All the Swag Go After Campaigns Fail? Everywhere," *The New York* Times, last modified March 5, 2020, www.nytimes.com/2020/02/25/us/politics/leftover-campaign-shirts-hats-mugs.html.

[5] Bassetti, "New Anxieties and Old Friends," 169.

[6] Martin Heidegger, *Poetry, Language, Thought* (New York: Harper Collins, 2001), 21.

[7] Heidegger, *Poetry, Language, Thought*, 21.

Figure 2.1   "... that which is only a thing, in an almost pejorative sense."

Florida in 2000, the mere and meaningless chad returned to public significance with a vengeance. Where it had been nothing or, rather, where it had stood as the mere antithesis of *something*, it appeared suddenly as a material representative of our hopes for, anxieties about, and even our basic awareness of the institutions that support and sometimes thwart "our collective capacities to imagine, build, and tend to a common world collaboratively."[8] It became something not merely to notice, but something to stare at with unnerving, pop-eyed attention (Figure 2.1). For the span of a few tense weeks, the chad was no longer a mere thing. It was an important thing, a public thing, a "pregnant" thing, and it was enough "to make you cry, my dear."[9] What, though, does it mean to take the chad or, for that matter, last year's ballot or a loser's bumper sticker or a defunct campaign's pin as a public thing? What does it mean to consider the

---

[8] Honig, *Public Things*, 38.
[9] When Ry Cooder covers Little Milton's 1970 "If Walls Could Talk" in 1974, he changes the lyrics slightly. Where Little Milton begins, "If walls could talk then I'm sure you'd hear / A lot of things that would make you cry, my dear," Cooder instead sings, "Well, if things could talk then I'm sure you'd hear / A lot of things to make you cry, my dear." The shift brings out, I think, an uncanniness latent in Little Milton's idea of talking walls, showing that a cheater's lament was always already a mediation on the eeriness of things: what kinds of things would things say if things could talk?

disavowed or the disruptive significance of electoral decisions, objects, and events when, from year to year, we hope that we won't have to consider them at all? "Lord," runs the Election Administrator's Prayer, "let there be a landslide."[10]

I want in this chapter to think about the importance of electoral things in mid-Victorian Britain, particularly in the years between 1832 and 1884 when a series of political and parliamentary reforms made casting a vote into a matter of both real hope and existential and institutional uncertainty.[11] Who got to cast a ballot, how they got to cast their ballot, and what their ballot finally got to mean were all questions regularly and passionately debated in Parliament, in a variety of intellectual circles, and in the popular press. As a result, the period I want to consider here was marked not only by its familiar engagements with the big issues of reform, representation, and the franchise, but also by its often obsessive and sometimes eccentric attention to the *thingly* details of electoral procedure.

With this, I want to place the nineteenth-century electoral ambit within the wider context of what Freedgood has identified as the "profusion, intensity, and heedless variety" of Victorian "thing culture." Arguing against a critical tendency to treat the "cavalcades of objects" that amble across the pages of the Victorian realist novel as *commodities*, which is to say as objects that mean something by virtue of their metaphorical and thus their subordinate relation to the larger logic of commodity exchange, Freedgood makes the case for an avowedly metonymic engagement with Victorian things, one that allows them to remain on a threshold between fact and fancy, between their status as "symbolically unencumbered" objects and the "largely fugitive" ideas that those objects contain. "A strong, literalizing metonymy can 'start' fictional objects into historical life and historicize our fictions against the grain of the kinds of allegorical meaning we already know how to find, read, and create."[12] On the one

---

[10] Quoted in Barton Gellman, "The Election that Could Break America," *The Atlantic*, November 2020, www.theatlantic.com/magazine/archive/2020/11/what-if-trump-refuses-concede/616424/.

[11] "The correspondence of voting system reform activity to suffrage expansion is most direct in the case of the United Kingdom. By far the most intense waves of reform activity emerged in response to the major Reform Acts of 1867 and 1884, each of which significantly expanded the franchise. On both occasions, electoral system choice emerged as a central point of contention, resulting in rifts between party leaders and the rank and file, as well as within party leadership. Throughout these debates, preferences for electoral systems turned on actors' calculations of whether workers would organize independently or join one of the established parties and rely on it to represent their interests." Amel Ahmed, *Democracy and the Politics of Electoral System Choice* (Cambridge: Cambridge University Press, 2013), 117–118.

[12] Freedgood, *Ideas in Things*, 1, 17. As with so much else in recent memory, attention to the fugitive materiality of the ballot reached new levels of absurdity as volunteers for the haphazard Arizona

hand, seeing electoral things – ballots, ballot boxes, pollbooks, etc. – as part of a wider Victorian thing culture will allow me to make some fresh connections between political and literary representation in the period: considering the *meaning* of a committee vote in George Eliot can help us to see differently what's at stake in the novel's realist representation of character; noticing the socially impacted, apparently illogical, but wholly familiar course of erotic desire in Trollope's Palliser Novels offers an unexpectedly rigorous challenge to at least one axiom of social choice theory (the "independence of irrelevant alternatives"). On the other hand, in addition to seeing possible relations or resemblances between the literary and electoral aspects of Victorian thing culture, I want to use something like Freedgood's metonymic method to tease out and track the significance of some other electoral things. More particularly, I want not only to see the idea in things but also to see ideas *as* things. Because, in other words, the curious recalcitrance of electoral practices and procedures can make otherwise ephemeral ideas look and feel unusually dense, it might make sense to approach what used to be called the history of ideas in terms that we tend to reserve for the more palpable textures of material culture.

Secular Magic

One doesn't need to look far to find the intensity and depth of Victorian investments in the details of electoral procedure. As a result of both the enactment and the practical downstream effects of the Reform Acts of 1832 and 1867 and an increased public engagement with voting as a practice, problem, politics, or contested right, there was, in Parliament, in the press, and well beyond a considerable amount of talk and writing not only about if and why some people or all people should be able to vote, but also about *how* they would vote if and when they finally could. Unsurprisingly, this apparently excessive attention to the matter of elections and electoral reform begins in earnest with Jeremy Bentham, who imagined his ideal "vote-receiving box" (as well as his "secret-selection box," his "voting cards," and other sundry elements) in characteristically exhaustive detail:

---

recount scrutinized ballots looking for "bamboo fibers" and, in at least one case, Cheeto stains, somehow imagining that either of these would have something significant to say about the larger legitimacy of the 2020 election. Jennifer Morrell, "I Watched the GOP's Arizona Election Audit. It Was Worse than You Think," *Washington Post*, May 19, 2021, www.washingtonpost.com/outlook/2021/05/19/gop-arizona-election-audit/.

A *Vote-receiving box* is a box of cast-iron, or other sufficiently strong and cheaper metal, if such there be.

I.   In form it is (supposed) a double cube, standing on one of its small sides.

II. In size, it is large enough to receive and keep concealed a number of *voting cards*, equal to that of the whole number of persons entitled to vote in the Polling District in which it is employed.

III. On the top, is a lid, which opens by a hinge, and when closed rests on a rim, so as to form on surface with the remainder of the plane into which it fits: in such sort, that when sealing wax, being dropt on it, has been impressed with a seal, the lid cannot be opened unless the seal is broken.

IV. In this lid is a slit, into which, at the time of voting, the cards are successively dropped. Near this slit rises a pin, on which slides a metallic plate, by which the slit is occasionally closed.

V.   In form and dimensions, the slit is so ordered, as to receive the cards with ease, without exposing the name to view, as they are dropt in, or afterwards.[13]

Here and elsewhere, Bentham's exact descriptions of unrealized voting paraphernalia do an uneasily double work. First, their material precision makes it possible not only to imagine – to *suppose* – but also, maybe, to visualize, to construct, and then to test the imaginary equipment under consideration:

> In size [the selection box] is (supposed) about two feet in length by one foot in width; and in depth, in front one foot, at the back 15 inches. . . . In the back board, is a plate of ground glass, for the letting in of light, without rendering any objects within it visible. . . . In each of the sides, is a hole, large enough to let in a hand with part of the fore-arm, in such sort that a man's two hands may meet within it to facilitate the selection of the intended name.[14]

If, in other words, these devices are only fictions, Bentham's willingness to treat supposition *as if* it were fact encourages the reader also to suspend disbelief and to enter fully into the thought experiment: What *would* it be like to put my hand into that machine? What would it mean, how would it look, what would it *feel* like? In this regard, "the instructional character" of Bentham's things encourage an "increased suppleness and capaciousness of

---

[13] Jeremy Bentham, *Bentham's Radical Reform Bill* (London: E. Wilson, 1819), 17–18.
[14] Bentham, *Radical Reform Bill*, 16–17.

our power to imagine" that Elaine Scarry associates with Huysmans, Hardy, and others: "Reading" in all three "entails an immense labor of imaginative construction."[15]

That said, whatever the fineness his attention to the putative materiality of *supposed* ballots and boxes, Bentham's descriptions are at last only imaginary; his are precise and schematic descriptions not only of things that do not yet exist but also of things that could not yet exist within the world as it was in 1819. Early critics of Bentham's voting schemes pointed to the threat of infinite regress that came along with his reliance on the eventual realization of implicit changes necessary and prior to the realization of the other changes for which he explicitly called. For instance, in *Ballot* (1839), his witty and influential attack on radical proposals for the secret ballot, Sydney Smith points to the tortoises-all-the-way-down nature of the Benthamite imagination:

> The answer of the excellent Benthamites to all this is, "What you say may be true enough in the present state of registrations, but we have another scheme of registration to which these objects will not apply." There is really no answering this Paulo post legislation. I reason now upon registration and reform which are in existence, which I have seen at work for several years. What new improvements are in the womb of time, or (if time has no womb) in the more capacious pockets of the followers of Bentham I know not: when I see them tried I will reason upon them.[16]

Seen in this context, the play between the only apparently modest schematic realism of Bentham's description and the wild unreality or, at least, the radical uncertainty of its political realization makes his vote-receiving box evocative less of the heavy-weather of discipline and punishment and more of the detailed, crazy, and negative utopias of Piranesi's *Carceri*; like Piranesi, this other, outlandish Bentham "exalts the capacity of the imagination to create models."[17] Miran Božovič, for one, takes this confrontation between the plainly schematic and the wildly suppositional as essential to Bentham's thinking: "the main thrust of the panopticon writings is that a certain reality – the panopticon prison – is sustained in existence by something that is utterly unreal, that is, by an imaginary non-entity; it is through its very non-existence that the non-entity sustains the reality in existence – if it were to exist,

---

[15] Elaine Scarry, *Dreaming by the Book* (New York: Farrar, Straus & Giroux, 1999), 34, 37.

[16] Sydney Smith, *Ballot* (London: Longmans, Green, & Co., 1871), 14.

[17] Manfredo Tafuri, *The Sphere and the Labyrinth: Avant-Gardes and Architecture from Piranesi to the 1970s*, trans. Pellegrino d'Acierno and Robert Connolly (Cambridge: Massachusetts Institute of Technology Press, 1990), 29.

the reality itself would disintegrate."[18] We'll want to keep track of this other, ecstatic Bentham – this, as it were, *auto-iconic* Bentham – as we move forward with our history of the Victorian vote; where, that is, some have sought to fit electoral reform into a familiar Foucauldian story of the making of the liberal subject, the unruly, model-happy, and sometimes *outré* efforts of the Victorian electoral imagination suggest something altogether stranger and less disciplined.

We might also consider Grote's Ballot Box, the mechanism George Grote designed with his wife Harriet in 1836 and shared with *The Spectator* in February 1837.[19] Best remembered for his influential twelve-volume *History of Greece* (1846–1856), Grote dedicated his fraught tenure as a parliamentary radical to the cause of the secret ballot, which he saw as essential to any successful electoral reform. As he wrote in the lead up to the 1832 Reform Act: "Every evil incidental to elections would be done away with, and the efficacy of the system as a means to good government greatly strengthened, if voters polled secretly, in small bodies, and in different places at the same time."[20] Between 1833 and 1839, Grote made six major speeches and offered six motions in favor of the ballot, which, paraphrasing Cicero, he celebrated as "the upholder of silent liberty."[21] As broadly eloquent as Grote was in his several speeches on the ballot, he also sweated the details, a fact evinced by his ballot box (Figure 2.2). In a pair of short pieces presented over two weeks in 1837, *The Spectator* not only described that box and its attendant processes in close detail but also seasoned that description with an unexpected soupçon of narrative suspense:

> Let us then suppose votes taken by Ballot, under direction of a Ballot Bill; and that our reader is about to give his vote. ... Upon getting in front of the box, he finds a screen on each side, to prevent his being seen; and opposite to him, at a moderate height, the names of the candidates upon a card (F), and a steel bodkin placed by him. The names are covered with a

[18] Miran Božovič, "Introduction," in Jeremy Bentham, *The Panopticon Writings* (London: Verso, 1995), 2.

[19] "We remained," writes Harriet Grote, "in London through the winter of 1836–1837. The agitation was very zealous all the autumn upon the subject of the Ballot. Grote and I spent a good deal of time in devising methods of taking votes, so as to ensure secrecy; at last a 'Ballot box' was perfected, and some forty or fifty models, in wood, distributed all over the kingdom." Harriet Grote, *The Personal Life of George Grote: Compiled from Family Documents, Private Memoranda, and Original Letters to and From Various Friends* (London: John Murray, 1873), 109.

[20] George Grote, *The Minor Works of George Grote*, ed. Alexander Bain (London: John Murray, 1873), 49.

[21] Grote, *Minor Works*, 28.

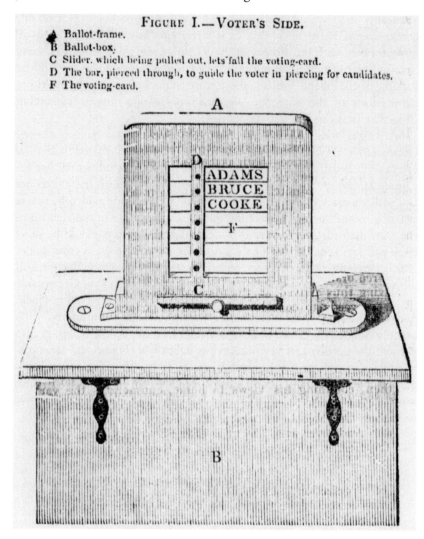

FIGURE I.—VOTER'S SIDE.

A   Ballot-frame.
B   Ballot-box.
C   Slider, which being pulled out, lets fall the voting-card.
D   The bar, pierced through, to guide the voter in piercing for candidates.
F   The voting-card.

Figure 2.2   "The card is marked; the vote is given!"

glass; how is he to touch the card? He sees the holes below the letter D; he thinks COOKE and ADAMS good Radicals, men of talent, of virtue, and of courage; and presses the bodkin-point into the holes opposite their names. The card is marked; the vote is given![22]

[22] "Ballot-Voting," *The Spectator*, February 25, 1837, 16.

Although Grote's close attention to the niceties of voting procedure was part of his larger political project, moments like these allowed his critics to paint him as a hobbyhorsical pedant, something *The Spectator* anticipated in the first of its two pieces: "if witlings find anything to ridicule in the minuteness necessary to make that process plain, they are perfectly welcome to fire their shot at the Ballot-box."[23] Grote's arch-antagonist Smith did exactly that and with evident and acid delight:

> It is possible, and perhaps not very difficult, to invent a machine, by the aid of which electors may vote for a candidate, or for two or three candidates, out of a greater number, without its being discovered for whom they vote; it is less easy than the rabid and foaming Radical supposed; but I have no doubt it may be accomplished. In Mr. Grote's dagger ballot box, which has been carried round the country by eminent patriots, you stab the card of your favorite candidate with a dagger. I have seen another, called the mouse-trap ballot box, in which you poke your finger into the trap of the member you prefer, and are caught and detained till the trap-clerk below (who knows by means of a wire when you are caught) marks your vote, pulls the liberator, and releases you.[24]

Smith, we see, not only refuses the secret ballot as mean, devious, or, as was said again and again, "unmanly" but also makes fun of it as somehow both minor and dangerous, both cutting and overnice; "does," wonders Smith, "Mr. Grote imagine, that the men of woods, forests, and rivers, – that they who have the strength of the hills, – are to be baffled by bumpkins thrusting a little pin into a little card in a little box? that England is to be governed by political acupuncturation [sic]?"[25] The suggestion here – that we ought to understand the ballot as an effeminate, implicitly "oriental," but nonetheless real threat to the pastoral earthiness of Anglo-Saxon virility – is borne out across the shifting style of Smith's prosody as he moves from the nearly iambic austerity of "woods, forests, and rivers" on to a fricative pile-up of alliterations, repetitions, and latinized diction.

Grote's "dagger," somehow both a "little pin" and something more formidable, both pricks and stabs, evoking the aggregative and, again, the "oriental" logic of death by a thousand cuts while also producing what might be history's first hanging chad. Smith's tacit invocation of the mix of dumb trust and anxious discomfort that comes with sticking one's finger into either a mousetrap or a mouse-hole, both of which the second

---

[23] "The Ballot Bill," *The Spectator*, February 18, 1837, 11.   [24] Smith, *Ballot*, 3.
[25] Smith, *Ballot*, 16.

machine seems to invoke, is queasily palpable. And, insofar the apparatus seems to cast both candidate and voter in one and the same role of trapped rat, it turns the election into the kind of undifferentiated existential morass that Plato had threatened so many years before: "it would seem to be a pleasant constitution . . . which distributes a sort of equality to both equals and unequals alike."[26] Indeed, the nervy ambivalence of Smith's assault was already there, waiting between the otherwise approving lines in *The Spectator*; a reference to Grote's electoral tool not as a "dagger" or "pin" but rather as a "bodkin" can only be read as a wry and self-consciously archaic allusion to the weapon with which Hamlet would "his full Quietus" have made and, thus, an invocation of the ultimately meaningless pairwise comparison of alternatives that is the subject of that great soliloquy. [27]

If, however, we're not sure that Grote's bodkin is necessarily the Bard's bodkin, a fuller reckoning with the word's connotations makes things more and not less complicated. The OED tells us that a bodkin was a craftsman's tool, "a small pointed instrument, of bone, ivory, or steel, used for piercing holes in cloth," which would seem to align the act of voting with the Chartist's manually-dexterous imaginary. It also tells us that a bodkin was a compositor's instrument, "an awl-like tool used to pick out letters in correcting set-up type," which underscores the fact that where open voting relied on the voice, the secret ballot had to be written (I'll come back to this distinction shortly). Finally, it turns out, too, that in Grote's own *History of Greece*, the bodkin appears as something like Smith's take on the dagger as both effeminate and deadly: "See the story," writes Grote in a note, "of the single Athenian citizen, who returned home alone, after all his comrades had perished in an unfortunate expedition to the island of Aegina. The widows of the slain warriors crowded round him, each asking him what had become of her husband, and finally put him to death by pricking him with their bodkins."[28] The bodkin comes, in other words, to a sharp point at which Chartist competence, Athenian democracy, revenge, rights, and writing come all and awkwardly together.

---

[26] Plato, *Republic* (Hackett Publishing Company, 1992), 228.

[27] Adams, Bruce, or Cooke? That is the question. Of course, properly speaking and from the perspective of some social choice theory, the question really *isn't*, "Adams, Bruce, or Cooke." That is, to track the group's feelings about Adams, Bruce, or Cooke, we'd need rather to break that question down into its constituent parts and present it as a series of comparable pairwise choices: Adams *or* Bruce, Adams *or* Cooke, Bruce *or* Cooke. From this perspective, a decision between three or four or twenty-four candidates is almost always *really* a series of discrete and comparable decisions between pairs of candidates. From this perspective, to be or not to be really is and almost always is *the only question.*

[28] George Grote, *History of Greece*, (London: John Murray, 1851), 5:130.

Similarly, Edward Leatham, the Liberal MP for Huddersfield who would go on to introduce the Ballot Act of 1872, also understood the vote and its reform both as a matter of many technical particulars and also, oddly, as a matter of taste: "I do not know," he said before Parliament in 1870, "that there is any object of human ambition except, perhaps, the production of a cup of coffee for breakfast, upon which the same amount of mechanical ingenuity has been lavished."[29] Reflecting in 1871 on the still unrealized secret ballot, Leatham again cast the issue in terms of its many details. He argued:

> I will go a step further, and say that, where the ballot has failed to realize fully the expectations of those who have advocated its adoption, that failure is clearly and solely due to faults of detail and imperfections of machinery. Since this is the case, perhaps it is not too much to assert that this whole question may be regarded as one of detail, and that there is no question which has of late come before the House of Commons demanding a closer attention to minutiae or a more thorough consideration of the facts within our reach.[30]

If Leatham comes off as a little defensive about his investment in the mechanical skill or technical attention necessary to realize a workable ballot, that's partly because of how one of his own more ingenious proposals had been received just a year before.

Looking, as Grote had looked, for a way to secure the secrecy of the secret ballot, Leatham took a peculiar page from the well-thumbed book of chemists, magicians, and secret agents: Mark the ballot, he suggested, with invisible ink! He laid out his idea to a receptive audience in 1871:

> The voter was to receive a ballot card, which to his eyes and the eyes of the political agents and everyone present was precisely identical with the voting card which was to be given to his neighbour. All through the process of polling, and the subsequent process of examination and counting the votes, there was nothing visible upon the card which could lead to its identification. But the card contained a secret, nevertheless, locked up in its bosom – if we may assume that the bosoms of cards are in their backs (Laughter). Upon the back of the card the presiding officer was directed to write the register number of the elector in a solution of chloride of cobalt. This solution possesses the peculiar property that at the maximum temperature of the atmosphere marks made with it are invisible, but when the marked

[29] 199 *Hansard Parliamentary Debates* (3rd ser.) (1870) col. 275, https://hansard.parliament.uk/ Commons/1870-02-14/debates/11007dae-9cef-4960-9088-7e7a216e835f/BallotBill.
[30] E. A. Leatham, *The Ballot – Technically Considered* (Manchester: National Reform Union, 1871), 5–6.

paper is submitted to a heat of 50 or 100 degrees above the ordinary temperature the writing becomes visible, and vanishes again when the temperature is lowered.[31]

References to (and sometimes recipes for) cobalt-based invisible inks appear regularly across the nineteenth century in popular chemistry books, encyclopedias, and guides to "the useful and domestic arts": "The first use of the solution of cobalt as an invisible ink is ascribed to Hellot," says John Henry Pepper in 1869's *The Playbook of Metals*. "The discoverer appears to have been a German named Stolberg, who probably met with the *kobalt* in his visits to certain mining districts, and trying the effect of aqua regia upon it, produced a red salt, that turned blue on exposure to heat."[32] It is striking "that Leatham held" on to his quirky faith in the power of practical chemistry, "which has solved so many other riddles," when he saw other technical innovations as ridiculous, dangerous, or needlessly complex:

> Even the magnetic telegraph has been pressed into the service, and it has been proposed to introduce the terrified elector alone and unprotected into the awful presence of a piece of mechanism so elaborate and imposing, so full of wires and balls, of wheels and dials and needles, that the unsophisticated bucolic mind, if it were able to form any conclusion as to what was going to happen, must have concluded not only that the vote was about to be registered, but the voter's portrait taken, his vote telegraphed to his landlord and to his agent, who probably would be waiting in the street, summoned by ring of bell.[33]

As opposed to the "awful" and Oz-like complexity of the magnetic machine, Leatham's alchemical solution is more attractive – if, at last, just as impractical – precisely because it seems to edge away from science and technology back toward the chthonic appeal of magic (it is not, I think, for nothing that "nothing visible upon the card" sounds something like another late-Victorian coinage: "nothing up my sleeve"). Less Frankenstein's monster than one of Prospero's spirits, Leatham's ballot is not only secret in its broadly institutional sense but also secret in the way that we imagine – or maybe hope – that people, souls and, indeed, secrets are secret: "the card contained a secret . . . locked up in its bosom."

---

[31] Leatham, *The Ballot*, 7–8.

[32] John Henry Pepper, *The Playbook of Metals: Including Personal Narratives of Visits to Coal, Lead, Copper, and Tin Mines; With a Large Number of Interesting Experiments* (London: George Routledge and Sons, 1869), 452.

[33] 199 *Hansard Parliamentary Debates* (3rd ser.) (1870) col. 275.

When, in that case, critics saw Leatham's proposal as "childish," they weren't far off; his boyish enthusiasm for a "hey presto!" moment of revelation turns the humble vote into a riddle or, rather, an example of what Simon During calls "secular magic," an object that would not only work but also heighten "our sensitivity to the play of puzzlement, fictiveness, and contingency" that underwrites modernity in general and modern democratic elections in particular.[34] Leatham's ballot can thus be seen as part of a longer and variously self-conscious effort to reckon with the various suspensions of disbelief that democratic systems require, an effort that would have to include Rousseau's "Japanese mountebank," the political-theorist-as-grisly-street-magician we met in a previous chapter; the riddling, childish, magical, and electoral works of Lewis Carroll; the mix of political economy and utopian fantasy that we find not only in William Morris's *News from Nowhere* but also in his less read fantasies of the same period; and also Ralph Ellison's invisible man, whose place outside or, rather, beneath civil society casts the racism that supports American democracy as the violent underside of secular magic: "You wonder whether you aren't simply a phantom in other people's minds. Say, a figure in a nightmare which the sleeper tries with all his strength to destroy."[35] As Rousseau, Carroll, Morris, Ellison, and Leatham seem to understand, one of the animating questions behind any vote, secret or otherwise, is how it can manage in whatever form to capture and then to count something as protean, as fleeting, and as fundamentally enigmatic as the human will. It may not be magic, but it is a mystery.

Goodbye to All That

While historians and critics have tended to overlook the seemingly minor and sometimes eccentric details of Victorian electoral thinking and electoral reform, some have tried recently to recover (1) the texture and holiday atmosphere of open elections as they existed before 1872, (2) the institutional turn to the secret ballot, (3) the "technologies of self" that came with that turn, and (4) the broader material culture of representative elections from 1832 to century's end. Malcolm Crook and Tom Crook write in a 2015 essay on "ballot papers and the practice of elections," that, "as work within an emergent 'material turn' suggests, practical considerations – considerations, that is of logistics, technology and discipline – are

---

[34] Simon During, *Modern Enchantments* (Cambridge, MA: Harvard University Press, 2002), 2.
[35] Ralph Ellison, *Invisible Man* (New York: Vintage, 1995), 4.

just as important as values, beliefs, and identities when it comes to understanding how societies function. Crudely, things, even 'little' things like paper, make possible 'big' ideas, structures, and identities."[36] For Crook and Crook, attention to the "controversial" "mobilization of pens, cubicles, and official papers" is crucial, first, because it allows the historian and critic to understand how institutions and individuals related practically to the idea of elections as well as to

> a wider nexus of agents and practices that have come to define representative democracy, beyond just parties, voter registration, and the provision of polling places. On the one hand, this extends to the development and reform of newspapers, national parliaments and established electoral cycles; on the other, to the development of bureaucracy and an administrative culture based on the currency of paperwork.[37]

Second – and this is especially important in the Victorian context – looking at the material and institutional details of the ballot as it was debated, designed, and then, finally, deployed allows one to "distinguish between the practice of using papers *per se*, and the practice of using them in secret."[38] As I will argue, there has been a tendency to understand questions about the nature and consequence of the Victorian ballot solely in terms of liberalism, privacy, and the public, in terms, that is, of the ballot *as a secret* as opposed to the ballot *as a thing*. Although there are, of course, good and familiar reasons to think about the political relation between secrecy and subjectivity, focusing on what was secret about the ballot at the expense of its materiality and procedural specificity has tended to distort the history and the consequence of Ballot Act of 1872. I'll come back to this shortly.

James Vernon's *Politics and the People* represents an important and early moment in what Crook and Crook refer to as the "material turn" in the analysis of elections as it attends to the matter of English political culture as an answer to some of conventional political history's shortcomings:

> What I am offering here is a new cultural history of the meanings of politics – a history of its subjectivities and identities, the ways in which politics defined and imagined people – which in turn provides, at least in my reading, a new narrative of nineteenth-century English political history. There is, then, little of the stuff of orthodox political history in this book. There is no discussion of organizations, personnel or policies of the national

---

[36] Malcolm Crook and Tom Crook, "Ballot Papers and the Practice of Elections: Britain, France and the United States of America, c. 1500–2000," *Historical Research,* 88(241) (August 2015), 532.
[37] Crook and Crook, "Ballot Papers," 560.   [38] Crook and Crook, "Ballot Papers," 531.

institutions of politics, not any detailed analyses of social and economic structures. Those traditional sources of political history which have tended to privilege the most literate and articulate members of the political nation have also been dispensed with, in favor of much neglected traces like ballads, banners, cartoons, handbills, statues, architecture, the uses of time and space, and the rich vein of ceremonial and iconographic forms.[39]

Vernon's account of the practices and paraphernalia of open voting in Britain is detailed, concrete, and alive to the ways in which the people could and often did adapt elections to their own shifting ends. The construction of the hustings, the "chairing" of winning candidates, the "elaborate decoration" of those chairs, the closing dinners, as well as the printed matter of posters, pamphlets, treating tickets, and ballot papers: all of these figure for Vernon as the props, practices, and public rituals that made voting before the secret ballot into a richly significant symbolic space in which candidates, electors, and the disenfranchised could act out "the various generic plots of romance, comedy, tragedy, and irony."[40] Essential to Vernon's sense of the importance of both "generic plots" and "electoral poetics" to the period is his suggestion that, as opposed to the buttoned-up and private version of voting that took shape after the 1872 Ballot Act, elections between 1832 and 1872 were contrapuntal affairs that played the unofficial energies of irony, femininity, humor, and even violence against the official presentation of open voting as nationalist proof of England as rugged, ancient, and free. More to the point, the raw and unruly publicity of the hustings gave the disenfranchised majority opportunities both to participate in elections and to travesty authorized expressions of political condescension. Writes Vernon:

> Here again the disenfranchised were able to turn the world upside down by pillorying those placed above them in the official political hierarchy. Like the canvass, polling turned a romantic electoral story into a carnivalesque comedy, it was the great leveller, and as such it formed an essential weapon in the armory of the disenfranchised, at least until the rationalizing introduction of the secret ballot in 1872.[41]

---

[39] James Vernon, *Politics and the People: A Study in English Political Culture c. 1815–1867* (Cambridge: Cambridge University Press, 1993), 6.
[40] Vernon, *Politics and the People*, 2–5.
[41] Vernon, *Politics and the People*, 81. The language of carnival also appears in Crook and Crook: "Underpinned by a shared sense of carnivalesque license, they involved electors and non-electors alike in lengthy campaigns characterized by extensive treating, feasting and drinking. The franchise was strictly limited, but non-electors were encouraged to assemble in and around the polling venue, where the polling booths and hustings were located. From here, crowds mocked, jeered and

Where, however, this open amalgam of ritual, parody, political participation, and heteroglossic play thrived before 1872, it gives way in Vernon's account to something decidedly less free. He continues:

> In this reading the Ballot Act did not herald the dawn of a great new democratic era in which the politics of individual opinion triumphed over the politics of influence and corruption. Instead, it has been read as part of the closing down of the public political sphere by officials who sought to replace the public and collective sphere with an increasingly private and individual male one. Central to this project was the official privileging of the political uses of print which enabled appeals to be directed at private individuals.[42]

Indeed, part of what made the introduction of the secret ballot not just possible but inevitable after decades of parliamentary failure was that it went from an avowedly *Radical* proposal, associated with Chartism, Bentham, Grote, and his "seriocomic" protégé F. H. Berkeley to a legibly *Liberal* proposal. "At that time," writes Elaine Hadley, the secret ballot "was detached from other sorts of radical electoral reforms, epitomized in the formation of the Ballot Society in 1853, and the ballot thereby became associated with mainstream liberalism and moderate reform."[43] This shift in political fortunes was tied to a related shift in the very meaning of the secret ballot: where Grote and others had seen the ballot as a way to protect voters from landlords, bosses, and bullies, its later liberal backers cast it as a way to protect the electoral process from the voters themselves. Arguing for the Ballot in 1860, the Liberal MP Hugh Childers noted that in Australia, where the secret ballot had been taken up in 1856 and which he offered to his colleagues as a model, "the prevailing evil was not so much intimidation as bribery."[44] John Stuart Mill was explicit about this shift in 1859, arguing that, "[t]hirty years ago it was still true that in the election of members of Parliament, the main evil to be guarded against was that which the ballot would exclude – coercion by landlords, employers, and customers. At present, I conceive, a much greater source of evil is the

applauded electors as they made their way to vote. At the same time, electors might arrive en masse in organized 'tallies,' wielding banners and wearing party ribbons, and to the accompaniment of music." Malcolm Crook and Tom Crook, "Reforming Voting Practices in a Global Age: The Making and Remaking of the Modern Secret Ballot in Britain, France and the United States, c. 1600–c. 1950," *Past & Present*, 212 (August 2011), 204.

[42] Vernon, *Politics and the People*, 157–158.

[43] Elaine Hadley, *Living Liberalism: Practical Citizenship in Mid-Victorian Britain* (Chicago: University of Chicago Press, 2010), 176.

[44] Hugh Childers, *The Ballot in Australia: A Speech Delivered in the House of Commons* (London: James Ridgway, 1860), 4.

selfishness, or the selfish partialities, of the voter himself."[45] The turn from radical to liberal accounts of the ballot thus represents an early instance of what I have called "the myth of rigging," the regular and perverse effort to cast voters as the greatest threat to the purity of elections, which is to say, the regular and perverse effort to cast democracy as a threat to itself. The myth of rigging exaggerates or invents instances of individual voters behaving badly to justify electoral "reforms" that make it harder for whole classes of people to vote. Those looking to hold on to power claim that elections have been haphazardly rigged by others in order to make it easier not only to rig them for themselves but also to rig them *systematically*.[46]

For Hadley, the secret ballot is emblematic of liberalism not only as a political "modality" but also as a way of living and thinking as a distinctively modern subject:

> With varying degrees of self-awareness, most supporters of the ballot were in fact promoting through the practices and promises of the ballot a much more circumscribed political arena than the periodic extensions of the franchise during this period might suggest. Through the ballot, popular politics as formerly understood would not only be sealed off in a little box – the balloting booth – but would also be spatially and cognitively delimited within the individual voter, thereby profoundly revising what could then be understood as the public sphere and its powerful resident, public opinion.[47]

We can, perhaps, see Hadley here as filling in the political details while also filling out the historical context of D. A. Miller's classic reading of *David Copperfield* as a book all about "boxes." "Characters in *David Copperfield*," says Miller, "are frequently coupled with boxes: bags, parcels, luggage."[48] As Miller goes on to argue, the proliferation of characters who "come with boxes because [they] come in boxes, as boxes" is evidence of "the subjective practice in which the oppositions of private/public, inside/outside, subject/ object are established."[49] Like the many boxes in *David Copperfield*, Hadley's "little box" both stands as representative of the logic of liberal subjectivity and serves as a useful discursive index of the wider epistemic shift – the "repressive hypothesis," if you will – that this new technology

---

[45] John Stuart Mill, *Thoughts on Parliamentary Reform* (London: John W. Parker & Son, 1859), 38–39.

[46] This two-faced myth was, of course, on vivid and frankly disgusting display after the 2020 election as Trump's lawyers sought to pull on picayune or phantasmatic threads of isolated electoral irregularities in order baselessly to conjure the shadow of a vast leftwing conspiracy.

[47] Hadley, *Living Liberalism*, 179–180.

[48] D. A. Miller, *The Novel and the Police* (Berkeley: University of California Press, 1988), 200.

[49] Miller, *Novel and the Police*, 201, 207.

would seem to exemplify. "The booths and boxes," says Hadley, "along with voter registration lists and election officials, nominating petitions and regulated polling days, strictly define both what constitutes electoral politics and what constitutes the politics of the elector; from this perspective, the booth seems more like a panopticon than a space of free thought."[50] The ballot box, in that case, appears as not only a significant object within liberal modernity but also as the index of the passage from one to another means of imagining the *meaning* of the vote or the voter as they figure within what Foucault once called "a correlative history of the modern soul."[51]

There are two complementary aspects of these arguments about the significance of the secret ballot that I'd like to explore. One is this case made about a relation between modern subjectivity and the ballot, and about where these two histories stand in relation to one another. That is, while both Vernon's and Hadley's claims about some kind of influence or resonance or analogy between specific practical procedural changes to the way people voted and a less concrete set of feelings about what politics and selves might have meant before and after the secret ballot are right, I'd like in what follows to put more pressure on what the Victorians thought about the details of elections. Seeing, as I will, the introduction of the secret ballot within the larger context of other technical debates about proportional representation and, in particular, what's now known as the Single Transferable Vote will help, I hope, to clarify and to specify some of what was at stake not only in the idea of self that the secret ballot assumed, but also in the turn from the vote understood as an essentially oral to an essentially written thing. What, I will suggest, was most important about the secret ballot was not that it was secret but rather than it imagined and assumed secrets as things that had to be written down.

Before and After

The other aspect of Vernon's and Hadley's argument that I want to address is an issue of *timing*. Both understand the Ballot Act of 1872 as an historical threshold, an event that separates a *before* from an *after* in British politics and culture. For Vernon, "the introduction of the secret ballot in 1872 transformed the cultural poetics of elections"; it serves, in

---

[50] Hadley, *Living Liberalism*, 211.
[51] Michel Foucault, *Discipline and Punish: The Birth of the Prison*, trans. Alan Sheridan (New York: Vintage Books, 1995), 23.

Figure 2.3   "... the voters are happily quite indifferent."

that case, as a sort of generic or, we could say with Bakhtin, a chronotopic divide, a line that marks out the difference between one way of thinking or one structure of feeling and another.[52] Similarly, Hadley sees this logic embodied in a "before-and-after" image "distributed by Berkeley's Ballot Society" (Figure 2.3):

[52] Vernon, *Politics and the People*, 157.

As one can see in part from [the] engraving ... the introduction of nominating petitions (which wholly eradicated public nominations) and the institutionalization of the ballot were intended, in part, to enforce social order. Nominating days involved the public nomination and declaration of candidates, who then delivered acceptance speeches before bipartisan crowds. Nominating petitions, by contrast, required a requisite number of signatures that were then submitted to electoral officials by a published deadline. As is emphatically evident in the before-and-after images provided by the Ballot Society, voting days, like nomination days, would also become less public. The spatial flexibility of the open air, the theatrical impact of the hustings platform, and the rowdy, undifferentiated mob would become rationalized under these reforms, their unpredictable energies redirected into the partitioned interior space of the polling station, with its railings, upholstered chairs, voting booths, and, tucked benignly in the corner, a small ballot box. The box quietly harbors the meaningfully silent, abstracted mark, not the vocal physical body, of an elector's choice. In this propaganda, a scene of public bacchanalia appears to be rather predictably civilized through the calming contours of a bourgeois interiority. The crowd is thinned out, and the electors are channeled into individual booths – all in all a homey space, both "discrete" and "discreet."[53]

Where the "before" image, offered as a view of the broken and unfair open election system, is rough and chaotic, the lower "after" image, offered as a view of what elections would or could be like after the proposed reforms, is calm, ordered, and "rather predictably civilized." The problem here is that the image is not (or it is at least not only) a representation of before and after, of elections as they were and of elections as they could or should be if England would only adopt the Ballot Society's proposals. It is not, as we saw with Bentham's box, an imaginative act of supposing what wasn't yet but that maybe could or should be. It is, rather, a representation of how other people were in fact voting *somewhere else*.

Although Hadley doesn't mention it, the caption written under the lower image makes this clear; not an effort to render what could happen next, the lower part of the engraving is instead a depiction of the "Mode of Election in the Australian Colonies." It's not a picture of the future; it's a picture of Australia! Anthony Trollope, who in fact opposed the secrecy of the secret ballot, wrote about Australian elections in terms that recall the pacific, lower half of Hadley's image: "The votes for both Houses are of course taken by ballot. In regard to the ballot in Victoria, it is as well to point out that its value consists not in any security afforded by secrecy, – as

[53] Hadley, *Living Liberalism*, 186.

to which the voters are happily quite indifferent; – but in the tranquility at elections which it ensures."[54] The relation between top and bottom is thus a comparison of contemporary voting systems, of voting as it was done differently in different places within the empire at midcentury. There is, in that case, not really a before or an after in the image; there is only the fraught and ideologically riven *now* of the comparative analysis of political systems separated not by time but by distance, power, and prestige; and, as Crook and Crook note, "during the nineteenth century, references to the voting practices of other regimes became more elaborate and numerous. Indeed, interest in earlier practices was displaced, if not entirely, by an interest in contemporary ones employed in other countries."[55] This inevitable confusion of time and space in political history is interesting enough; what's more important for us, "now and around here," is the specific influence of the "Australian Ballot" or, as it was also called, the "Victorian Ballot" on English politics leading up to and in the year of the Ballot Act, 1872.

The plan for the modern secret ballot, first developed and enacted in Australia in the 1850s, more or less adopted in England in 1872, and then taken up – as we shall see – in the US, was the brainchild of an emigrant lawyer with deep ties to the philosophical radicalism of Bentham, J. A. Roebuck, and James Mill. Before ending up in Australia, Henry Samuel Chapman was born in England and lived and worked in both Amsterdam and Canada. After a long, close, and varied association with radical activists and thinkers at home and abroad, Chapman passed the Bar in England in 1841 and then emigrated to New Zealand in 1843. After serving as a judge at Wellington, he accepted a position as Colonial Secretary in Tasmania in 1852 and then practiced law privately in Victoria. He was elected to Victoria's Legislative Council in 1855, where he took up the work of drafting a working proposal for electoral reform and the implementation of a secret ballot.[56] "Eventually, and with great reluctance, the government adopted the system for the election in 1856 of Victoria's first parliament."[57] Chapman, who "had an extensive knowledge of constitutional law in Britain, Canada, and the United States," was, like Bentham, Grote, and Leatham before him, less concerned with the value of secrecy as such

---

[54] Anthony Trollope, *Victoria and Tasmania* (London: Chapman & Hall, 1875), 117.

[55] Crook and Crook, "Reforming Voting Practices," 212.

[56] For more on Chapman's history and his connections with philosophical radicalism, see R. S. Neale, "H. S. Chapman and the 'Victorian Ballot,'" *Australian Historical Studies*, 12(48) (1967), 506–521.

[57] Judith Brett, *From Secret Ballot to Democracy Sausage: How Australia Got Compulsory Voting* (Melbourne: Text Publishing, 2019), 23.

than with the various procedural devices that secrecy would require.[58] Judith Brett writes that:

> The novel part of Chapman's plan was not the secrecy itself but the means by which the secrecy was achieved: the government-provided ballot paper. Traditionally governments would issue the writs, but otherwise not be involved in running elections. It was left to the candidates and their committees or parties, or to the voters themselves, to organize ballot papers. All the polling booth needed was a ballot box to put them in. Now the government would oversee the whole operation. The printed ballot papers listed the names of the candidates, and voters crossed out those they rejected. . . . Chapman's plan required further innovation. How and where was the ballot paper to be filled in? What would prevent the watchful eyes of the candidates' electoral agents from checking how people voted? Chapman's proposal was this. The voter would pick up a ballot from the polling clerk, who would mark his name off the roll and sign the back of his ballot to prevent fraud. The voter would then pass into an inner room where he would vote in private, with pen, ink, and blotting paper provided. He would then return to the polling clerk and put his folded ballot in the box.[59]

It was this model that, after much discussion made its way from Victoria into English parliamentary debate and, finally, into law.

One of the first English references to Australia in relation to the ballot came in 1860 when, as I've mentioned, Hugh Childers talked up the new system in his own inaugural speech before the House. First begging his colleagues' pardon and then referring to his own tenure alongside Chapman on Victoria's Legislative Council, Childers described the process:

> After the nomination, the returning officer sends to a public officer – I think the Clerk of the Peace – a requisition for a number of voting papers equal to that of voters on the roll. On the face of each paper is printed a list of the candidates, with instructions to the voter to strike off those for whom

---

[58] Crook and Crook, "Reforming Voting Practices," 219.

[59] Brett, *From Secret Ballot to Democracy Sausage*, 22–23. Also see Peter Brent, "The Australian Ballot: Not the Secret Ballot," *Australian Journal of Political Science*, 41(1) (March 2006): 39–50; Julian Go, "Empire, Democracy, and Discipline: The Transimperial History of the Secret Ballot," in *Crossing Empires: Taking U. S. History into Transimperial Terrain*, ed. Kristin L. Hoganson and Jay Sexton (Durham, NC: Duke University Press, 2020), 93–111; and Alan Ware: "The essential elements of this system were that the ballot paper was printed by the state, and not by the candidates or parties, it was available only at the place of balloting and at the time of voting, and a ballot paper could not legally be removed from the balloting place." Ware, *The American Direct Primary: Party Institutionalization and Transformation in the North* (Cambridge: Cambridge University Press, 2002).

he does not poll; and on the back the returning officer signs his name. When the elector comes up to vote, and after the usual questions have been put to him, the returning officer writes at the back of a voting paper the number of the elector on the roll, and hands it to him. The voter takes the paper to a table, not overlooked by the poll clerks or the public, and after erasing the necessary number of names, folds it, brings it back, and drops it into the ballot box in front of the returning officer.[60]

Over the course of the next decade, parliamentary discussions of voting reform and the secret ballot returned frequently to the subject of Australia, to the differences between Australian, American, and other elections, to the "Australian ballot," the "Victorian ballot," and the wily and worrisome "Tasmanian Dodge."[61] The eventual passage of the Ballot Act in 1872 was greatly facilitated by the report of Lord Hartington's Select Committee, which had "questioned witnesses from France, Italy, Greece, the United States, and Australia" and argued "that corruption, treating and intimidation by priests and landlords took place to a large extent at both parliamentary and municipal elections in England and Ireland; and that the ballot, if adopted, would probably not only promote tranquility at elections, but protect voters from undue influence, and introduce greater freedom and purity in voting, provided secrecy was made inviolable except in cases where a voter was found guilty of bribery, or where an invalid vote had been given."[62] The point here is that the difference at the heart of the debates leading up to the 1872 Ballot Act wasn't or wasn't only the imaginative or epistemic difference between how things were and how they should be; it was, rather, a comparative difference between national characters, contemporary systems, and, in the case of England and Australia, the ostensible center and edges of empire.

---

[60] 156 *Hansard Parliamentary Debates* (3rd ser.) (1860) col. 790, https://hansard.parliament.uk/ Commons/1860-02-09/debates/e21e374e-8034-476b-a5a1-ca31b725b5f7/GloucesterCityAndWa kefieldElections—Leave?highlight=after%20nomination%20returning%20officer%20sends% 20public%20officer#contribution-9a8c207b-859d-4923-8e6b-e1887e701fa5.

[61] For more on the "Tasmanian Dodge," also known as the "endless chain," see Eldon Cobb Evans, *A History of the Australian Ballot System in the United States* (Chicago: University of Chicago Press, 1917): "By some method or other an official ballot is removed from the polling-place and is marked by a vote-purchaser on the outside. This marked ballot is given to a bribed elector who votes that ticket and brings back the one given to him by the ballot clerk unmarked. This process is repeated over and over again, and so gets its name of the endless chain" (72). Trollope's friend and whist partner W. E. Forster described it this way in the House on April 12, 1872: "a paper was taken out of the polling booth and imitated, while another paper marked under exterior influence was inserted into the ballot box."

[62] Evans, *Australian Ballot System in the United States* (Chicago: University of Chicago Press, 1917), 18; 1911 *Encyclopedia Britannica*.

The "Australian Ballot" is thus not only a thing but also a *transimperial* thing. As Sukanya Banerjee puts it, the concept of transimperial is important because, unlike transnational or world-systems theories, a "transimperial approach posits a relation of comparison, connection, and contiguity between different imperial constituencies."[63] As opposed to models that privilege "flow and mobility," the transimperial attends to the stickiness, the "groundedness" of things that don't move so easily, of things that don't "readily circulate," of things like the ecological givens and generic conventions that Banerjee explores in her essay on the relation between indigo cultivation and theatrical representation in nineteenth-century Calcutta. Indeed, the potential category mistake embedded in the Australian Ballot's other name – the "Victorian Ballot" – is a neat expression of the resistant and thingly character of electoral procedures in and around 1872. Like indigo or "Negro head tobacco," or like some especially recalcitrant but nonetheless peripatetic literary conventions, the thickly transimperial and transnational itinerary of a particular ballot design or of the concept of secrecy itself suggests something about the history of practical electoral reform in the nineteenth century that, if it doesn't entirely overturn the before-and-after logic of our more familiar genealogies, at least forces us to confront its character and what it might mean for the history of political theory, subjectivity, and representation.[64]

In fact, a full reckoning with the awkward and double sense of "Victorian" in "Victorian Ballot" would have to address several intriguing facts:

1. The fact that a significant number of English emigrants – including Henry Samuel Chapman – were or had been radicals or Chartists who moved or were transported to Australia during the 1830s and 1840s.

---

[63] Sukanya Banerjee, "Transimperial," *Victorian Literature and Culture*, 46(3–4) (Fall/Winter 2018), 927.

[64] Elaine Freedgood's account of the *barely* hidden presence of Australia and the "extermination" of Australian Aborigines behind the seemingly innocuous detail of Magwitch's "Negro head tobacco" in *Great Expectations* is useful here not only because of its method but also because it helps us better to see what we have forgotten about what the Victorians simply knew about Australia; where Freedgood had at first expected that Australia and colonial violence would emerge as another instance of the Victorian repressed, "turning from *Great Expectations* to the Victorian periodical press, one finds a massive chronicling of Australia in general and of Aboriginal everyday life – and death – in particular, beginning in the 1830s and persisting through the 1860s, the decade of the novel's publication." As is the case with "Negro head tobacco," the surprisingly transimperial character of the "Victorian" secret ballot and thus of secrecy itself would have surprised almost no one in England in 1872. Freedgood, *Ideas in Things*, 84. For more on the local recalcitrance of literary and novelistic convention, see Roberto Schwarz, *Misplaced Ideas: Essays on Brazilian Culture*, trans. John Gledson (London: Verso Books, 1992).

This not only facilitated the early and relatively unproblematic embrace of the ballot in Victoria but also suggests something interesting about what we might think of the "uneven development" of Chartism in the nineteenth century. Where, in other words, many accounts assume that Chartism had more or less died out by about 1850, its colonial afterlife and eventual reappearance at home in the discrete and, as it were, domesticated form of a tangible ballot design might encourage us to think differently both about the nature of comparative political history in general and, more to the point, about Chartism's place in the history of the international and imperial Left.

2. The fact that the need for electoral reform in Australia was not only the result of political agitation but also a byproduct of the discovery of gold in Victoria. Australia had adopted the 1832 Reform Act's property qualification of ten pounds, which was meant to "exclude most working men"; because, however, "the goldrush inflation" pushed rents higher and higher, there was an unplanned and sudden expansion of the electorate.[65] As a result, universal manhood suffrage happened nearly by accident in some parts of Australia, a fact that necessitated both quick political thinking and the practical reorganization of elections; this, we now know, is where Chapman and his procedural innovations came in. In a fuller account, we would need to see how the contingent but seemingly inevitable electoral path opened by this "accidental" achievement of universal manhood suffrage would reach both a logical end and a perverse limit in 1902, when a parliamentary act gave the vote to all British subjects over the age of 21, regardless of gender, while simultaneously and systematically *disenfranchising* Australia's Aboriginal peoples. On the one hand, this meant that Australia became the first country to embrace national women's suffrage, decades before England would manage the same thing with the Representation of the People Act of 1928. On the other hand, and as a result of the same 1902 Franchise Act, Aboriginal people were subjected to an Australian equivalent of Jim Crow, and their "voting rights [were] tied to various tests, such as literacy, financial status or receipt of public assistance."[66] The Janus-faced nature of the 1902 Act, at once surprisingly progressive and yet also grossly reactionary, points to ways in which both electoral and Victorian things need to be viewed within a thick context of imperial

---

[65] Brett, *From Secret Ballot to Democracy Sausage*, 15–16.
[66] Brett, *From Secret Ballot to Democracy Sausage*, 71, 72.

conquest and political liberalism, global trade and local prejudice, women's suffrage and white supremacy.

3. The fact that this messy and unexpected mix of imperialism, emigration, inflation, racism, and the expropriation of natural resources somehow came together to force the appearance of an especially rickety "technology of self." This is not only striking but might also offer us another way to think about the co-implication of the novelistic character and colonial treasure in, just for instance, *Great Expectations*; when the revelation of Magwitch's gold forces Pip to realize that his benefactor was not only a convict but also a man, he is, in a sense, only doing in the novel what Victoria's Legislative Council had done five years before. The story of Magwitch's passage from minor "warmint" to a fully drawn character makes, oddly enough, more sense when seen in relation to the transimperial story of the relation between empire, political personhood, gold, and the secret ballot.

Understanding the simple facts that the ballot came from somewhere and that, when it went somewhere else (the US, the Philippines, etc.), it looked a little different and did different things as it went helps us better to see the loaded particularity of the 1872 Ballot Act. Not just the abstract index of a paradigm shift, the Ballot Act represented an effort to negotiate class and class conflict on the threshold of something at least closer to real representative democracy; it was a way to process both the fact and the changing contours and significance of a radical intellectual history that found itself preserved, reworked, and, in a sense, domesticated in 1872; it also represented, almost by the way, a real change in how it was that institutions understood, codified, and relied upon ideas about what the human will was and how more than one human will could or should be added up to represent the general will of a group.

While, in other words, this shift does seem to toe the Foucauldian line, the stakes, the complexity, and, at times, the essential incoherence of Victorian efforts to imagine a system that might represent and coordinate the will of the individual and the will of the group also exceeds and distorts and, as it were, smudges that Foucauldian line, helping to account for both the historical particularity and the aesthetic desire that stand just behind the vote. We've already begun to see how this works in relation to the ballot's jaggedly transimperial circuit. In what follows, I want to return to some of the more technical or abstruse efforts to realize political representation before and after 1872. Seeing the overlap between political and aesthetic representation before, after, and beyond the secrecy of the secret ballot will, I hope, help to show how the *written ballot* became a thing and how that thing helped to shape our expectations and anxieties about what a person is when one person decides along with other persons about what the world should be.

An Extraordinary Machine

In a previous section, I considered the unusual or the excessive attention to detail that seemed characteristic of several Victorian efforts to imagine, envision, or suppose the devices and machines on which elections after reform and the implementation of a secret ballot would rely. For Bentham, Grote, Leatham, and others, thinking about elections, how they should work, and what they could and should mean required thinking with special and *suppositional* intensity about the material details of ballots, ballot boxes, voting booths, pencils, pens, ink, and so on. I tried then to show how attending to the nature, design, and significance of these electoral things opens onto other ways of understanding the history behind and the hopes for electoral reform in general and the secret ballot in particular. Recognizing, in other words, that the secret ballot was really an "Australian" or a "Victorian" ballot thickens our sense of the prove-nance, significance, and, as it were, *reality* of electoral reform. In this section, I want to turn to another, different but related kind of electoral thing, what John Stuart Mill, Thomas Hare, and others imagined as "the machinery of representation." In so doing, I'll also return to a question I raised earlier: what did it mean that, with the ballot, a vote became not only a secret but also an essentially written thing?

In the 1850s, Thomas Hare – autodidact, lawyer, eccentric, and all-around self-made man – began laying out meticulous plans for electoral reform that sought to reimagine who would vote, where they would vote, how they would vote, how their votes would be counted, and what their votes would ultimately mean. His primary concern was that, because the post-1832 electoral system relied on competition between strong political parties operating in artificially circumscribed geographic areas, votes and elections simply could not represent the real will or interests of either the individual or the group. That is, even though there were more electors with a vote after reform, those new electors still had very little actual choice: more votes, it turned out, did not mean more choice. Because the range of candidates and thus the range of interests that those candidates represented were wholly limited by place, party, and the backroom influence of party grandees, individual votes could not really represent the real will of voting individuals; and, if those votes were not really representative, they couldn't, when taken in aggregate, really represent the full and real will – the general will, if you will – of the nation taken as a whole.

Hare's solution was, as I will discuss in a moment, brilliant, complicated, and meticulously, maybe even obsessively wrought. These are just its main points:

1. Instead of only voting for candidates within their given, local constituency, electors would be able to vote for candidates put forward from anywhere in the country. Election officials would register all candidates and prepare and circulate an approved and "gazetted" list of all candidates from which electors would then take their pick.[67]

2. Although each elector's vote would ultimately count *only once* as support for *only one* candidate, the elector was encouraged to list several candidates in a ranked order of preference on a ballot paper also provided by election officials.

3. To identify winners, election officials ("scrutineers") would count votes cast for a winning candidate up to and only up to what Hare referred to as a *quota*, the minimum number of votes a candidate would need within a given election to be guaranteed a seat. In the motion he put forward in 1867, Hare's chief supporter, John Stuart Mill defined the quota as "a number equal to the quotient obtained by dividing by 658 [the total number of MPs in the House in 1867] the total number of votes polled throughout the kingdom at the same election, and if such quotient be fractional, the integral number next less."[68] Once a candidate had reached that quota, that candidate would be considered elected, and subsequent votes for that candidate would not be counted.[69]

---

[67] "Of course," writes Vernon Bogdanor, "the vast majority of electors would, no doubt, name candidates who lived within their local constituency and who were personally known to them. But there would be a significant and important minority, including, for Hare, the educated minority, who would name candidates from elsewhere." Bogdanor, *The People and the Party System: The Referendum and Electoral Reform in British Politics* (Cambridge: Cambridge University Press, 1981), 106.

[68] J. S. Mill, *Personal Representation. Speech of John Stuart Mill, Esq., M.P., Delivered in the House of Commons, May 29, 1867* (London: Henderson, Rait, & Fenton, 1867), 5.

[69] Soon after Mill's speech, H. R. Droop proposed a revision to the internal workings of Hare's machine. Instead of dividing the total number of votes by the total number of seats, Droop suggested that one should instead begin by dividing the total number of votes by the total number of seats *plus one*, and then one should add *one more* to the result of that first division. In an election where a million voters had to fill 658, calculating Hare's quota would result in 1520 necessary votes and Droop's quota would result in 1518 necessary votes. From one

4. Because, however, electors would have indicated second and subsequent choices on their ballot papers, those unconsidered first *votes* would not result in wasted *ballots*. Instead, when faced with an already elected first choice, officials would count the elector's second choice as their first choice. As the counting continued, officials would continue to work across and down the ballots, navigating the ranked preferences of electors as more and more candidates met the quota and found seats in parliament.

As Hare, Mill, and others saw it, this scheme had several clear benefits.

1. It prevented two kinds of electoral "wastage." First, where the results of simple majority elections can and often do leave nearly half of all voters more or less unrepresented, the combination of a national field and the reduced caucusing power of the major parties would, they suggested, lead to a greater, indeed, a proportional representation not only of *majorities* but also of *minorities* within parliament. This would not only – and this was dear to Mill's heart – counteract the threat of majority tyranny, but also ensure that minority votes really counted. Second, just as Hare's scheme meant that *minority* votes were not wasted, so did it mean that *majority* votes were not wasted. Although we tend to think that more is always better in elections, once a candidate reaches a certain numerical threshold, every vote past that threshold is technically (if not rhetorically) a wasted vote. If a candidate can win with 125 votes, 126 votes does not make that candidate win *better* or win *more*. It makes sense, in that case, to transfer those otherwise wasted votes to the next strongest candidate. "If," writes

perspective of the candidate receiving either 1520 or 1518 votes, the systems are almost the same. From, however the perspective of subsequent candidates who might inherit a winning candidate's unneeded votes, two votes might mean the difference between winning and losing a seat. Conceptually, Droop's innovation leans into one aspect of Hare's system; because his quota identifies a numerical winner slightly sooner, it allows more votes to pass on to a second or third candidate. Taking Hare a small step forward, Droop emphasizes the *breadth* of a voter's preferences. What's more, Kenneth Benoit has shown that – practically and at scale – Hare quotas are slightly better at representing the range of interests or positions in a given area while Droop quotas offer a slight advantage to candidates associated with large political parties. In close elections or in evenly split representative bodies, a few votes or a few seats can, of course, have enormous consequences. This is more evidence that the minor or tacit details of electoral procedure can have unexpectedly significant effects: "the results," says Benoit, "should remind researchers and electoral systems designers alike that electoral formulas, even apparent minutiae such as quota denominators and numerical series, are more than inconsequential mathematical details." Kenneth Benoit, "Which Electoral Formula Is the Most Proportional? A New Look with New Evidence," *Political Analysis* 8 (4) (2000) 388. Also see, H. R. Droop, "On Methods of Electing Representatives," in *Journal of the Statistical Society*, June 1881, 141–202.

Hare, "a popular candidate should receive, as is most likely to be the case, the suffrages of a very much larger number of electors than the number of the quota, it would follow that the excess of votes would be lost, if means were not provided for enabling the electors to transfer their votes, on that contingency, to some other candidate."[70]

2. Hare's scheme would also radically reduce the incentive either to intimidate or to bribe electors, two of the primary concerns that drove the contemporary push for the secret ballot. Where, in other words, the local significance of the individual vote within close, restricted elections meant that it had a particular, legible, and, as it were, saleable value, the significance of the individual vote within the context of a national election leavened with the ranked play between first, second, and third choices meant that, while the individual vote became *more* valuable to the elector, whose whole preference was more fully and richly represented, and *more* valuable to the state, which could wring more meaning out of it, it became *less* valuable to those who would try unduly to influence an election.

3. Maybe most importantly, Hare's scheme would, with its geographic breadth, its comparative bent, and its ability to bypass the distorting pressures of local interests and political parties, allow the results of an election and thus the whole House of Commons to stand as a living and, as it were, *realistic* reflection or representation of the many ideas, interests, conflicts, and beliefs that defined a complex and robust national culture. Hare made this point in characteristically euphoric terms:

> A representative assembly, chosen under a system thus free and expansive, would be a reflex of the feeling and intelligence of the people. Gradually elevated in character by the constant operation of the process of comparison which is so powerful in every department of science, by the introduction of the most distinguished men, and by the elimination of the inferior, it would become a national Walhalla, worthy to form a branch of that parliament which, having its origin in the depth of past ages where all records are

---

[70] Thomas Hare, *A Treatise on the Election of Representatives, Parliamentary and Municipal* (London: Longman, Brown, Green, Longmans, & Roberts, 1859), 145. As I'll discuss in Chapter 3, the idea that votes cast for a candidate more than those necessary simply to win are wasted votes has changed in recent years. That is, as questions of legitimacy and post-election litigation have become more and more vexed, the importance of winning by a landslide has increased. As became all too clear in 2020 and 2021, when every election is liable to be challenged in court, it's no longer enough to win; you have, rather, to win big.

shadowy and doubtful, has rolled on, gathering strength and dignity in its course, down to our own days, and become the great model of constitutional government, the envy or admiration of all civilized nations.[71]

Although not adopted at the time (give my regards to Walhalla), Hare's scheme for proportional representation was widely discussed and impressed several influential public figures (Herbert Spencer, Alexander Bain, Thomas Hughes, John Lubbock, and, most importantly, Mill). Following the interest in his 1857 pamphlet, Hare went on in 1859 to publish the much longer *Treatise on the Election of Representatives*, which ran into several editions, sold more than 1,500 copies, spawned the British Proportional Representation Society, and led to "a copious literature ... for the promotion or discussion of Hare's electoral system which attracted attention in many parts of the world."[72] Known now as the Single Transferable Vote (STV), something close to Hare's scheme is actually used in a few places – "the Republic of Ireland since 1921, Malta since 1947, and once in Estonia in 1990" – and "has long been advocated by political scientists as one of the most attractive electoral systems."[73]

There are a few different ways to think about the significance of Hare's scheme. First, like Grote's box and Leatham's ink, Hare's scheme was regularly criticized – even mocked – for its meticulousness, its complexity, and for the almost manic overelaboration of its details; as a result, we can see Hare's method as another part of the electoral thing culture that I've begun to describe. Because, however, Hare's system is more an idea, arrangement, or model than it is an evidently discrete object – a box, bodkin, or bottle of ink – it encourages us to think differently about the relation between things and ideas in the period. What is the difference between ideas and things, between things and ideas? As we've already begun to see, the *rules* of electoral design are interesting and challenging in part because they seem to refuse that difference. That you have to rank your choices on a ranked-choice ballot isn't exactly an idea (you don't really think about it unless you must) and it isn't exactly a thing either (you can't touch or see or smell a rule *qua* rule); this, I think, is why this material and these problems are so interesting: they make – for me at

---

[71] Hare, *Election of Representatives*, 160.

[72] Jenifer Hart, *Proportional Representation: Critics of the British Electoral System, 1820–1945* (Oxford: Clarendon Press, 1992), 24.

[73] Andrew Reynolds, Ben Reilly, and Andrew Ellis, *Electoral System Design: The New International IDEA Handbook* (Stockholm: International Institute for Democracy and Electoral Assistance, 2005), 71. For more on the workings and virtues of STV, see David M. Farrell, *Electoral Systems: A Comparative Introduction* (London: Palgrave, 2011), 119–152.

least – new, enlivening methodological demands on the history of ideas.[74] Second, in addition to its fairly radical revision of what votes mean both individually and when they're taken together in aggregate, Hare's plan relied on a *written* ballot in ways that had important consequences for the emergence of a new relation between writing and political subjectivity. Because, in other words, an elector could fill a ballot paper with anywhere from one name to "all the names on the gazette list, though this might, according to Hare, amount to two or three thousand," it would have been practically impossible both for electors *to speak* their vote and, even more so, for election officials to manage aurally the complex, sequential tabulation that those complex votes would require.[75] So, unlike the secret ballot, where writing could serve as a way simply to translate and thus to preserve the secrecy of vote that *could otherwise have been spoken*, the flexible preference schedule on which Hare's scheme relied fundamentally on writing as political representation's primary mode.[76] Where the secret ballot needed writing because writing allowed electors really – if paradoxically – to say what they meant and what they would have said out loud if only they were allowed, Hare's ballot paper assumed the deep and thus essentially *unsayable* complexity of an elector's preference as an existentially written thing. Hare's inadvertent embrace of the elector's vote and, thus, of the elector's political subjectivity as necessarily written and thus unspeakable might be his most important, if least acknowledged (indeed, wholly unacknowledged, as far as I can tell) contribution to electoral theory and intellectual history.

As a result, and this is my third point, Hare's method both relied on and had significant if unintended consequences for thinking about the aesthetics of political representation as well as the politics of aesthetic representation. Let me begin to explain what I mean with a turn to the *language* of electoral reform: the word "machinery" comes up again and again in relation to Hare's proposals for proportional representation. In addition to its place in the title of the 1857 pamphlet, it shows up in Mill's essay on Hare ("this done, the rest of the machinery would work of itself"), in Henry Fawcett's more user-friendly summation of Hare's theory ("the

---

[74] As I was finishing this book, New York held its first ranked-choice mayoral election, an apparently upsetting innovation that spawned more than a few pieces that spoke to the odd status of electoral rules: "Let's look," says one calming and interactive overview, "at an election where six candidates – **A, B, C, D, E**, and **F** – received votes." Sarah Almukhtar, Jazmine Hughes, and Eden Weingart, "How Does Ranked-Choice Voting Work in New York?," *The New York Times*, April 22, 2021, www.nytimes.com/interactive/2021/nyregion/ranked-choice-voting-nyc.html.

[75] Hart, *Proportional Representation*, 35.   [76] Hart, *Proportional Representation*, 35.

existing machinery of representation entirely disregards the amount of support which a candidate receives"), in Simon Sterne's application of Hare's ideas to the American context ("representative government, therefore, is not an original organic form, but a machinery necessitated by modern civilization"), in H. R. Droop's "On Methods of Electing Representatives" ("the election of representatives has become, in modern times, a most important part of all political and social machinery"), in John Lubbock's work for the Proportional Representation Society ("the whole representative machinery of the country is constructed upon a principle so erroneous that the motive power cannot be augmented without throwing the entire machine out of gear"), and so on.[77]

At first glance, it seems clear that Hare and the others use the term in its broadly procedural sense: "The workings, organization, or functional equipment of a system, institution, subject, etc." (OED). Insofar as political representation is a system or institution or a part of another system or institution, it relies on a discrete set of procedures that can allow for the conversion of the unprocessed desires, beliefs, or interests of individuals into a recognizable set of social choices, decisions, or programs; it is thus necessary to identify and to understand the "machinery of representation" – the steps or processes that exist between the thing itself (in this case the will of the voter) and the thing's appearance as an and in a form of effective political representation – before that machinery could be endorsed, improved, or replaced. If, though, that is the term's dominant sense for Hare and his followers, other connotations seem nonetheless to creep in. There is, first, the sense of machinery not as a metaphor for systems that are *like* machines but, rather, as what it simply is: a machine is a machine is a machine, "a complex device, consisting of a number of interrelated parts, each having a definite function" (OED). Indeed, the profound intricacy of Hare's idea, its reliance not only on different and differently connected axioms, clauses, and claims but also on a coherent if fantastically elaborate set of procedures, was immediately striking to his readers: "Hare's book," writes Jenifer Hart in reference to his 1859 work, "is a strange and uneasy amalgam of broad general reflections on such subjects as government, society, public opinion, and divine law, and meticulous details in the form of thirty-three extremely technical clauses

---

[77] Mill, *Thoughts on Parliamentary Reform*, 52; Henry Fawcett, *Mr. Hare's Reform Bill Simplified and Explained* (London: James Ridgway, 1860), 11; Simon Sterne, *On Representative Government and Personal Representation* (Philadelphia: J. B. Lippincott & Co., 1871), 24; H. R. Droop, "On Methods of Electing Representatives," in *Journal of the Statistical Society*, June, 1881, 141; John Lubbock, *Representation* (London: Swan Sonnenschein & Co., 1885), 80.

of an electoral law with explanations of how it would work."[78] This almost inescapable sense of Hare's work as something especially and maybe needlessly complex often encourages Hare, Mill, Fawcett, and others to protest too much and to claim that, despite appearances, the machine really was pretty simple. "It is," says Hare, "of importance that the proposed form of voting should not in the smallest degree perplex or complicate the business of voting."[79] "Seldom," says a somewhat defensive Mill, "has it happened that a great political idea could be realized by such easy and simple machinery; and there is not a serious object, nor a genuine difficulty, of however slight a nature, which will not, we think, be found to have been foreseen and met."[80] "The danger," he suggests elsewhere, "is lest the inevitable prominence of the mechanical arrangements should confuse the mind of a mere cursory reader, and enable the scheme to be represented as too complex and subtle to be workable."[81]

In 1867, while unsuccessfully presenting the idea to the House as an improvement on the going reform, Mill took this argument even further, suggesting that when people "take it into their heads" that Hare's plan was a complex instead of a simple machine, they were, in fact, caught in the grip of a category mistake:

> People who have merely heard of Mr. Hare's plan have taken it into their heads that it is particularly hard to understand and difficult to execute. But the difficulty is altogether imaginary: to the elector there is no difficulty at all; to the scrutineers, only that of performing correctly an almost mechanical operation. Mr. Hare, anxious to leave nothing vague or uncertain, has taken the trouble to discuss in his book the whole detail of the mode of sorting the voting papers. People glance at this, and because they cannot take it all in at a glance it seems to them very mysterious. But when was there any act of Parliament that could be understood at a glance? And how can gentlemen expect to understand the details of a plan unless they first possess themselves of its principle? If we were to read a description, for examples, of the mode in which letters are sorted at the Post-office, would it not seem to us very complicated? Yet, among so vast a number of letters, how seldom is any mistake made.[82]

The immediate response to Mill's speech showed that his anxiety about what people had "taken into their heads" had not been unfounded.

---

[78] Hart, *Proportional Representation*, 31.   [79] Hare, *Election of Representatives*, 147.
[80] Mill, *Thoughts on Parliamentary Reform*, 46.
[81] John Stuart Mill, "Recent Writers on Reform," in *Dissertations and Discussions: Political, Philosophical, and Historical* (New York: Henry Holt, 1874), 4:83.
[82] Mill, *Personal Representation*, 11.

A polite Viscount Cranborne thanked Mill but admitted that "all instinctively felt that it was a scheme that had no chance of success. It was not our atmosphere – it was not in accordance with our habits; it did not belong to us."[83] A decidedly less polite Serjeant Gaselee insisted that "the House could come to no practical conclusion by discussing these philosophical eccentricities," and asked that they "turn from the amusement they had that night to more serious business."[84] In short, Mill's colleagues took Hare's machinery as others had taken Grote's box or Leatham's ink: as complex, overnice, eccentric, exotic, fantastic, and, finally, more trouble than it was worth. Like Grote's box, Hare's machine appeared to many members of the House less like a hammer, saw, or an inclined plane and more like a Rube Goldberg device or Jean Tinguely's self-destroying device. Hare's machine seemed to be a thing that valued complexity – detail, difficulty, paradox – for its own sake. It was, perhaps, with Gaselee and others in mind that Mill wrote in his *Autobiography* that "anyone who does not feel the want which the scheme is intended to supply; anyone who throws it over as a mere theoretical subtlety or crotchet, tending to no valuable purpose, and unworthy of the attention of practical men, may be pronounced an incompetent statesman, unequal to the politics of the future."[85] To paraphrase: a lot of things seem complicated when you're stupid.

There is, I think, yet another connotation of the word "machinery" at work here. In addition to the procedures basic to a complex institutional system or to a composite thing made up of discrete but interrelated parts, machinery can also refer to the "contrivances employed for effect in a literary work" (OED). It can, in other words, refer to the conventions and the imaginative labor necessary to produce literary or dramatic art; machinery, as Hare must have understood, is what one needs to produce not only political representations but also the aesthetic representations on which political thinking often relies. What's most striking about Mill's exhortation to his colleagues in Parliament is that it took the form not only of a technical or a practical suggestion but also of an invitation to make an imaginative "leap into the dark." The apparent impracticability of Hare's system was, Mill suggested, an effect not of its objective design but rather of the viewer's subjective and scalar relation to an apparently convoluted

[83] 187 *Hansard Parliamentary Debates* (3rd ser.) (1867) col. 1357, https://hansard.parliament.uk/Commons/1867-05-30/debates/3ec24b72-e81e-4855-be93-cf3f1d821256/CommitteeProgressMay28?highlight=more%20serious%20business#contribution-60d27b13–23d4–495d-8153-31a2150e1f4e.

[84] 187 *Hansard Parliamentary Debates* (3d ser.) (1867) col. 1360–1361.

[85] John Stuart Mill, *Autobiography* (London: Penguin, 1990), 194.

but finally coherent object. In order, then, to overcome a false first impression of hopeless complexity, the reader or listener needed, first, to act *as if* Hare's scheme were simple to arrive at the real but conceptually deferred fact of its real, if oblique simplicity. Here fiction works not as an imaginative alternative to things as they really are but as the roundabout, dilatory, and nonetheless necessary route one needs to take to get at what really is and always really was the case. It is, as it were, a suppositional realism.

In a way, the state of conceptual suspension that Mill encourages in his readers and listeners – this thing might not make sense now, but have faith, hang in there, and it someday will – reminds me of "the experience of being in error" that Scarry associates with beauty seen in its difficult but real relation to truth. As she argues in *On Beauty and Being Just*, when one recovers from the "error" of having before thought of a beautiful thing as unbeautiful, that recovery is a matter not of seeing a new thing but rather of seeing an old thing – and the whole of the world that contains that old thing – in a new way; for Scarry, "a beautiful object is suddenly present, not because a new object has entered the sensory horizon bringing its beauty with it . . . but because an object, already within the horizon, has its beauty, like late luggage, suddenly placed in your hands."[86] For Mill, the elegance and institutional sublimity of Hare's scheme work in a similar way; although it can look ungainly or ridiculous at first, once you come to appreciate the machine's order, its effects, its beauty, it will change your world. If it seems like a stretch to see a technical plan for proportional representation as having anything to do with the palm fronds and other beautiful things in Scarry's book, consider Hare's own, intensely lyrical description what political representation would mean once reformed and realized:

> The representation in its theory, or in any worthy view of it, should be of all that is best and most instructed, omitting, as far as the separation is possible, all that is ignorant and vicious. The representative embodiment is to be of man, approaching, as near as his infirmity of thought and will permits him to approach, his pristine dignity, when, –

> In their looks divine
> The image of their glorious Maker shone,
> Truth, wisdom, sanctitude, severe and pure
> (Severe, but in true filial freedom placed),
> Whence true authority.

---

[86] Elaine Scarry, *On Beauty and Being Just* (Princeton, NJ: Princeton University Press, 2001), 16.

The design is to represent the qualities with which man is divinely gifted, – the noble heritage of his nature, – not their absence and negation. Such an assembly should present "the awful image of virtue and wisdom of a whole people collected into a focus."[87]

The passage is not only insistently literary, drawing with sympathetic and cultured enthusiasm on Milton and Burke, but also something like an aesthetic theory in and of itself. For Hare, political representation isn't merely a matter of capturing preferences, balancing interests, and counting votes; it is also a process that sorts, selects, and orders its raw materials so as to reveal the available and immanent truth of those materials while also working them into something both "awful" and new. Hare sounds here something like Trollope's Mr. Monk, a Radical MP who sees political representation in similarly aesthetic terms: a "great authority," he says to Phineas Finn in *Phineas Finn*, "has told us that our House of Commons should be the mirror of the people. I say, not its mirror, but its miniature. And let the artist be careful to put in every line of the expression of that ever-moving face."[88] And indeed, the lines Hare takes from Milton come from a passage that not only casts Adam and Eve in pure, unashamed, and still unmediated form but also presents that purity as seen from Satan's degraded point of view. Rather than treating purity as a privileged form of presence, Milton treats it rather as a mediated representation of a thing, as the thing that Satan sees as he looks, "undelighted, all delight," at the scene. As a focalizing, mediating, literary presence standing necessarily between the reader and Paradise, Satan is, as it were, Milton's machinery of representation, an unwilling contrivance necessary to the larger logic of the divine plan.[89]

There is something almost Coleridgean about Hare's view of the machinery of political representation, something that recalls the synthesis of active power and passive perception that Coleridge saw as essential to the imagination. It seems to have been this organic, this synthetic quality to Hare's plan which, in addition to the answers it offered to the questions of the day, captivated Mill just as Coleridge's work had captivated and sustained him thirty years before. In his speech before the House, he imagined the effects of Hare's scheme in wildly ambitious terms:

[87] Hare, *Election of Representatives*, 161–162.
[88] Anthony Trollope, *Phineas Finn*, ed. Simon Dentith (Oxford: Oxford University Press, 2011), 268. Hereafter abbreviated *PF* and cited parenthetically.
[89] This, of course, is an absurdly condensed version of Stanley Fish's classic argument in *Surprised by Sin: The Reader in Paradise Lost* (Cambridge, MA: Harvard University Press, 1967).

> It would be a healing, a reconciling measure, softening all political transitions, securing that every opinion, instead of conquering or being conquered by starts and shocks, and passing suddenly from having no power at all in Parliament to having too much or the contrary, should wax or wane in political power in exact proportion to its growth or decline in the general mind of the country. So perfectly does this system realize the idea of what a representative government ought to be, that its perfection stands in its way, and is the great obstacle to its success.[90]

Mill's argument is peculiar, to say the least; if, he suggests, the measure fails, it will be because it is too good, too excellent, too perfect. What could be the problem with a machine as beautiful as Hare's machine? Maybe it's just too beautiful for you.

Taken on its own, the strange mingling of technocratic detail and aesthetic longing that characterizes both Hare's and Mill's experiments in proportional representation is suggestive enough. As we have seen, Hare's writing on the subject was somehow both fastidious and barely constrained, both a scrupulous account of electoral procedure and a passionate "leap into the dark." Just consider the ordering – the compositional machinery – of his 1857 pamphlet: as presented there, Hare's plan has twelve parts (that number would swell to thirty-three by 1859). Instead, though, of laying them out in one or another order, Hare opts for a curiously erratic design: "The scheme," he says, "is comprised in twelve clauses. They are numbered in the order in which they would logically stand if embodied in an act, but they are inserted in the order most convenient for explanation."[91] As a result, the sixth clause appears before the third and after the second, a discursive reshuffling of and answer to the imaginary act's unwritten story. This would seem maybe unnecessary and certainly eccentric in any case, but falling, as it does, in an essay on the possibility, necessity, and value of putting one's preferences into some kind of order, it feels doubly loaded; it feels like a tacit acknowledgement of the unofficial energies, dreams, or desires running beneath the official logic of proportional representation.

In a similar if more tragic vein, Hart speculates that "the rather unbalanced avidity with which" Mill embraced Hare's scheme may have had its own deeper and more extreme sources: "When Mill first read Hare's *Treatise* in January 1859, his wife [Harriet Taylor] had only recently died ... and he was suffering acutely from this crushing calamity."[92] It

[90] Mill, *Personal Representation*, 15.
[91] Thomas Hare, *The Machinery of Representation* (London: W. Maxwell, 1857), 16.
[92] Hart, *Proportional Representation*, 53.

is, of course, impossible to know what, other than its undeniable logistical appeal, drove Mill to Hare, his machinery, and the idea of proportional representation; and, even were it possible, such an endeavor might be inadvisable or wrong even to try. That said, there are two aspects to Hart's feeling that there might be more to Mill's feelings for Hare's machinery about which I want to think. First, it is instructive to think here about Mill's late embrace of Hare's scheme in relation to the better-known ideas on women's suffrage which he developed in collaboration with Taylor, and, at last, published as *The Subjection of Women* (1869). Although that book is more immediate, more sustained, and more serious (it has certainly been taken more seriously as an argument), it sets the table, as it were, for his embrace of Hare's almost weirdly procedural scheme. What's striking, in other words, about Mill's argument in *The Subjection* is that, because he refuses any stable definition of character or identity before the shaping work of education, he must also refuse identity as pertinent to the question of who votes. His argument isn't, in other words, that women ought to be admitted to the suffrage because women *qua* women ought to be represented or that elections are a means of registering and managing real differences between people; his argument is, rather, that a good representational procedure is good because it renders the difference between one kind of person and another moot:

> In the case of election to public trusts, it is the business of constitutional law to surround the right of suffrage with all needful securities and limitations; but whatever securities are sufficient in the case of the male sex, no others need be required in the case of women. Under whatever conditions, and within whatever limits, men are admitted to the suffrage, there is not a shadow of justification for not admitting women under the same.[93]

We can see, in other words, how Mill's radical agnosticism about the prior or foundational reality of identity and his lifelong commitment to logical coherence for its own sake would have led him from a polemic about women's suffrage to his late and pronounced embrace of Hare's complicated and abstract scheme. Rather than look later for procedures that could address the fact of existing social problems and inequities, Mill sought to invent procedures the logical consistency of which would obviate the need to consider social categories. In a sense, Mill's and Taylor's move carves out a space between two divergent tactical futures for the suffragist movement as well as for political movements more generally: When it

---

[93] John Stuart Mill, *The Subjection of Women*, in *The Basic Writings of John Stuart Mill*, ed., Dale. E. Miller (New York: Modern Library, 2002), 177.

comes to political representation, does one start with identity and then find the rule that fits, or does one start with rule, hoping that a good one will somehow render identity unnecessary?

Second, there might be something less certain to say about what might connect the fact of Mill's *personal loss* with the idea behind Hare's ballot paper. In addition to its political value, what Hare's scheme brings to the vote is the promise that an indefinitely long and necessarily written list of diverse, competing, and variously balanced preferences would say more about the truth of the voter and the voter's feelings than the largely canned choice between two figures chosen in advance by their respective political parties. As I will discuss in greater detail in the following section, Hare's ballot paper raised important and importantly novelistic questions about what people – as citizens and subjects – could think and feel as well as about what methods, what representative machinery, might be best suited to capture the complexity, intensity, incoherence, and significance of those thoughts and feelings. The unfulfilled promise of Hare's ballot paper was, in that case, the suggestion that it might be able to capture and convey something about the feelings of others and about one's own feelings that couldn't be or hadn't been captured before, that it could avoid the waste of feelings and thus, as it were, the loss of loss. For Mill, who famously associated his deepest depression with the inability or the unwillingness to write, the promise of the ballot paper as a form of writing that might be capable of representing and thus working dispassionately through that "most unexpected and bitter calamity" might have offered a profoundly personal as well as a practically political appeal.

A Miniature of the People

I've written throughout this book about how modern elections depend on the suppositional posture of imaginative fiction. From the beginning, the idea of representative government – the idea that the will of one person could somehow stand in for and *represent* the will of another person or another group of people – relied on a willing suspension of disbelief that aligns thinking about elections with the various political and aesthetic discourses that Edmund Morgan, Catherine Gallagher, and others have associated with the modern rise of fictionality. Although aspects of the premises, procedures, and outcomes of modern elections will always strain or even beggar belief, for a representative democracy to work, its participants must act *as if* those premises, procedures, and outcomes are not only coherent and real but also legitimate. This brings us back to what Bernard

Williams calls the Basic Legitimacy Demand (BLD); because, taken to its logical limit, all political (as opposed to moral or ethical) legitimacy is both necessary and, as it were, existentially groundless, participants in political systems based on the idea of consensus as opposed to the threat or application of brute force must act *as if* the political legitimacy of those systems is not only binding but also real. They must agree to make it real. Thinking about this necessary and, as it were, paradoxically *honest* relation between fiction and legitimacy can help, I think, to make sense of the legal and logistical nightmare that followed the 2020 election. Trump and his lawyers used gross, ham-handed lies about voting (a specter is haunting our voting machines: it is the socialist ghost of Hugo Chavez!) to call juvenile but effective attention to the delicate, the subtle fictionality of voting, which, in turn, undermined a sense of political legitimacy that depends on a shared suspension of disbelief. If, when, and how the pieces of something so necessary and yet also so fragile come back together again are, as I write, open and alarming questions.

We've seen over the course of this chapter how some electoral things in mid-Victorian Britain relied on and activated a mix of imaginative or suppositional play and political realism. In Bentham, Grote, Hare, Mill, and others, the work of designing elections and electoral systems fell somewhere between "facticity and fantasy," between the work of making procedures conducive to the practical realization of electoral reform and an imaginative investment in possible objects, possible ideas, and possible futures, the details of which seemed sometimes to exceed their role in any possible political program. Bentham's box, Grote's dagger, Leatham's ink, Hare's machinery: these are electoral things that point, on the one hand, to an imaginative excess that is inseparable from the idea of political repre-sentation and, on the other hand, to a significant family resemblance that electoral theory shared with the period's preeminent discourse of sus-pended disbelief: the novel. Indeed, the play of facticity and fantasy, of pragmatism and suppositional excess that I've associated with the extraor-dinary machines of Victorian reform could as easily apply, say, to Trollope's fiction, in which, as J. Hillis Miller suggests, "Trollope empha-sizes the way his acts of imagination were rule-bound, made to submit to the laws of internal consistency, continuity, probability, and modera-tion."[94] I've discussed Hare's sense that political representation ought

---

[94] J. Hillis Miller, *The Ethics of Reading: Kant, de Man, Eliot, Trollope, James, and Benjamin* (New York: Columbia University Press, 1987), 83.

not only to reflect but also to purify or even to beautify what it sought to represent: "the representative embodiment is to be of man, approaching, as near as his infirmity of thought and will permits him to approach, his pristine dignity." This view, although cast in Hare's characteristically high-spirited style, was not his alone. I've mentioned that Trollope's Mr. Monk made much the same argument in *Phineas Finn*. This same – active and aesthetic – view of political representation found previous expression in the work of one of the concept's chief architects; in *The Federalist Papers* (No. 10), Madison argued for the mediating effects of representation, which, he argued, would "refine and enlarge the public views by passing them through the medium of a chosen body of citizens, whose wisdom may best discern the true interest of their country and whose patriotism and love of justice will be least likely to sacrifice it to temporary or partial considerations."[95] Seen in these terms, the results of a representative election ought to be not an accurate or immediate reflection of one or another opinion, interest, or preference; they ought instead to be something mediated, different, and better.

It is not, I think, a coincidence that similar claims were made about another of the Victorian period's essential forms, the novelistic character. Although, we could turn here to the long line of critics who have written about the special typicality of the realist character in the nineteenth-century novel (Georg Lukács, Ian Watt, Catherine Gallagher, Diedre Lynch, Alex Woloch, etc.), it seems better or at least apropos to look to an unsigned 1869 review of *Phineas Finn*, one of Trollope's most explicitly political novels:

> It has been objected to Mr. Trollope that his creations are too like real life for literature, – that what one really wants in literature are men and women not so much representative of average men and women, as typical of them, with something, however, of intensity and force and clearness of outline, which belongs more to exceptional than to average men and women, but which is necessary in order to furnish keys to human nature in general. It is said that Mr. Trollope's sketches are so like to those whom one actually meets in society that one learns no more from them than we should learn from those whom we actually meet in society. We do not think that Mr. Trollope is fairly open to this charge. His characters are usually quite as marked and strong in relation to modern society, as are Fielding's in

[95] James Madison, "No. 10," in Alexander Hamilton, Madison, John Jay, *The Federalist Papers*, ed. Ian Shapiro (New Haven, CT: Yale University Press, 2009), 51.

relation to the more sharply classified and more strongly contrasted types of character of a far less uniformly developed and far more localized and provincialized state of society.[96]

The anonymous reviewer draws a contrast here between the "representative" and the "typical"; where the former would simply reflect or hold a mirror up to people as they are, the latter distills, accentuates, purifies. This early anticipation of the Lukácsian claim – that the novel "must give central place throughout to all that is typical in characters" – is striking on its own.[97]

It is, however, more striking when we consider that *Phineas Finn*, the novel that occasioned this critical notice, is itself a novel not only about literary but also about political representation, a relation that is made exceedingly plain in Mr. Monk's description of Parliament as it is and as it should be. A "great authority," he writes in his long letter to Phineas,

> ... has told us that our House of Commons should be the mirror of the people. I say, not its mirror, but its miniature. And let the artist be careful to put in every line of the expression of that ever-moving face. To do this is a great work, and the artist must know his trade well. In America the work has been done with so coarse a hand that nothing is shown in the picture but the broad, plain, unspeaking outline of the face. As you look from the represented to the representation you cannot but acknowledge the likeness; – but there is in that portrait more of the body than of the mind. The true portrait should represent more than the body. With us, hitherto, there have been snatches of the countenance of the nation which have been inimitable, – a turn of the eye here and a curl of the lip there, which have seemed to denote a power almost divine. There have been marvels on the canvas so beautiful that one approaches the work of remodelling it with awe. But not only is the picture imperfect, – a thing of snatches, – but with years it becomes less and still less like its original. (*PF*, 268)

Referring almost directly to Hare's machinery of representation, he casts political representation as a work of refined and undeniably aesthetic portraiture that, at its best, might make legible in the local details of face ("a turn of the eye here and a curl of the lip there") the deeper meaning of the whole person. Of course, the dream of total legibility remains just that, a dream, leaving the turn of an eye or the curl of a lip to stand as the same kind of isolated indexical riddle that underwrote Robert Browning's "My

---

[96] Unsigned notice in *The Spectator*, quoted in Donald Smalley, *Anthony Trollope: The Critical Heritage* (London: Routledge, 1995), 310.

[97] Georg Lukács, *The Historical Novel* (Lincoln: University of Nebraska Press, 1983), 139.

Last Duchess"; like the enigmatic "spot of joy" marking the image of the dead and presumably murdered Duchess's cheek, the isolated and somehow morbid physiognomic details of the modern body politic captured by the House of Commons seem to Monk to invite interpretation, appreciation, misinterpretation, ridicule, and possibly ruin.

"He Hardly Knew How"

How, in that case, should we understand the uncertain representational potential of the individual vote in relation to the equally uncertain representational potential of the novelistic character? Before turning back to *Phineas Finn*, I want to consider another of the period's great novels of parliamentary reform, *Middlemarch*. Although George Eliot's greatest novel is in some obvious sense *about* the 1832 Reform Act, its partial expansion of the franchise, and thus voting, it doesn't really attend to the details of elections in the same way that *Phineas Finn* attends to them. Although we follow Will Ladislaw as he works with intermittent energy to return Mr. Brooke to Parliament as a reform candidate for the town of Middlemarch, Brooke's spectacularly tongue-tied failure on the hustings brings his campaign to an early end and pushes the details, processes, and actual act of voting pretty far into the novel's background. To understand how Victorian voting in fact worked, one should look instead to almost any of Trollope's novels or to *Our Mutual Friend* or even to Eliot's other novel about 1832, *Felix Holt, the Radical*.

That said, although it lacks the national consequence of a Reform Act, one fully represented election does appear in the novel. In the early days of Tertius Lydgate's association with the banker Nicholas Bulstrode, he is called upon to cast a vote for the new chaplain of the infirmary he oversees with Bulstrode, Brooke, and other Middlemarch notables. The choice is between Lydgate's new acquaintance, Mr. Farebrother, and Bulstrode's man, Mr. Tyke. Although he leans initially toward Tyke despite his developing personal regard for Farebrother, Lydgate hesitates, finding the decision less politically difficult than personally galling: "But whichever way Lydgate began to incline, there was something to make him wince; and being a proud man, he was a little exasperated at being obliged to wince."[98] The issue is less about the relative merits of two candidates, about which Lydgate as yet knows very little, than about how other people

---

[98] George Eliot, *Middlemarch*, ed. Rosemary Ashton (New York: Penguin, 1994), 180. Hereafter abbreviated *MM* and cited parenthetically.

will see and interpret his vote and the interests that vote will appear to indicate. Ultimately, he ends where he began and votes for Tyke; he does so, however, out of neither conviction nor convenience, but rather in a moment of zero-sum spite.

Coming late into the committee room, Lydgate is left to cast the tie-breaking vote. Before he does, the phlegmatic Wrench chides him:

> "The thing is settled now," said Mr. Wrench, rising. "We all know how Mr. Lydgate will vote."
>
> "You seem to speak with some peculiar meaning, sir," said Lydgate, rather defiantly, and keeping his pencil suspended.
>
> "I merely mean that you are expected to vote with Mr. Bulstrode. Do you regard that meaning as offensive?"
>
> "It may be offensive to others. But I shall not desist from voting with him on that account."
>
> Lydgate immediately wrote down "Tyke." (*MM*, 186)

Denying the good Farebrother a much-needed income, Lydgate's vote continues to make him wince long after it is cast:

> The affair of the chaplaincy remained a sore point in his memory as a case in which this petty medium of Middlemarch had been too strong for him. How could a man be satisfied with a decision between such alternatives and under such circumstances? No more than he could be satisfied with his hat, which he has chosen from among such shapes as the resources of the age offer him, wearing it at best with a resignation which is chiefly supported by comparison. (*MM*, 186)

What happens here? Eliot's quick sartorial take feels inadequate insofar as it attributes Lydgate's consternation to the historically limited nature of any and every choice. Because, that is, we can choose only between the options that time and circumstance provide, no choice can be truly objective or free; and Lydgate, whose chief fault is his inflated sense of independence from social and material constraints, *would* chafe at the idea of choice as wholly conditioned by historical contingency (those incompletely disavowed material constraints are what Eliot refers to as Lydgate's characteristic "spots of commonness"). This sketchy analysis, however consonant with the novel's larger sense of the limits of historical agency, doesn't really account for what's odd about Lydgate's vote. Lydgate doesn't vote for Tyke simply because he has to vote for *someone*; rather, he votes for him because he wants, in a moment of pique, to show Wrench and the others that he doesn't care what they think. He votes against his inclination but not necessarily in his interest in order to petulantly assert his agency.

Lydgate's wince-inducing vote is thus an example of problems essential to the political representation of social preference. What *part* of Lydgate – his public spirit, his personal interest, his claim to autonomy, his *amour propre* – is in fact represented by his vote? Given Lydgate's divided and avowedly irrational sense of what's at stake, which *person* in the person of Tertius Lydgate votes when he votes for Tyke over Farebrother? Lydgate's problem is thus an example of what Hadley takes as immanent to debates that led up to Britain's eventual adoption of the secret ballot:

> the persistence of personation as a topic of debate, and therefore its persistence as a 'problem' for liberalism, suggests that the ballot unsuccessfully addresses a social alterity that once was and could be again the perilous or promising place of politics: as if the liberal citizen must always register in the possibility of personation his own representational inadequacy.[99]

That is, in and around 1872, when Eliot was finishing *Middlemarch*, it was not clear that it was possible to represent oneself as a single and rational person in the form of a single vote. Arguing against the secret ballot in 1861, Mill wrote that, "[t]hough the community, as a whole, can have (as the terms imply) no other interest than its collective interest, any or every individual in it may. A man's interest consists of whatever he takes an interest *in*. Everybody has as many different interests as he has feelings; likings or dislikings, either of a selfish or of a better kind."[100]

Eliot's sense of the internally divided and finally incoherent nature of Lydgate's vote anticipates the Joseph Schumpeter's skeptical account of "the classical theory of democracy" in *Capitalism, Socialism, and Democracy* (1942):

> ... we still remain under the practical necessity of attributing to the will of the individual an independence and a rational quality that are altogether unrealistic. If we are to argue that the will of the citizens per se is a political factor entitled to respect, it must first exist. That is to say, it must be something more than an indeterminate bundle of vague impulses loosely playing about given slogans and mistaken impressions.[101]

In order for the individual vote to count and to be counted as a representation of a discrete social preference, we have to imagine the person as a bearer of individual, autonomous, and legible preferences; and, because *his*

[99] Hadley, *Living Liberalism*, 227–228.
[100] John Stuart Mill, *Considerations on Representative Government* (Charleston: BiblioBazaar, 2007), 147.
[101] Joseph A. Schumpeter, *Capitalism, Socialism, and Democracy* (New York: Harper Perennial, 2008), 253.

preference is an incoherent and ironic mix of public feeling, private interest, and personal pique, Lydgate cannot cast his vote as a single representation of a singular preference: he came to his ballot not with an opinion but rather with "a vexed sense that he must make up his mind" (*MM*, 178).

As interesting as this moment is in and of itself, it is characteristic both of Lydgate's behavior and, I think, Eliot's wider sense of the nature of literary character as a powerful and yet limited representational form. Take, for instance, Lydgate's youthful experience with the actress Madame Laure in Paris. Having fallen casually and, as it were, disinterestedly in love with the idea as opposed to the real person of Laure ("as a man is in love with a woman whom he never expects to speak to"), everything changes when, one night, a performance with her leading man and husband goes terribly wrong:

> At the moment when the heroine was to act the stabbing of her lover, and he was to fall gracefully, the wife veritably stabbed her husband, who fell as death willed. A wild shriek pierced the house, and the Provencale fell swooning: a shriek and a swoon were demanded by the play, but the swooning too was real this time. Lydgate leaped and climbed, he hardly knew how, on to the stage, and was active in help, making the acquaintance of his heroine by finding a contusion on her head and lifting her gently in his arms. (*MM*, 151)

The moment is, as the narrator suggests, an important one in Lydgate's history because it is more proof of the unstable mix of motives that drive him. He leaps and climbs, *he hardly knows how*, because there is no single, knowable cognitive or emotional impetus at work here: He leaps both because he is really brave and because he *sees* himself as really brave, and these are not the same thing; he leaps because he had been in love in one way, but is now suddenly in love in another; he leaps because he already understood himself as a man of action; maybe not *this* kind of action, but there you are. In other words, Lydgate hardly knows why he leaps because no one can ever *really* know why they leap when they do.

This is brought to a sharp and paradoxical point when, later, Lydgate pressures Laure to marry him. To rebuff him once and for all, Laure admits two things: first, that her husband's death was really an accident – "My foot really slipped" – and, second, that she nonetheless "meant to do it." What's unnerving about this moment is not that the melodramatic Laure killed her husband (that is, after all, what melodramatic Laures do), but rather that she embodies an impossible but still operable thing: the paradox of the meant mistake, the intentional accident. "Lydgate, strong man as he was, turned pale and trembled" (*MM*, 153). What's upsetting about Laure isn't that, as a murderer and a criminal, she is so different from Lydgate. After all, when at the novel's end his maybe malign medical neglect abets Bulstrode's passive murder of the alcoholic Raffles, Lydgate, too, becomes a murderer who didn't or didn't *exactly* mean it. No, what's upsetting about Laure is rather that she and Lydgate are *the same*: They are both characters whose several incommensurate motives make it impossible to know and thus represent why they want what they want and, thus, why they do what they do.

On the one hand, Lydgate's problem might be, as Schumpeter would have it, a problem with people. That is, even if one were able to design an election or a ballot or a set of democratic procedures that could adequately capture the will of an individual, the individual needs in the first place to have a will and to be able to articulate that will if an election, ballot, or set of democratic procedures is to have any definite meaning. For the skeptical Schumpeter, individuals can be expected to have strong, positive feelings, opinions, preferences about the things closest to them: family, friends, private concerns, etc. As, however, one moves out from the center of those immediate cares to the social circumference, things take on an increasingly "fictitious" quality:

> This reduced sense of reality accounts not only for a reduced sense of responsibility but also for the absence of effective volition. One has one's phrases, of course, and one's wishes and daydreams and grumbles; especially, one has one's likes and dislikes. But ordinarily they do not amount to what we call a will – the psychic counterpart of purposeful responsible action.[102]

In these terms, Lydgate's vote poses a representational problem because there is nothing definite in him to represent; as a result, Lydgate's lack of coherence or clarity stands both as a precocious answer to the methodological hubris of rational choice theory and as an implicit suggestion about how we might imagine a complementary relation between literature and politics. If, that is, elections are good at doing business but bad at understanding what people need or want from their business, maybe novels, which are good at people and maybe bad at business, can help to fill in the gaps. Maybe – just maybe – novels, because they can help us understand what people mean, could, after all, help us live more democratically.

---

[102] Schumpeter, *Capitalism, Socialism, and Democracy*, 261.

On the other hand – and more sensibly – Lydgate's problem might not be a problem with people but with elections and electoral theory. If Lydgate's vote couldn't get at what Lydgate really felt, maybe that's because it was the wrong kind of vote; maybe it was a representational form essentially unsuited to the real content or nature of those feelings. What, after all, is a vote supposed really to represent? Is it the expression or embodiment of an interest, opinion, belief, hope, wish, or preference? If, for instance, one thinks of a vote as the index of a belief, one might think also that a vote works best when it is understood in terms of its definite epistemic potential, when it is seen as contributing to an aggregative or a deliberative process aimed at arriving at a true or at least more true answer to one or another question about the world. As Condorcet's Jury Theorem suggests, (1) if a vote is viewed as a conveyer of definite epistemic potential, and (2) if the voter is understood as someone with a better than 50 percent chance of being right, then every vote added to an aggregate of votes will bring the whole election's chance of being right closer and closer to 100 percent. This is a usefully upbeat way to think about elections and, if taken seriously, it requires us to design ballots and the questions that ballots ask in very particular ways; it requires us to construct a ballot that would allow one to differentiate between a right and a wrong answer to a clear question. If, however, one thinks of a vote as the index of a preference instead of a belief, then the jury theorem will not apply, and one will both expect very different things from elections and design those elections in very different ways. Because, for instance, one doesn't imagine a preference as right or wrong in the same way that a belief can be right or wrong, adding up votes that are reports of preferences won't bring us closer to a better answer or a better situation; an election based on the aggregation of preferences will only tell us what more people *prefer*, regardless of whether what they prefer is truer or better. Unlike beliefs, which derive their value in opposition to other beliefs, preferences are understood as existing on a continuum with other preferences. This is, first, why elections based on preferences are especially amenable to ranked-choice balloting and, second, why theorists who favor preference over belief understand even votes for a single candidate as just the visible tip of a preferential iceberg made up of all other possible choices and comparisons. When, in these terms, I vote for candidate A, I am really if tacitly saying that I prefer candidate A over candidates B, C, D, E, and so on. The point here is that, even if we accept that Lydgate the voter has something real to express (a belief, preference, hope, wish, interest), if the form of vote with which he is presented is unsuited to that *something*, then we will end up once again with dissonance, incoherence, and frustration. And, if we see the problem with voting as a problem with the *form* instead of the ultimate *content* of a given election or ballot, then novels might not be in such a great position to help us after all. If some votes are better than others at capturing aspects of character, the same will be true of novels and other aesthetic forms. In this case, we might look to the relation between literature and democracy not to try and fix one or the other but rather in order better to understand what representation is and what it both can and can't do. The relation can help us once again recognize and work within the limits of some systems on which we must rely to represent ourselves to and for other people. The novel probably won't and can't do much to "help us to live more democratically," but perhaps it can help us to see to understand, and, thus, to manage democracy's formal limits.

Phineas Finnorama

As I've begun to say, Anthony Trollope's *Phineas Finn* (1869) offers an unusually sustained reflection on the nature of and the relations between literary and political forms of representation. The second of his six Palliser novels, *Phineas Finn*, follows the early political career of the titular son of an Irish doctor, who comes to London to study law; he more or less stumbles into a Liberal seat in the House of Commons; he worries often, if not all that seriously, about what he should believe and what he should say; he falls in and out of love with four women; he fights a duel; he gives some speeches; he takes a job with the government as a political appointee; and, after bucking the party line on Irish tenant rights, he resigns, returns to Ireland, becomes a poor-law inspector, and marries the first of his four loves: the "simple pretty Irish girl" back home.[103] I want to talk about the novel's relation to the forms of political representation in three related ways: first, in terms of the secret ballot, which anchors one of the novel's major subplots; second, in terms of the novel's novelistic take on the tension between political independence and party politics; and third, in terms of a question about the nature of preference that unexpectedly connects Trollope's novel with some arcane musings over the nature of political representation.

Although several issues related to parliamentary reform come up over the course of *Phineas Finn*, the most important in terms of both its effect on the novel's plot and its broader thematic consequence is the debate on the secret ballot. Although Trollope's book precedes the passage of the

---

[103] Anthony Trollope, *An Autobiography* (Oxford: Oxford University Press, 1980), 318.

Ballot Act by three years, as we have seen, arguments about the subject had come up regularly in Britain since the 1830s. Trollope, like Phineas and his mentor Mr. Monk, was no fan of the ballot. While running his Quixotic campaign for a House seat in Beverley, Trollope had gone against the interest of both his potential constituents and his party when he talked down the increasingly popular secret ballot, which he "hated" as "unmanly": "But a Liberal, to do any good at Beverley, should have been able to swallow such gnats as those. I would swallow nothing, and was altogether the wrong man."[104] In this both Trollope and Phineas echo many of the period's ethical or characterological arguments against the secret ballot, the idea that English electors should say and say publicly what they wanted and why they wanted it: the elector should simply say what the elector really meant. As Monk puts it, "My idea is . . . that every man possessed of the franchise should dare to have and to express a political opinion of his own; that otherwise the franchise is not worth having and that men will learn that when all so dare, no evil can come from such daring. As the ballot would make any courage of that kind unnecessary, I dislike the ballot" (*PF*, 148). For Monk, an election is not only an opportunity for electors to say what they mean about a given issue or candidate but also a form that can motivate saying's relation to meaning in a special and politically potent way; more than just an isolated act of social choice, an election is a rare and maybe unique opportunity to capture the otherwise mobile play between one's private and public life, of what one thinks, what one does, and who one is. For Monk, elections catalyze character.

As framed by Monk, Trollope's resistance to the secret ballot is thus not only political but also especially novelistic. Although we often think about the novel in terms of its special capacity to represent aspects of other lives that would otherwise remain secret (as if secrets were somehow essentially different or more valuable than other things we can know about a person), the novel in fact works because it refuses the ethical or ontological difference between public and private, secret and revealed. The novel, in other words, depends on the notion that it can, when it wants, show us *both* what a character says *and* what a character means because these are, at least for the novel, made of the same stuff. It is this medium-specific relation between meaning, saying, and doing that allows the novel to wring drama, irony, and suspense out of character even in the near absence of plot; and this, the *passion* of character – its commitments, its bad faith, its

[104] Trollope, *Autobiography*, 188.

mystifications, its human potential, and its slow or sudden development – is Trollope's bread and butter. "Mr. Trollope," wrote an anonymous reviewer of *Phineas Finn*, "thoroughly understands the art of putting his characters through their paces."[105] A century later, J. Hillis Miller writes in similar terms that, "the essence of novel-writing … is for Trollope the production of characters, not of plots."[106] It makes sense, in that case, that, when Trollope and Monk articulate their support for open instead of secret voting, they do so in a way that casts the secrecy of the secret ballot as a problem for character and as a failure of political and aesthetic representation: the secret ballot makes it impossible to see the relation between saying and meaning, and thus threatens to make a vote into a form especially resistant to the novel.

Indeed, one of the main plots of *Phineas Finn* turns on Phineas's struggle not just to say what he means but to do so in the House of Commons where the relation between the two is a matter of urgent political and, I want again to argue, aesthetic significance. To speak in Parliament in *Phineas Finn* is, in other words, not merely a matter of saying what one means in a persuasive manner; it is, rather, to choose and to live in or as one of several different characterological or rhetorical relations between the two. When, for instance, Phineas is first approached by his friend Barrington Erle with the suggestion that he run for a seat in the House, he lets Erle know that he will, regardless of party or patron, always say just what he means: "Let me assure you I wouldn't change my views in politics either for you or for the Earl, though each of you carried seats in your breeches pockets. If I go into Parliament, I shall go there as a sound Liberal, – not to support a party, but to do the best I can for the country. I tell you so, and I shall tell the Earl the same" (*PF*, 17). At this early, untested moment, Phineas embraces the ideal or, perhaps, the fantasy of nonfigural, immediate political speech, speech that would erase any distance between meaning and saying.

This goal would seem merely creditable were it not for the facts, first, that it is exactly this effort that proves to be the defining challenge of Phineas's career and, second, that his pledge to say what he means is met immediately with the pragmatic Erle's disgust:

> he hated the very name of independence in Parliament, and when he was told of any man, that that man intended to look to measures and not to men, he regarded that man as being both unstable as water and dishonest as

---

the wind. ... A member's vote, – except on some small crotchety open question thrown out for the amusement of crotchety members, – was due to the leader of that member's party. (*PF*, 18)

(The reader will remember that, in his *Autobiography*, Mill despaired that "practical men" had seen Hare's scheme of proportional representation as "a mere theoretical subtlety or crotchet.") For Erle, the political speech of a person ought not to represent what that person means; it ought rather to represent and thus support what the party means. In this case, an MP must speak both in figural terms and *as* a kind of figure, as, that is, a kind of living *synecdoche*, a part that exists to stand in for the whole; to do anything else would be self-serving, eccentric, crotchety.[107]

There are other examples: the showy Radical Turnbull seems sometimes to say things more for effect than because he means them and, as a result, threatens the House again and again with the short-circuiting violence of *catachresis*. There is also Mr. Kennedy, whose disquieting social taciturnity comes together with his considerable political power to make for an oddly *aporetic* rhetorical style. It is the wily conservative leader Daubeny (Trollope's take on Disraeli) who fully embraces politics and political speech as a species of poetic play. Disraeli's opponents in fact referred to him as a "perfect will-o'-the wisp" and a "political gamester"; Daubeny, similarly, is always ready with "some sharp trick of political conjuring, some 'hocus-pocus presto' sleight of hand" (*PF*, 169). Even when discussing something as earthy and pragmatic as the proposed dissolution of seven rotten boroughs, Daubeny manages to make "a beautiful speech about ... the seven sins, and seven stars, and seven churches, and seven lamps" (*PF*, 169). It is, perhaps, this skill with figural language and figuration as such that, in *Phineas Redux*, allows Daubeny – as it also allowed Disraeli – to take a "leap into the dark" and trope a recognizably liberal attachment to reform into an unexpected conservative victory. Indeed, "leap into the

---

[107] I referred earlier to Josiah Ober's argument that the classical Athenian concept of political representation is probably best understood as a form of *synecdoche*, "a figure of speech in which a part stands for and refers to a whole, or vice versa. Each of the various institutional 'parts' of the citizen body ... could stand for and refer to the whole citizen body." We might also consider Hélène Landemore's brief discussion of the conceptual history of representation in *Open Democracy*: "The then central theological question – whether and how Christ could be said to be 'embodied,' or represented in the Holy Communion – occasioned a conceptual breakthrough in making it possible to think of representation as a commonly agreed upon convention relating two objects without any kind of pictorial resemblance." Landemore's gesture toward the strong figurality of the Holy Communion makes one wonder about the *political* history of Auerbach's "Figura." Josiah Ober, "Review Article: The Nature of Athenian Democracy," *Classical Philology*, 84(4) (October 1989), 330–331; Landemore, *Open Democracy: Reinventing Popular Rule for the Twenty-First Century* (Princeton, NJ: Princeton University Press, 2020), 62–63.

dark" is both an enlightening trope for the conservative Disraeli's unexpected turn to electoral reform in 1867 and a nice figure for figurality itself, for the risk always entailed in making the leap from vehicle to tenor. In each of these cases, the relation between what one means and what one says isn't simply a matter of truth or untruth. It is, rather, a way to lay claim to the power of a particular set of figures and thus to a particular relation to political character understood as a rhetorical and aesthetic form. What matters to the politician is *how* you say what you maybe mean.

This sense of politics as a space in which to articulate oneself is especially apparent in the case of Phineas's several efforts to speak in public. With his first try, he agrees to give his maiden speech in the House and to speak against the secret ballot but loses his nerve at the last moment and gives his spot over to another. Although he had prepared carefully for the speech, when the time comes, he almost physically crumbles. He becomes, in Hadley's phrase, "distracted in thought and unmanned":

> Now he found that he could not remember the first phrases without unloosing and looking at a small roll of paper which he held furtively in his hand. What was the good of looking at it? He would forget it again in the next moment. He had intended to satisfy the most eager of his friends, and to astound his opponents. As it was, no one would be satisfied, – and none astounded but they who had trusted in him. (*PF*, 148)[108]

It is, of course, no coincidence that, when Phineas finds he cannot say what he means, it is in the context of a debate about the secret ballot, in which he meant to say but he could not say that it is important to say what you mean. In three subsequent speeches – one on reform, another on potted peas, and then one again on reform – he improves gradually until, curiously, speaking before the House turns out to have been no big deal all along. Lacking Turnbull's showy intensity or Daubeny's gift of rhetorical prestidigitation, Phineas settles quickly into the role of a steady, capable, and effective political operative, someone who speaks well, knows when to speak, knows not to say too much, and, until he finally breaks rank on Ireland, does effective party work on the House floor: "words were very easy to him, and he would feel as though he could talk for ever. And there quickly came to him a reputation for practical usefulness" (*PF*, 301). Indeed, almost as soon as he "finds his legs" as a speaker, he loses interest in speaking and takes on the position of Under-Secretary for the Colonies, a job defined less by the quality of its speech than by the reading and

---

[108] Hadley, *Living Liberalism*, 272.

writing it demands: "books and newspapers," "maps of all the colonies," "a heap of papers," and facts "jotted down." On his way out the door, he takes a moment to remind his private secretary, "just tie up those papers, – exactly as they are" (*PF*, 388).

This shift from politics and character as spoken to politics and character as written is important in *Phineas Finn*. In addition to Phineas's own career move from the House floor to a government office (and he loves his office), we should recall both that we don't hear much of the many things we are told people say in session and that the novel's most coherent and important political statement comes in the form of the long personal letter Monk sends to Phineas, a letter that Trollope presents whole, from its dated header to its closing signature: "Yours, always faithfully, JOSHUA MONK." Similarly, during and after his first truly successful speech before the House, we don't hear or read a word of it; we do, however, get to share in Phineas's belated and oddly vicarious experience of reading what he said the night before: "He read every word of the debate, studiously postponing the perusal of his own speech till he should come to it in due order. . . . Then, as he was putting up the paper, he looked again at his own speech, and of course read every word of it once more" (*PF*, 278). In both cases, although his people say that authenticity is a matter of really saying what you really mean, Trollope puts his trust in the written word; and, whatever Trollope might have had to say against the authenticity of the secret ballot, he had, nonetheless and as a novelist, to take character and its honest expression as things essentially written.

Even the novel's title seems to reveal tensions immanent to this play of political speech and political writing. Because "Phin" is a familiar short form of Phineas, the titular character's name could be plausibly rendered as the homophonic pair "Phin Finn," which, while unremarkable in writing, would sound like a baby's babble, a comic song, or an unintentional repetition when spoken. The difference both between "Phin" and "Finn" and thus between "Phin Finn," "Phin Phin," and "Finn Finn" is thus a difference that can only really register in writing; and, insofar as that difference is, in this case, the difference that makes character (it is his name, after all), it suggests something important about where writing might short-circuit – in the novel and elsewhere – the longed-for identity between what one means, what one says, and who one is. Trollope seems to push this tacit riddle to a sort of quietly comic extreme in the title of his sequel: *Phineas Redux*. Because, as the OED tells us, "redux" means "experienced or considered for a second time," the title might be read as "Phineas Phineas" or, perhaps, "Phineas Finn Phineas Finn"; if, once again, we consider "Phin" as a familiar form of Phineas, that gets us either to "Phin Phin" or to "Phin Finn Phin Finn," which would sound like "Phin Phin Phin Phin" or "Finn Finn Finn Finn," either of which would be absurd. A more muted but no less significant version of this same problem comes up early in *Phineas Finn* when Barrington Erle first proposes that Phineas seek a seat in Parliament. Erle raises the possibility because he has heard that the Hon. George Morris, MP for the Irish pocket borough of Loughshane, had a falling out with his brother and patron, the Earl of Tulla. We could, in that case, say that Phin Finn owes his parliamentary career to the sovereign authority of Erle's Earl, which is absurd, but, again, only when you say it.

The Qualities of a Swan

This play of speech and writing would seem like so much deconstructive fun were it not for the fact that a vote's status as a spoken or written thing was also one of the most important if almost unnoticed electoral questions to emerge from the age of Victorian reform. In the case of the secret ballot, the problem takes one important and spectacular, but still relatively limited form. Where the old system of open, public, spoken voting sustained the illusion if not the reality of an elector saying only what an elector meant, the written secret ballot either made or revealed (depending on your perspective) an existential gap between saying and meaning. In these terms, the ballot emerges not only as a convenient and, by this point, entirely self-evident logistical answer to bribery, undue influence, electoral harassment, and so on, but also as an unexpected fellow traveler to other, more abstruse ideas about the nonidentity of the subject with itself, ideas that we associate with the "masters of suspicion": Marx, Nietzsche, and Freud. By either making or revealing the vote's nonidentity in space (the vote isn't counted *where* it is cast), its nonidentity in time (the vote isn't counted *when* it is cast), and the nonidentical nature of practical political intention (one can't know, when and where it is finally counted, exactly *why* a vote was cast), the secret ballot represents an important shift in how we think about voters and their votes. Even so: while the secret ballot was surely different from the open vote, they were nonetheless continuous in an important sense: although one is secret and the other is not, both versions of the vote imagine the voter has having something sayable to say.

The same cannot be said of another kind of voting to which Monk refers in his long letter to Phineas Finn. Although he dismisses it quickly, Monk brings up, if only to put it back down, Hare's complex machinery of

proportional representation. The reader will remember that Hare's innovation, which Mill took up with so much gusto, relied on a few interlock-
ing parts: (1) MPs would no longer represent set geographic areas, but
would instead be chosen from a single national list – a "schedule" – of all
eligible candidates: the elector, says Hare, will "have a schedule furnished
to him, containing the names, not only of the candidates for his own
particular constituency, but of the candidates for all the other constituencies in the kingdom."[109] (2) While the vote of a single voter would finally
count only once as support for only one candidate, each voter would be
provided with a "voting paper" of Hare's design and encouraged to
produce a ranked list of as many candidates as that voter liked: "In the
blank spaces opposite the several numbers on the above form the elector
will insert either one or more names."[110] (3) Once a candidate received the
minimum number of votes necessary to be elected to the House (what
Hare called a "quota," arrived at by dividing the total number of electors
by the number of seats in the House), that candidate's name would be
struck from subsequent voting papers and the remaining names on the
remaining voting papers would be reordered to reflect the winning candidate's absence. The process would be repeated, candidates would be
elected, and names would be struck until all seats were filled.

I've already talked about Hare's system at length, so I will stress just one
aspect of his plan here: because voters were encouraged to list as many
candidates as they could responsibly recognize, rank, remember, and
recommend, an individual vote could quickly reach a level of complexity
so great that it would be impossible either to speak or to hear that vote.
The need to know and manage ten, twenty, a hundred, or more candidates
in a significantly ranked order tacitly assumed that the extant meaning of a
vote was or at least could be too complex and multifarious either to say or
to hear. Where the secret ballot had to be written because writing would
secure its simple, sayable, but socially fraught meaning, Hare's ballot could
exist *only* in writing precisely because it was not sayable. Where, in other
words, the secret ballot represented a shift in the social significance of an
otherwise sayable vote, Hare's ballot represents a shift in the very essence of
political subjectivity as a kind of content and the elector's vote as a kind of
form. What it means *to mean something* in the context of Hare's machinery
becomes something complex enough to outstrip previously available
models of will, interest, belief, or preference. It is, in this way, a machinery
designed to meet the complexity and maybe the incoherence of the

[109] Hare, *Election of Representatives*, 149.   [110] Hare, *Election of Representatives*, 149.

specifically modern political character. "It is plain," writes Hare in his *Treatise*, "that as the intelligence of the country has advanced, we have been receding from anything like a real representation, because it has become every year less possible for the rude forms of an earlier age to convey the varieties of expression that have in modern times been called into existence."[111] Voting had begun to fail because it was a form unsuited to the new complexity of its content. A new content demands a new form: the Single Transferable Vote.

This might seem like a lot to hang on a passing reference to Hare's scheme in Monk's letter. What's striking, though, is how thoroughly the novel seems to demand or even to resemble Hare's voting paper. From the very beginning of *Phineas Finn*, efforts to assess and to name the value of people and things are understood in terms of comparative relations between implicitly or explicitly ranked preferences. In a way that recalls the structure of the Bennet family in *Pride and Prejudice*, Phineas's father had

> a costly family, five daughters and one son, and at the time of which we are speaking, no provision in the way of marriage or profession had been made for any of them. Of the one son, Phineas, the hero of the following pages, the mother and five sisters were very proud. The doctor was accustomed to say that his goose was as good as any other man's goose, as far as he could see as yet; but that he should like some very strong evidence before he allowed himself to express an opinion that the young bird partook, in any degree, of the qualities of a swan. (*PF*, 8)

On the one hand, the emergence of the son as a "hero" against the implicitly comparative field of his five sisters recalls – of course, with a difference – Alex Woloch's influential reading of Austen's novel as the story of how one character among many can *become* a protagonist.[112] On the other hand, the father's sense of his son's value is, as it were, ordinal as opposed to cardinal; where another father might say that my son is a swan because he is my son, thus imagining that "swan" named a quality fixed within the person of that son ("swan" would name son in the same way that *six* names the number of Finn's children), the wise Mr. Finn sees swanhood instead as an index of a son's untested *comparative* value relative

[111] Hare, *Election of Representatives*, 152.
[112] Alex Woloch, *The One vs. the Many: Minor Characters and the Space of the Protagonist in the Novel* (Princeton, NJ: Princeton University Press, 2003), 43–125.

to the value of other sons ("swan" *might* name the son in the way that *sixth* names one child's ordinal position in relation to the other children).

This sense of value as ordinal instead of cardinal appears throughout the novel. For instance, after his initial excitement at finding himself in Parliament fades, Phineas begins to realize that he needs not only to succeed but also to distinguish himself from other MPs and, more to the point, from the other *Irish* members of Parliament: "There were O'B— and O'C— and O'D—, for whom no one cared a straw, who could hardly get men to dine with them at the club, and yet they were genuine members of Parliament. Why should he ever be better than O'B—, or O'C—, or O'D—? And in what way should he begin to be better?" (*PF*, 24). The first thing to say is that this is another instance of value understood in ordinal as opposed to cardinal terms. To succeed in Parliament seems, at this early moment, to succeed in ranked, comparative relation to O'B—, O'C—, and O'D—; to succeed is, in other words, to emerge ultimately as O'A—. Trollope, of course, takes this a little further and makes what seems to me an especially novelistic joke. On the one hand, the use of O'B—, O'C—, and O'D— as the names of Phineas's competitors foregrounds their status not as individuals but rather as barely differentiated tokens, the same kind of tokens *The Spectator* relied on when, in its February 1837 illustration of Grote's ballot box, it imagined the competing candidates, **A**dams, **B**ruce, and **C**ooke. On the other hand, Trollope's use of the same Irish "O" before each of the other letters manages to make the ethnic particularity of Irishness work not to offset the almost pure abstraction of B, C, and D but rather somehow to accentuate it; instead of helping to mark out the difference between one person and another, the repeated Irish "O" seems rather to intensify abstraction, turning O'B—, O'C—, and O'D— into types of a token or tokens of a type, neither of which Phineas wants to be. If A, B, C, and D represent barely differentiated tokens, O, in this case, represents a barely significant type; an O'A— would, in that case, be undifferentiated token of an insignificant type. It would, in that case, be wrong to say that Phineas wants to emerge from the parliamentary scrum as an O'A—; he wants rather to play a different game, to escape the set, and to represent a different kind or a different measure of value: a protagonist, a hero, a swan.

At a related moment, one of Phineas's several love interests, Violet Effingham (A, B, C, D, E, Effingham), is asked by her well-heeled battle-axe of an aunt, Lady Baldock, what she thinks of Phineas Finn; Violet responds with characteristic spirit that he is "A1, I may say; – among young men, I mean."

"Violet," said Lady Baldock, bridling up, "I never heard such a word before from the lips of a young lady."

"Not as A1? I thought it simply meant very good."

"A1 is a nobleman," said Lady Baldock.

"No, aunt; – A1 is a ship, – a ship that is very good," said Violet.

"And do you mean to say that Mr. Finn is, – is, – is, – very good?"

"Yes, indeed. You ask Lord Brentford, and Mr. Kennedy. You know he saved poor Mr. Kennedy from being throttled in the streets."

"That has nothing to do with it. A policeman might have done that."

"Then he would have been A1 of policemen, – though A1 does not mean a policeman." (*PF*, 315–316)

Phineas does, it seems, get at last to be an A (an A1 instead of an O'A—), but, as Violet's jokey demeanor suggests, the nature and real value of even that accomplishment remains up for grabs. First, as a term of nautical art, A1 is strongly comparative, a designation used by Lloyd's Register since 1834 to indicate the quality of a ship's hull and fittings relative to quality of other ships: "It is to be distinctly understood," says the 1898 edition of *Lloyd's Register of British and Foreign Shipping*, "that the numerals prefixed to the letter **A** do not signify terms of years, but are intended for the purpose of comparison only; the **A** character assigned being for an indefinite period, subject to annual and periodical Survey as hereinafter described."[113] Second, when the term is repurposed as slang, it becomes even more fungible, working as well to compare not only ships with ships or boys with boys or cops with cops but also, potentially, anything with everything. Indeed, Violet's conversion of A1 into slang recalls a great passage from Balzac:

> The boarders, resident and non-resident, came in one by one, exchanging greetings and those trifles which, in certain circles in Paris, pass for wit, though their main component is foolishness, and their merit consists above all in gesture and pronunciation. This sort of slang changes all the time. The catchword on which it is based never lasts more than a month. A political event, a high Court trial, a street song, an actor's antics, anything can provide material for this form of humor which consists above all in taking ideas and words like shuttlecocks and batting them to and fro. The recent invention of the Diorama, carrying optical illusion a stage further than the Panoramas, had prompted the comic practice in some artists' studios of adding "*rama*" to words and a young painter who frequented the Maison Vauquer had injected the infection there.

---

[113] *Lloyd's Register of British and Foreign Shipping: Rules & Regulations for the Construction and Classification of Steel Vessels* (London: Lloyd's Register, 1898), 33.

"Well, *Monsieurre* Poiret," said the Museum man, rolling his r's, "how is your delicate *healthorama*?"[114]

As is the case with Balzac's *Balzacorama*, while Violet's A1 *appears* to distinguish one thing from another, it in fact imagines absolutely everything as a possible member of the same low-stakes set, thus flattening potentially significant difference into a night in which all cows are blackorama. To get at the special value of a special thing, A1 may be eminently, perfectly useful, but it is not really all that special.

Blondes or Brunettes

What each of these cases demonstrates is not necessarily that value doesn't exist in the world of *Phineas Finn* but rather that agreeing either with others or with oneself about the value of a thing and where that value stands in relation to the value of other things is too complicated to be easily represented by a single cardinal term, whether it be protagonist, swan, O'A —, or A1. Although there are many other examples of this implicit reliance of ordinal ranking as opposed to cardinal definition at work throughout *Phineas Finn*, the most important of them is the one that motivates the whole of the novel's plot. As I mentioned before, one of the more unusual things about Trollope's novel is the number of Phineas's running love interests. Where novelistic representations of desire tend to be structured around the triangle, either where one character must choose between two clearly delineated alternatives (Darcy or Wickham, Rebecca or Rowena, Flora or Rose, Gwendolen or Mirah, George Vavasor or John Grey) or where a character's desire is a mimetic and erotic reflex of another character's desire for the same object, Phineas is at one point or another tenably in love with four different women, each of whom stands as a viable, which is to say a comparable option. Writes one anonymous reviewer about the maybe unsavory complexity of Phineas's situation:

> So, again, of the four ladies amongst whom he flutters about, without distinctly knowing when he passed from one to the other; – we contend that he must have had some either true or false self-measurement in regard to this matter also. He must have either recognized that what he called love was not worth much, and was a faint watery sort of sentiment, – or he must have been a great adept in painting up the circumstances so as to excuse

[114] Honoré de Balzac, *Père Goriot*, trans. A. J. Krailsheimer (Oxford: Oxford World Classics, 1999), 45.

himself for his many transitions, and to persuade himself that there was a clear and well-marked water-shed dividing the opposite water-courses of his various loves.[115]

Although Trollope's representation of Phineas's behavior seems to make this reviewer a little seasick, the lines manage nonetheless to capture something about the formal and psychological complexity of *Phineas Finn*, about its skeptical refusal of the fairy-tale logic of two paths, two boxes, two loves, etc., and about its related embrace of an account of preference capable of at least recognizing the competing force of good intentions, bad faith, sour grapes, mixed motives, and the fluid vagaries of affective intensity.

Of course, it's easy and right to dismiss or travesty the blunt and misogynistic blonde-or-brunette logic that seems to anchor the novels of Scott, Dickens, Eliot, and so many others. Flaubert, indeed, does just that with characteristic economy in his *Dictionary of Received Ideas*, where we read under the entry "BLONDES," "Hotter than brunettes. (See BRUNETTES.)," and under the entry "BRUNETTES," "Hotter than blondes. (See BLONDES.)." Luring one into the potentially endless paratextual cul-de-sac of blondes-brunettes-blondes or brunettes-blondes-brunettes, Flaubert manages both to preserve and to shatter the novel's juvenile need to square the circle of logic and desire. We might also think of *Jane Eyre*, where Brontë relies on the structure of an either/or choice but pushes that choice to and maybe past its logical limit; as Gilbert and Gubar demonstrated long ago, *Jane Eyre* helps reveal a systemic madness that was already at work within the conventional and apparently tame architecture of the blonde woman and the brunette. *Phineas Finn*, which, of all Trollope's novels, seems most consciously to resemble *Waverley*, does something different and, in its way, more difficult. Instead of simply mocking or deconstructing the damaged and misogynistic folk logic of blonde-brunette, Trollope preserves the symbolic power of that *donée* in the form of an initial central "choice" between Laura, the fiery redhead, and Violet, the funny blonde, but then places that choice within a field of other, ramifying choices in a way that both recognizes the seductive ideological allure of simple explanations and also reveals the real limits of simplicity as a way of accounting for the complexity of desire and modern life.

---

[115] Quoted Smalley, *Trollope: The Critical Heritage*, 310–311.

In part, we can see Trollope's skeptical innovation as part of a larger "marginalist revolution" in literary representation, one brought recently to light by Regina Gangier, Catherine Gallagher, Amanpal Garcha, and others. "Where," writes Garcha, "earlier novelists generally depict characters who face a series of binary, or 'yes or no,' decisions, later ones increasingly show choice as far more expansive and thus at times bewildering, as characters contemplate many, simultaneously available options at once."[116] Garcha goes on to align these "representations of individual minds in a state of wondering indecision" with the rise of neoclassical economists (Carl Menger, W. S. Jevons, Alfred Marshall, and others) who were less focused on the output of producers than on the preferences of consumers. He suggests:

> the differences between the late-century economic writing by Jevons, Marshall, and Menger and the literary representations of decision-making in Trollope and Hardy are often less significant than their commonalities. Each sees the individual's capacity to decide between a number of available, commensurable options as central to humans' mental activity; and each associates (the economists much more directly) this capacity with consumption in the marketplace.[117]

Taken as an example of the consumer's "inexact, difficult, or futile" but nonetheless necessary ranking of individual preferences, Phineas's dubious handling of his several love affairs reveals him not – or at least not only – as a gold-digger or cad but rather as the novelistic equivalent of the desiring subject of neoclassical economics; another Victorian child of Matthew Arnold's "Hamlet and Faust," Phineas is not the hero of an epic action but rather the characteristically modern individual, trying and maybe failing to know what he really wants when he can want so, so many things.

Phineas's conundrum becomes even clearer when we move back from the wide field of neoclassical or marginalist accounts of relative utility to the narrower but related world of modern electoral theory. Alongside a series of more direct and spectacular debates about parliamentary reform and the secret ballot, some writers and a few MPs were seriously considering the more abstruse promise of Hare's representational machinery. I've also already argued that what's most important about Hare's system is its reliance on a "voting paper" that, because it was essentially written as

---

[116] Amanpal Garcha, "Choice," in *From Political Economy to Economics through Nineteenth-Century Literature: Reclaiming the Social*, ed. Elaine Hadley, Audrey Jaffe, and Sarah Winter (London: Palgrave, 2019), 198.
[117] Garcha, "Choice," 213.

opposed to spoken, could, he claimed, better capture and represent the complexity of modern political subjectivity. What allowed Hare's "voting paper" to represent this complexity was an apparently simple but powerful relation between, on the one hand, its invitation to rank many candidates and, on the other, its ultimate status as single vote for a single candidate. It worked because it recognized both the feeling that it was and should be difficult to make a choice when confronted with a number of differently valued but still viable alternatives and the fact that one had finally to make a single choice with one's vote; dialectically balancing the multifarious nature of modern preference with the need nonetheless to choose and to act, Hare's system and his voting paper are remarkable and nuanced things, capable of preserving the essential and modern inconsistency of an individual's commitments, interests, hopes, and preferences while nonetheless resulting in a logically defensible social choice. It is also, as it turns out, a surprisingly useful way to render and to understand the wayward loves of *Phineas Finn*.

"I'll Take the Blueberry!"

At the risk of seeming as callous as Phineas, what would it look like to run his romantic history through Hare's machinery? The exercise is not as ridiculous as it might first seem; if Hare's "voting paper" worked because it could register a range of preferences while still resulting in a single choice, that same tension between several viable and real preferences but only one choice is exactly the tension that motivates the marriage plots of *Phineas Finn*. Phineas's first candidate is his first love, "the simple pretty Irish girl," Mary Flood Jones: "a little girl about twenty years of age, with the softest hair in the world, of a color varying between brown and auburn, – for sometimes you would swear it was the one and sometimes the other; and she was as pretty as ever she could be" (*PF*, 20). Because he knows her first, we'll refer to Mary Flood Jones as **A**. His second candidate is the worldly and political Lady Laura Standish:

> She was in fact about five feet seven in height, and she carried her height well. There was something of nobility in her gait, and she seemed thus to be taller than her inches. Her hair was in truth red, – of a deep thorough redness. .... Her face was very fair, though it lacked that softness which we all love in women. Her eyes, which were large and bright, and very clear, never seemed to quail, never rose and sunk or showed themselves to be afraid of their own power. (*PF*, 31)

Because he meets and falls in love with her second, we'll refer to Lady Laura Standish as **B**. His third candidate is "an orphan, an heiress, and a beauty," Violet Effingham:

> She was small, with light crispy hair, which seemed to be ever on the flutter round her brows, and which yet was never a hair astray. She had sweet, soft grey eyes, which never looked at you long, hardly for a moment, – but which yet, in that half moment, nearly killed you by the power of their sweetness. Her cheek was the softest thing in nature, and the colour of it, when its colour was fixed enough to be told, was a shade of pink so faint and creamy that you would hardly dare to call it by its name. Her mouth was perfect, not small enough to give that expression of silliness which is so common, but almost divine, with the temptation of its full, rich, ruby lips. Her teeth, which she but seldom showed, were very even and very white, and there rested on her chin the dearest dimple that ever acted as a loadstar to men's eyes. The fault of her face, if it had a fault, was in her nose, – which was a little too sharp, and perhaps too small. (*PF*, 76)

Because he meets and falls in love with her third, we'll refer to Violet Effingham as **C**. His fourth and final candidate is the rich and beautiful widow, Madame Max Goesler:

> She was a woman probably something over thirty years of age. She had thick black hair, which she wore in curls, – unlike anybody else in the world, – in curls which hung down low beneath her face, covering, and perhaps intended to cover, a certain thinness in her cheeks which would otherwise have taken something from the charm of her countenance. Her eyes were large, of a dark blue colour, and very bright, – and she used them in a manner which is as yet hardly common with Englishwomen. . . . Her nose was not classically beautiful, being broader at the nostrils than beauty required, and, moreover, not perfectly straight in its line. (*PF*, 304)

Because he meets and falls in love with her fourth, we'll refer to Madame Max Goesler as **D**.

There is of course, a great deal too much to say about these passages and about Trollope's way of describing women in general and the women central to his love plots in particular: his sense of the "varying" color of Mary Flood Jones's hair as opposed to the "deep and thorough redness" of Lady Laura Standish's; the system of value tacitly implied by relation between "clear eyes," "grey eyes," "large eyes," "bright eyes"; the place of the nose as a special exception to the rule of beauty, as feature that is somehow *more* attractive when it deviates from aesthetic norms; and so on. For now, though, I want to notice and distinguish between two kinds of complexity that characterize Trollope's system. The first complexity is qualitative: as I've begun to describe here, Trollope's introduces qualities into his account that both invite and resist meaningful comparison. Each of the women has eyes, and having eyes makes them comparable in those terms; how, though, can one meaningfully compare brightness with largeness with greyness with clearness? The particular qualities embedded in these modifiers make it hard to engage in the quantitative ranking that the novel seems to encourage. I'll come back to this in a minute.

The second complexity is quantitative. Despite his attention to qualitative details, Trollope's reliance on a quantitative architecture remains striking. Consider the care with which he not only imagines these four women as parts of a single system or set but also imagines that system or set as one that builds in self-consciously rickety terms on the simpler folk duo of blonde-brunette. With a crude, almost ham-handed sense of "wait, there's more" structural elaboration, Trollope gives us not just the duo – blonde-brunette – but rather the related but far more complicated quartet, blonde/light-brunette/redhead/dark-brunette. Although the difference seems like a simple one, it is, I think, an instance where an apparently modest increase in quantity represents a real shift in the complexity and the quality of the system at hand. Where blonde or brunette (**A** or **B**) is an almost gratuitously simple choice, the work of assessing the relative value of **A** in relation to the relative values of **B**, **C**, and **D** when each of those values is not only complex but also almost impossibly complex. Although Trollope's reference to their hair and its different colors would seem to suggest a single measure against which and thus a single set within which to compare their value, the women in *Phineas Finn* are not nickels, dimes, and quarters; even seen as literary characters as opposed to human beings, they are nonetheless too complicated to reduce to a place in a defined ordinal ranking.

At the novel's beginning, Phineas is more or less in love with Mary Flood Jones: **A**. As, however, he begins to navigate the world of parliamentary politics, he begins more and more to recognize the value of Lady Laura Standish, her intelligence, and her connections: **B**. At this point, he would rank the two in this way:

1. **B**: Lady Laura Standish
2. **A**: Mary Flood Jones

B>A

Relatively early in the novel, Phineas proposes to and is refused by Lady Laura, who chooses instead – and disastrously – to marry the rich and strange Mr. Kennedy; he also begins to realize that life as an MP is expensive. As a result, he decides that he is in fact in love with Violet Effingham: **C**. At this point, the ranking would look as follows:

1. **C**. Violet Effingham
2. **B**. Lady Laura Standish
3. **A**. Mary Flood Jones

C>B>A

So far, so good. When, however, Phineas proposes to Violet, she turns him down and instead marries Lady Laura's brother, the violent and horsey Lord Chiltern. Late in the novel, he meets the beautiful and powerful and rich Madame Max, who – unlike Lady Laura and Violet – signals her real romantic interest in Phineas, who in turn, seems very much to admire Madame Max. At this point, it seems reasonable to expect that the novel will complete the series already suggested by its first three moments of romantic possibility, a turn that would result in the sequence:

D>C>B>A

What happens instead is surprising on several levels. Rather than marrying or for that matter proposing to the eminently eligible Madame Max, Phineas returns home to Ireland and to his first love, whom he marries. This leaves us at last with the unexpected preference schedule:

1. **A**. Mary Flood Jones
2. **C**. Violet Effingham
3. **B**. Lady Laura Standish
4. **D**. Madame Max Goesler

A>C>B>D

When I say this is unexpected, I am referring only partly to the plot of *Phineas Finn*, although that is also a problem. In his *Autobiography*, Trollope admitted that he came to the end of his writing with little idea about how he should end his novel:

> It is all fairly good except the ending, – as to which till I got to it I made no provision. As I fully intended to bring my hero again into the world, I was wrong to marry him to a simple pretty Irish girl, who could only be felt as an encumbrance on such return. When he did return I had no alternative but to kill the simple pretty Irish girl, which was an unpleasant and awkward necessity.[118]

Indeed, *Phineas Redux* begins with Mary's death, which finally clears the way for a marriage with Madame Max.

[118] Trollope, *Autobiography*.

As surprising, disappointing, or cruel as Mary's fate is at the end of one novel and the beginning of another, it is, perhaps, less strange than what happens within the ordinal syntax of our ranking. When Madame Max enters the picture, it changes the order of Phineas's preferences, but not in a way we could have foreseen. Instead of simply taking the top position in the ranking and completing the sequence implied by the plot up to that point, her presence instead leads to something not only unsatisfying (to Trollope, anyway) but also apparently irrational: the introduction of the new alternative **D** leads to an apparently unrelated preference reversal within the pairwise comparisons **B>A** and **C>A**. Like T. S. Eliot's "bit of finely filiated platinum . . . introduced into a chamber containing oxygen and sulphur dioxide," the introduction of alternative **D** somehow modifies the relative values of **A**, **B**, and **C**, rewriting the relations between them, while remaining itself somehow unchanged and independent of them.

There's a story people tell about Columbia University philosopher, Sidney Morgenbesser. Sitting at a restaurant, he asks a waitress if they have any pie. She says that they have apple pie and blueberry pie. Morgenbesser says, "I'll have the apple." The waitress returns a minute later and tells him, "You know what, we also have cherry pie." "In that case, I'll take the blueberry!" This unexpected and apparently irrational shift runs against what Kenneth Arrow refers to as the "independence of irrelevant alternatives," one of several conditions that, as we shall soon see, he takes as axiomatic to the putative coherence of democratic elections. Arrow takes it, in other words, as a minimal condition necessary to electoral coherence that, if voters prefer **A>B>C**, the addition or the subtraction of an alternative **D** to or from the set should not affect the pairwise relations that already exist between the other terms in the set. Why, after all, would the introduction of cherry pie make blueberry more appealing than apple, when apple had been more appealing than blueberry before? Why, in Trollope's vulgar calculus, does the apparently irrelevant introduction of the dark-haired Madame Max change his mind about the unrelated ordering of blonde over brunette or brunette over blonde?

If this feels like a crude way to think about matters of the heart, that's because it is crude, and deliberately so. Although it might make sense at first blush to consider Morgenbesser's switch from apple to blueberry as simply irrational, that reading only holds if we accept a harshly limited definition of rationality. Why, on a given day, would the late and apparently irrelevant appearance of cherry pie overturn his previously stated preference for apple over blueberry? Maybe it's because the cherry pie reminds him of a time when he shared blueberry and cherry pie (but not apple pie) with a favorite uncle; maybe it's because, even though he doesn't like cherry pie, its late appearance reminds him that he does quite like the "erry" sound that "cherry" shares with "blueberry" and not "apple," the sound thus adding something to the savor of the pie; maybe it's because he is a diehard Aristotelian and, when presented with options **A**, **B**, and **C**, he will always and as a matter of principle move to the middle; or maybe it's because, as a funny philosopher interested in the independence of irrelevant alternatives, he prefers logical perversity to his favorite flavor of pie.

The point is that, while these possible causes are not generalizable rules that others could or would use to choose between different kinds of pie, neither are they simply irrational; they may be wholly personal and thus illegible to others, but they are not *necessarily* incoherent. What they are, however, is *intransitive*; they are rational rules that work fine for the individual but that cannot work as a rational basis for interpersonal comparisons between individuals. This is why Arrow insists on the independence of irrelevant alternatives as one of his criteria. It is not because he believes that people can't make decisions that are both rational and intransitive – of course they can – but rather because he understands that the content of those kinds of decisions cannot be rationally compared or aggregated; they cannot, in that case, be useful to the production of social choices that are both rational and democratic.[119] We can think of this as an apples-to-blueberries problem.[120] This is why Arrow opts to focus not on the content of any given preference but rather on the simple form of the *preferential relation* that exists between two options; although one cannot compare the nature, origins, or intensity of one's preference for brunettes, blondes, or blueberry pie, one can compare the restricted and almost purely formal pairwise comparisons that underwrite bare statements of preference. With this, Arrow builds on a mode of self-conscious methodological reduction advocated by Vilfredo Pareto fifty years earlier. He says:

[119] Kenneth J. Arrow, *Social Choice and Individual Values* (New Haven, CT: Yale University Press, 2012), 9: "The viewpoint will be taken here that interpersonal comparison of utilities has no meaning and, in fact, that there is no meaning relevant to welfare comparisons in the measurability of individual utility."

[120] Annie McClanahan offers a nice summary of what she identifies as the microeconomic position: "Microeconomics does more than just insist on the unknowability of mental states: it also reduces the scope of the meaningful individual actions to a relatively narrow orbit (consumer choices), establishes in advance a set of normative criteria to apply to those actions (maximization of utility), and understands choices and wants relatively rather than absolutely (not only does it not matter *why* I love apples, but it also doesn't really matter *how much*, only whether I prefer them to oranges). McClanahan, "Methodological Individualism and the Novel in the Age of Microeconomics, 1871 to the Present," *Timelines of American Literature*, ed. Cody Marrs and Christopher Hager (Baltimore: Johns Hopkins University Press, 2019), 352.

> The fact that there can be choices relieves us from having to examine the motives. It is enough to note the fact of the choice ultimately made by the individual without going into the psychological and metaphysical implications. If a dog is eating its soup and is thrown a piece of meat, it leaves the soup and takes the meat. However often this experiment is repeated, the dog's reaction is the same. That is a fact, and it is the only point which I wish to emphasize. It can be expressed in the phrase that this dog *prefers* the meat to the soup, but provided that it is made quite clear that the term *prefers* does not introduce the slightest suggestion of a new idea going beyond the pure expression of the fact.[121]

Although an evolutionary biologist or a pet psychologist could and should ask *why* the dog eats the meat, and although Jack London, Aesop, or La Fontaine could say something about what eating the meat means, *as an economist*, Pareto brackets those otherwise interesting questions in order to provide a methodologically stable means of identifying and measuring the equilibrium of, which is to say the social relation between, individual preference relations.

In order, though, for those bare statements of preference (**A>B**, **B>C**, **C>D**) to maintain their transitivity and thus their value as a basis of comparison between statements, schedules, and votes, they need to remain stable over time and in the face of new information. If, however, **A>B** can flip – even for real and rational reasons – then **A>B** loses its value as a stable foundation for the aggregation of individual preferences and thus the making of rational social choices; and, without that or some other stable foundation, it becomes impossible to build a bridge between the complex and only apparently irrational rationality of an individual's choices and the shared rationality of a group's choice or the general will. This is why, for Arrow, the catalytic effect of ostensibly irrelevant alternatives is not a psychological impossibility but rather a methodological impediment to the institutional possibility of rationally designed and rationally conducted democratic elections. This is also why Arrow concludes that a reliable or universal method for producing perfectly consistent choices is in fact not possible "where the wills of many people are involved."[122]

Left there, we could take the exaggerated place of Phineas's romantic vagaries in a novel about politics, political choice, and electoral reform as a

---

[121] Vilfredo Pareto, "Summary of Some Chapters of a New Treatise on Pure Economics by Professor Pareto," *Giornale degli Economisti e Annali di Economia* 67(3) (December 2008), 457.
[122] Arrow, *Social Choice*, 2.

precocious test of the limits of democratic rationality; Phineas's rational irrationality could be offered as living proof of the problems that the unruly desires of real individuals will always pose to efforts either to aggregate the preferences of the many into some version of the one or to identify what really constitutes the welfare of a group. And, of course, Trollope does often seem skeptical of both the coherence and the various motives that drive his various politicians to pursue their various courses and, more to the point, to cast their votes as they do. If, for instance, the emotionally stunted Plantagenet Palliser's long-running obsession with decimal coinage seems like the displaced expression of some other, some deeper need, that's because it probably is. In this way, we could take *Phineas Finn* as an early expression of Arrow's impossibility theory, his sense – sharpened in the increasingly strident work of William Riker and others – that elections maybe can't ever be both reliably rational and really democratic. That said, Trollope, whatever his local reservations, never really doubted the value of Parliament and the inherent nobility of a parliamentary career; he writes in his *Autobiography* that

> I have always thought that to sit in the British Parliament should be the highest object of ambition to every educated Englishman. I do not by this mean to suggest that every educated Englishman should set before himself a seat in Parliament as a probable or even a possible career; but that the man in Parliament has reached a higher position than the man out, – that to serve one's country without pay is the grandest work that a man can do, – that of all studies the study of politics is the one in which a man may make himself most useful to his fellow-creatures, – and that of all lives, public political lives are capable of the highest efforts.[123]

Despite his lifelong and, really, unparalleled attention to the quirks, inconsistencies, and pathos of intention, he remained a believer not only in one or another political program but also in an ideal of political representation – in, that is, a possibility that Arrow and his followers would subsequently resist: the idea that there is a form of elected government that can, at its best, really and rationally represent both the will and the interests of the people.

This is where we need to come away from Arrow and Pareto and back to Trollope's contemporary, Thomas Hare, and his ornate machinery of representation. Although the list of ranked candidates on Hare's "voting

---

[123] Trollope, *Autobiography.*

paper" looks almost exactly like the similar schedules one can find in Pareto, Arrow, Riker, and others, the meaning of that list is something entirely different. Where Arrow's lists work because they capture (and only capture) the value-neutral preference relations that exist between a set of given options, Hare's list works because, when coupled with his quota and his admittedly elaborate process, it captures so much content. When one fills out a Hare ballot, one isn't simply stating a preference relation, **A>B>C**. One is, instead, saying something that cannot be reduced to **A>B>C**, something like this: "Although I value **A** because of how **A** thinks about **X**, I also value **B** because **B** has a lot of relevant experience; and, even though I disagree with some of what **C** says about **Y**, **C** and I belong to the same club and that's meaningful to me, so I'm glad that I can register **C**'s other type of value, too." Because, in other words, the system asks the elector not simply to state a preference or a series of preferences but rather to acknowledge and to record a living and mobile record of interests, hopes, beliefs, intensities, and associations that will not be reduced to a preference, and, what's more, because the machinery allows for the content of those interests, hopes, beliefs, intensities, and associations to be represented institutionally at a level of detail that transcends not only any single statement of preference but also the very logic of party, the system is capable of registering without reducing the *character* of an electorate. "The design," says Hare of his machine, "is to represent the qualities with which man is divinely gifted, – the noble heritage of his nature, – not their absence and negation. Such an assembly should present 'the awful image of virtue and wisdom of a whole people collected into a focus.'"[124]

Hare's machinery is the most complex of the many electoral things I've considered in this chapter because it recognizes and seeks formally to capture what's consistent and inconsistent, rational and irrational, typical and singular, general and particular, humdrum and nearly divine about the political character of both the individual and the group. It is complex because it accepts the work of realistic political representation as an aesthetic and, we might say, novelistic project, as an effort not to bracket, to rationalize, or to overcome the electorate but rather to recognize and, as it were, to respect the quirks, hopes, and desires of the electorate. It is a thing that tries to treat both individual voter and the "whole people" as characters in terms especially resonant to readers of novels in general and,

---

[124] Hare, *Election of Representatives*, 162.

we could say, to readers of Trollope's novels in particular. That Hare, Mill, and, in his way, even Trollope tried and might actually have managed to pull this off is compelling if not conclusive proof that, if we want to understand the full complexity of Victorian political reform, we should try also to think differently about elections, characters, novels, and some other extraordinary machines.

CHAPTER 3

Late Returns
Lewis Carroll and William Morris

I have been engaged writing about Elections very constantly lately.
—Lewis Carroll, 1873

Don't vote.
—William Morris, 1895

In the last chapter I looked at several more or less reasonable – as well as several more or less outlandish – attempts to make representative democracy work. From the "suppositional" designs of ballot boxes to the intricacies of Hare's machinery to the representational aspirations of the realist novel, the *things* I considered were variously committed to the idea that, given the right system, one could accurately represent the will of a single individual and then somehow aggregate the accurate representations of many individuals into yet another, accurate second-order representation of the will-of-all. As the figures I looked at understood, this isn't easy – first, because any effort to represent the will of an individual relies on a complicated and maybe impossible set of assumptions about what an individual is and, second, because, even if one could settle on a way to represent an individual, arriving at a meaningful second-order representation of the aggregation of other representations is itself wickedly difficult. Before one could settle on an electoral design for parliamentary and other elections, one had to decide whether political representation was supposed to represent what individuals thought, what different types of individuals thought, what the state thought, what a party thought, what a strategic coalition of parties thought, what different places thought, what simple majorities thought, or what the people as *le Peuple* thought. These were and still are hard problems. Despite that, the figures I looked at *believed* in parliamentary democracy; they believed in its power, its potential, and its seemingly limitless capacity for expansion and reform.

That said, a belief in parliamentary democracy and, more to the point, a belief in the effectively representative character of the British Parliament was always precarious. On the one hand, to believe in the legitimacy of British Parliament in the present, one had to ignore its recent and unruly past. To put one's faith in any given government, in the idea that a particular Conservative or Liberal platform could somehow, here and now, represent everyone, one had to ignore, forget, or at least finesse the antic whipsawing between the formation and dissolution of government coalitions that characterized British politics in the second half of the century. What could the logic, form, or legitimacy of parliamentary representation really *mean* when the content of that representation could and would shift fundamentally from month to month or from day to day? When the political relation between tenor and vehicle – between a parliament and a people – was anything but stable? When the will of the people looked really *like* a unicorn at one moment and really *like* a lion at the next? "Very like a whale."

This uncertainty about the relation between Parliament, party, and people became acute in 1867 when, at least partly to kneecap Gladstone, Disraeli not only embraced the Liberal cause of parliamentary reform but also pushed it up to and past its expected political limits. On the other hand, to believe in Parliament as a body that could represent the *whole* of a people, one had also to forget its earliest days, its violent, tactical, and contingent emergence as an economic and political alternative to the waning power of both the prince and the people.[1] For the socialists William Morris and E. Belfort Bax, "the meaning of the great struggle which took place in England between the King and the Parliament" was to be found not in "the profession of an almost pedantic devotion to the quasi-historical constitution, which was, nevertheless, in the main a figment of the period" but rather in "the creation of a powerful middle class freed from all restrictions that would interfere with it in the pursuit of individual profit."[2] For Morris and Bax, Parliament represented and had *always* represented private property and not the people. In order, then, to believe in Parliament as a timeless, universal, and real representative of a whole people, one had to willingly suspend disbelief and act *as if* Parliament were something it was not and could never be. Seen from this perspective, Parliament was another one of the discourses of suspended disbelief I've been talking about. Parliament was a fiction.[3]

---

[1] See Barrington Moore, Jr., *The Social Origins of Dictatorship and Democracy: Lord and Peasant in the Making of the Modern World* (Boston: Beacon Press, 1993), 3–39.

[2] William Morris and E. Belfort Bax, *Socialism: Its Growth & Outcome* (London: Swan Sonnenschein & Co., 1893), 114, 115, 119–120. The essays in Morris and Bax's book first appeared serially in *The Commonweal* from 1886–1888 under the name *Socialism from the Root Up*.

[3] The most thorough, probably the greatest, and certainly the most acerbic account of a parliament reaching its political and *figural* limits remains Marx's *Eighteenth Brumaire*: "They were," he writes of

This necessary state of suspension might help account for the splendidly suppositional quality of the "electoral things" I looked at in Chapter 2. For Bentham, Grote, Mill, Hare, and others, the immanent and almost touching fragility of parliamentary democracy was both a political challenge and an imaginative opportunity. It led to what we might think of as a kind of DIY utopianism, an aesthetic stance that both accepts the resistance and the reality of a given historical arrangement and, at the same time, takes that resistance as an opportunity to counter or to supplement the given with something else, something other, something more. Although it's easy to overlook, one can sometimes catch a glimpse of a topsy-turvy utopianism at work behind or within the dry-as-dust pieties of Victorian reform. G. K. Chesterton recognized this:

> The Victorians had to invent a sort of impossible paradise in which to indulge in good logic: for all serious things they preferred bad logic. This is not paradoxical, or at any rate, it was they who made the paradox. Macaulay and Bagehot and all their teachers taught them that the British Constitution ought to be illogical – they called it being practical. Read the great Reform Bill and then read *Alice in Wonderland* – you will be struck by the resemblance of *Alice in Wonderland*.[4]

Indeed, one of the things I'll explore in what follows is what exactly it means to see a book like *Alice* not as one or another cryptic or unconscious response to or rejection of the everyday politics of the period, but rather as an especially concentrated, practical, thus an especially true expression of that everyday politics. Says Matthew Wolf-Meyer:

> Social theory and speculative fiction are two sides of the same coin. It is not the case that social theory is the sole provenance of academics nor that speculative fiction is that of science fiction writers. Both traditions ask us to imagine worlds that can be described and depicted, and ask us as audiences to imagine the rules that undergird a society and its human and more-than-human relationships.[5]

What would it mean, in that case, to see the weird utopianism of *Alice's Adventures in Wonderland* or *The House of the Wolfings* or *News from*

the French National Assembly in 1851, "therefore reduced to moving within strictly parliamentary limits. And it took that peculiar malady which since 1848 has raged all over the Continent, *parliamentary cretinism*, which holds those infected by it fast in an imaginary world and robs them of all sense, all memory, all understanding of the rude external world . . . ." Karl Marx, *The Eighteenth Brumaire of Louis Bonaparte* (New York: International Publishers, 1963), 91.
[4] G. K. Chesterton, "Both Sides of the Looking-Glass," in *The Listener* (November 29, 1933).
[5] Matthew J. Wolf-Meyer, *Theory for the World to Come: Speculative Fiction and Apocalyptic Anthropology* (Minneapolis: University of Minnesota Press, 2019), 5.

Nowhere as an applied response to the logic and limits of parliamentary representation in the later part of the nineteenth century? To see either Carroll or Morris as a working agent of what Jose Muñoz (after Ernst Bloch) identifies as "concrete" as opposed to "abstract" utopianism, to see either as, to use Muñoz's lovely and fitting phrase, "the solitary oddball who is the one who dreams for the many"?[6] If that might – and it will – result in different readings of these books, it will also force us to look differently at political representation itself, to see it no longer as a historical or institutional given but rather as something unstable, imaginative, and curious.

In this chapter I want to consider two versions of what happened in late Victorian Britain when a quietly tactical or provisional belief in the fictions of parliamentary representation seemed to waver or approach a kind of limit, when it became harder if not quite impossible to suspend disbelief in the universality, disinterestedness, good intentions, or, simply, representative capacity of Parliament. Although one might have expected regular efforts at parliamentary reform and the expansion of the franchise to have secured and renewed Parliament's reputation as a representative body, several waves of electoral reform served instead to raise more doubts and to bring the makeshift quality of the system into greater relief. This was partly because the reforms begun in 1832 led not only to more representation and *perhaps* to more democracy but also to the increased influence, aggression, and cunning of political parties. With more voters and fewer secure boroughs, political parties now had to compete for seats that had once been held safely in pocket; as a result, they modified old and developed new parliamentary and extra-parliamentary institutions and methods: party leaders, party whips, party agents, party associations, party caucuses, etc. Daniel Ziblatt writes that "the impact of competition after 1832 was itself reinforced and moderated by political parties' gradual accumulation of political skills and resources."[7] Although Trollope could still write in 1883 that "to sit in the British Parliament should be the highest object of ambition to every educated Englishman," even he had begun to feel that the party tail was wagging the parliamentary dog.[8] Describing one of the cannier MPs in *Phineas Finn*, he writes that, "according to his theory of parliamentary government, the House of

---

[6] Jose Muñoz, *Cruising Utopia: The Then and There of Queer Futurity* (New York: New York University Press, 2009), 3.

[7] Daniel Ziblatt, *Conservative Parties and the Birth of Democracy* (Cambridge: Cambridge University Press, 2017), 66.

[8] Anthony Trollope, *An Autobiography* (Oxford: Oxford University Press, 1980).

Commons should be divided by a marked line, and every member should be required to stand on one side of it or on the other."⁹ And in *Doctor Thorne*, he observes with morbid curiosity as the perfectly named and barely scrupulous election agents, Mr. Nearthewinde and Mr. Closerstil, test the limits of the "purity of election" in Barchester:

> We strain at our gnats with a vengeance, but we swallow our camels with ease. For what purpose is it that we employ those peculiarly safe men of business – Messrs Nearthewinde and Closerstil – when we wish to win our path through all obstacles into that sacred recess, if all be so open, all so easy, all so much above board? Alas! the money is still necessary, is still prepared, or at any rate expended. The poor candidate of course knows nothing of the matter till the attorney's bill is laid before him, when all danger of petitions has passed away. He little dreamed till then, not he, that there had been banquetings and junketings, secret doings and deep drinkings at his expense. Poor candidate! Poor member! Who was so ignorant as he! 'Tis true he has paid such bills before; but 'tis equally true that he specially begged his managing friend, Mr. Nearthewinde, to be very careful that all was done according to law! He pays the bill, however, and on the next election will again employ Mr. Nearthewinde.¹⁰

"For most contemporaries and historians," says Elaine Hadley, "the Second Reform Bill marks the beginning of the end of parliamentary governance of the status quo and the bumpy emergence of, among other trends, the governance by public opinion via mass political gatherings, newspapers, party bureaucracy … "¹¹ If the figures I looked at in Chapter 2 believed in or, at least, if they *did not disbelieve* in the disinterested ground of parliamentary democracy, that stance became harder to sustain as the party – an entity defined by its interestedness and raw partisanship – came to hold more and more sway in political life.

In what follows I want to think about what we might see as a late or mannerist phase of British parliamentary democracy, a transitional stage during which practices, styles, and rules seemed to become exaggerated, recondite, or residual. As, in other words, the parties took more and more control over the *content* of political opinion and political life, the *forms* of parliamentary democracy became more interesting for some and more absurd for others. This is one reason why, after the attentive realisms of Eliot and Trollope, I want to consider a pair of writers who moved easily if

---

⁹ Anthony Trollope, *Phineas Finn*, ed. Simon Dentith (Oxford: Oxford University Press, 2011), 18.

¹⁰ Anthony Trollope, *Doctor Thorne* (Oxford: Oxford University Press, 1980), 293.

¹¹ Elaine Hadley, *Living Liberalism: Practical Citizenship in Mid-Victorian Britain* (Chicago: University of Chicago Press, 2010), 295.

unexpectedly between political theory and speculative fiction: William Morris and Lewis Carroll. In both cases, their more famous works of fantasy fed into and were fed by a deep engagement with the character, structure, and historical limits of parliamentary democracy. In addition to his *Alice* books and his solid if undistinguished work as a professional mathematician, Carroll was a sophisticated and, in time, a profoundly influential theorist of the function of committees, the machinery of elections, and the logic of proportional representation; although he understood himself as a good if mild conservative, his thinking about elections and representation was in fact radical and maybe a little perverse. When Carroll looked at parliamentary democracy, he saw ironies, contradictions, and paradoxes, some of which would come to shape some of the more skeptical and dominant varieties of subsequent electoral theory. And, while Morris is remembered as many things – a novelist, a designer, a printer, a poet, a critic, a patron, one or another kind of socialist – his considerable place within the history of late-century socialism was not, as it is sometimes cast, the result of his well-meaning if wooly-minded readiness to bankroll more serious but cash-poor comrades. It was instead his hard, tactical resistance to parliamentary representation and to the idea of voting as such that made him not simply a wealthy and thus welcome fellow traveler but rather a potent, sharply divisive, and sometimes inexplicable figure within the world of British socialism and social democratic politics. That he managed to invent a new and influential kind of fantasy novel while fully engaged with the world of practical politics is, I will suggest, no coincidence.

I want thus to consider some obvious political and theoretical differences between Carroll and Morris and, at the same time, to look at how their dissimilar thinking reflects and helps to explain aspects of the same political context. On the one hand, Carroll and Morris couldn't be more different. Where Carroll was shy, reserved, and a political and dispositional conservative, Morris was loud, gregarious, and probably the most visible and arguably most consequential British socialist of his day; where Carroll was deeply and emotionally (if sometimes also ironically) dedicated to a range of institutions *qua* institutions – the Hebdomadal Council, university committees, and his college common room – Morris was notable among other socialists not only for his thoroughgoing refusal of *the system* but also for his reluctant but resigned acceptance of political violence as a tactical and historical necessity. That said, Carroll and Morris are contemporary, crucial, and difficult figures in the history of speculative fiction; both are curiously restrained or "concrete" utopian thinkers; and both are surprisingly central to the history of thinking about voting and elections. For Carroll, this meant watching forms break free from their content, to see them come allegorically or more-than-allegorically to life; as Adorno said of Beethoven's late quartets, in Carroll's novels as well as in his political theory, "the conventions find expression as the naked representation of themselves."[12] Carroll's Wonderland is, after all, a place where, having been reborn in the form of white rabbits, mock turtles, and march hares, social conventions roam tetchily free. Carroll's is, as it were, a paradoxically unruly utopia of rules. Morris, on the contrary, wants to remake, expand, or push at the limits of the rules so that the content of life might better and more freely realize itself. For Morris, the modern world is a sham because its rules and conventions work for the rich and pinch at the poor; they force life into uncongenial, unproductive, and unkind patterns; the modern world is a bad and shoddy form, and it needs a lot of work. Nowhere is the utopia we'll get to once we get on with that work. As I will argue in the next two sections, Carroll and Morris both use the modest but radical resources of fantasy to engage with a logic of parliamentary democracy as it reaches one kind of limit. Although they come to different conclusions, they both rely on an unlikely and unfinished synthesis of imaginative fiction and political analysis to reflect on the nature and bounds of shared belief at a moment of significant uncertainty. To make this case I will need, once again, *to speak excessively* about the history, the forms, and the feeling of electoral theory after reform.

A quick word on the duple structure of both this chapter and Chapter 4: although it would have been possible and maybe simpler to present the following sections on Carroll and Morris as separate chapters, I have decided instead to treat them as two halves of the same piece of writing. Each half is, as the reader will soon see, a pretty full, indeed, maybe an overfull reckoning with the personalities, histories, and issues at hand. Thinking of Raymond Williams's discussion of J. S. Mill's paired essays on Bentham and Coleridge in *Culture & Society*, I hoped that allowing these two different but related figures to speak across but also within a single chapter could be a useful writerly and readerly exercise. As Williams argues, even if Mill couldn't manage to synthesize the two sides of his personality, that thwarted but necessary effort led to something worth saying. I can only hope for a similar effect here. I ask the reader to hold these figures conceptually suspended to invite comparison and, thus, to

---

[12] Theodor W. Adorno, "Late Style in Beethoven," in *Essays on Music*, ed. Richard Leppert, trans. Susan H. Gillespie (Berkeley: University of California Press, 2002), 566.

discover something new while also keeping hold of historical particularity. I will return to this structure with Ralph Ellison and Kenneth Arrow.

3.1 WHAT THE TORTOISE SAID TO ACHILLES

"If **A** and **B** and **C** are true, **Z** *must* be true," the Tortoise thoughtfully repeated. "That's *another* Hypothetical, isn't it? And, if I failed to see its truth, I might accept **A** and **B** and **C**, and *still* not accept **Z**, mightn't I?"

> —Lewis Carroll, "What the Tortoise Said to Achilles" (1895)

Caucus-Racing

What does it mean to turn to *Alice's Adventures in Wonderland* (1865) to think about the form, function, and procedural details of the British electoral system after midcentury? On the face of it, *Alice* would seem to have little to say about the selection and election of candidates, the ongoing expansion of the franchise, and the nuts and bolts of electoral processes – less, anyway, than its near contemporaries *Felix Holt, the Radical* (1866) and *Can You Forgive Her?* (1865), or, as we have already seen, *Middlemarch* (1871–1872) and *Phineas Finn* (1867–1868). Where those novels deal explicitly with elections, electoral reform, and the ups and downs of individual political careers, *Alice's Adventures in Wonderland* would seem, because of its calculated appeal to children and thus its deliberately fantastical distance from the real world, to have little to say about democracy, never mind the practical details of electoral procedure. It is, in that case, "curiouser and curiouser" that alongside its wonderful creatures, its sudden and sometimes violent bursts of nonsense, and its beautifully absurd set pieces, we would find something as mundane and crassly political as a caucus-race.

After Alice nearly drowns in her own tears, she washes up on shore amongst a small group of similarly sopped animals: there is a mouse, a lorry, an eaglet, a duck, and a dodo. When confronted with the difficulty of drying off, the Dodo offers a peculiar but attractive solution, suggesting that electoral theory can indeed be a dry affair:

> "What I was going to say," said the Dodo in an offended tone, "was, that the best thing to get us dry would be a Caucus-race."
> "What IS a Caucus-race?" said Alice; not that she wanted much to know, but the Dodo had paused as if it thought that SOMEBODY ought to speak, and no one else seemed inclined to say anything.

"Why," said the Dodo, "the best way to explain it is to do it." (And, as you might like to try the thing yourself, some winter day, I will tell you how the Dodo managed it.)

First it marked out a race-course, in a sort of circle, ("the exact shape doesn't matter," it said,) and then all the party were placed along the course, here and there. There was no "One, two, three, and away," but they began running when they liked, and left off when they liked, so that it was not easy to know when the race was over. However, when they had been running half an hour or so, and were quite dry again, the Dodo suddenly called out "The race is over!" and they all crowded round it, panting, and asking, "But who has won?"

This question the Dodo could not answer without a great deal of thought, and it sat for a long time with one finger pressed upon its forehead (the position in which you usually see Shakespeare, in the pictures of him), while the rest waited in silence. At last the Dodo said, "EVERYBODY has won, and all must have prizes."[13]

As with so much in Wonderland, the rules of the Dodo's caucus-race are coherent, transparent, and yet perfectly ridiculous. Although it doesn't go anywhere, the narrator takes care to make the race a reproducible thing, an event that could be restaged because it has rules and because those rules are at least notionally repeatable: "you might," says the narrator, "like to try the thing yourself, some winter day" (*AW*, 26). So, to return to the larger curiosity: what is an electoral process that is at once vaguely recognizable, procedurally precise, and perfectly ludicrous doing in Wonderland?

The caucus-race was in fact a late addition to Carroll's novel, not appearing in the first draft, and it replaced a too-cute scene of Alice and Dodo "snugly" drying off by a fire in a small cottage. If the scene is almost certainly an improvement, what kind of improvement is it? We might imagine that the word-mad Carroll saw the caucus as better not only because of its antic energy but also because of its inherently Wonderlandian sound. The repetition of the hard c's and soft sibilants in "caucus-race" produces a twinned effect characteristic of Wonderland. Not only does it anticipate the pervasive and chiastic looking-glass logic of Tweedledee, Tweedledum, and others, but it also seems especially appropriate coming from a bird with its own doubled and necessarily stammered name: "Dodo."[14] We might, then, want to hear an embodied resistance

---

[13] Lewis Carroll, *Alice's Adventures in Wonderland and through the Looking-Glass*, ed. Peter Hunt (Oxford: Oxford University Press, 2009), 26. Hereafter abbreviated *AW* and cited parenthetically.

[14] "Dodo" was a nickname that Carroll gave himself in order to mark both his felt physical awkwardness and his lifelong stutter. As Marc Shell puts it, "the dodo could neither walk the talk nor talk the walk." Marc Shell, *Stutter* (Cambridge, MA: Harvard University Press, 2009), 81.

clucking away beneath the word's hard phonetic skip: cau-cus. Indeed, given the fact that the caucus-race is run mostly by birds, maybe it's simply a typically good-bad joke: what better race for a bunch of birds than a CAW-cus race? And if a "caw" sounds better coming from a raven than it does from a dodo, we need wait for only a few pages before exactly that bird makes its inky appearance. Soon after the race is run, the Mad Hatter offers his famous riddle without an answer, "Why is a raven like a writing desk?" (*AW*, 62). One possible answer: because neither ran the caucus-race.[15]

But "what," as Alice says, "IS a caucus-race?" Or what, rather, was the caucus-race to Lewis Carroll? What Carroll would have had in mind is not the anachronistic electoral process still followed in certain American states, but instead an ad hoc and maybe secret meeting at which party leaders choose candidates who will later be put up before the public for general election. It is, as it were, the "election" before the election. The word "caucus" is of obscure but definitely American origin, and it was often discussed in relation to its aggressively glottal sound. George Troup, Governor of Georgia, wrote in 1823 that, "[Caucus] is not an English word. It is not to be found in our dictionary, and, being an uncouth word and of harsh sound I hope never will."[16] Too bad for Troup, the word does appear in our dictionaries, and the OED's first example of its use comes from a 1763 entry in John Adams's diary:

> This day learned that the caucus club meets, at certain times, in the garret of Tom Dawes, the adjutant of the Boston regiment. [...] There they smoke tobacco till you cannot see from one end of the garret to the other. There they drink flip, I suppose [...]. And selectmen, assessors, collectors, wardens of fire-wards and representatives are chosen before they are chosen at the town.[17]

---

[15] Another possible solution to the riddle, "Why is a raven like a writing-desk?" We know from the Mad Hatter that it is a riddle without an answer. And, because riddles are usually written in reverse, that is from the answer *back* to the question (like mystery novels or crossword puzzles), we could say that the Hatter's riddle is a riddle written in reverse or rather a reversed reversal: a riddle without an answer is written not from right to left (from answer to question) but from left to right (from question to answer). In that case, the raven is like a writing-desk when both words begin with the letter "r." It isn't a writing desk; it's a righting-desk. That is to say, the Hatter's riddle was written on a righting-desk (from left to right) instead of a lefting-desk (from right to left), which given the backwards logic of the riddle, is the desk upon which regular riddles are written; in other words, a left desk is the right desk for writing riddles.

[16] Quoted in Edward J. Harden, *The Life of George M. Troup* (Savannah, GA: E. J. Purse, 1859), 172.

[17] Quoted in C. S. Thompson, *An Essay on the Rise and Fall of the Congressional Caucus as a Machine for Nominating Candidates for the Presidency* (New Haven, CT: Yale University Press, 1902), 14.

Scattered etymological efforts have produced other different and differently strained theories. Some have seen it as a derivation from "kaukos," the modern Greek word for a "cup," evoking the boozy atmosphere of early caucuses; some suggest that it is a corruption of "caulkers," suggesting its relation to secret meetings of seditious ship-workers on the eve the American Revolution; still others say the word comes from the Algonquin "cau-cau-as-u," or "one who advises."

For the very British Carroll, the word would certainly have carried with it some of the American political scene's more exotic and, for him, unpleasant connotations: Andrew Jackson's battle with King Caucus, the nineteenth-century rise of machine politics, the gross corruption of Boss Tweed and Tammany Hall. In *Latter-Day Pamphlets*, Thomas Carlyle writes, "Cease to brag to me of America, and its model institutions and constitutions. To men in their sleep there is nothing granted in this world: nothing, or as good as nothing, to men that sit idly caucusing and ballot-boxing on the graves of their heroic ancestors, saying, 'It is well, it is well!'"[18] One politically calculating character in Bulwer-Lytton's 1853 novel, *My Novel, or Varieties of English Life*, says, "I think of taking a hint from the free and glorious land of America, and establishing secret caucuses. Nothing like 'em."[19] The word had taken on a more pointedly pejorative sense in Britain during the 1870s when Disraeli used it to cast aspersion on the electoral practices of Birmingham Liberals: "The policy of the politicians of the Midland capital will bring upon us the *caucus* with all its evils."[20] Around the same time, a contributor to the *Times* wrote, "Caucus is by no means a pretty word, much less a sensible one, to be added to our vocabulary. But if it be adopted at all let us make right use of it, that is, not to apply it to an open but to a secret meeting."[21] With all this in mind, we might think that Carroll chose to associate the Dodo's nonsensical race with a caucus in order to evoke the imagined wild-west character of nineteenth-century American politics and the difference between a solidly parliamentary ethos and what was frequently cast, by contrast, as a dangerously democratic system. Or maybe he just liked its sound.

---

[18] Thomas Carlyle, *Latter-Day Pamphlets* (London: Chapman, 1898), 20.
[19] Edward Bulwer-Lytton, *My Novel, or Varieties of English Life* (Boston: Little, 1892), 136.
[20] Alfred F. Robbins, "'Caucus' in English Politics," *Notes and Queries*, ser. 8-VI, (147) (October 20, 1894), 310.
[21] George Lawton, *The American Caucus System: Its Origin, Purpose, and Utility* (New York: Putnam, 1885), 8.

Absurdity and Repugnance

With all that said, the caucus did have a more precise meaning for Carroll, one that will require some detailed reconstruction. To begin with, William Empson mentions the caucus and what it might have meant to Carroll in "The Child as Swain," his great essay on *Alice* in *Some Versions of Pastoral*:

> We then have the Caucus Race (the word had associations for Dodgson with local politics; he says somewhere, "I never go to a Caucus without reluctance"), in which you begin running when you like and leave of when you like, and all win. The subtlety of this is that it supports Natural Selection (in the offensive way the nineteenth century did) to show the absurdity of democracy, and supports democracy (or at any rate liberty) to show the absurdity of Natural Selection.[22]

Empson's primary point here – that there is to be found in *Alice* a demanding argument about the paradoxical relation between, on the one hand, democracy, freedom, and intention and, on the other, nature, necessity, and constraint – is itself wonderfully and characteristically subtle. For now, however, I want to focus on Empson's apparently prosaic and by-the-way remark that, for Carroll, the term had something probably to do with "local politics" and his own reluctance ever to "go to a Caucus."

The phrase, as Empson *almost* remembers it, does appear in the notes to one of the many squibs Carroll wrote and circulated around Oxford, a satirical poem he called "The Election to the Hebdomadal Council" (1866). Peter Hunt, the editor of the 2009 Oxford University Press edition of *Alice's Adventures in Wonderland and Through the Looking-Glass*, follows Empson, similarly glossing the caucus-race with this: "In 1866, Dodgson published a satirical pamphlet on *The Elections to the Hebdominal* [sic] *Council*, which contained in a footnote 'I never go to a *caucus* without reluctance: I never write a canvassing letter without a feeling of repugnance to my task'" (*AW*, 261). For both Empson and Hunt, Carroll's apparent "repugnance" helps to account for the otherwise inexplicable appearance of the Dodo's race as a *caucus-race*; although any image of animals running a wild race willy-nilly could have suggested the paradox of freedom and necessity that Empson admires, the by-the-way addition of the *caucus* let Carroll leaven and motivate that core paradox with some topical and ironic disdain. Absurdity was the benign form that real repugnance took when it passed from the grubby scrum of "local politics" into nonsense world of Wonderland, when a repressed political animus returned sublimated in the antics of fairy-tale animals.

---

[22] William Empson, *Some Versions of Pastoral* (New York: New Directions, 1950), 255.

The problem, however, is that both Empson and Hunt appear to have misremembered or to have misread Carroll's pamphlet. Although a cursory look might have suggested that the usually oversubtle Carroll had felt an unusually blunt need to register his revulsion, the line, as is the case with all of Carroll's notes to the poem, is in fact taken from Goldwin Smith's *The Elections to the Hebdomadal Council* (1866), an earnest open letter addressed to C. W. Sandford, the Senior Censor of Christ Church College that Carroll explicitly travesties in his poem. As opposed, then, to a simple and, as it were, gut repudiation (let's call it a "hebdominal" repudiation), the line is instead part of a trickier and more involved figural management of Oxford politics in relation to the nature of institutional and political representation writ large. Seen in this light, the Dodo's caucus-race isn't simply an absurd expression of real repugnance ("I never go to a *caucus*"). It is rather a nonsensical and proleptic representation of another, parodic representation of someone else's repugnance (the representation of a representation of a reaction). Given the fact that the caucus-race in *Alice* appeared the year *before* both Smith's letter and Carroll's parody of it, it may have seemed to a bemused Carroll that Oxford was dutifully if unconsciously reenacting his already imagined absurdity. Life imitates art and all must have prizes!

At one level, the point of Carroll's joke is straightforward enough. Smith's heartfelt letter to his colleagues is both a general call for university reform and, more immediately, a procedural complaint about a recent election of two Conservative members to the Hebdomadal Council, the body responsible since the University Act of 1854 for overseeing university administration, finances, and property. Smith's problem is that, because members of the Council were elected by the whole Convocation (that is, all university graduates) and not just its current and specifically *academic* stakeholders, those elections not only were decided on inexpert grounds but also were especially subject to political manipulation and conservative "wire-pulling." In effect Smith was echoing an argument that William Gladstone, who had represented Oxford as a Liberal until 1865, had made a few years before:

> Let the House remember that there is already one vicious element in a University constituency with which all those who have been connected with University elections cannot fail to be practically acquainted. ... I refer to the disposition towards College combinations, and the working out, through those combinations, of selfish wishes and limited views, instead of adopting the broader views connected with the whole University.[23]

---

[23] 164 *Hansard Parliamentary Debates* (3d ser.) (1861) col. 836, https://hansard.parliament.uk/Commons/1861-07-12/debates/9bdd489b-ab18–4b39–8f9f-ca81907e5452/UniversityElectionsBill.

This potential for caucusing and combination was, Smith suggests, especially pronounced in Oxford because of the disproportionate numbers of university-trained, nonacademic, and broadly conservative clergy living outside the city. As a result of this and other factors, he suggests, the conservatives were simply better able to round their people up and get them to a meeting; They were thus able to install council members who were not, in his view, representative of the university's "academical" community and what he understood as that community's almost necessarily progressive values. Without a real representation of those values, he suggests the university could not keep up either with continental and American scholarship or with rising, rival institutions like the University of London: "The system of education here, as everywhere else, is, owing to the growth of science and other great changes in the intellectual world, in a transition state. The relations of the Universities to national education generally, are also evidently about to undergo resettlement, and the process will involve questions which it will require real academical statesmanship to solve."[24]

After raging for a page or two against the rise of the conservative caucus in Oxford and against caucuses in general, Smith proposes an administrative redrawing of the university electorate that Carroll takes, with good reason, as caucusing by another name: "To save the University from going completely under the yoke," says Smith, "to keep one-third of the places in her governing body open to men who will serve her for herself, we shall have to combine."[25] In his verse paraphrase of Smith, Carroll writes, "To save beloved Oxford from the yoke, / (For this majority's beyond a joke,) / We must combine, aye! hold a *caucus*-meeting, / Unless we want to get another beating."[26] We might think in that case that, as opposed to expressing any special love or hate for the political caucus, Carroll's poem was aimed at that more traditional target of literary satire: the benighted and overearnest hypocrisy of another. I want, however, to suggest that there's more at work here and that the problems posed by majorities, decisions, and the caucus went deep into Carroll's thinking. As we will see, this becomes clearest when we read Carroll's satire and his fiction alongside his important but often neglected work on preference aggregation and

[24] Goldwin Smith, *The Elections to the Hebdomadal Council: A Letter to the Rev. C. W. Sandford, M. A.* (Oxford: James Parker & Co., 1866), 5.
[25] Smith, *Hebdomadal Council*, 6.
[26] Lewis Carroll, "The Elections to the Hebdomadal Council," in *Notes by an Oxford Chiel* (Oxford: James Parker and Co., 1865–1874), 12.

proportional representation.[27] As Carroll understood, a caucus was significant as something other than a funny sound or a sordid ploy because it implied a different and disturbing way of thinking about the very meaning of a majority. Where idealists saw numerical majorities as the natural representatives of general will, caucusers saw numerical majorities as a sophisticated way to advance the interests of a minority or a strategic coalition of minorities. After the caucus and in a way the paradoxical Carroll would have appreciated, a majority was not a majority: $A \neq A$. Carroll was beguiled by the fact that one could both follow the rules and use those rules to make a majority that wasn't one. As we will see, that interest is a thread that runs through his writing on politics, his world-making, and his everyday life.

My Old School

Read alongside his several other Oxford squibs, "The Election to the Hebdomadal Council" emerges as a comic expression of Carroll's serious and sometimes officious commitment to the rules that underwrote the institutional management of Christ Church College. He sat on the college's Governing Board, was Curator of its Common Room, and, although he cared little for wine, took up the management of the college's cellar with strange assiduity.[28] He also entered with gusto into college discussions of

---

[27] The form taken by this relative neglect is an interesting thing. For one, it's not an even neglect. While literary critics either make rare and passing mention of his electoral theory or ignore it altogether, Carroll's work on committees (more, perhaps, than his work on proportional representation) is enormously important to the history and the practice of social choice. This begins, as we shall see, with Duncan Black's rediscovery of the work in the 1940s and 1950s. This disciplinary difference is marked by the fact that, where critics tend to refer to Carroll as "Lewis Carroll," social choice theorists almost always refer to him as "Charles Dodgson," as if it were important to maintain the fiction that the Alice books and the electoral theory were written by two different people. For instance, in the index to Amartya Sen's *Collective Choice and Social Welfare*, he appears not as "Carroll, Lewis (C. L. Dodgson)" but rather as "Dodgson, C. L. (Lewis Carroll)." Although Carroll might have liked this – Alice, we know, "was very fond of pretending to be two people" – the situation is more complicated. While the earlier work on committees was signed "Dodgson," he tended to sign the later, equally technical work on proportional representation with "Carroll." In part, this is because, where the earlier work was mostly written within the context of local controversies at Oxford, the later work was circulated more widely. There's, of course, a lot more to say about Carroll's play with names. For now, I'll just say that the convention of using the one name to talk about his fiction and the other to talk about his theory isn't supported by the record. This is why, with only slight reservations, I have opted to refer to him as "Lewis Carroll" throughout.

[28] Duncan Black writes that, "During the first year of office he wrote 800 letters enquiring about wines, enquiring about the best temperature, ventilation and dampness for the cellars, in his violet ink, and made inventories of the bins and racks, to be able to trace the movement of a single bottle from bin to bin and from the cellar to the Common Room. ... He then devised a liqueur measure

H. G. Liddell's proposals for several architectural renovations. In 1855 the reformist Liddell had replaced Thomas Gaisford as Dean (he was, of course, also the father of Carroll's young friend and muse, Alice Liddell). Carroll had liked and sympathized with Gaisford's time-serving, if-it-ain't-broke attitude and, some time after the publication of *Alice*, had a decisive if still somewhat obscure falling-out with the Liddells and, in particular, with his reform-minded Dean. For instance, in "The New Belfry of Christ Church, Oxford," a satirical and aphoristic catalogue of thirteen ways of looking at one of the Dean's innovations, he mocked the new-fangled structure with characteristic obscurity, writing that "the word 'Belfry' is derived from the French *bel*, 'beautiful, becoming, meet,' and from the German *frei*, 'free, unfettered, secure, safe.' Thus the word is strictly equivalent to 'meat-safe,' to which the new Belfry bears a resemblance so perfect as almost to amount to coincidence."[29] In addition to its ugliness, the new belfry was an especially visible emblem of Liddell's desire to reform the old, hidebound Oxford ("oh no, Keble and Pusey won't do ... ") and thus spoke to deeper questions about the nature and meaning of history, tradition, and convention. It suggested, along with other proposals, that times were changing, and Carroll didn't much like change.

More importantly, the discussions around Liddell's proposals led to one of Carroll's earliest systematic writings on elections and preferences: "Suggestions as to the Best Method of Taking Votes, Where More Than Two Issues Are to Be Voted On" (1874). Written and printed in haste before an important meeting of the college's Governing Body about the proposed belfry, "Suggestions" is one of several moments when college practice, national politics, and the meaning of majorities came together for Carroll. In this case, the immediate need for a best or at least a better practice for taking votes followed from the group's inability to come to a clear conclusion about which of several architectural proposals ought to be adopted: "evidence," writes Duncan Black, "is overwhelming that acute difference of opinion existed among the members, with agreement only on the need that a decision should be taken."[30]

---

which he wanted the Common Room butler to use in making his charges. It was a ruler, graduated in shillings and pence, which the butler would stand upright by the bottle, and read off to the nearest penny the amount served." Duncan Black, *A Mathematical Approach to Proportional Representation: Duncan Black on Lewis Carroll*, ed. Iain McLean and Alistair McMillan (New York: Springer, 1996), 30, 32.

[29] Lewis Carroll, "The New Belfry of Christ Church, Oxford," in *Notes by an Oxford Chiel* (Oxford: James Parker & Co., 1865–1874), 7.

[30] Duncan Black, *The Theory of Committees and Elections* (Cambridge: Cambridge University Press, 1958), 206.

The Governing Body was presented on June 18, 1874 with four options – Mr. Jackson's Tower (**A**), Mr. Bodley's Gateway (**B**), a fresh design from Mr. Bodley (**C**), and Mr. Deane's Arcade (**D**). The group then voted and found itself deadlocked when none of the four proposals could command a majority of its 23 members: Option **A** got nine votes, **B** got two votes, **C** got seven votes, and **D** got five votes. While it may have seemed obvious initially that **A** had won with the largest number of first-place votes, Carroll felt that something was off. That is, even though **A** clearly got more first-place votes than **B** or **C** or **D** when all four were voted on in a single round (**A** was in other words a plurality as opposed to a majority winner), Carroll saw that that outcome might not represent the real preference of the committee. He suspected that the winner may not have been the winner, and that the committee may not have meant what it seemed nonetheless to have said. The majority was not the majority. (In fact, it turned out that **C** and not **A** was the real winner, as I will explain.) How then do you decide what a committee really means when what it means is not what it says? "You should say what you mean," said the March Hare. "I do," replied Alice, "at least – at least I mean what I say – that's the same thing, you know." "Not the same thing a bit!" said the Hatter (*AW*, 61).

To see how this actually works, imagine a starker but related set of choices, where **A** is stopping construction on the new belfry, **B** is painting the new belfry blue, **C** is painting the new belfry red, and **D** is painting the new belfry green, and where, as in the case the real vote, **A** gets nine votes, **B** gets two votes, **C** gets seven votes, and **D** gets five votes. Although it would again appear from this first, simple count that the committee preferred **A** – no belfry – to all other choices, it is clear in this case that, if one put the question of color aside, the majority must probably prefer *some* belfry to no belfry at all and that it would in fact probably prefer it by a wide margin. If one stops counting at the end of the first round, the plurality winner **A** would seem to be but might not be what the committee really prefers. The winner might not be the winner, and what the committee seems to have said is not what the committee in fact meant. Carroll's problem, then, was to establish a system that could recognize essential, insuperable, and, as it were, uncountable differences between different options (apples-to-oranges differences of definition, interest, context, intensity, etc.) and yet still produce a reasonable and recognizable decision. Faced with this difficulty, Carroll arrived at an ingenious scheme, which he describes in "Suggestions."

After voting once and seeing that an easy and absolute majority was not possible, a committee should, suggested Carroll, run through a series of pairwise comparisons between each of its several options: "This course is suggested in the hope that by it some one issue may be discovered, which is preferred by a majority to every other taken separately. For this purpose, any two may be put up to begin with, then the winning issue along with some other, and so on."[31] Indeed, after Jackson (**A**) received his initial plurality of votes, another vote was taken on the pair *Jackson* v. *Bodley* (**A** v. **C**); while Jackson held on to his nine votes, *everyone else* cast theirs for Bodley, giving him a real majority. Despite first appearances, it wasn't even close. In the case of the belfry, running the four options through this pairwise process allowed the committee to see that, even where there was no clear winner, it could nonetheless arrive at the committee's calculable and demonstrable preference for **C**, even though **A** had at first received more first-place votes; where **A** was a plurality winner, **C** *emerged* as the majority winner of the election when the election was understood as a measure of the committee's whole preference and not as a dumb tally of first-place votes. As we saw with the question of the caucus, Carroll uses the case of the belfry to ask deeper questions: what does a majority mean, and what do *I* mean when *I* am either part or not part of that majority? Although debates about the look of the new belfry or the makeup of the Hebdomadal Council might seem too insular or donnish to be of much consequence to anyone living beyond the confines of Carroll's college and university, they were only apparently idiosyncratic expressions of some urgent and essential problems with people and politics. They help to explain not only the question of what the caucus could have meant to Carroll but also the question how history, politics, theory, and aesthetics can come practically together at moments of institutional uncertainty.

The Idea of a University

Of course, it makes sense that arguments around representation, party affiliation, and the relation between national and borough politics would seep into, influence, and aggravate what might otherwise have been quiet questions of college and university administration. As a result of the long and even chummy connection between the university and government (by 1865 at least ten Prime Ministers had come from Christ Church alone), the Oxford Movement and its national significance, Oxford's splendid and

---

[31] Lewis Carroll, *The Political Pamphlets and Letters of Charles Lutwidge Dodgson and Related Pieces: A Mathematical Approach*, ed. Francine F. Abeles (New York: The Lewis Carroll Society of North America, 2001), 44–45.

tone-deaf association with a set of increasingly residual social values, and an unfolding reckoning between Oxbridge, newer universities, scientific controversy, and university reform, what could have been quiet, collegiate disputes about promotions, scheduling, and capital expenditure instead became high-pressure proxies for national debates about religion, tradition, and political reform. Another factor that brought these factors together, making this political confluence of town and gown unavoidable, was the fact of William Gladstone's long and increasingly fraught relationship with Oxford, which he had represented in the House of Commons from 1847 until his loss in the general election of 1865.

In some ways, Gladstone was an emblematic Oxford man. Like his father before him, Gladstone attended Christ Church, finishing in 1831 and managing a double first in Classics and Mathematics. He "occasionally watched both cricket and rowing," was President of the Debating Society, and made school friends with other notables like Pusey and F. D. Maurice.[32] After graduating and serving more than ten years as a Conservative Member for the borough of Newark, Gladstone changed parties and represented Oxford for nearly two decades, winning seven elections, first as a Peelite and then as a Liberal. In 1865, after nearly forty years of association with the university, he lost his long-held seat to the Conservative Gathorne Hardy. Gladstone's electoral relationship to Oxford in general and more particularly in the *annus horribilis* of 1865 was peculiar for a few reasons. First, unlike his seat in Newark, where he had come from, or the one South Lancashire, where he went immediately after, Oxford was not a parliamentary borough but a university constituency. This meant that where almost all other House seats were tied firmly to particular if sometimes contested geographic areas, a university constituency was instead defined by *a certain type of person*, namely a university graduate, regardless of where that person lived: "The franchise," wrote Edward Freeman in 1883, "is open to all academic citizens who have reached full academic growth, to all who have put on the *toga virilis* as the badge of having taken a complete degree in any faculty."[33] According to Blackstone, "it was King James the First who indulged [the universities] with the permanent privilege to send constantly two of their own body; to serve for those students who, though useful members of the community, were neither concerned in the landed nor the trading interest; and to

---

[32] Roy Jenkins, *Gladstone: A Biography* (New York: Random House, 2002), 23.
[33] Edward A. Freeman, "University Elections," *Contemporary Review* 43(1) (January 1883), 25.

protect in the legislature the rights of the republic of letters."[34] In practice this meant that, while voting took place within the city of Oxford, far-flung members of the constituency were invited to make a trip back to vote, as, in fact, far-flung members of the Convocation had come to vote against a promotion for the philologist Max Müller a few years before.[35] And so, although Gladstone had managed to navigate these choppy waters for almost two decades, a few new factors contributed to his fall in 1865. Most importantly, between the elections of 1859 and 1865, Parliament had changed the rules governing Oxford elections to accommodate the peculiarity and, more to the point, the unique placelessness of university electors.

Seeing that it was difficult and expensive for many members of the constituency – especially the "poor country clergy" – to vote, members of both Houses argued that procedures needed to be altered in order to reflect the eccentric character of the electorate and, as a result and for the first time, some British electors were entitled to vote both by proxy and by mail. Writes one of Gladstone's early biographers:

> By the irony of fate, a Liberal measure was destined to operate most injuriously against Mr. Gladstone. Only in the previous Parliament an Act was passed on the instigation of a well-known member of the Liberal party, by which the election for the Universities was authorized to be made by means of voting papers, transmitted through the post or otherwise to the Vice-Chancellors, and a period of five days was allowed for keeping open the poll.[36]

As a result, then, of the University Elections Act of 1861, nonresident electors and, in particular, nonresident members of the clergy were

---

[34] William Blackstone, *Commentaries on the Laws of England* (Chicago: Callaghan & Company, 1884), 1:174.

[35] In 1860 the brilliant and popular Müller was in competition with the less impressive but more institutionally legible M. Monier Williams for the lucrative position of Boden Professor of Sanskrit. Although it was of course an academic and highly specialized position, the whole of the Oxford Convocation was, as with the case of elections to the Hebdomadal Council, invited to vote on the matter. As a result, an elaborate pressure campaign unfolded, resulting in manifestos, committees, personal and professional endorsements, letters to the *Times*, and, at last, special trains arranged to cart members of the Convocation to town. "Müller," writes Linda Dowling, "drew his support from most of the dons; in the less cosmopolitan precents outside Oxford, however, the argument that Müller was 'not English' told heavily against him." As a result, she writes, of "the Oxford Tories who disliked his liberal politics," the "university conservatives who hoped to win one battle against 'Germanizing' reform," and the local Anglican clergy, the highly respected Müller lost his election to Monier Williams, 833 to 610. Dowling, "Victorian Oxford and the Science of Language," *PMLA* 97(2) (March 1982), 164.

[36] George Barnett Smith, *The Life of the Right Honourable William Ewart Gladstone: Popular Edition* (London: Cassell, Petter, Galpin & Co., 1880), 323.

suddenly able to vote easily and without much expense, a development that Thomas Hare, for one, took as a tremendous step forward: "No symptom of the progress of thought amongst public men, on the amendment of the representation, is more encouraging that the Act of the last session, enabling the members of the university to vote without leaving their abodes, or their ordinary duties, or incurring the expense and inconvenience of a journey to Oxford, or Cambridge, or Dublin."[37] As a result of what Gladstone, *pace* Hare, cast as "as strange and startling ... innovation," the 1865 Oxford election not only saw a record turnout – "nearly double that at any former election" – but also experienced a proportional shift away from resident to nonresident voters: against the nearly 4000 votes cast, "the resident body consisted of some 250 persons."[38] And, partly because that enlarged electorate was considerably more conservative than was the case in previous elections, Gladstone lost: "a dear dream," he lamented, "is dispelled."[39]

What was most surprising about both the University Elections Act of 1861 and its consequences in the 1865 Oxford election was, paradoxically, just how unsurprising it all was. In debate in both the House of Commons and the House of Lords, those in favor of the law and those against the law both saw that, although it did nothing really to expand or to redraw the franchise, it was nonetheless likely to alter the character of the electorate fundamentally. On the one hand, admitting that the proposal had some logistical advantages, the Bishop of Oxford argued that it would disfigure the very logic of university representation:

> One great objection to the Bill was that the Member for a University was intended to represent the University itself. Now, the special life of a University was embodied in the resident members rather than in those who, living at a distance, were subject probably to alien influences, and might exercise their franchise at variance with the interests and sympathies of the institution to represent which their Members were intended.[40]

On the other hand, supporters like John Dodson, who had first proposed the measure, and Hare, who subsequently applauded it, also understood

---

[37] Thomas Hare, "Suggestions for the Improvement of Our Representative System: The University Elections Act of Last Session," in *Macmillan's Magazine, Vol. V. November, 1861–April, 1862*, ed. David Masson (Cambridge: Macmillan & Co., 1862), 295.

[38] Smith, *Gladstone*, 324.

[39] Richard Aldous, *The Lion and the Unicorn: Gladstone vs. Disraeli* (New York: W. W. Norton, 2007), 150.

[40] 164 *Hansard Parliamentary Debates* (3d ser.) (1861) col. 1469, https://hansard.parliament.uk/Lords/1861-07-25/debates/e95a4857-6198-40c6-83c8-4a2679ba9f99/Committee.

that this procedural change could have serious political byproducts. Writes Hare:

> The action of non-resident members in the local business of the universities has not always been in accordance with the views, or opinions, of the more intellectual of the resident body, and there is little doubt that it would be better that such business, which has no analogy with the choice of representatives in Parliament, should be more exclusively reserved for resident members. It is possible, however, that some of those who, in Parliament, voted for or against the Bill, might have been influenced by the supposition, that the country clergy would be found less liberal in their political creed, and that the reception of their votes with greater facility might strengthen the Tory, or weaken the Whig, party in a future contest.

By changing the rules, the University Act would change the meaning of the university majority.

Aside, though, from its immediate consequences for Liberals, Conservatives, and the Right Honourable William Gladstone, the University Elections Act raised more difficult questions that must, I think, have fed into Carroll's growing sense of what was not only crass but also weird and maybe even wonderful about a caucus as a machine for remaking majorities. First, the Election Act and its consequences made yet another argument for the remarkable and sometimes occult power of electoral rules. Outmatched as it was by contemporary efforts to expand the franchise, to embrace a secret ballot, or to do away with the rotten boroughs, the House's decision to tinker with the mechanics of voting in a couple of college towns must have seemed insignificant to most. That said, and as Carroll saw firsthand, making even a small change to how people voted could and did rewrite the meaning both of those votes and that electorate; in this and other cases, the rules not only reveal but also sometimes *make* the meaning of an election. As we will see, Carroll's writings both about the often-hidden power of the procedures governing elections as well as about the absurd and yet high-stakes rules that order life in Wonderland are concerned fundamentally with the almost occult power of process.

Second, the nature of these changes and their effects raised an even more difficult set of questions about the idea of political representation. What, given the oddity of its design, was the Oxford constituency supposed really to represent? Was Oxford a place, a history, an idea, character, an intellectual commitment, or a religious belief? "The University of Oxford has interests, feelings, a general corporate being, distinct from the city of Oxford, just as the city of Oxford has interests, feelings, a general corporate being, distinct from the county of Oxford."[41] The placeless and protean character of the Oxford constituency made it possible if bewildering for one or another person simply to *decide* that it was best represented by the Broad Church Liberals, the High Church Tories, expatriate academics, the "poor country clergy," or whatever other combination or caucus one might care to imagine and then to wrangle. And, if parliamentary representation aimed to represent and to aggregate one or another kind of intention, what did the fraught and formally riven nature of the Oxford constituency mean for either representation or intention? What is an intention? What is a representation? Is it possible really to say or really to do what one means? These questions are, as we will see, central not only to Carroll's late and significant work on parliamentary representation but also to imaginary worlds in which an essential difference between saying and meaning was imagined both as an existential threat and, I'll argue, as a political opportunity.

The Lion and the Unicorn

As we have begun to see, each of these cases loomed large in Carroll's mind. Elections to the Hebdomadal Council, questions about promotions, college admissions, and capital expenditure, and Oxford's peculiar fusion of town and gown politics encouraged him to develop concepts and practices that could be used to understand and to rationalize votes, preferences, and elections. At the same time, these ideas and events fed Carroll's other less practical work, not only his many topical satires but also, as we will see, *Alice's Adventures in Wonderland* and *Through the Looking-Glass*. As a result, Carroll offers a concentrated example of the electoral imagination at work; he shows both how the consequential and yet minor details of electoral procedure could achieve fictional and even fantastic expression, and how those fantasies could find their way back into the real world of politics and remake what they would otherwise only represent. Before turning back to Carroll's caucus-race, let's stick with Gladstone for a moment to see more clearly how imagination and procedure, figures and rules, efficacy and absurdity, fantasy and facticity came together for Carroll.

As I've already suggested, if Gladstone was an outsized figure everywhere in Britain, he loomed especially large in Oxford. This is apparent in Carroll's "Dynamics of a Parti-cle," where he treats the heightened and,

---

[41] Freeman, "University Elections," 23.

to Carroll, somewhat hysterical atmosphere around the 1865 election with mathematical mock seriousness. In one section he offers, as a kind of proleptic gag, some of his first systematic observations on voting, offering a taxonomy of ridiculous methods for casting votes. There is the *invertendo*, when someone "came all the way from Edinburgh to vote, handed in a blank voting-paper, and so went home rejoicing"; the *dividendo*, when someone, "who being sorely perplexed in his choice of candidates, voted for neither"; and the *alternando*, when someone voted "for and against Mr. Gladstone, alternate elections."[42] In 1868, Carroll came up with a number of suggestive anagrams on the whole name, William Ewart Gladstone. One casts Gladstone as a Liberal breaker of idols, a thing certainly at odds with Carroll's Oxford: "Wilt tear down *all* images?" Another imagines him as something out of a topical amalgam of *Don Quixote* and *The Origin of Species*: "A wild man will go at trees." And yet another manages to capture both the fiery promise of the Gladstone persona and what Carroll might have seen as the humble, deflated truth of its political realization: "Wild agitator! Means well."[43]

Although it appears they have done so without much proof, readers have often taken Carroll's depiction and, even more, Tenniel's illustration of the never-ending quarrel between the Lion and the Unicorn, as images of Gladstone and Disraeli, who, whatever their relation to the image, had in fact spent decades beating one another "all round the town." Richard Scully – following Michael Hancher – points out that there is little evidence to support the association and that the idea seems to have come – again – from a throwaway line in Empson: "I think," he writes in "The Child as Swain," that Disraeli "turns up again as the unicorn when the Lion and the Unicorn are fighting for the Crown."[44] Although Scully is of course right that the animals don't look much like the men, Empson's thought does get at something important about Carroll's ongoing effort to capture in word and image a kind of ceaselessly revolving conflict that was characteristic of party politics under the two leaders. As simple allegory or caricature it might fail; as part of a broader

---

[42] Lewis Carroll, "The Dynamics of a Parti-cle," in *Notes by an Oxford Chiel* (Oxford: James Parker & Co., 1865-1874), 11–12.

[43] Robert Douglas-Fairhurst, *The Story of Alice: Lewis Carroll and the Secret History of Wonderland* (Cambridge, MA: Harvard University Press, 2016), 161.

[44] Richard Scully, "The Lion and the Unicorn – William Gladstone and Benjamin Disraeli through William Empson's Looking-Glass," *International Journal of Comic Art* 15(1) (Spring 2013), 323–337; Michael Hancher, *The Tenniel Illustrations to the "Alice" Books*, (Athens: Ohio University Press, 1985); Empson, *Some Versions of Pastoral*, 257.

effort to render political conflict in aesthetic form, it remains suggestive, to say the least. Even more curious is the existence of a riddle popular among "small boys" and some Tories in 1867: "Why is Gladstone like a telescope? Because Disraeli draws him out, looks through him, and shuts him up."[45] Aside from its unmistakably Wonderlandian sound (why *is* a raven like a writing-desk?), the image of the one man shutting the other up like a telescope seems to have come directly from Alice, who, wishing to do the same thing to herself, half hoped that she might come across "a book of rules for shutting people up like telescopes" (*AW*, 13). Because *Alice* comes a couple of years before the riddle, it raises the uncertain but tantalizing possibility that Carroll, who had thought so much about Gladstone, had created imaginative forms that really shaped how others thought about him, too.

And then there's the Mad Hatter, who has been often, if also somewhat spuriously, associated with Gladstone. Martin Gardiner writes assuredly in *The Annotated Alice* that "[t]here is good reason to believe that Tenniel adopted a suggestion of Carroll's that he draw the Hatter to represent one Theophilius Carter, a furniture dealer near Oxford (and no grounds whatever for the widespread belief at the time that the Hatter was a burlesque of Prime Minister Gladstone)."[46] Although Gardiner's confidence was well earned, I'm not sure we should be so hasty. First, Gladstone was neither everyone's Prime Minister nor yet the "People's William" in 1865; he was still "only" the Chancellor of the Exchequer and a losing candidate in an election that touched Carroll and Carroll's college in very immediate, very spectacular ways. So, even if the Hatter is not Gladstone, it would be less absurd than Gardiner suggests for someone to think so. This may be why the liberal *Spectator*, still smarting from its hero's electoral loss, "took the Mad Hatter to be a caricature of Gladstone" when Carroll's book first appeared.[47] Second, even if the Hatter was in fact modeled on the eccentric local, Theophilius Carter, and not on Gladstone, it seems that Carter had in fact modeled *himself* on Gladstone; according to one acquaintance, Carter "was the living image of the late W. E. Gladstone, and, being well aware of the fact, was always careful to wear the high collar and black stock so often depicted in *Punch* in cartoons of

---

[45] Philip Magnus, *Gladstone: A Biography* (New York: E. P. Dutton & Co., 1954), 189.
[46] Martin Gardiner, ed., *The Annotated Alice* (New York: W. W. Norton, 2015), 83.
[47] Roger Lancelyn Green, introduction to *Alice's Adventures in Wonderland and through the Looking-Glass*, by Lewis Carroll (Oxford: Oxford University Press, 1998), xviii.

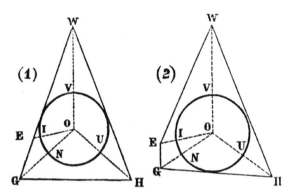

Figure 3.1   "Wilt tear down *all* images?"

the 'Grand Old Man.'"[48] If the Hatter is not a copy of Gladstone but rather a copy of a copy of Gladstone, where would that leave Gladstone, already humiliated in 1865? "I ca'n't go no lower," said the Hatter: "I'm on the floor, as it is" (*AW*, 101).

If, however, speculations about the real Hatter are fun but probably frivolous, what's more interesting and important is how the possible relation between Carroll's imagination and local politics reveals a logic, a *way of thinking* that runs across Carroll's work. After pages of ersatz axioms and definitions, "The Dynamics of a Parti-cle" at last presents its theory of the 1865 election in the form of two diagrams (Figure 3.1).[49] To simplify what is an intentionally and obstinately complicated image: the circle (UNIV) is the university as it exists or will exist in relation to its representation in Parliament. The triangle (WHG) that contains the circle represents the field of possible electoral outcomes. The three lines that make up the triangle are candidates: the unchallenged William Heathcote (WH), Gathorne Hardy (GH), and William Ewart Gladstone (WEG). The lines that touch the circle are the winners. There's too much to say about Carroll's somewhat labored (almost Lacanian!) image. What's important is, first, that it represents the election and its candidates as a set of related but different letters, a convention Carroll will later exploit to its fullest in his technical works on elections. Second, the triangle is an oddly active image, a set of places around which the eye must again and again revolve if the image is to have any meaning. Because each of the three names shares at least one letter with the previous or the subsequent name,

---

[48] Quoted in Hancher, *Tenniel Illustrations*, 101.   [49] Carroll, "Parti-cle," 22.

you can't see one without also seeing another; to read the political field as represented by the triangle is to find that each position is never only itself but is rather the end of the former or the beginning of next. The meaning of the election is, in other words, both dynamic and relational, something that Carroll will explore in greater and more earnest detail in subsequent works on elections and their paradoxes. To be a candidate is, in some sense, to be always already on the move; it is here that we can find the *idea* as opposed to the *image* of the Hatter at work in Carroll's political imagination. A parliamentary election is, in other words, nothing but a Mad Hatter's tea party (a tea parti-cle!), an occasion at which participants move from seat to seat regularly and according to rule but, finally, without much reason:

> A bright idea came into Alice's head.
> "Is that the reason so many tea-things are put out here?" she asked.
> "Yes, that's it," said the Hatter with a sigh: "it's always tea-time, and we've no time to wash the things between whiles."
> "Then you keep moving round, I suppose?" said Alice.
> "Exactly so," said the Hatter: "as the things get used up."
> "But what happens when you come to the beginning again?" Alice ventured to ask.
> "Suppose we change the subject," the March Hare interrupted, yawning. "I'm getting tired of this. I vote the young lady tells us a story."
> (*AW*, 64–65)

If one can't finally say whether or not the Mad Hatter is really like Gladstone (or really like someone who was really like Gladstone), it is certainly the case that the Hatter, the March Hare, and the Dormouse share more than a year with WH, GH, and WEG: they share a lived tension between structure, motion, and meaning that gives one's place in things relational significance if not much independent sense.

Do Bats Eat Cats?

In 1876, Carroll produced his most influential work on the theory of majorities, "A Method of Taking Votes on More Than Two Issues." In it, he refined and modified the "suggestion" he had made during the belfry debate two years before. He did this for a few different reasons. The first and most immediate was occasional and somewhat poignant. In the previous year Max Müller announced that he planned to give up his Professorship of Comparative Philology in order to return to Germany and pursue his studies without the burden of college work and teaching: "If," he wrote to the Duke of Albany, "I had continued to discharge my duties as Professor of Comparative Philology, I should have to surrender my Sanskrit studies altogether."[50] Müller's friends knew that a renewed focus on his life's work was only part of the story. He was still smarting from his loss of the Boden Chair in 1860 ("clerical intrigues and petty jealousies, alas!"), so when he heard in 1875 that his old nemesis Monier Williams was set to receive an additional honorary degree from the university, it was more than his already wounded pride could take. "I think," he wrote, "my time in England is nearly up. I doubt whether I ought to stay longer. I am only tolerated at Oxford, allowed to help when I am wanted, but never helped when I want help."[51] Faced with the threat of his resignation, Müller's friends and supporters, the classicist Benjamin Jowett and Liddell chief amongst them, came up with a plan to allow him to remain in Oxford without teaching. Müller would continue his work on the *Rig-Veda*, would not have to teach, and yet would be able still to draw half of his salary; the remaining half would then be used to hire a "deputy," who would take up Müller's slack.

Although he had been a friend to Müller and his family, Carroll thought that this arrangement made little sense and would do damage to the new deputy, to the Professorship, and to the college: "for surely," he said in one of a few broadsheets he circulated during the controversy, "the very proposal to invite the new Professor to do the work for half the present salary, is to say, by implication, that the work has been hitherto overpaid – against which suspicion I, for one, desire to record my protest."[52] Anticipating "a widespread feeling of dissatisfaction," a fractious debate, another potentially inconclusive vote, and, painfully, the need to vote personally and publicly against the interests of a good friend, Carroll turned his mind back to committees, parliamentary procedure, and, now, the possible bad faith of other electors.[53] On February 15, the day of Müller's meeting, Carroll circulated the last of his broadsheets on "The Professorship of Comparative Philology," and spoke before the Convocation: "I had not meant to speak, but the advocates of the Decree persisted so much in praising Max Müller, and ignoring the

[50] Nirad C. Chaudhuri, *Scholar Extraordinary: The Life of Professor the Rt. Hon. Friedrich Max Muller, P. C.* (New York: Oxford University Press, 1974), 230.
[51] Chaudhuri, *Scholar Extraordinary*, 231.   [52] Chaudhuri, *Scholar Extraordinary*, 234.
[53] "Dodgson photographed Max Müller and was a friend of his family." Gillian Beer, *Alice in Space: The Sideways Victorian World of Lewis Carroll* (Chicago: The University of Chicago Press, 2016), 152.

half-pay of the Deputy that I rose to ask them to keep more to the point. The Decree was carried by 94–35."[54]

If, however, the occasion was awkward and immediate, the questions raised and addressed in "A Method" went deep into the theory of majorities and elections. Part of this touched on the problem of the "sophisticated" or "strategic" voter. First, Carroll saw that, where personal feelings or uncertainty were at issue, electors might be unwilling to go out on a limb against a sympathetic candidate or proposal; to spare the feelings of others or to spare themselves the trouble of much thought, they might vote against or at least vote somewhere alongside their real opinions, interests, or beliefs. Similarly, if an elector saw that an unpopular opinion had no chance of winning, that elector might decide that resistance was both futile and costly, and thus choose to vote without practical consequence against their own real inclination. Like Alice with the March Hare, electors could find it hard both to say what they meant and to mean what they said; they might, as a result, decide to avoid the issue and simply say something else. A truly representative election would, in that case, need to guard against the pressure that comes with the very existence of other people. Carroll thus recommended that the first round of voting be managed "on paper and not openly": "each elector," he wrote, "not knowing exactly how others are voting, has less inducement to vote contrary to his own opinion."[55]

Second, because, as we have seen, Carroll understood the strong effects that procedures could have not only on the course but also on the outcome of elections, he saw that it was important to minimize the power that more sophisticated voters could wield over their less savvy counterparts: "my own opinion is that it is better for elections to be decided according to the wish of the majority than of those who happen to have the most skill in the game."[56] This "skill" takes at least two forms in Carroll's writing in 1876. On the one hand, he saw that, because an election is *like* a game even if it isn't one, sophisticated players would have a strategic advantage over their more ingenuous peers. For instance, Carroll understood that, in an election run on the pairwise model he outlined in 1874, a "good" player should *always* follow this rule: "In any division taken on a pair of issues neither of which you desire, vote against the most popular."[57] Even if this rule couldn't always reflect one's real opinions (you should vote against the

[54] Robert D. Sutherland, *Language and Lewis Carroll* (Ann Arbor: University of Michigan, 1970), 45.
[55] Carroll, *Political Pamphlets and Letters*, 57.	[56] Carroll, *Political Pamphlets and Letters*, 57.
[57] Carroll, *Political Pamphlets and Letters*, 57.

most popular option even if you recognize the most popular option as the better option), undermining a strong candidate who is not *your* candidate is always the smart move. The problem here is not only that this results in a bad representation of the real feelings of the electorate and that it arguably favors the fortunes of the mediocre, but also that it gives an unfair advantage to voters with "the most skill in the game."

On the other hand, in the same way that good players can identify rules *always* to follow, so can they see, as others can't, the value of setting the agenda and, in this case, determining the order in which votes are taken. Consider again the simplified example of the belfry, where voters had to choose between **A**, **B**, **C**, and **D**, when **A** was "no belfry" and **B**, **C**, and **D** were three different colors. Seen through *to its end*, that election would always reveal, wherever one began and however one asked the question, that even though **A** got more top votes in the first round, those votes did not in fact reflect the real will of the committee. This would become clear almost immediately if one started Carroll's process with the color votes, pitting **B** against **C**, **B** against **D**, and so on. At the end of those first rounds, a majority would probably emerge around one color and a majority in favor of a belfry would be shown immediately to outnumber those against the belfry *per se*. If, however, one started instead with the pairs, **A&B**, **A&C**, and **A&D**, one would have to go pretty far into the process before the fundamental weakness of **A** would become evident. It could be easy in that case for a "sophisticated" voter rhetorically to exploit the early but, at last, only apparent strength of **A** and to suggest prematurely that the committee had seen enough and that there was no reason to continue on with the count. That would of course be a false conclusion, but, at the end of a long meeting, it might be a persuasive or at least welcome conclusion. When other voters don't know better, beginning with one comparison instead of another can give a particular candidate or issue an unearned but nonetheless real edge.[58] Again, general awareness both of this rule as a rule *always* to follow and of its possible downstream effects would have to be built into any fair and representative electoral procedure.

---

[58] Arrow: "In the case of legislatures, the paradox takes a more concrete form. The formal procedure is to reduce the procedure which ultimately leads to a decision to a sequence of binary choices: motion, amendment, amendment to amendment, and so forth. (In practice, of course, there is a good deal more flexibility.) At each stage, majority voting makes the choice. But if there is no Condorcet winner, the order of amendments determines the outcome." Kenneth Arrow, "The Functions of Social Choice Theory," in *Social Choice Re-examined*, ed. Kotaro Suzumura (London: Palgrave Macmillan, 1996), 5.

If, however, Carroll's analysis of sophisticated voting and agenda-setting were remarkable, the most significant aspect of his 1876 paper appeared in its discussion of cyclical majorities: "majorities may be 'cyclical,' e.g. there may be a majority for **A** over **B**, for **B** over **C**, and for **C** over **A**."[59] What Carroll found is that even after one runs a proper and full series of pairwise comparisons, it can turn out that, instead of finally uncovering a group's rational if initially obscure preference, the process can rather reveal a paradoxical situation where no one wins because "each [beats] the one next following," and the election ends not with a determinate result but rather in the barren and ostensibly alogical cul-de-sac, **A B C D A B C A D**. Although it seems that Carroll arrived at this startling point independently, he had in effect rediscovered a paradox that had unsettled the Marquis de Condorcet in his *Essai sur l'application de l'analyse à la probabilité des decisions rendues à le pluralité des voix* (1785). He had, in other words, rediscovered Condorcet's Paradox or the tendency of some elections to cycle and thus not to produce a winner. Let me explain how a cyclical majority might work in practice. Imagine that we ask eleven voters to rank their choices between four candidates or four issues in order of preference and that we end up with the following results:

Voter 1 votes: **A>B>C>D**
Voter 2 votes: **A>B>C>D**
Voter 3 votes: **A>D>B>C**
Voter 4 votes: **A>D>B>C**
Voter 5 votes: **D>C>A>B**
Voter 6 votes: **D>C>A>B**
Voter 7 votes: **D>B>C>A**
Voter 8 votes: **C>D>B>A**
Voter 9 votes: **C>D>B>A**
Voter 10 votes: **C>D>B>A**
Voter 11 votes: **B>C>D>A**

A few problems reveal themselves. First, if we were to count votes in the way we do in simple first-past-the-post elections, **A** would win straightaway with four votes. Because, however, **A** did not win the six votes necessary to secure an absolute majority, Carroll's scheme would have us move on to a series of pairwise comparisons. Proceeding alphabetically, we learn first that **A** beats **B**, **B** beats **C**, and **C** beats **D** ("beats" here means

[59] Carroll, *Political Pamphlets and Letters*, 49.

that an option is preferred by at least six voters). It might make sense to stop at this point because, as Condorcet argues, "when a man compares two individuals and prefers the second to the first, and then, on comparing the second with a third, prefers the latter, it would be self-contradictory if he did not also prefer the third to the first."[60] We expect, in other words, the preference relations between **A**, **B**, **C**, and **D** to be *transitive*. We can't, however, stop there because, if we continue to ask the question, who is preferable to whom, it turns out not only that **A** beats **B**, **B** beats **C**, **C** beats **D** but also that **D** beats **A**! The election is thus essentially indeterminate: no one wins and no one loses. Or, as the Dodo says at the end of the caucus-race, "EVERYBODY has won, and all must have prizes." We could think also of Alice, musing groggily as she tumbles down the rabbit-hole: "And here Alice began to get rather sleepy, and went on saying to herself, in a dreamy sort of way, 'Do cats eat bats? Do cats eat bats?' and sometimes 'Do bats eat cats?' for, you see, as she couldn't answer either question, it didn't much matter which way she put it" (*AW*, 11).[61] It is, I think, not for nothing that when **A**lice asks, "**D**o **C**ats **E**at **B**ats?," it gets us the mixed-up but still contiguous series **A**, **D**, **C**, **E**, **B**; and, while it might not matter to a drowsy Alice, it must matter to us to find that **ADCEB =ADBEC** because a world in which the one is equal to the other must be an indeterminate world at the very least. What do we do when the majority is not the majority?

Carroll of course recognized that a result as strange as a cyclical majority would seem unlikely to many. He says:

> I am quite prepared to be told, with regard to the cases I have here proposed, as I have already been told with regard to others, "Oh, *that* is an extreme case: it could never really happen!" Now I have observed that this answer is always given instantly, with perfect confidence, and without any examination of the details of the proposed case. It must therefore rest on some general principle: the mental process being probably something

---

[60] Marquis de Condorcet, "On Elections," in *The Democracy Sourcebook*, ed. Robert A Dahl, Ian Shapiro, and José Antonio Cheibub (Cambridge: Massachusetts Institute of Technology Press, 2003), 315.

[61] We might, thinking back to my discussion of Trollope, Hare, and Pareto in Chapter 2, also think of Carroll's joke here as a play between the list as an ordinal or as a cardinal system. Where the first leans only on the sequential relation between the three terms, the latter leans on their independent value. The charge, in other words, of seeing that "it doesn't much matter" comes from the confusion of these different systems. Carroll clearly understood this and, indeed, begins *Alice's Adventures* with a similar gesture. In his otherwise sentimental prefatory poem, "All in the golden afternoon," he refers to the three Liddell sisters, "Ah, cruel three!," as Prima, Secunda, and Tertia, a move that recognizes sisters as cardinal values while setting them within an ordinal scheme.

like this – "I have formed a theory. This case contradicts my theory. *Therefore* this is an extreme case, and would never occur in practice."[62]

Carroll's question here is, what are we to do with an unlikely but unnerving possibility? What does it mean that a cycle probably won't but maybe could happen? With this Carroll anticipates a conceptual or dispositional divide that structures much subsequent electoral theory. That is, while almost all social choice theorists assume that there is *some* chance that a cycle will occur (William Riker sees them lurking around every corner, while Gerry Mackie sees them as remote and thus trivial possibilities), what seems really to define differences within the field is one or another attitude toward the idea of possibility itself. That is, while some writers see a remote possibility as just that, a possible but practically negligible occurrence that ought not fundamentally shape our attitudes about elections or preferences, others seem constitutionally incapable of ignoring any logical possibility once it has been raised. Indeed, for someone like Carroll, the fact that a possibility is remote or exotic or extreme only makes it *more* beguiling and thus somehow *more* real. This is perhaps the difference between the person who can use a cracked but working smartphone covered in tape or clingwrap without much minding and the person who *needs* to replace the thing not simply when it shows a single scratch but because it shows a *single* scratch: for that second person, the single scratch becomes the phone's singular *thing*. This, it seems to me, is a fundamental difference in dispositions, and, although it cannot be part of a field because it comes, as it were, before the field, it is nonetheless an imaginative and intuitive force we need to understand.

To return to the upshot of Carroll's analysis of cycles: there are three related points to make. First, as was the case with agenda-setting earlier, if one doesn't know that cyclical majorities are even possible, one won't look for them; and because one wouldn't necessarily ask the last question (could it be that, after everything, **D** somehow preferable to **A**?), one might not realize that an election had in fact ended with a cycle and not a determinate result, and one might give the win to **A** when **A** was not in fact the winner. Whether or not they are likely to happen, even a remote possibility of cyclical majorities occurring is reason enough to develop procedures to deal with them when they do.[63] Second, although Carroll writes here and in his

---

[62] Carroll, *Political Pamphlets and Letters*, 54.

[63] Carroll offered a simple solution to the problem of cycles. Returning to our sample election, imagine that Voter 11 shifts preferences, putting **D** ahead of **C**. This simple swap breaks the cycle, allowing **D** to emerge as preferable to all and thus as the definitive winner of the election. What

subsequent work on proportional representation to reform elections, he does so in what will turn out to be a dangerous way. Because he begins with an encounter with logical extremity, with the identification of a disturbing paradox, his work risks upsetting or undermining exactly the kinds of reform to which he was otherwise committed. More recent work on cyclical majorities and the ostensible "impossibility" of social choice – in Kenneth Arrow, Anthony Downs, James Buchanan, Riker, and others – has tended to see the possibility of cycles as a skeptical argument *against* models of democracy based in deliberation, justice, or social welfare (I'll do more to distinguish between Arrow and Downs and the darker, more nihilistic work of Riker and Buchanan in Chapter 4).[64] Daniel Rogers paraphrases the "strong" version of the argument like this: "Majoritarianism yielded . . . only 'a fundamental and inescapable arbitrariness,' as Riker put it, an endless chaotic play of logrolling and vote cycling as factions won and lost control of the agenda."[65] As opposed, that is, to seeing a voting cycle as reason for everybody to have prizes, Riker, following and, as it were, weaponizing Carroll, argued that the remote but nonetheless real possibility of voting cycles meant that democratic procedure not only admitted the possibility of but in fact *relied upon* the lurking and irrational presence of the dictator: "This conclusion appears to be devastating, for it consigns democratic outcomes – and hence the

Carroll proposes then is to "count the number of swaps that each candidate in a cycle would need in order to come out on top, and declare the candidate who requires the fewest swaps the winner." The problem is, the number of computations that one would need to manage to figure out the winner in even a middle-sized election would be so great as to become intractable; complexity theorists call this an NP-hard problem (a nondeterministic polynomial-time hard problem); that means that it is a problem at least as hard as the hardest problem possible in a given set, which means it is a problem essentially too hard to solve. Carroll's solution to the problem is, thus, both perfectly logical and perfectly impossible. The authors of a paper on Carroll's solution that demonstrates this difficulty rightly suggest that, "We think Lewis Carroll would have appreciated the idea that a candidate's mandate might have expired before it was ever recognized." If, however, this scheme is impracticable, it is important to take his swap system as evidence of his larger and real commitment to breaking the cycle; it is, I think, a commitment to the political that goes beyond his occasional writing on elections. J. Bartholdi, III, C. A. Tovey, and M. A. Trick, "Voting Schemes for Which It Can Be Difficult to Tell Who Won the Election," *Social Choice and Welfare* 6 (2) (1989), 157–165.

[64] Riker: "In the late 1960s, however, a wide variety of philosophers, economists, and political scientists began to appreciate how profoundly unsettling [Arrow's] theorem was and how deeply it called into question some conventionally accepted notions – not only about voting, the subject of this work, but also about the ontological validity of the concept of social welfare, a subject that, fortunately, we can leave to metaphysicians." William Riker, *Liberalism Against Populism: A Confrontation between the Theory of Democracy and the Theory of Social Choice* (Long Grove, IL: Waveland Press, 1988), 115–116. For more in this vein, see Gerry Mackie's "hall of quotations" in *Democracy Defended* (Cambridge: Cambridge University Press, 2003), 10–15.

[65] Daniel T. Rogers, *Age of Fracture* (Cambridge, MA: Harvard University Press, 2011), 86–87.

democratic method – to the world of arbitrary nonsense, at least some of the time."[66] He continues:

> Hence a social arrangement is indeterminate when a cycle exists. When the arrangement is indeterminate, the actual choice is arbitrarily made. The selection is not determined by the preference of the voters. Rather it is determined by the power of some chooser to dominate the choice or to manipulate the process to his or her advantage.[67]

Or, as Alice says to the King, "That's not a regular rule: you invented it just now" (*AW*, 105). This is why, despite his sometimes-officious commitments to institutional and parliamentary reforms, it might make sense to think about Carroll and *Alice* in relation to what Carl Schmitt once called the crisis of parliamentary democracy: His sense of and delight in paradox for its own sake threatened sometimes to overwhelm his interest in really reforming the institutions with which he was concerned. And, as we can see everywhere in Wonderland, it can be hard to tell the difference between the genial making and following of rules and the sheer, dictatorial exercise and abuse of power.

Third, Carroll is, I think, making a more general, more difficult, and (to me) more hopeful argument about politics, democracy, and the imagination. A thing like a cyclical majority is paradoxical, upsetting, weird, and, as Riker notes with dark relish, nonsensical.[68] While that all might seem like reason not to believe in the possibility or the likelihood of cyclical majorities, for Carroll thinking right up to and even past the limits of sense is both characteristic and essential. For Carroll, cyclical majorities were not merely possible if unlikely realities; they were, rather, immanent proof that what we tend to accept as reasonable and real about intentions, preferences, and institutions are often illusions that get in the way of our seeing

---

[66] Riker, *Liberalism Against Populism*, 119. Gerry Mackie traces and counters the academic influence of this idea in *Democracy Defended*: "Although democratization is the main trend in the world today, the main intellectual trend in American political science is the view that democracy is chaotic, arbitrary, meaningless, and impossible" (2–3).

[67] Riker, *Liberalism against Populism*, 120. William Poundstone calls Riker "the Joe McCarthy of Condorcet cycles": "Riker presented democracy as a shell game. The 'marks' (voters) put up with voting only because they *believe* it's a fair game. The smart operators who run the show know how easily it's rigged. Every 'paradox' of voting is an opportunity for insiders to force the outcome they desire." William Poundstone, *Gaming the Vote: Why Elections Aren't Fair (and What We Can Do about It)* (New York: Hill & Wang, 2008), 180–181. For more on Riker, his sources, and his influence, see S. M. Amadae and Bruce Bueno de Mesquita, "The Rochester School: The Origins of Positive Political Theory," *Annual Review of Political. Science* 2 (1999), 269–295; see also, Rogers, *Age of Fracture*, 85–90.

[68] Albert O. Hirschman, *The Rhetoric of Reaction: Perversity, Futility, Jeopardy* (Cambridge, MA: Harvard University Press, 1991).

things as they really are. As his colleague Augustus De Morgan put it, "All that is thinkable is possible; all that is impossible is unthinkable: that is, so far as our knowledge can go."[69] In order to see past or through the bad "grown-up" realism of this theory or that convention, one needs to seek out and to confront varieties of the real that, like "the Jabberwock, my son," assert their reality most powerfully just when they approach the edge of the unthinkable and confound our expectations about what reality really is or what it ought really to be like. To put this in other terms: for someone like William Riker the fragility of a procedure or a rule suggests that we ought to reject or to replace that procedure or rule; for Carroll, however, the fragility, delicacy, and absurdity of rules is ultimate proof of their value.

What makes a rule absurd is the fact that it is, in the last instance, based on nothing: "That's not a regular rule: you invented it just now." When, however, the choice is between a rule based on nothing *and* the nihilism of nothing at all, between a shared, if fragile procedure *and* the abuse of power wielded for its own sake, it becomes even more important to understand, to reform, even to care for the rules we have. The caucus-race is good and fun not because it is a game *without* rules but rather because it is a game the rules of which have been set weirdly free to enjoy themselves. Carroll's conservatism was the conservatism of traditions, relations, conventions, and local rules, a conservatism of family, the college common room, an organized wine cellar, and the game properly played. Carroll, it seems clear, was a conservative not because he believed that any given rule was essentially good; he was a conservative because he saw or felt or feared that the alternative to a rule was violence, chaos, nonsense. In the face of political reform, cultural change, and the waning of social tradition, Carroll found ways to embrace rules *because* they had begun – as forms – to break free from the shifting conditions that had once given them their meaning. A paradox is not, in that case, a reason to abandon or to doubt democracy; a paradox is a reason, rather, to care for it all the more.

A Toad in a Stone

That said, the originality, the intensity, and – in time – the influence of Carroll's sporadic work on elections and parliamentary representation still begs some questions. Although I have pointed to several local occasions

---

[69] Quoted in Gillian Beer, *Alice in Space: The Sideways Victorian World of Lewis Carroll* (Chicago: The University of Chicago Press, 2016), 55.

and events that seem to have encouraged Carroll to dedicate himself to the more and less systematic study of elections and preferences, the work nonetheless seems improbably *sui generis*. Although much social choice theory has had at least to refer to Carroll's writing on elections since the appearance of Duncan Black's *The Theory of Committees and Elections* in 1958, the work hasn't made much of an impression on literary critics. On the one hand, it is easy to see why: the strange mix of college parochialism and logical abstraction that characterizes these pamphlets makes them hard both to place and to understand. On the other hand, a close engagement with them shows not only where they are in dialogue with the political climate as well as with Carroll's other work but also how they possess a singular imaginative force that is striking and valuable in and of itself. I want, then, to end this section by thinking more about where writing like this comes from and how we might be able to understand its place both in and in-between literary history and the electoral imagination.

I've already mentioned the fact that Carroll managed *independently* to rediscover the paradox that had troubled Condorcet a century before. That we know or think we know that Carroll never read Condorcet is due to the work of Duncan Black, to whom I have referred more than once. In the course of his own work as an economist and lecturer working at the Dundee School of Economics and the University College of North Wales, Bangor, Black had also independently "discovered" Condorcet's and then Carroll's paradox in the 1940s, an experience he remembered as a kind of intellectual malady: "On finding that the arithmetic was correct and the intransitivity persisted, my stomach revolted in something akin to physical sickness."[70] Although Black had, like Carroll had before him, arrived at his idea without much intellectual support, he was, unlike Carroll or, later, Arrow, deeply and, as it were, emotionally interested in the secret history of his idea, an interest that took him back to Condorcet, Borda, Edgeworth, Carroll, and others: "Black's contribution to restoring the lost intellectual history of the eighteenth century is immense."[71] It was as if, faced with and sickened by the outlandishness of his own imagination, Black wanted to make a place for himself, to invent an intellectual history or a "family romance" that might make sense of things and give him and

---

[70]   Black, *A Mathematical Approach*, xii.
[71]   Iain McLean, Alistair McMillan, and Burt L. Monroe, "Editor's Introduction," in Duncan Black, *The Theory of Committees and Elections,* by Duncan Black, ed. Iain McLean, Alistair McMillan, and Burt L. Monroe (New York: Springer Science & Business, 1998), xxviii.

his orphan idea a home.[72] It was as part of this historical project that he visited Oxford in order to see for himself what Carroll had thought and read when he had his own outlandish idea:

> [W]e can prove almost beyond doubt that he was unacquainted with the works of [Condorcet and Borda], because when we examined the volume of the *Histoire de l'académie royale des sciences* for 1781, containing Borda's article, in the Christ Church Library, we found that its pages were still uncut; and this is surely the copy, if any, which Dodgson would have consulted. And it seems clear enough that if he did not read Borda neither did he read Condorcet . . . while there was no copy of Condorcet's *Essai sur l'application de l'analyse* . . . in the Christ Church Library, we found that in the copy in the Bodleian one of the pages of a section on elections was uncut. . . . His work owes almost nothing to his predecessors.[73]

As Black searched the Christ Church archives for evidence of Carroll's theoretical independence, he also came across "three letter books in an old cupboard, with copies of letters that Carroll had written when he was Curator of the Common Room."[74] Alongside the letters, Black also found an envelope filled with newspaper clippings, including a number from the *Times* in 1862 commenting on a story about "a frog [that] has been put on display which was supposed to have been embedded in a block of coal."[75] For Black these letters were significant because they seemed to him to explain Carroll's thinking when he came up with the Frog-Footman in *Alice's Adventures in Wonderland*: "There is no doubt," he says with extraordinary confidence, "that the provenance of the Frog-Footman is the letter to *The Times*."[76] Although it seems a stretch to say *for sure* that Carroll somehow got from a frog in coal to the terrible stupidity of the Frog-Footman, it does seem clear that, as he thought about the character and origin of Carroll's ideas, Black was himself invested, and deeply so, in states of suspended animation as a telling aspect of intellectual history. Condorcet had an idea in 1785 and it went more or less missing, encased in uncut pages, for a century; Carroll had the same idea independently in 1876 and it, too, went more or less missing until, in the 1940s, Duncan Black got sick thinking about the intransitivity of cyclical majorities. This sense of an idea as a toad in the stone, as a thing that lived and might live again, but only after the passage of a long and lonely age, is even more poignant when seen in relation to Black's own troubled career.

---

[72] See Sigmund Freud, "Family Romances," in *The Standard Edition of the Complete Psychological Works of Sigmund Freud, Volume IX (1906–1908): Jensen's "Gradiva" and Other Works*, 235–242.
[73] Black, *Theory of Committees and Elections*, 193–194.   [74] Black, *Mathematical Approach*, 5.
[75] Black, *Mathematical Approach*, 5.   [76] Black, *Mathematical Approach*, 8.

A brilliant, "unworldly," and "somewhat lonely" character, Black had always been something of an outsider. Hailing from a working-class town outside of Glasgow, he labored, like other Scottish academics of the period, at the edges of the British university system: "in Britain," remembers R. H. Coase, "his ideas met everywhere with skepticism or hostility."[77] His career, writes S. M. Amadae, "was one of isolation and instability."[78] This sense of displacement and resistance became all the more pronounced when he submitted a paper on voting cycles, coauthored with R. A. Newing, to the journal *Econometrica* in November 1949. The journal sat on the piece until 1951, only a few months after Kenneth Arrow published his *Social Choice and Individual Values*, which, although it appeared first, covered ground that Black had surveyed for almost a decade. When William B. Simpson finally wrote back on the journal's behalf, he told Black that they would take "the paper for resubmission on condition that the authors acknowledged Arrow's results."[79] "Black," say Iain McLean and Alistair McMillan, "was very angry at what he saw as a denial of priority [and] withdrew the paper."[80] What's more, notes Amadae, "Black's outrage was complete when he learned that Simpson played another professional role as assistant director of research at the Cowles Commission in Chicago, where Arrow worked."[81] "The effect on Black of [the *Econometrica*] decision was," remembers Coase, "profound. He became suspicious of the motives of others and retired within himself, largely devoting himself in his researches to an historical study of the thought of his predecessors, above all, Lewis Carroll."[82] (It is, incidentally, too good to be true that when you try to manage and to notate the priority of Arrow, Black, and Carroll, you end up either with **C, B, A** or **C, A, B**.)

It makes a kind of sense that it was in the wake of this disappointment that Black then made the odd but somehow inevitable decision to devote years to the study of another anxious, imaginative, and retiring man. In a long series of finished, unfinished, and infrequently read writings, he thought and wrote about Carroll's work on social preferences and cyclical majorities, about his contributions to the theory and practice of

---

[77] R. H. Coase, Foreword to *Theory of Committees and Elections*, xi.
[78] S. M. Amadae, *Rationalizing Capitalist Democracy: The Cold War Origins of Rational Choice Liberalism* (Chicago: University of Chicago Press, 2003), 125.
[79] Iain McLean and Alistair McMillan, introduction to *A Mathematical Approach to Proportional Representation: Duncan Black on Lewis Carroll*, ed. Iain McLean and Alistair McMillan (New York: Springer, 1996), xvii–xviii.
[80] Black, *Mathematical Approach*, xvii.   [81] Amadae, *Rationalizing Capitalist Democracy*, 123.
[82] R. H. Coase, Foreword to *Theory of Committees and Elections*, xiv.

proportional representation, and, as we saw with his speculations on the stony toad and the Frog-Footman, about the logical and electoral sources of *Alice's Adventures in Wonderland* and *Through the Looking-Glass*. When we think now about why it was that Carroll's clippings about the toad in the stone fired Black's critical imagination, what seems more important than any demonstrable relation to the appearance of the Frog-Footman is, on the one hand, what it might have suggested about the idea of Black's own living essay held eerily suspended in the calcified medium of *Econometrica* and, on the other hand, how it might have supported an image of the journal's editor standing with great power and vast stupidity athwart the threshold of Black's spoilt career: "'There's no sort of use in knocking,' said the Footman" (*AW*, 51).

What's striking about Black's work on Carroll is that, both as an intellectual historian and an especially intrepid if also reckless kind of literary critic, he approaches the relation between Carroll's creative and analytical work in unexpected, idiosyncratic, and somehow persuasive terms. That is, where critics have often looked to Carroll's work as a mathematician and a logician in order to trace the appearance of similar ideas, patterns, or forms in the *Alice* books, where they have, in other words, asked how the one might have influenced the other, Black was instead interested in finding a common and, as it were, avowedly inexplicable source for all of Carroll's thinking. Black believed that, for all of its logical clarity and analytical power, Carroll's work on elections was, like the *Alice* books, motivated in its depth, originality, and intensity by feelings and desires too strange or shameful ever to own directly: "in his best writing, Carroll is himself in the dark as to what he is writing about."[83] Carroll's many writings on elections and preferences, work that turned on how we might imagine or invent procedures that would let us say what we really wanted or really meant, were for Black strange and compensatory proof that Carroll would not, could not manage as much himself.

On the one hand, Black was thinking about the difficult and frankly discomfiting problem of Carroll's relationship with the young Alice Liddell and her two sisters. While evidence suggests that his attachment to Alice and to other children was innocent *in its way*, it was clear to Black, as it has been clear to so many, that the relationship was nonetheless overcharged with feelings of affection, need, loss, and desire that rendered it queasily unsustainable. It was, Black suggests, the uncomfortable fact of this

---

[83] Black, *Mathematical Approach*, 14.

relation and its fallout that partly drove Carroll to spend years symptom-
atically pestering Dean Liddell with squibs, broadsheets, pamphlets, and
new schemes for taking votes and making majorities. On the other hand,
Carroll's real but necessarily inchoate sense of his own feelings and their
intensity led him to a far more substantial engagement with the relation
between saying, meaning, and wanting in the *Alice* books as well as in his
writing on elections. Says Black:

> It appeared to refer to committees and did so: but it referred at the same
> time to a subject that was still closer to him, his own feelings and thoughts.
> He was symbolizing, it seems to me, and putting into logical form,
> something which cannot be expressed in the ordinary extensional Logic,
> but requires another form of Logic, intensional Logic, or, as we may call it,
> the Logic of Intensity.[84]

For complicated but crucial reasons, the reliable representation of *intensity*
has been, for some, the holy grail and, for others, the third rail of electoral
theory; if it's easy enough to represent the simple fact that I prefer coffee to
tea, it is far more difficult to represent *why* and *how much* I prefer it. To
represent intensity is, in other words, to move not only into the fraught area
of the "interpersonal comparison of preferences and utilities" but also into
the psychologically rich, imaginatively demanding, and potentially endless
work of representing character. Carroll, suggests Black, had to think about
voting because available forms of voting so often failed – as Thomas Hare
and others had seen before him – to account for the richness, thickness,
intensity, oddity, or perversity of individual preferences. They could not
contend with what, *in the individual*, must exceed the individual or leave the
individual undone. In order to represent the will of a group, one had to
wrestle with the real but somehow unrepresentable intensity of individual
feelings and desires; but, as Black saw, Carroll had also to think about
elections because, whether it be with a vote or a word, and whether it be in
committee, Parliament, or our dealings with other people, it is always a
struggle really to say what one really means or what one really wants.

3.2   THE EARTHLY PARADOX

> Parliamentary leaders must get used to being dragged through the
> dung-hill of lies and intrigue, or they will be of little service to
> their party.
>   —William Morris, "Notes on Passing Events" (1886)

[84] Black, *Mathematical Approach*, 41.

Don't Vote!

Just as Lewis Carroll was turning his antic and sometimes angsty attention to some of the deepest paradoxes of political representation and preference, another Oxford graduate was also writing about the meaning and mechanics of parliamentary democracy. In a halfpenny pamphlet printed on behalf of the Socialist League at the end of 1885, Carroll's contemporary William Morris exhorted "the working-men electors of Great Britain" not to vote: "DO NOT VOTE AT ALL, but consider what you can do for your class *without voting.*"[85] He goes on to review the several parties competing in the general election, arguing that the choice between parliamentary Conservatives, Liberals, and Radicals was, in the final analysis, no choice at all. He insists:

> Working men! Keep away from the poll altogether! DO NOT VOTE! You are governed as a lower class by an upper class; let the class that governs you take all the responsibility of its government, and itself bear all the fear and the hatred that may come of it! The one thing which the ruling classes desire, whether they be Conservative, Liberal, or Radical, is to make you the accomplices of your own enslavement. We show you the snare: avoid it, and DO NOT VOTE.[86]

From 1883, when he first became a socialist, until the end of his life, a sharply pronounced distaste for all political parties and a tactical resistance to parliamentary contests were defining aspects of Morris's thinking about democracy, activism, and class struggle. Having crossed what he called "the river of fire" into the commitment to socialism that would define his life, Morris not only rejected Parliament as a representative institution but also attacked it regularly with an irony, an intensity, and a consistency that, at a distance, can seem excessive or even strange. Florence Boos notes that, "traditionally, the most difficult to understand of Morris's tactical convictions is his deep opposition to electoral politics."[87] In the *hundreds* of essays and topical notes he prepared for *Commonweal* between 1885 and 1900, he came back and back again to the essential bad faith and procedural constipation of Parliament, to the mendacity of all political parties, and to what he took as the narcissistic, two-faced, or shabby pranks of Liberal and Radical party grandees like Gladstone, Joseph Chamberlain, and John Bright. Indeed, his "policy of abstention" not only pitted him

---

[85] William Morris, *For Whom Shall We Vote?* (London: Commonweal, November 1895), 2.

[86] *For Whom Shall We Vote,* 5.

[87] Florence Boos, introduction to *William Morris's Socialist Diary,* by William Morris, ed. Florence Boos (London: The Journeyman Press, 1985), 6.

against the establishment but also put him repeatedly and, at times, disastrously at odds with other socialists. In the first instance, it was largely his disagreement with H. M. Hyndman over the question of voting that led to his 1884 break with the Social Democratic Federation (SDF) and the subsequent formation – with E. Belfort Bax, Eleanor Marx, Edward Aveling, and others – of the Socialist League; writes Fiona MacCarthy:

> The fundamental argument was over the means of achieving Socialism. It was between the members who believed in some sort of parliamentary action, the view of the impatient, opportunistic Hyndman, and the more purist Socialists who supported a longer-term programme of social agitation and education, leading to a more informed and therefore more genuine consensus in the end.[88]

And then – after all that and in the wake of the Fourth Annual Conference of the Socialist League in 1888 – Marx, Aveling, A. K. Donald, and a few others broke away from Morris to form their own "independent splinter group," the Bloomsbury Socialist Society, and to "contest seats" at the national and municipal levels while cultivating relationships of convenience with the SDF, the Fabian Society, and trade unionists.[89]

All these groups, seen either together or apart, combined varying levels of skepticism about parliamentary politics with a pragmatic willingness to caucus, to strike deals, to support candidates, and to take wins where they could get them. Morris, however, was adamant:

> The moderate Socialists or those who can see nothing but the transitional period therefore, believe in what may be called a system of cumulative reforms as the means towards the end; which reforms must be carried out by means of Parliament and a bourgeois executive, the only legal power at present existing, while the Communists believe that it would be a waste of time for the Socialists to expend their energy in furthering reforms which so far from bringing us nearer to Socialism would rather serve to bolster up the present state of things; and not believing in the efficacy of reforms, they can see no reason for attempting to use Parliament in any way; except perhaps by holding it up as an example to show what a contemptible thing a body can be which poses as the representative of a whole nation, and which really

[88] Fiona MacCarthy, *William Morris: A Life for Our Time* (New York: Alfred A. Knopf, 1995), 493.
[89] Yvonne Kapp, *Eleanor Marx*, Vol. 2 (New York: Pantheon Books, 1976), 265. See also Mark Bevir, *The Making of British Socialism* (Princeton, NJ: Princeton University Press, 2011), 103: "At the next annual conference the Marx family circle who dominated the Bloomsbury branch proposed a motion that would allow individual branches to choose whether or not to run candidate in elections. Morris had tried to avoid a split, but when forced to act, he now proposed a purist anti-parliamentary amendment. The amendment was passed, and the Bloomsbury branch withdrew from the League."

represents nothing but the firm determination of the privileged or monopolistic class to stick to their privilege and monopoly till they are *forced* to relinquish it.[90]

The problems of the present, says Morris again and again and again, won't be managed through compromise, coalitions, "palliative measures," or what the Fabians called "permeation" (sometimes "possibilism").[91] Because, he argues, the problem is the whole social system as it stands *here and now*, any effort to improve the living conditions of the proletariat within the structures of and with the legal means available to that system can serve only to obscure the essential problem and, thus, to extend the life of exactly the conditions against which socialists claimed to stand in moral opposition. For Morris, those counterproductive "palliative measures" included minor adjustments to the length of the working day, targeted wage increases, and other largely symbolic parliamentary concessions to accommodationist trade unions; as Morris saw it, these fixes wouldn't really improve the lives of working people, the conditions under which they worked, or the kinds or work they produced. What they would do, however, was to dilute or to delay the ability of working people both to see their shared condition as *the* productive class and, thus, to recognize their power to change their living conditions on their own: "the real business of Socialists is to impress on the workers that they are a class, whereas they ought to be Society; if we mix ourselves up with Parliament we shall confuse and dull this fact in people's minds instead of making it clear and intensifying it."[92] A vote in Parliament or a vote for a parliamentary

[90] William Morris, "The Policy of Abstention," in William Morris, *How I Became a Socialist*, ed. Owen Hatherly and Owen Holland (London: Verso Books, 2020), 128. See also, "Whigs, Democrats, & Socialists," in William Morris, *Signs of Change*, ed. May Morris (London: Longmans, Green, & Company, 1895), 33: "Those who think that they can deal with our present system in this piecemeal way very much underrate the strength of the tremendous organization under which we live, and which appoints to each of us his place, and if we do not chance to fit it, grinds us down until we do. Nothing but a tremendous force can deal with this force; it will not suffer itself to be dismembered, nor to lose anything which really is its essence without putting forth all its force in resistance; rather than lose anything which it considers of importance, it will pull the roof of the world down upon its head."

[91] Peter Gay on "permeation": "Socialist institutions, so the theory runs, begin to permeate capitalism even while the latter system is at its height. The area of communal action is steadily increasing in size and significance. This is cause for great hope, for it demonstrates that the transformation of capitalism into Socialism can proceed in gradual and nonviolent fashion. The Fabian concept of 'municipal Socialism,' according to which city-owned gas and water works are milestones on the road to Socialism, is one expression of this doctrine." Gay, *The Dilemma of Democratic Socialism* (New York: Columbia University Press, 1962), 221.

[92] William Morris, "Socialism and Politics (An Answer to 'Another View')," in William Morris, *Political Writings: Contributions to Justice and Commonweal, 1883–1890*, ed. Nicholas Salmon (Bristol, England: Thoemmes Press, 1994), 100.

representative was, in that case, not only useless; for a socialist, a vote was a means that worked directly, logically, and inevitably against its own putative end. For Morris, a socialist's vote was, in and of itself, a contradiction in terms. It was not only dangerous but also a kind of nonsense. Don't vote, he said; don't vote.

The Policy of Abstention: A Necessary Digression

I want to take a brief detour and consider what it might mean in general to tell someone or to tell oneself not to vote, and then consider what it meant for William Morris to say so. As we've already seen, Morris was neither the first nor the last person to express skepticism about the value of democracy in either its direct or its representative forms. The suggestion that political voting might be useless, dangerous, or somehow counterproductive goes back at least to Plato and has run alongside and beneath the international expansion and consolidation of democratic norms like a long and darkling tone. As is the case with both voting and rigging, however, the meaning of "don't vote" shifts from person to person and context to context. Before, in that case, looking more clearly at what Morris meant when he said, "don't vote," I want briefly to consider three different but related senses of the phrase. This will, I hope, help to clarify both what it can mean and, more importantly, how a maybe essential lack of clarity or definition has sometimes muddled and sometimes motivated the imperative, Don't Vote. What's more, this is another opportunity to acknowledge how the problems of the past remain problems of the present.

DV_1: Counting Noses

The first sense of Don't Vote! (DV_1) is perhaps the most familiar and the one closest to Morris's; it takes the meaning of voting as a matter of shifting categories, perspectives, or levels of abstraction. As we've already seen, Morris saw the choice between Tories, Liberals, and Radicals as false (1) because, whatever the apparent or epiphenomenal differences between their respective positions, any and every candidate implicitly supported the existence of Parliament simply by virtue of running; (2) because Parliament supported private property, then any and every parliamentary candidate was effectively supporting private property; and, (3) because any and every candidate was effectively supporting private property, *then* a socialist, i.e. someone committed fundamentally to the abolition of private property, could support neither Parliament nor its candidates:

> Here, say the politicians, vote for *this* or for *that*. Is there no third course, you say, but to vote for a piece of reaction or a piece of inaction? None, they answer; your business is to have your nose counted on one side or other of the business that we nose-counters have made for you: if you object, you are a faddist, a crank, a person ignorant of "practical politics."[93]

Faced with what he understood as a choice that wasn't one, Morris chose rather to abstain. Although, as I will argue, Morris based his purist's resistance to voting and parliamentary politics on coherently, if controversially, socialist grounds, his position nevertheless put him increasingly on the side of the anarchist elements in the Socialist League, a situation that made him uncomfortable and that led finally in 1890 to his own break with both *Commonweal* and the League. Even so, the clearest and most familiar expressions of DV₁ are probably those articulated across a long and broadly anarchist tradition. In "On Representative Government and Universal Suffrage" (1870), Mikhail Bakunin wrote that

> It was generally expected that once universal suffrage was established, the political liberty of the people would be assured. This turned out to be a great illusion. In practice, universal suffrage led to the collapse, or at least the flagrant demoralization, of the Radical party, which is so glaringly obvious today. ... The whole system of representative government is an immense fraud resting on this fiction.[94]

Peter Kropotkin, one of Morris's good friends, mocked the parliamentary Socialists in 1903:

> Vote! Greater men than you will tell you the moment when the self-annihilation of capital has been accomplished. They will then expropriate the few usurpers left, who will own everything, and you will be freed without ever having taken any more trouble than that of writing on a bit of paper the name of the man whom the heads of your faction of the party told you to vote for![95]

---

[93] Morris, quoted in Boos, 7; William Morris, "Counting Noses," in William Morris, *Political Writings: Contributions to Justice and Commonweal 1883–1890*, ed. Nichoals Salmon (Bristol: Thoemmes Press, 1994), 371.

[94] Mikhail Bakunin, *Bakunin on Anarchism*, ed. Sam Dolgoff (Montreal: Black Rose Books, 1980), 220.

[95] Quoted in Ruth Kinna, "Kropotkin's Theory of Mutual Aid in Historical Context," *International Review of Social History* 40(2) (1995), 265–266.

In 1911, Emma Goldman, writing *against* women's suffrage, lamented:

> The poor, stupid, free American citizen! Free to starve, free to tramp the
> highways of this great country, he enjoys universal suffrage, and, by that
> right, he has forged chains about his limbs. The reward that he receives is
> stringent labor laws prohibiting the right of boycott, of picketing, in fact, of
> everything, except the right to be robbed of the fruits of his labor. Yet all
> these disastrous results of the twentieth-century fetich have taught woman
> nothing.[96]

In 1973 Jean-Paul Sartre published a short piece called, "Elections: A Trap
for Fools": "Why am I going to vote? Because I have been persuaded that
the only political act in my life consists of depositing my ballot in the box
once every four years? But that is the very opposite of an act. I am only
revealing my powerlessness and obeying the power of a party."[97] Whether
expressed by a Socialist or an Anarchist, DV_1 argues that because *the system*
is corrupt, either because it is dedicated above all else to the protection of
private property or because the coercion of states is an essential evil
whatever a given state's ostensible character, any choice made within the
established and artificially limited terms of *the system* must also be corrupt.
So, don't vote.

DV_2: Carrying Coals to Newcastle

The second sense of Don't Vote (DV_2) is sometimes invoked to support
DV_1, but it also appears in many contexts beyond and often well to the
right of the socialist's or anarchist's conviction that a choice between any
two candidates for office will always be empty when the office itself is the
problem. This is the argument that voting simply isn't worth the effort or,
to put it more precisely, that it is irrational to vote.[98] Because, the thinking
goes, in large elections the value or the utility of an individual vote can
seem to approach zero, the real costs of voting can and probably will

---

[96] Emma Goldman, *Anarchism and Other Essays* (New York: Mother Earth Publishing Association,
1911), 204.

[97] Jean-Paul Sartre, "Elections: A Trap for Fools," *New Indicator*, 6(4) (November 4–17, 1980): 4.

[98] For another, plummier version of this same idea, see W. H. Morris Jones, "In Defence of Apathy:
Some Doubts on the Duty to Vote," *Political Studies* 2(1) (1954): "But the presence of an apathetic
part of the electorate is even more than a sign of understanding and tolerance of human variety; it
may also have a beneficial effect on the tone of political life itself. ... A State which has 'cured'
apathy is likely to be a State in which too many people have fallen into the error of believing in the
efficiency of political solutions for the problems of ordinary lives" (37). For Jones, who might
deserve a page or two in Hirschman's *Rhetoric of Reaction*, a little democracy is good; a lot of
democracy is, paradoxically, not only bad but also somehow totalitarian.

outweigh the benefits of voting. "The greater the number of voters," writes Jeremy Bentham, "the less the weight and the value of each vote, the less its price in the eyes of the voter, and the less of an incentive he has in assuring that it conforms to the true end and even in casting it at all."[99] In the context of rational choice models, the term "benefit" refers to the power that an individual vote will have, first, to determine the outcome of any given election and, second, to shape public policies that will have a direct effect on the voter. The term "cost" refers to any expenditure of money, effort, or time incurred as a result of voting. Although public choice theorists tend to focus on what they call "information costs," these forms of expenditure must also include travel expenses, time away from work, social effects, etc.

The classic distillation of this problem, often referred to as the "paradox of voting," is to be found in Anthony Downs's 1957 *An Economic Theory of Democracy*: "since," he writes, "the returns from voting are often miniscule, even low voting costs may cause many partisan citizens to abstain."[100] Seen from a purely economic point of view, a potential voter might do the math and determine that voting simply isn't worth the trouble. Because, however, Downs accepts as given the idea that democracy is good and thus the idea that people should vote, the practical upshot of his argument is first, that the costs of voting should be reduced as far as possible and, second, that those costs should be equally distributed across a population: "When voting is costly, its costs may outweigh its returns, so abstention can be rational even for citizens with party preferences. In fact, the returns from voting are usually so low that even small costs may cause voters to abstain; hence tiny variations in cost can sharply redistribute political power."[101] If, in other words, even "tiny variations" can make it more irrational for *some* voters to vote than for others, that is a social as opposed to a logical or an economic problem, and it ought to be addressed as such. For Downs, Don't Vote! isn't a political or an ethical imperative but rather a response to conditions that can be understood as more rational in some cases than in others given how things work for some people and not others "now and around here."

Although Downs's work has been used to support many arguments about the meaning, conduct, and outcome of elections, aspects of his

---

[99] Quoted in Jon Elster, *Explaining Social Behavior: More Nuts and Bolts for the Social Sciences* (Cambridge: Cambridge University Press, 2015), 409.
[100] Anthony Downs, *An Economic Theory of Democracy* (Boston: Addison Wesley, 1957), 265.
[101] Downs, *Economic Theory of Democracy*, 274.

argument have been taken up with special and, I would argue, myopic intensity by libertarians, anarcho-capitalists, and other democratic skeptics.[102] These writers tend to limit engagement with Downs's argument to the question of "information costs" without attending much to the question of other social costs (transportation, time, wages, etc.). As a result, they tend to focus on the idea of the problem of "the ignorant voter," the person who, when faced with the low benefits of voting and the high costs of learning enough *to vote well*, will make the perfectly rational decision not to learn anything but to vote anyway.[103] And – they say – if, as a society, we both argue that one has a moral responsibility to vote and yet acknowledge that it would be irrational (too costly) for everyone to learn enough to vote well, then we're left with a democracy that will inevitably produce bad, uninformed policies. The solution? We should, they argue, tell people who don't or can't know enough to vote well, Don't Vote! "Many politically active citizens," writes Jason Brennan, "try to make the world better and vote with the best of intentions. They vote for what they believe will promote the common good. However, despite their best intentions, on my view, many are blameworthy for voting. Although they are politically engaged, they are nonetheless often ignorant of or misinformed about the relevant facts or, worse, are simply irrational. Though they intend to promote the common good, they all too often lack sufficient evidence to justify the policies they advocate. When they do vote, I argue, they *pollute* democracy with their votes and make it more likely that we will have to suffer from bad governance."[104]

The first question that this begs, of course, is, who gets to establish and police the norms that would allow us to distinguish good from bad governance? In the work of Brennan, Bryan Caplan, and Ilya Somin, democratic elections are understood as essentially epistemic affairs, systems designed – however badly – to produce the best answer to some explicit or

---

[102] See Jason Brennan, *Against Democracy* (Princeton, NJ: Princeton University Press, 2017) and *The Ethics of Voting* (Princeton, NJ: Princeton University Press, 2012); Bryan Caplan, *The Myth of the Rational Voter: Why Democracies Choose Bad Policies* (Princeton, NJ: Princeton University Press, 2011); and Ilya Somin, *Democracy and Political Ignorance* (Stanford, CA: Stanford University Press, 2016).

[103] This is, as we have seen, an old but persistent kind of calumny. "In summary," wrote Eugene Burdick in 1959, "the voting studies etch a portrait of the contemporary voter as a person who votes with relatively high frequency, but on very low information, with very little interest, and with very low emotional involvement in the entire process. The act of voting seems divorced from any coherent set of principles." Eugene Burdick, "Political Theory and the Voting Studies," in *American Party Politics: Essays and Readings*, ed. Donald G. Herzberg and Gerald M. Pomper (New York: Holt, Rinehart, & Winston, Inc., 1966), 400.

[104] Brennan, *Ethics of Voting*, 5.

implicit question. This view of elections as epistemic or, to use Brennan's frankly repellent phrase, as *epistocratic* assumes some of the same premises found, on the one hand, in Condorcet's interest in seeing elections as part of a larger and essentially progressive move toward real, rational, and inevitable social ends and, on the other, more recent attempts to use Condorcet's jury theorem as the basis for a theory of functioning epistemic democracy. It is because they see the point of elections as arriving at correct answers to social questions that they can argue that some definite measure of epistemic competence is necessary to "voting well" and thus to producing "good policy."

There are, it seems to me, a few problems at work in this line of thinking.

1. It is simply not the case that every election or, for that matter, many elections can be understood as primarily epistemic, which is to say as cooperative efforts to find a correct answer to some explicit or implicit question. As we have already seen, the problem of what it is that a vote is meant to represent – a belief, preference, protest, opinion, interest, wish, and so on – is an open one, and wishes and interests cannot be tested against an assumed epistemic standard in the same way that beliefs *perhaps* could be. What's more, what arguably distinguishes politics from other kinds of human endeavor is exactly that, where biology, chemistry, or even economics are rightly in search of a right answer, the practice of politics exists because, as Charles Larmore puts it, "reasonable people, precisely in virtue of exercising their reason in good faith and to the best of their abilities, tend to come to contrary opinions when they consider, especially in some detail, what it is for instance to live well."[105] In this description, politics exists not to overcome or to resolve conflict but rather to create conditions under which the results of collective decisions can be recognized as legitimate even or especially where epistemic resolution is impossible and where conflict will continue to exist. Unless Brennan and company can demonstrate that all or even many votes are best understood as epistemic and thus properly falsifiable, their analysis can have only limited descriptive or normative value. And, even if all elections were epistemic, which they are not, the establishment of an "epistocracy" or a Coleridgean clerisy wouldn't make practical sense. The point of such

---

[105] Charles Larmore, *What Is Political Philosophy?* (Princeton, NJ: Princeton University Press, 2020), 133.

an exercise would, I imagine, be to identify voters with a higher chance of being right about things (say, right 80–90 percent of the time); aggregating those fewer but "better" votes would, the argument goes, produce a higher likelihood of "good" social choices. The problem of course is that it would be impossible and grotesque to establish and to police the norms that would allow one to distinguish in advance who would be more likely to be right. The logical, never mind ethical, weaknesses of whatever model you care to think of – trial and error, educational history, socioeconomic access to said education, a sanitized Jim Crow style literacy test, review by some appointed council of elders – are so glaringly apparent that they don't, frankly, warrant much serious discussion.[106] If, in that case, we did decide that all elections are epistemic – and they are not all epistemic – the obvious and least costly solution would be to rely on Condorcet's jury theorem or "the wisdom of crowds," which tells us that, if individual voters have only a 50.1 percent chance of being right (just better than a coin toss), aggregating more and more of those voters will approach a group that has a 100 percent chance of being right, without needing first to establish any spurious norm.[107] The solution, in other words, to this particular fantasy of a problem would be *more* and not *less* participation in elections. But, since all elections are not epistemic, even this saner response doesn't really take us all that far.

2. These arguments rely, as I have said, on the claim that in large elections individual votes will in most cases have almost no value. Because the idea that my vote could be *the* vote that tips the scale in an election is almost always a fantasy, it is simply a mistake to imagine that my vote could be *more* important, never mind *more* decisive, than any other vote; indeed, it is essential to the transitivity of elections to treat and to understand every vote *qua* vote as identical. This argument about the low utility of the individual vote works well enough in the context of a particular kind of election, that is, in a

---

[106] If, by the way, these arguments seem merely academic, they resurfaced – and more than once – after the 2020 election in, shall we say, a more public-facing form in the pages of the *National Review*, wherein Kevin Williamson makes the frankly troglodytic argument that everything would be a lot better if a lot of other people just didn't vote. Why? Because he thinks a lot of other people are stupid: "Voters – individually and in majorities – are as apt to be wrong about things as right about them, often vote from low motives such as bigotry and spite, and very often are contentedly ignorant." Williamson, "Why Not Fewer Voters?," *National Review*, April 6, 2021, www .nationalreview.com/2021/04/why-not-fewer-voters/.

[107] See Hélène Landemore, *Democratic Reason: Politics Collective Intelligence, and the Rule of the Many* (Princeton, NJ: Princeton University Press, 2013).

first-past-the-post election where the difference between winning by one vote or by a million votes is practically meaningless. When it becomes clear that one candidate or party has reached or will reach that quota, it would be rational for every subsequent voter to abstain. This is why, for instance, it can be hard to get people to the polls in California. As, however, recent years have shown, for elections to be won without the threat of protracted litigation or lingering illegitimacy, candidates need not only to win but also to win big. Peter Salib and Guha Krishnamurthi write that,

> the mechanics of post-election litigation complicate core assumptions of the traditional economic argument that voting to change outcomes is irrational. In particular, we show that it is not *just* the tipping-point, half-plus-one vote that affects an election's outcome. Rather, in reasonably close races, *many* votes have the potential to change the outcome. This changes the math substantially, making it possible that at least *some* votes should rationally be cast in expectation of having an electoral effect.[108]

Because, in other words, litigation and legitimacy questions have expanded the horizons of what counts as a meaningful vote in US elections, they have put pressure on logical assumptions that underwrite the economic paradox. What's more, if the effects of litigation and voter skepticism have altered the calculus of consent, the model works even less well with other kinds of elections: in ranked choice elections, in the proportional models I looked at in the previous chapter, in the "majority judgment" model recently proposed by Michel Balinski and Rida Laraki, and in others.[109] That's not to mention situations, like Australia's, where voting is compulsory and, thus, the question of voting-costs vs. voting-benefits is mooted. In all of these cases, votes are not wasted, or at least not wasted in the same way, because they are understood to count differently. They are valuable not simply because they get a candidate across a line, but because they also figure in a larger effort to represent and, as it were, to appreciate the preferences or the judgment of a group. Brennan's assumptions about the value of votes and his arguments about the nature of ignorance simply wouldn't work in elections where the meaning of a vote is explicitly neither strictly epistemic nor zero-

---

[108] Peter Salib and Guha Krishnamurthi, "Post-Election Litigation and the Paradox of Voting," forthcoming in *University of Chicago Law Review* and cited with authors' permission.

[109] See Balinski and Laraki, *Majority Judgment: Measuring, Ranking, and Electing* (Cambridge: The Massachusetts Institute of Technology Press, 2010).

sum. So, in short, the case for asking some putatively "ignorant" voters to abstain (DV_2) based on some asserted epistemic norm only works with some restricted kinds of election, and, even then, it doesn't work all that well.

3. Finally, because, as I have said, these accounts tend to restrict discussion of the opportunity costs of voting to "information costs," they strategically limit our sense of the meaning and the history of voting. If, that is, we did decide to restrict our definition of cost in this way, looking only at the time and effort taken by an individual to minimize ignorance about a given question or candidate, it would make the math a whole lot easier. Deciding to limit the meaning of "opportunity costs" to a single input would, in other words, allow one to sidestep knotty questions of transitivity and the interpersonal comparison of utilities that have otherwise bedeviled electoral theory. What's more, *information costs* are peculiar because of the degree to which they prioritize "personal responsibility" over social questions of equity and access. That is, even if it were the case that information about political decisions were equally available to all (and that, of course, is very far from being the case), managing that broadly available information still takes "time, trouble, and thought."[110] As a result, even were information made equally available to all, it would still make sense to ask whether or not it would be equally *rational* for everyone to make the same use of that available information. Limiting voter opportunity costs to information costs thus allows one to imagine that the paradox of voting would remain unchanged even in the face of increased equity amongst the different parts of an electorate. Putting aside the stark fact that radically unequal access to education and information is an endemic problem in the US and elsewhere, a more accurate reckoning with a range of voter opportunity costs would have to factor in questions of time, transportation, impact on wages and reputation, and conditions of basic access; that more accurate reckoning would, it seems to me, have to come to the conclusion that the best way to adjust the social imbalance between the costs and benefits of voting is not to encourage some significant percentage of the popular to abstain (DV_2), but rather to work to lower all of the assorted costs of voting: to make it easier to get to the polls, to have time to get to the polls, and to cast ballots when casting

---

[110] William Morris, "The Beauty of Life," in *The Collected Works of William Morris, Vol. 22*, ed. May Morris (London: Longmans, Green, & Company, 1910), 75.

ballots would otherwise be hard. Let me put it this way: If (1) there is, in fact, an imbalance between the social costs and the social benefits of voting and (2) the social benefits of voting are a fixed quantity, the (3) we can and should address the imbalance by working on what is *not* fixed: the social costs. This is, it seems to me, what Downs had in mind when he first observed the "paradox of voting," and coming to the other conclusion – that, because voting has been *made* difficult, the people for whom it has been made difficult should go ahead and not vote – is perverse, to say the least.

Taken together, questions about the costs, the benefits, and the ultimate rationality of voting must open up onto a set of larger and longer historical disputes about what a vote or an election could or should mean. Aside from dealing with problems *within* the rational choice account, we need also to remember how that account emerged as a specific and ideologically potent alternative to other, equally coherent models proposed by communitarians, welfare economists, socialists, and social democrats. That is, where classical liberalism and rational choice theorists tend to understand the vote as an expression of individual preference that is *like* one's individual preference for chicken or fish, two doors or four, Coke or Pepsi, others have imagined votes as performative and, as it were, provisional ways of signaling belonging to a community, nation, class, species, or even to a general will. Because these other models of election don't see the vote as an expression of individual preference, they aren't subject to the same assumptions that we find at work in Downs, Brennan, and others. I don't need necessarily to say here that one model is better than another; what I do need to say is that the existence of other at least logically coherent systems must make most universalizing claims about voting and rationality specious. I need also to say is that the difference between liberal and communitarian models for thinking about the meaning of a vote was enormously important to William Morris and that, as I will soon show, that difference shaped his thinking not only about politics but also about art and design.

DV₃: Don't Vote Because You're You

The third sense of Don't Vote! (DV$_3$) will require less discussion here both because I will come back to it in close detail in Chapter 4 and because its "logic" is so entirely stark. As we have seen in the US since Jim Crow and with renewed intensity in the wake of new voter suppression laws stemming from the bogus fraud claims of the 2020 election, any and every putative expansion of the franchise (to people of color, to women, to the working classes, etc.) tends to usher in immediate legal and extra-legal efforts to make voting harder and to say to potential new voters, Don't Vote![111] Although, as I suggested in the previous section, there are definite limits to the rational choice model, it can help to explain the logic consistently at work behind modern efforts at voter suppression and voter intimidation.

As opposed to *reducing* the social costs of voting in relation to its ostensibly fixed social benefits, voter-suppression tactics from the grotesque demands of Jim Crow county clerks to the litigious machinations of Hans von Spakovsky and John Fund, to more recent efforts on the part of State Legislators from Iowa, Arkansas, Georgia, Texas, and elsewhere have sought to make it more difficult for some people to vote and thus *to increase* social costs; and, because even "tiny variations in cost can sharply redistribute political power," poll taxes, literacy tests, voter-ID laws, restrictions on voting times, polling places, and absentee ballots, not to mention more blatant forms of extra-legal intimidation are likely to have a nonnegligible effect on how and in what numbers some people vote. While the starkest US efforts at voter suppression and intimidation have been aimed at communities of color, the longer international history of democratic elections shows that almost every expansion of the franchise has been followed by a reaction which, surprisingly or not, almost always takes the same form.[112] More voters thus tend to mean more rules; more rules mean higher opportunity costs for *some* voters; and higher opportunity costs for some voters mean fewer votes from those voters. As I said, I will come back more directly to the sordid history of voter suppression and voter intimidation in the Chapter 4. For now let me say, first, that in

---

[111] Referring to efforts on the part of members of the Arizona State Legislature, Arizona Secretary of State Katie Hobbs said, "What we are seeing this year, especially, is a Republican majority that has the closest margin that there's been in the legislature in decades. And the majority of that majority being dissatisfied with the outcome of the election and simply doing everything that they can to make it harder for people to vote." Quoted in Tierney Sneed and Matt Shuham, "How the Far-Right's Dream of Undermining Arizona's Mail Voting Turned into a Reality," *Talking Points Memo*, March 17, 2021, https://talkingpointsmemo.com/news/how-the-far-rights-dream-of-undermining-arizonas-mail-voting-turned-into-a-reality; see also Nolan D. McCaskill, "After Trump's Loss and False Fraud Claims, GOP Eyes Voter Restrictions across Nation," *Politico*, March 15, 2021, www.politico.com/news/2021/03/15/voting-restrictions-states-475732.

[112] Just for instance, in the 1860s and 1880s in Britain, members of Parliament faced with the economic expansion of the franchise began to wonder aloud about the competence of poorer voters and, even more, the likelihood that they would probably commit some kind of fraud. Don't forget the Tasmanian Dodge!

order to think properly about Morris's apparently blunt imperative, Don't Vote!, we need to think not only about the character of these different definitions but also about how they often rely on one another. Given the complex history of voting rights and ideas about the meaning and efficacy of votes in Britain, the US, and elsewhere, one has to see that any one intention behind Don't Vote! needs to be thought of in relation to some or all of the others.[113] Second, as I end this necessary digression and turn back to Morris and his own dogged efforts to define his socialism against the imperative to vote for members of Parliament or to lobby for the votes of members in Parliament, I'll want to understand what Don't Vote! meant to him.

English Questions

Of course, it makes sense that Morris and other British Socialists would have seen their politics in relation to procedural questions about who gets to vote, when they get to vote, and how they get to vote. Although the seemingly inevitable – if gradual and often bloody – extension of demo-cratic prerogatives and attendant calls for universal suffrage were, as Tocqueville had already seen in 1840, broadly endemic to the experience of European and American political modernity, nineteenth-century Britain seemed to have a special taste for thinking through the procedural niceties of elections. As Thomas Carlyle put it with characteristic disdain, "The English people are used to suffrage; it is their panacea for all that goes wrong with them; they have a fixed-idea of suffrage. Singular enough: one's right to vote for a Member of Parliament, to send one's 'twenty-thousandth part of a master of tongue-fence to National Palaver,' – the Doctors asserted that this was Freedom, this and no other."[114] This widely shared emphasis on the vote *qua* vote was partly a result of the lengthy and, as it were, slow-motion character of British electoral reform. Although

---

[113] For instance, Morris's sometimes writing partner E. Belfort Bax employs the "epistocratic" logic of what I've called DV_2 in order to strengthen the socialist case for DV_1: "Supposing there were a referendum or poll of all the people of England to-morrow, it would be of little avail on any but the very simplest issue. For so long as there is inequality of education and of natural conditions and the majority are at a disadvantage in respect of these things, they are necessarily incapable of weighing the issue before them. Their very wants are but vaguely present to their minds and in their judgment as to the means of satisfying them they are at the mercy of every passing wind." Bax, "The Will of the Majority," in *The Ethics of Socialism* (London: Swan Sonnenschein & Co., 1902), 121.

[114] Thomas Carlyle, "Parliamentary Radicalism," in *Chartism and Past and Present* (London: Chapman & Hall, 1870), 55.

politicians and commentators regularly returned to the anxious and stadial
language of an electoral "leap into the dark," the protracted and prolonged
movement through distinct but overlapping periods of reform (1832,
1867, 1872, 1884, 1918, 1928, with many minor adjustments in between)
kept the everyday details of elections and parliamentary design at the
forefront of English political thought for at least a century.

We can, for instance, see both the fact and the extent of this influence in
the experience and afterlives of Chartism. Part of what differentiated
Chartism from contemporary movements on the European Left was not
only its particular relationship to questions of democratic representation
writ large but also its attention to the fine-grained details of electoral
procedure. Consider, for example, that the published *People's Charter* of
1838 opens not with the stirring language of truths held self-evident or of
specters haunting Europe, but with a highly detailed and schematic
rendering of a "Balloting Place" and a "Ballot Box." Here, then, is another
instance of the at once pragmatic and yet "suppositional" imaginative
intensity that I described in Chapter 2. This emphasis on the mechanics
of the vote was, says Dorothy Thompson, the result partly of the fact that
"the provincial leadership of early Chartism was to a very large extent
recruited from men whose reputations as 'town radicals' was based on the
manhood suffrage movement in the Reform Bill period, and who had a
continuous history of agitating on radical issues in the years between."[115]
And, although Chartism faded quickly as a coordinated national movement, its effects and, perhaps, something of its style returned in the 1860s
to exert an influence not only on the English working Left, where
"Chartist memories had not disappeared," but also on Gladstonian
Liberalism, for which "Chartism received a certain aura of respectability
[as it offered] a contrast between the bad old days of the Corn Laws and
the blessings of free trade."[116] Put simply, the vote *qua* vote stood at the
center of the English political imaginary, and so it makes sense that, when
early converts like Hyndman and others sought to define themselves as
English Socialists, they would see the vote as having both a considerable
pragmatic and a symbolic power. It made sense that, for Hyndman – who,
unlike Morris, retained warm feelings for Britain's imperial grandeur –
voting was a political necessity as well as a charged ethical, symbolic, and
national value.

---

[115] Dorothy Thompson, *The Dignity of Chartism* (London: Verso Books, 2015), PAGE.
[116] Thompson, *Dignity of Chartism*.

Despite a tendency to associate him with the broadly middlebrow pleasures of rolling meadows, medieval workshops, museum gift shops, and going "round the Maypole high," Morris's socialism was, as opposed to Hyndman's, resolutely international. His first entry into practical politics came with his unexpected participation in the Eastern Question Association (EQA). Appalled at reports of the Turkish abuse of Bulgarian Christians, wary of rising jingoist support for imperial war against Russia, and stirred by Gladstone's 1874 pamphlet, *The Bulgarian Horrors and the Question of the East*, Morris threw himself wholeheartedly into the movement, giving speeches, writing letters, and even becoming the EQA's treasurer. Although the issue was a Liberal *cause célèbre*, one that not only resuscitated Gladstone's moribund career but also attracted the high-profile support of Ruskin, Carlyle, Rossetti, and others, Morris took the thing up with characteristically all-in intensity: "I who am writing this," he said in a letter to *The Daily News*, "am one of a large class of men – quiet men, who usually go about their own business, heeding public matters less than they ought, and afraid to speak in such a huge concourse as the English nation, however much they may feel, but who are now stung into bitterness by thinking how helpless they are in a public matter that touches them so closely."[117] Despite its strong start, the EQA quickly lost steam. After reaping its immediate political benefits and feeling a jingoist shift in the winds of national sentiment, Gladstone lost his taste for the issue and hung increasingly back from public events. And even A. J. Mundella, the Radical MP for Sheffield and Chairman of the EQA's Executive Committee, seemed to lose his nerve: "I have had a sleepless night," he wrote after a setback, "and feel a weaker man in *every way* this morning, but I shall put a good face on it, and go into the fight following my own convictions regardless of all consequences."[118] As E. P. Thompson notes, "Such professions – as is usual with politicians – were a prelude to his backing out altogether."[119] Morris, who had given his ingenuous all to the cause, took the inevitable break-up and betrayal of the movement especially hard, feeling "full of shame and anger at the cowardice of the

---

[117] William Morris, *The Collected Letters of William Morris, Volume I: 1848–1880*, ed. Norman Kelvin (Princeton, NJ: Princeton University Press, 2016), 325. E. P. Thompson writes that, "Gladstone, who had retired in a disgruntled mood from the leadership of the Liberal Party after his defeat in 1874, saw in the popular agitation a matchless opportunity for rehabilitating the Party and strengthening his own hand against the aristocratic Whigs, Lords Hartington and Granville, who had resumed its leadership." E. P. Thompson, *William Morris: Romantic to Revolutionary* (Oakland, CA: PM Press, 2011), 205.

[118] Quoted in Thompson, *William Morris*, 222.   [119] Thompson, *William Morris*, 222.

so-called Liberal party."[120] "This," concludes Thompson, "was Morris's first introduction to the political world. It was an experience which was likely either to teach him many lessons or to drive him off in disgust."[121]

I want to highlight two aspects of this first, thwarted brush with political organization and agitation. Morris's sharp and, importantly, his *shamed* sense of disillusionment is crucial here (the word "shame" appears something like ten times in his brief letter to the *Daily News*). Morris came away from the EQA not merely with a sense of the practical limits of parliamentary parties but also with a feeling that he had been made a fool. That wasn't going to happen again. And, although the EQA came to grief, Morris never lost his establishing sense of politics as necessarily international and anti-imperial; although he had still much to say about Hyde Park, what Matthew Arnold was up to, and the discovery of "Coal in Kent," his emphases and outlook in *Commonweal* remained defined by a series of events and ideas that exceeded any narrowly English frame: the Paris Commune, the experiences of expatriate Russian and Austrian comrades like Sergius Stepniak and Andreas Scheu, Irish home rule, Stanley's atrocities in Congo, the trial of the Haymarket Anarchists in Chicago, and so on. This meant, first, that despite Morris's considerable, even overwhelming love for English craft, culture, and history, he didn't – with a few exceptions – identify much with a local radical tradition that ran from the Levellers through the Chartists to the trade unions, parliamentary radicals, and, in time, to the Labour Party.[122] Second, because Morris understood socialism as an essentially international movement, he saw individual parliaments, national governments, and even the promise of "State Socialism" necessarily as impediments to struggle. Because revolution had to exceed the context of the nation and its institutions, even well-meaning efforts to make use of those institutions would strengthen them and, thus, defer a reckoning with the brutal character of either nationalism or international capitalism: "all the rivalries of nations have been reduced to this one – a degraded struggle for their share of the spoils of barbarous countries to be used at home for the purpose of increasing the riches of the rich and the poverty of the poor."[123] No matter how helpful in the short term, national governments were means antithetical to what Morris understood as the only possible end of socialism: "a change,"

---

[120] Thompson, *William Morris*, 220.   [121] Thompson, *William Morris*, 225.

[122] See Morris's passing – and often slighting – comments on the Levellers, the Chartists, etc. in Morris and Bax, *Socialism*.

[123] William Morris, "The Manifesto of the Socialist League," in William Morris, *Journalism: Contributions to Commonweal, 1885–1890*, ed. Nicholas Salmon (Bristol: Thoemmes Press, 1996), 4.

he wrote in the *Manifesto of the Socialist League*, "which would destroy the distinctions of classes and nationalities."[124] And, imperialism, he said, "is simply the agony of capitalism driven by a force it cannot resist to seek for new and ever new markets at any price and any risk."

The Strange Game

In *News from Nowhere*, the time-traveling William Guest is walking through the future streets of London with his new friend and guide, the handsome Dick. "Why," he exclaims, "there are the Houses of Parliament! Do you still use them?" After laughing out loud, Dick gets hold of himself and responds:

> I take you, neighbour; you may well wonder at our keeping them standing, and I know something about that, and my old kinsman has given me books to read about the strange game that they played there. Use them! Well, yes, they are used for a sort of subsidiary market, and a storage place for manure, and they are handy for that, being on the waterside.[125]

After his dispiriting experience with Gladstone, Mundella, and the EQA, Morris never lost his conviction that Parliament was of an essentially bad odor; and, if you spend your time in a shit house, you will end up smelling like shit. That said, although Morris saw Parliament as fundamentally abject, he could never really look away. Although one might have imagined that he would ignore the details of a parliamentary politics that he saw as feckless at best, quite the opposite was true: despite – or maybe because of – his disgust at Parliament as an institution, Morris followed its movements, foibles, and intrigues with a rubbernecker's eye for grisly detail. As is clear from his hundreds of entries in the regular "Notes on News" section of *Commonweal*, he was in fact a dedicated and canny reader of political reporting in *The Times*, *The Pall Mall Gazette*, and *The Daily News*. In her footnotes to Morris's briefly-kept *Socialist Diary* of 1887, Boos writes that Morris was especially fond of the *Daily News*. "Its emotional, editorializing tone brought out responsive traits in his character, and he engaged in a daily struggle with its contents. Although of course he disapproved of its hostility to Socialism, he tended to accept its interpretations ... of parliamentary and foreign events."[126]

---

[124] Morris, "Manifesto of the Socialist League," 3.
[125] William Morris, *News from Nowhere*, in *The Collected Works of William Morris, Vol. 16*, ed. May Morris (London: Longmans, Green, & Company, 1910), 32.
[126] *William Morris's Socialist Diary*, ed. Florence Boos (London: The Journeyman Press, 1985), 20.

Because some of Morris's best and best-known socialist writings (*A Dream of John Ball, News from Nowhere, Socialism from the Root Up*, etc.) appeared there first, it can be easy to overlook his *other* work for *Commonweal*: the truly enormous amount of occasional journalism he managed to produce especially after the paper moved from a monthly to a weekly format on May 1, 1886. Although these short and sharply critical entries were by design less consequential than his longer prose pieces, Morris's weekly observations on current events, sustained without pause over several years, were work that undoubtedly defined his everyday experience of being a socialist. Always presented as a running series of a dozen or so discrete paragraphs, each separated by a single centered line, the "Notes on News" section was usually the first thing readers would see when they picked the journal up, a design decision that contributed to the urgency, the immediacy, the *presentness* of the paper as a whole.[127] Sometimes individual paragraphs would stand alone as quick and brutal takes on Gladstone, the Suez Canal, the Bishop of Limerick, a poisoning in Chiswick, or "a show of pet dogs . . . at St. Stephen's Hall"; at other times, three or more paragraphs would add up to make an improvised short essay on Home Rule, Free Speech, or, in one instance, the *real* meaning of Albrecht Dürer's "Knight and Death": "The armed man on the war-horse is riding towards no victory, but a shameful death; he has come to the 'net end of all his villanies'; and the awful *thing* that follows him is a tangible image of the crimes of his past life; his greed, rapine, cruelty, fraud, and reckless violence."[128]

In a way, the literalized line breaks that punctuate Morris's continuous and yet oddly arhythmic performance in "Notes on News" anticipate what Alex Woloch has cast as the similarly broken prose form of the weekly column George Orwell published in the *Tribune* between 1943 and 1947:

> In organizing the columns around these gaps, Orwell subtly moves a break that rests outside the text (that looming imperative, imposed on newspaper writing, to end according to an imminent deadline) into the column itself. The internal truncations work, in this way, to register the present, but only unsatisfactorily or incompletely so – almost grasping that exteriority *most* inexpressible within the weekly column (as these breaks limn the very contours *of* the column form) and fragmenting writerly expression in the process.[129]

---

[127] The section, which often also included paragraphs from other contributors, was initially called "Notes on Passing Events" until early 1887 when it became "Notes on News," which it remained until after Morris left *Commonweal* more than three years later.

[128] William Morris, "Notes on News," in William Morris, *Journalism: Contributions to Commonweal, 1885–1890*, ed. Nicholas Salmon (Bristol: Thoemmes Press, 1996), 204.

[129] Alex Woloch, *Or Orwell: Writing and Democratic Socialism* (Cambridge, MA: Harvard University Press, 2016), 199.

In "Notes on News," Morris's line breaks do a similar kind of work as, on the one hand, they solidify the critical standpoint of the socialist critic who can survey the field as some kind of totality and thus see how the apparently disconnected parts hang really together – can thus see what show dogs have to do with Suez – and, on the other hand, they embody and heighten the status of the capitalist present as immanently incoherent, disjointed, and riven with the contradictions that Morris understood as the proper objects of socialist theory, analysis, and practice.[130]

As it appeared first in *Commonweal*, I think we need to read the title of *News from Nowhere* alongside "Notes on News" and to see the resonance between them in two ways. First, we need to understand that *News from Nowhere* is itself a lot more topical than it might otherwise seem; references to Parliament as a manure house, to the heated arguments taking place "up at the league," to the imagined revolutionary events of 1952 were aimed first at a very particular readership steeped in the investments, gossip, and intraparty conflicts that had defined British socialism in the 1880s. Second, the "news" in *News from Nowhere* is, I think, meant to stand as an explicit and dialectical alternative to its printed neighbor: the "news" in "Notes on News." An example of a more general "osmosis between journalism and fiction within the socialist periodical," it represents, on the one hand, a historical break between the conflicts of a fractured capitalist present and the coherence and utopian promise of the commu-nist future: someday, Morris seems to suggest, the news will be different and better.[131] On the other hand, the title also represents an important kind of historical continuity; although the news will be different and better, it will still be the news: whatever else it is, the future will be detailed, pragmatic, interesting, and real. It will be historical. I'll come back to this relation between details and utopia in Morris shortly.

If Morris's general distaste for Parliament first took hold after his demoralizing experience with the EQA, it was solidified as a necessary and necessarily socialist *strategy* in the wake of the "Tory Gold" episode of 1885, in which "it was revealed that two S.D.F. candidates, Jack Williams

---

[130] We might take this as the textual or editorial equivalent of an urge that Matthew Beaumont takes as characteristic of nineteenth-century utopian thinking and writing, the urge "to totalize a fragmentary and reified society by seeing it from the standpoint of an alternative future." Matthew Beaumont, *Utopia Ltd.: Ideologies of Social Dreaming in England 1870–1900* (Chicago: Haymarket Books, 2009), 171.

[131] Deborah Mutch goes on to note that "a great deal of contemporary history was absorbed and re-narrated within the serialized socialist fiction at the end of the nineteenth century." Mutch, "Re-Righting the Past: Socialist Historical Narrative and the Road to the New Life," *Literature & History* 18(1) (Spring 2009), 17.

in Hampstead and John Fielding in Kensington, had been funded by the Tories to 'make running' (as Morris put it) for the Tories by spoiling the Liberal vote."[132] It came out that Hyndman and his right-hand man, Henry Hyde Champion, had accepted £340 from the intrepid Maltman Barry, who managed somehow to live both as a Marxist and yet also as a paid agent for the Tory party; "Citizen Barry," who had been there "with Karl Marx and . . . the First International Working Men's Association" in 1871, was said to be "the most Marxian of Tories and the Toryest of Marxians."[133] The affair seriously dented the reputations of both Hyndman and the erstwhile Champion, and it "produced a general feeling of disgust."[134] Champion was especially damaged by the event: H. W. Lee described him in *Justice*, the official journal of the SDF, as having been an "earnest, self-sacrificing, hard-working and single-hearted comrade" until his "fatal intimacy [with] Mr. Maltman Barry," whom Lee cast as a "mephistophelian influence."[135] Mark Bevir writes that, in later years, "Champion was . . . notorious for his part in the 1885 scandal over Tory Gold in the S.D.F."[136] Morris, as we have seen, took the whole affair as confirmation that socialism and parliamentary ambition don't mix, and the Fabian Annie Besant used it to humiliate a hapless member of the SDF: "Force indeed! What is your revolutionary strength in London; may we not gauge it by your fifty votes or so, at the late Election – and bought and paid for with Tory gold?"[137] In the aftermath of this episode, Champion and Barry went together to join Keir Hardie's Independent Labour Party, where they continued to be regularly suspected of working secretly with and for the Tories in order to "nobble" the Lib-Labs.

Spoilers

Although we might want to dismiss the Tory Gold scandal as an unseemly but trivial passage in the up-and-down history of the British Left, I think that it did more to cement Morris's resistance to parliamentary tactics, and it did so for a more precise, technical, and, as it were, logical reason.

[132] MacCarthy, *William Morris*, 533.
[133] W. Hamish Fraser, *Scottish Popular Politics* (Edinburgh: Edinburgh University Press, 2001), 136.
[134] Paul Thompson, *The Work of William Morris* (New York: Viking Press, 1967), 203.
[135] A. E. P. Duffy, "Differing Policies and Personal Rivalries in the Origins of the Independent Labour Party," *Victorian Studies* 6(1) (September 1962), 46.
[136] Bevir, *Making of British Socialism*, 208.
[137] "The Fabian Society – Nationalizing Accumulated Wealth," *The Practical Socialist* 1(1) (January 1886), 15.

Indeed, it brings him closer to Carroll. When Barry shifted resources from the Tories to the SDF to hurt the Liberals, he was engaged in a kind of strategic vote splitting, an effort to introduce or to assist a third "spoiler" candidate in order only to weaken one of the first two. He thus introduced or, rather, exploited a basic means-ends problem in elections: although we tend to imagine support for a candidate as a narrow means to a specific end (the eventual election of the supported candidate), it can, under certain circumstances, make perverse sense to support *another* candidate in order really to support your own. The putative means thus become alienated from the real ends. Of course, the real, imagined, or manufactured threat of third-party spoilers has been a perennial part of electoral systems. Remember, just for instance, Ross Perot in 1992, Ralph Nader in 2000, and Jill Stein in 2016; and, when Kanye West announced his quixotic run for president in 2020, *The New York Times* reported that, "Because a variety of allies and supporters of President Trump [were] working on the ground to advance his campaign, many Democrats [viewed] his candidacy as a dirty trick by Republicans."[138] Although easy to dismiss as a "dirty trick" or a bad joke, it's important to see the practical appeal, the cold rationality, and even the historical inevitability of these and other kinds of strategic voting. Although we might want people simply to vote their conscience, to match their means to their ends, if some voters know or can guess how other voters will vote and, moreover, can *use* that knowledge to help their preferred candidate, it is, perhaps, unreasonable to expect them to act as if they didn't know what in fact they do.

Imagine, for instance, I'm asked to rank my preference between options **A**, **B**, and **C**, and I happen to like them in just that order: **A**>**B**>**C**. It would seem logical to simply state as much, just as it would have seemed logical for Barry to have supported the Tories if what he really wanted was for the Tories to win. The problem, however, is that if I *really* prefer **A**, but have a feeling that the impressive **B** might have an edge over **A**, voting

---

[138] Danny Hakim and Maggie Haberman, "Kanye West's Perplexing Run as a Potential 2020 Spoiler," *The New York Times*, September 16, 2020, www.nytimes.com/2020/09/16/us/politics/kanye-west-president-2020.html. In 2020, Frank Artiles, a Florida Republican operative, paid a friend $50,000 to change his party affiliation from Republican to Independent and to have his name included on a state senatorial ballot in order to "siphon off votes" from the Democratic incumbent. The plan worked: "In November, Senator Rodríguez, an effective legislator who had crusaded for Florida to face the climate change crisis, lost to the Republican challenger, Ileana Garcia, by a mere 32 votes out of more than 215,000 that had been cast. Alex Rodriguez had received 6,382 votes and played the spoiler." Patricia Mazzei, "How a Sham Candidate Helped Flip a Florida Election," *The New York Times*, March 19, 2021, www.nytimes.com/2021/03/19/us/florida-senate-race-fraud.html.

sincerely might not achieve my preferred result. I might, in that case, think it best to vote **A**>**C**>**B** even if I think that **B** is nearly as good as **A** and that **C** is a truly terrible or even dangerous candidate. While such a ranking doesn't reflect my real feelings, it would increase the likelihood of my preferred outcome; the false vote would, in some practical sense, be truer to my preference, if not to my beliefs. You'll remember that Lewis Carroll identified exactly this strategy as a problematic rule: "In any division taken on a pair of issues neither of which you desire, vote against the most popular."[139] Some version of this problem is *probably* present in all voting systems: sometimes the best way to get what I really want is, paradoxically, to act *as if* I wanted something else.[140] "In essentially all voting systems," says Jon Elster, "situations can arise in which a voter, by voting for an alternative other than her first-ranked one, can bring about an outcome that she prefers to the one that would have occurred had she voted sincerely."[141]

This is an especially hard problem for democracy because it forces the voter to negotiate a relation between two real, different, and sometimes incommensurate imperatives: the imperative, on the one hand, to represent one's preference honestly and the imperative, on the other, to see one's preference realized. For Morris this problem was even harder. Part of what defined his politics was the sense that socialist practice was first and foremost ways to counter and, at last, to overcome the alienated and essential falseness of the age, a falseness he saw at work, as E. P.

---

[139] Carroll, *Political Pamphlets and Letters*, 57.

[140] "It can be shown," writes David Miller, "that there is virtually no decision rule that is not vulnerable to strategic manipulation if some voters choose to act in this way." Miller, "Deliberative Democracy and Social Choice," in *Democracy*, ed. David Estlund (Oxford: Blackwell, 2002), 294.

[141] Elster, *Explaining Social Behavior*, 410. Exactly this situation is used at the start of Robert Downey's 1969 satire, *Putney Swope*. Immediately after the chairman of the board of a New York advertising agency drops dead at a meeting, the surviving members vote to replace him: "The corporate bylaws make it very clear that the only way we can determine a new chairman is by democratic process. Paragraph 68 specifically states that nobody can vote for himself. That's what it says, so that's where it's at." After the votes are counted, Putney Swope, the lone Black member of the board, is elected nine votes to two: "We all voted for him because we thought no one else would vote for him." In other words, because everyone wanted to win, but no one could vote for himself (the board is entirely male), they all voted for Swope assuming, because they themselves were racists, that the racism of the other members would mean that a vote for Swope was a vote for an unelectable candidate and, thus, not really a vote against themselves. The plan backfires, and Swope takes over the agency, changing its name to Truth and Soul and making it, at least initially, into a revolutionary and antiracist collective. Although the racial and radical politics of *Putney Swope* are a mess, to say the least, its establishing reliance on a failed effort at strategic voting makes a suggestive case for the relation between race, desire, late capitalism, and social choice at the tail end of the 1960s. I'll come back to some of this in the next chapter.

Thompson puts it, in "the squalor and anarchy which he passed through in London and the great towns," in "the degradation of its architecture," and in "the sham and hypocrisy pervading its manners and thought."[142] "It is a shoddy age," said Morris. "Shoddy is king. From the statesman to the shoemaker, all is shoddy!"[143] The problem with political representation in Parliament was, in that case, not only that Liberals, Tories, and Radicals were equally in the mediated thrall of their party interests as opposed to the immediate interests of the people, but also that the nature of electoral representation forced even the most sincere voters to live insincerely: representation was shoddy.[144] Because, explains Morris, parliamentary socialists need to put election and re-election ahead of organization and education, they have to put the *game* of winning votes and making majorities ahead of the *work* of "making socialists," e.g., the work of helping to catalyze the as-yet quiescent class-consciousness – what E.P. Thompson would later call the "nameless solidarities" – of the proletariat.[145] As a result, parliamentary socialists had to tell voters (who are not yet socialists) what they *wanted* to hear rather than what they *needed* to hear:

> starting from the same point as the abstentionists they have to preach an electioneering campaign as an absolute necessity, and to set about it as soon as possible: they will then have to put forward a programme of reforms deduced from the principles of Socialism, which we will admit they will always keep to the front as much as possible; they will necessarily have to appeal for support (i.e. votes) to a great number of people who are not convinced Socialists, and their programme of reforms will be the bait to catch those votes: and to the ordinary voter it will be this bait which will be the matter of interest, and not the principle for whose furtherance they will be interested to act as the instrument . . . it will [as a result] be impossible to deal with him honestly.[146]

To "catch" votes, the socialist candidate would need to represent their real beliefs as something different from or something simpler than what they

---

[142] Thompson, *William Morris*, 40.

[143] From a 1892 interview with William Morris, by "Quinbus Flestrin" for the *Clarion*; quoted in Thompson, *William Morris*, 108.

[144] Joseph Schumpeter paraphrased the purist's position with characteristic neatness: "mere political democracy is of necessity a sham." Schumpeter, *Capitalism, Socialism, and Democracy* (New York: Harper Perennial, 2008), 235.

[145] Quoted in Tim Rogan, *The Moral Economists: R. H. Tawney, Karl Polanyi, E. P. Thompson, and the Critique of Capitalism* (Princeton, NJ: Princeton University Press, 2017), 156.

[146] William Morris, "The Policy of Abstention," in *How I Became a Socialist*, ed. Owen Hatherly and Owen Holland (London: Verso Books, 2020), 138–139.

really were. Because even honest politicians have to fool voters in order to win their votes, the voters would become fools and not socialists. For Morris's socialist, to vote was to accept a lie.

Adam Przeworski argues in *Capitalism and Social Democracy* that this problem was as much mathematical as ethical. Because "the prediction that the displaced members of the old middle classes would either become proletarians or join the army of the unemployed did not materialize," "the proletariat was not and never became a numerical majority of voting members of any society."[147] As a result, it was simply not possible to imagine a situation in which parliamentary representatives of the proletariat could hope to lay claim to a secure voting majority within any Parliament. Without even the dimmest prospect of claiming that institutional power, socialist representatives would have necessarily to compromise and to form coalitions with other representatives whose interests could not align directly with the interests of the working class.

> Electoral success requires that class structure be conceptualized in terms of propensity of mobilization and support; it requires socialist parties to adhere to the broadest conceivable concept of the proletariat and even to go beyond this broad concept by emphasizing similar life situations and 'parallel interests.' In search for electoral support socialist parties appeal to members of other classes as they organize workers into a class.[148]

> It is now clear that the dilemma comes back with a vengeance within the very system of electoral competition. The choice between class purity and broad support must be lived continually by social democratic parties because when they attempt to increase their electoral support beyond the working class these parties reduce their capacity to mobilize workers.[149]

For Morris, who clearly saw and anticipated Przeworski's dilemma, parliamentarianism wasn't a better or worse tactical choice; it was, rather the institutional embodiment of contradictions that both characterized and maimed the present: "electioneering," he wrote in an open letter signed in 1885 by the members of the new Socialist League, "would have deprived us of the due services of some of our most energetic men by sending them to our sham parliament, there to become either nonentities, or perhaps our masters, and it may be our betrayers."[150]

---

[147] Adam Przeworski, *Capitalism and Social Democracy* (Cambridge: Cambridge University Press, 1985), 23.
[148] Przeworski, *Capitalism and Social Democracy*, 75.
[149] Przeworski, *Capitalism and Social Democracy*, 28.
[150] Quoted in Kapp, *Eleanor Marx*, Vol. 2, 64.

Just as the Tory Gold episode revealed the strategic compulsion potentially at work in the logic of all elections, so did the experience of socialists running for Parliament and the necessary confusion of means and ends that went along with it suggest to Morris not only that ambitious politicians might occasionally fall into dishonesty but also that the representative core of parliamentary democracy was itself a lie; or, rather, it was a form that, because it put life at odds with itself, was essentially indirect and duplicitous. If the point of socialism was to make it possible to work and to live truly, any political system that relied, first, on the willful confusion of ends and means and, second, on a fissure between the free and authentic intention of an individual and that intention's necessarily distorted appearance in the carnival mirror of party politics was not only tactically resistant to socialist values but also logically antithetical to socialism as such. Morris wrote with Bax,

> Thus is carried out the crowning sham of modern politics under the absurd title of Representative Government, and the name of democracy is used to cloak an oligarchy more or less extended, while once more all decent people who may profess an interest in politics are expected to range themselves under one or other of the great political parties, now become almost less than mere names, the very shadows of shadows.[151]

Small Is Beautiful

Although he had more in common, both politically and temperamentally, with his friend Peter Kropotkin than with Hyndman and others at the SDF, Morris was not himself an anarchist.[152] Although he refused what he saw as Parliament's interested abuse of authority, he was against neither social authority nor even coercion *as such*:

> experience shows us that wherever a dozen thoughtful men shall meet together there will be twelve different opinions on any subject which is not a dry matter of fact (and often on that too); and if those twelve men want to act together, there must be give and take between them, and they

---

[151] Morris and Bax, *Socialism*, 13.

[152] The question of how exactly to define Morris's politics is and has been an open one. He has been associated with socialism, communism, anarchism, anarcho-communism; he's been cast as a Marxian, a proto-Marxian, a post-Marxian; and while some see his position as dreamily utopian, others see it as pragmatic to a fault and still others take it as mere nostalgia. While these debates are interesting and do a lot to get at the history both of the British Left and the critical reception of Morris and the Arts and Crafts movement, it seems to me that Morris – as I've tried to show – was actually pretty clear about what he stood for.

must agree on some common rule of conduct to act as a bond between them, or leave their business undone. And what is this common bond but authority – that is, the conscience of the association voluntarily accepted in the first instance.[153]

"The fatal flaw of anarchism," says Ruth Kinna, "was illustrated, he suggested, by the inability of anarchists to show how individuals might enter into a process of decision-making and, therefore to develop any practical socialist alternative."[154] The question for Morris was, thus, how to imagine institutional rules that would allow individuals to resolve conflicts and to realize practical consensus *without* the alienating indirection of political representation.

Of course, Morris's long experience as a businessman, an editor, and a political organizer had given him practical insight into the difficult art of herding cats. As Michael Martel argues, Morris's various disputes with others in the SDF and the Socialist League had made him keenly and *imaginatively* aware of the need for modes of administration that might split the difference between practical management and local autonomy. On the one hand, this took the form of Morris's ultimately doomed efforts to sustain the League's defining and, as it were, centralized antipathy to parliamentary politics while acknowledging the differences of opinion that began to emerge within the League's various branches. It was this tension that led to the defection of Marx and Aveling's Bloomsbury faction. On the other hand, if the practical realization of a working system of management was harder than it looked, Morris also turned – in the mode *almost* of involuntary and compensatory wish fulfillment – to imaginative, past and future representations of collective action. He turned, oddly enough, to the mote. Martel writes:

> Believed to be the primary mode of British governance before the Norman invasion, the mote represented to Victorian advocates of local self-governance an institution rich with associations of Anglo-Saxon self-determination and anti-centralism. Until the eleventh century, the mote served as an assembly wherein a locality's citizens would collectively deliberate upon courses of action affecting the entire community. According to George Laurence Gomme, the ancient folk mote served as the "primary

---

[153] William Morris, "On Communism and Anarchism," in *How I Became a Socialist*, ed. Owen Hatherly and Owen Holland (London: Verso Books, 2020), 161. Morris's example, of course, anticipates the opening frame narrative of *News from Nowhere*.

[154] Ruth Kinna, "Anarchism, Individualism, and Communism: William Morris's Critique of Anarcho-Communism," in *Libertarian Socialism: Politics in Black and Red*, ed. Alex Prichard, Ruth Kinna, Saku Pinta, and David Berry (London: Palgrave Macmillan, 2012), 36.

assembly composed of all the thanes of the shire, and not a representative assembly composed of elected members."[155]

As proof of a real or imaginary but certainly an *other* time's better ability to manage people and their preferences, the mote appears again and again in Morris's late work; "for Morris," says Martel, "the archaic folk mote offered a model for communistic self-governance, both locally and trans-locally."[156]

The mote occupies the social and procedural center of Morris's 1889 proto-fantasy novel, *The House of the Wolfings*:

> Yet you must not think that their solemn councils were held there, the folk-motes whereat it must be determined what to do and what to forbear doing; for according as such councils, (which they called Things) were of the House or of the Mid-mark or of the whole Folk, were they held each at the due Thing-steads in the Wood aloof from either acre or meadow, (as was the custom of our forefathers for long after) and at such Things would all the men of the House or the Mid-mark or the Folk be present man by man.[157]

The mote-form, although not named as such, returns in *A Dream of John Ball*, which opens with "a goodish many people" "coming into the village street ... by twos and threes," a more or less spontaneous gathering that will lead to the Peasants' Revolt of 1381. Finally, and probably most importantly, the mote turns out to be the better form eventually redis-covered by the dreamt future in *News from Nowhere*; as Guest's tutor, the old man Hammond, explains (I'll quote this passage at some length):

---

[155] Michael Martel, "Romancing the Folk Mote: William Morris, the Socialist League, and Local Direct Democracy," in *Useful and Beautiful: Newsletter of the William Morris Society* (Summer 2018), 11.

[156] Martel, "Romancing the Folk Mote," 7.

[157] In a discussion of the origins of democracy in Europe, the democratic theorist Robert Dahl writes, "In the ... town of Steinkjer [in Norway] you can still see a boat-shaped ring of large stones where Viking freemen regularly met from about 600 CE to 1000 CE to hold an adjudicative assembly called in Norse a *Ting*. ... At the meeting of the Ting the freemen settled disputes; discussed, accepted, and rejected laws; adopted or turned down a proposed change of religion ... and even elected or gave approval to a king – who was often required to swear his faithfulness to the laws approved by the Ting." Robert A. Dahl, *On Democracy, Second Edition: With a New Preface and Two New Chapters by Ian Shapiro* (New Haven, CT: Yale University Press, 2015), 18. And Hélène Landemore uses a similar example at the start of her *Open Democracy*: "To the Icelandic Vikings, who invented a different form of it in Northern Europe ... democracy meant gathering every summer in a large field south of Reykjavik known as Thingvellir, the place of their annual parliament, and talking things through until they reached decisions about their common fate." Landemore, *Open Democracy: Reinventing Popular Rule for the Twenty-First Century* (Princeton, NJ: Princeton University Press, 2020), 1.

"Well," said he, "let us take one of our units of management, a commune, or a ward, or a parish (for we have all three names, indicating little real distinction between them now, though time was there was a good deal). In such a district, as you would call it, some neighbours think that something ought to be done or undone: a new town-hall built; a clearance of inconvenient houses; or say a stone bridge substituted for some ugly old iron one, – there you have undoing and doing in one. Well, at the next ordinary meeting of the neighbours, or Mote, as we call it, according to the ancient tongue of the times before bureaucracy, a neighbour proposes the change, and of course, if everybody agrees, there is an end of discussion, except about details. Equally, if no one backs the proposer, – 'seconds him,' it used to be called – the matter drops for the time being; a thing not likely to happen amongst reasonable men, however, as the proposer is sure to have talked it over with others before the Mote. But supposing the affair proposed and seconded, if a few of the neighbours disagree to it, if they think that the beastly iron bridge will serve a little longer and they don't want to be bothered with building a new one just then, they don't count heads that time, but put off the formal discussion to the next Mote; and meantime arguments *pro* and *con* are flying about, and some get printed, so that everybody knows what is going on; and when the Mote comes together again there is a regular discussion and at last a vote by show of hands. If the division is a close one, the question is again put off for further discussion; if the division is a wide one, the minority are asked if they will yield to the more general opinion, which they often, nay, most commonly do. If they refuse, the question is debated a third time, when, if the minority has not perceptibly grown, they always give way; though I believe there is some half-forgotten rule by which they might still carry it on further; but I say, what always happens is that they are convinced, not perhaps that their view is the wrong one, but they cannot persuade or force the community to adopt it."[158]

There are a few things to notice about the passage.

First, despite the reasonable impression that Morris's socialism was really just a stalking horse for his hoary Englishness, his masculinist craftsman's nostalgia, or, to use Wendy Brown's resonant phrase, his growing "left melancholy," this account of the mote doesn't really feel like it is *only* a comforting return to an old and trusted model.[159] While the *word* is old, Hammond's use of it seems less rooted in a longed-for return to a more authentic past than it is proof of the form's dialectical play of recognition and alterity, its active and, as it were, argumentative difference from the structural as opposed to the temporal limits of "bureaucracy"; the word works, that is, as a means of imaginatively suturing the future to the

---

[158] Morris, *News from Nowhere*, 103.   [159] Quoted Rogan, *Moral Economists*, 171.

past so as to define and reject the capitalist present. With this Hammond offers a historical example of what John Plotz has identified as an *emergent residualism* that animates Morris's thinking about design and typography. He writes:

> Morris wants to make use of a fixed and available past in order to create, and play around with, a flexible and protean present, but his conception of the present design work always strives to retain within it a sense both of the real nature of the dimly discernible past and of the innovations and originality that are required to make a new manifestation that effectively recreates some aspect of the older work.[160]

Second, for Morris, the mote exists not only to make decisions when decisions need to be made but also to manage and, as it were, to sustain conflict, which Morris takes as necessary to human society. Morris is again using the mote to work dialectically, to suggest that, while the future will be better, different, more compassionate, it will also remain human; it will have its conflicts, but we will manage those conflicts; it will be a better future, but it will remain *our* future. This sense of the revolution and of revolutionary history as both continuous and disjointed helps, I think, to get at some of what is difficult, and, as E. P. Thompson argued, fundamentally *human* about Morris's socialism.

Third, Hammond's account of the mote's rules is highly and unexpectedly comprehensive. Closer to *Robert's Rules of Order* than to *The Lord of the Rings*, the mote in *News from Nowhere* reveals Morris's peculiar investment in the paradoxically humdrum details of his utopia, in the reality not only of *the future* but also of the quotidian procedures according to which life, conflict, and desire will be organized in that future. Robert Elliott notes rightly that Morris "clearly recognizes that old Hammond's long discourse . . . is painfully wooden. It deals with the prescriptive materials: the customs, the mode of life, the politics . . . of the new society and how these came about."[161] "In Nowhere," writes Matthew Beaumont, "history is made not in the macro-events of an evolving civilization but in the micro-processes of daily life. Utopia, Morris implies, redeems history as the process by which we produce and reproduce ourselves in our everyday lives."[162] I'll come back to the importance of desire and everyday detail in a bit.

---

[160] John Plotz, *Semi-Detached: The Aesthetics of Virtual Experience since Dickens* (Princeton, NJ: Princeton University Press, 2017), 167.

[161] Robert C. Elliott, *The Shape of Utopia: Studies in a Literary Genre* (Chicago: University of Chicago Press, 1970), 109.

[162] Beaumont, *Utopia Ltd.*, 179.

Although Morris's motes – imagined as part of both the distant past and the utopian future – can seem willfully esoteric or fanciful, can seem, as I said before, like instances of mere wish-fulfillment (they do almost always appear in or as dreams in Morris), the idea of small, face-to-face, or "unitary" democracies as both existentially distinct and especially viable has had a long life in democratic theory. Greek political theorists, faced with the expansion of city-states, argued about how big the *polis* could get before really participatory democracy would become impossible: was it two thousand? was it ten thousand? was it *sixty* thousand, as was the case "at the height of Athenian democracy in 450 BCE"?[163] Even as he worked to imagine the essential, amalgamated, and fungible rightness of the general will, Rousseau still regretted the loss of something closer, simpler, and more direct: "When we see among the happiest people in the world bands of peasants regulating the affairs of state under an oak tree, and always acting wisely, can we help feeling a certain contempt for the refinements of other nations, which employ so much skill and mystery to make themselves at once illustrious and wretched?"[164] In 1871, while arguing in favor of Thomas Hare's "machinery of representation," Simon Sterne pointed to the mote both as the origin of and as a model for good representative government: the "folk mote was not a city rabble, but a staid gathering of friends and neighbors, which not only satisfied the postulate of Aristotle, but went further, in never becoming even so numerous as to induce confusion."[165] In the mode of Victorian stadial pseudo-ethnography, Gomme's *The Village Community* recalled "examples of the old village-moot assembling in the open air under a tree" in order to align a mode of direct democracy with "a stage of development long prior to the political stage . . . a survival from prehistoric times."[166] Having seen first-hand the

---

[163] Robert A. Dahl, *On Democracy* (New Haven, CT: Yale University Press, 2008), 106.

[164] Jean-Jacques Rousseau, *The Social Contract*, trans. Maurice Cranston (London: Penguin Classics, 1968), 149.

[165] Simon Sterne, *On Representative Government and Personal Representation* (Philadelphia: J. B. Lippincott & Co., 1871), 25.

[166] George Laurence Gomme, *The Village Community, with Special Reference to the Origin and Form of Its Survivals in Britain* (London: Walter Scott, 1890), 110, 2. The moot makes an unexpected but related return in Sarah Corbin Robert's historical introduction to a 1970 edition of her father-in-law's *Robert's Rules of Order*. "From analogy with the customs of other Germanic tribes, it is supposed that freemen were accustomed to come together in the 'Village-moot,' to make 'bye-laws' for their village, and to administer justice. These groups also chose men to represent them at the 'Hundred-moot' of the district, which acted as a court of appeal and arbitrated intervillage disputes. Still higher in authority, and similarly constituted, was the 'Folk-moot,' which was also the citizen army of the tribe." Sarah Corbin Robert, introduction to *Robert's Rules of Order*, by Henry Martyn Robert, ed. Sarah Corbin Robert (New York: Scott, Foresman, 1970), xxviii. We'll have occasion to return to the Roberts in Chapter 4.

development of rules for "face-to-face, consensual decision making" in various New Left collectives in the 1960s, Jane Mansbridge argued in *Beyond Adversary Democracy* for the need to recover "another, older understanding of democracy," in which "people who disagree do not vote; they reason together until they agree on the best answer. Nor do they elect representatives to reason for them. They come together with their friends to find agreement. This democracy is consensual, based on common interest and equal respect. It is the democracy of face-to-face relations."[167] Faced with the increasingly centralized "giantism" of postwar industry and trade, the progressive economist E. F. Schumacher sold a lot of books in 1973 arguing that *Small Is Beautiful*: "people can be themselves only in small comprehensible groups. Therefore we must learn to think in terms of an articulated structure than can cope with a multitude of small-scale units."[168] Reflecting more neutrally about the necessary and inverse relation between state size and democratic possibility, Robert Dahl posits a fixed "law of time and numbers": "The more citizens a democratic unit contains, the less that citizens can participate directly in government decisions and the more that they must delegate authority to others."[169] Seen in relation to these other figures (and these are just a few), Morris can seem less like a dreamer than one in a sustained tradition of democratic theorists; however unfeasible in practice, his repeated invocation of the mote puts him in a long line of serious thinking about the necessary relation between political systems and social scale.

Morris did in fact work with characteristic sincerity and seriousness both to support and to realize small-scale models of social organization. In 1874, he wrote to a friend, "but look, suppose people lived in little communities among gardens and green fields ... and studied the (difficult) arts of enjoying life, and finding out what they really wanted."[170] Although he wrote and edited and argued, Morris saw his "open-air work," his direct, unmediated face-to-face appeals to potential socialists as most important: "He spoke at scores of open-air meetings, chaired them, carried the banner, sold literature, took round the hat for collections. He acted as a sandwichman, between placards advertising *Commonweal*."[171] Morris's

---

[167] Jane J. Mansbridge, *Beyond Adversary Democracy* (Chicago: University of Chicago Press, 1983), 21, 3.
[168] E. F. Schumacher, *Small Is Beautiful: Economics as if People Mattered* (New York: Harper Perennial, 2010), 71, 80.
[169] Dahl, *On Democracy* (2008), 109.
[170] Quoted in Thompson, *Morris: Romantic to Revolutionary*, 194.
[171] Thompson, *William Morris*, 424.

daughter, May, remembered "my father in his loose blue serge suit and soft felt hat speaking, a little nervously at first, but warming to his work as the crowd drew closer, and by the end of his 'turn' answering objectors and scoffers with vigorous repartee and picturesque chaff of his own."[172] In 1889, he offered mild and mildly surprising praise for the newly established County Councils, which

> in the great towns and especially in London are showing signs of life and a tendency towards Socialism which were certainly never looked for by the Tory party who brought in the bill which created them; and it may be well hoped that they will form a rallying point for the people against the centralizing bureaucratic Parliament which in England is sure to be reactionary up to its last days.[173]

"Morris," writes Fiona MacCarthy, "welcomed [them] as the step back in the direction of the populist Althing, the old Parliament of Iceland."[174] Crucial to Morris's development and, really, to the development of serious socialist thought in Britain were the regular Sunday lectures and the boozy dinners that followed at Kelmscott House:

> Almost every important Socialist thinker of the period spoke in the Coach House, most of them many times. Stepniak, Kropotkin, Lawrence Gronlund, Graham Wallas, Annie Besant, Sidney and Beatrice Webb, Sydney Olivier, later Ramsay MacDonald and Keir Hardie. Walter Crane gave memorable lectures, using a blackboard and chalk. The most regular performers were Bernard Shaw and Morris himself.[175]

Oscar Wilde, H. G. Wells, and W. B. Yeats also attended. As important as any of the lectures or events was Morris's management of the space as the practical embodiment of an idea about socialism, a radical and yet oddly modest sense that the means and the ends of socialism were or at least ought to be the same: Socialism for Morris was a serious, direct, honest way of living well with, for, and toward other people.

Direct Democracy

The story of Morris's institutional relation to socialism is often cast as a series of scalar reductions. When he joined the SDF in 1883, he was

---

[172] May Morris, introduction to *The Collected Works of William Morris, Vol. 20*, ed. May Morris (Cambridge: Cambridge University Press, 1913), liii.
[173] William Morris, "The Progress of English Socialism," in *How I Became a Socialist*, ed. Owen Hatherly and Owen Holland (London: Verso Books, 2020),164.
[174] MacCarthy, *William Morris*, 580.   [175] MacCarthy, *William Morris*, 522.

joining a group that must have seemed big to him and was supposed to only get bigger; that was, of course, what Hyndman wanted and, in the end, it was what Morris resisted. When he and his comrades broke away to form the Socialist League in 1885, they opted for something smaller, but better: without the distraction of Hyndman's parliamentary aspirations, without the distraction of *making a party,* they could focus on the close and pedagogical work of *making socialists.* But then, with the departure of the go-getting Bloomsbury faction, on the one hand, and the rising profile of increasingly violent anarchist elements within the League, on the other, Morris himself broke away to form the "necessarily low-key" Hammersmith Socialist Society.[176] The Society – the smallest yet – represented both a retreat from the tiring tactical squabbles of the previous decade and a recommitment to the methods of direct propaganda and pedagogy that Morris had always preferred. In the 1890 "Statement of Principles of the Hammersmith Socialist Society" (notice that it is just a statement and not yet another manifesto), Morris explicitly eschews the promise of direct action in favor of the "low-key" reality of direct education:

> We believe then, that it should be our special aim to make Socialists, by putting before people, and especially the working-classes, the elementary truths of Socialism; since we feel sure, in the first place, that in spite of the stir in the ranks of labour, there are comparatively few who understand what Socialism is, or have had opportunities of arguing on the subject with those who have at least begun to understand it; and, in the second place, we are no less sure that before any definite *Socialist* action can be attempted, it must be backed up by a great body of intelligent opinion - the opinion of a great mass of people who are already Socialists, people who know what they want, and are prepared to accept the responsibilities of self-government, which must form a part of their claims.[177]

He put this in more homely terms in his last lecture notes in 1895: we had, he said, "better confine ourselves to the old teaching and preaching of Socialism pure and simple, which I fear is more or less neglected amidst the . . . futile attempt to act as a party when we have no party."[178] Caught between the characterological indirection of parliamentary representation and the anarchist's equation of direct action with spectacular violence,

---

[176] MacCarthy, *William Morris,* 589.
[177] William Morris, "Statement of Principles of the Hammersmith Socialist Society," in Oscar Lovell Triggs, *Chapters in the History of the Arts and Crafts Movement* (London: Industrial Art League, 1902), 134.
[178] Quoted in Thompson, *William Morris,* 622.

Morris whittled his socialism down to an increasingly pure and, for some, an increasingly quixotic imperative: the imperative, as Miguel Abensour puts it, to "teach desire to desire, to desire better, to desire more, and above all to desire in a different way."[179] For Morris, alienation, reification, and ideology were most importantly what prevented people not simply from *having* a good life but rather from *wanting* or even *knowing how to want* a good life: bodily health, the enjoyment of the natural world, satisfying work, time to learn new things, objects that were both useful and beautiful, etc. This desire to desire was for Morris tied up with the ornamental. "We must," he said, "begin to build up the ornamental part of life – its pleasures, bodily and mental, scientific and artistic, social and individual – on the basis of work undertaken willingly and cheerfully, with the consciousness of benefitting ourselves and our neighbors with it."[180] This deep belief is why, before becoming a socialist and when faced with the "complete degradation" of the minor arts, he formed Morris & Co. and, "with the conceited courage of a young man [set out] to reform all that"; he set out, in other words, to make things worth wanting. It is also why, when he became a socialist, he understood the future as earthy, tangible, playful, practical, and full – but not overfull – of useful and beautiful things: "First you must be free, and next you must learn to take pleasure in all the details of life: which, indeed, will be necessary for you, because, since others will be free, you will have to do your own work."[181]

Although the language of teaching "desire to desire" feels a little abstract, one can see why the usually gruff E. P. Thompson was taken with Abensour's argument, with his sense that Morris's utopianism and his socialism, his unshakeable commitment to "making socialists," should be understood as efforts simply to put people in a better position to say what they really wanted and – having learnt to say it – to go ahead and make it happen. Although it seems like it should be easy, simply saying what you want is often really hard, and this is all the truer for people who want and have wanted things – basic things, human things – that society won't give them: working people, people of color, women, gay, queer, and trans people, etc. Although this problem is systemic, which is to say it is a problem that has run wide and deep, it often finds, as Morris understood, concentrated expression in the limits of the vote. When one is asked to

---

[179] Quoted in Thompson, *William Morris*, 790.

[180] William Morris, "Useful Work vs. Useless Toil," in *The Collected Works of William Morris, Vol. 23*, ed. May Morris (London: Longmans, Green, & Company, 1910), 111.

[181] Quoted in Thompson, *William Morris*, 93; William Morris, "The Society of the Future," in *How I Became a Socialist*, ed. Owen Hattherly and Owen Holland (London: Verso Books, 2020), 148.

vote between **A** and **B**, and neither **A** nor **B** can say what one really wants to say, it not only stacks the deck against some and not others but also creates or reveals a more fundamental rift between what one wants and what one can have, what one wants and what one can express, who one is and who one has to be in order simply to be counted. Amartya Sen has cast this problem in terms of a relation between "voice and social choice."[182] Although we rely on elections and similar processes to make shared social decisions, those processes are informationally poor *by design*; if we are to count up, to aggregate, and to compare a lot of votes, those votes *cannot* carry the kinds of information or significance – intensity, history, bad faith, suffering, sacrifice, desire – that could complicate or undermine their comparability even as they would add to their reality and to their meaning. Although critics on both the left and the right have often taken this aspect of elections as a cause for outrage, resignation, or gloom, Sen understands these necessary structural limits as an opportunity *to widen* the informational parameters of social choice in order to reckon with welfare as well as preference. Instead of looking for a new system, Sen suggests, we should let more of what we and others *want* into the system we have.

Contemporaries often took note of Morris's hearty, no-nonsense directness, his "bluff self-assertive decision, vigorous application to detail, matter-of-fact workmanship."[183] They told the story of when, after "resigning his directorship of the Devon Great Consols Company," he "put his top-hat on a chair, and sat down on it."[184] "His robust bearing," says E. P. Thompson, "and a slight roll in his walk led him to be mistaken more than once for a sailor."[185] Henry James remembered him as "short, burly, corpulent, very careless and unfinished in his dress ... He has a very loud voice and a nervous restless manner and a perfectly unaffected and businesslike address. His talk indeed is wonderfully to the point and remarkable for clear good sense." James's 1869 visit with Morris had, he wrote, "a strong peculiar flavor of its own."[186] Although this recurrent emphasis on his cheery plain-speaking supports entirely legitimate critical readings that see Morris, his politics, and his art as privileged, chauvinist, nostalgic, or blinkered, a similar emphasis on directness as a value finds more subtle and, it seems to me, more significant expression in his work as a poet, artist, and designer.

---

[182] Amartya K. Sen, *The Idea of Justice* (Cambridge, MA: Harvard University Press, 2009), 87–114.
[183] Thompson, *William Morris*, 88.   [184] Thompson, *William Morris*, 192.
[185] Thompson, *William Morris*, 88.
[186] Henry James, *Selected Letters*, ed. Leon Edel (Cambridge: The Belknap Press, 1987), 24.

Victorian reviewers praised his poetry, often wooden or mawkish to modern ears, as "distinct and direct ... clear and pellucid."[187] When he took up different kinds of work, he tried, first and foremost, to make his materials entirely themselves:

> I have tried to produce goods which should be genuine so far as their mere substances are concerned, and should have on that account the primary beauty in them which belongs to naturally treated natural substances; have tried for instance to make woollen substances as woollen as possible, cotton as cotton as possible, and so on; have used only the dyes which are natural and simple, because they produce beauty almost without the intervention of art; all this quite apart from the design in the stuffs or what not.[188]

Even more, as he moved away from his early, Pre-Raphaelite work in painting and poetry into printing, design, and – I want to add – political activism, he was also and, in every case, moving away from a representational and toward an increasingly *ornamental* style. Although his wallpapers of course featured "gardens and fields, and strange trees, boughs, and tendrils," his designs didn't really refer to some other thing: the wallpaper was wallpaper, and that had, crucially, to be enough. "While," write Charlotte and Peter Fiell, "Morris's designs were non-illusionistic – thus remaining true to their materials – his naturalistic patterned repeats flowed freely and seamlessly into one another to create rhythmic and balanced overall patterns."[189] Indeed, Morris's later naturalism was less a matter of representing nature than capturing what he saw as its fecund self-sufficiency. His mature wallpapers

> are quite as naturalistic as the first, but now generally based on a subtly concealed but strong underlying pattern which gives their easy curves the reality of growth. They do not look absolutely flat, but rather as if arranged within a depth of about an inch. ... One untypical client, a small tradesman, conveying to a visiting East End clergyman his "great delight in the Morris paper with which his room was covered," put his finger on it: "seems as if it was all a-growing."[190]

When he set up the Kelmscott Press in 1891, his first concern was to design a type that, while being beautiful, would, above all, let the books have their say:

> And here what I wanted was letter pure in form; severe, without needless excrescences; solid, without the thickening and thinning of the line, which

---

[187] Quoted in Thompson, *William Morris*, 135. [188] Quoted in Thompson, *William Morris*, 100.
[189] Charlotte & Peter Fiell, *William Morris: A Life of Art* (Köln: Taschen Books, 2020), 61.
[190] Paul Thompson, *Work of William Morris*, 108.

is the essential fault of the ordinary modern type, and which makes it difficult to read; and not compressed laterally, as all later type has grown to be owning to commercial exigencies.[191]

Indeed, his long effort at the *Kelmscott Chaucer*, the edition that Edward Burne-Jones aptly praised as a "pocket cathedral," wasn't aimed at saying something *else* or something *new* about Chaucer's writing; it was aimed rather, and with paradoxically gorgeous and minimal interference, at letting Chaucer say for himself what he meant: "I want," said Burne-Jones to his daughter, "particularly to draw your attention to the fact that there is no preface to Chaucer, and no introduction, and no essay on his position as a poet, and no notes, and no glossary; so that all is prepared for you to enjoy him thoroughly."[192] For Morris, *Chaucer* was Chaucer.

In each of these cases, Morris sought increasingly to make art that might "build up the ornamental part of life," to make things that one could want for their own sake and not for what they otherwise meant or otherwise said.[193] If, in the first instance, he sought to make objects – furniture, tiles, books, wallpaper, etc. – that could be worth the wanting, when this effort came inevitably to grief, he turned his attention to the more fundamental and more difficult work of creating the social conditions under which people could learn that they *deserved* to want what was worth the wanting: "Both my historical studies and my practical conflict with the philistinism of modern society have forced on me the conviction that art cannot have a real life and growth under the present system of commercialism and profit mongering."[194] In both cases, *ornament* was not a passive retreat from or a decadent alternative to life, politics, or reality; it was, rather, a way to make a socialist's and an activist's connection between the cultivation of class consciousness and what E. P. Thompson calls "the education of desire."[195] In *The Making of British Socialism*, Mark Bevir argues that "Morris's anti-parliamentarianism derived from his aesthetic and moral ideals" and not

---

[191] William S. Peterson, *The Kelmscott Press: A History of William Morris's Typographical Adventure* (Berkeley: University of California Press, 1991), 82

[192] Quoted in Charles LaPorte, "Morris's Compromises: On Victorian Editorial Theory and the Kelmscott Chaucer," in *Writing on the Image: Reading William Morris*, ed. David Latham (Toronto: University of Toronto Press, 2007), 209. LaPorte goes on in his excellent essay to point to ways in which Morris's desire for textual directness in the Kelmscott Chaucer was in fact belied by questions and contradictions that he sought strategically to minimize, in part by leaning on the "bibliographic," at the expense of the "linguistic," sense of the text.

[193] Cheryl Wall and Zora Neal Hurston.

[194] William Morris, *The Collected Letters of William Morris, Volume II*, ed. Norman Kelvin (Princeton, NJ: Princeton University Press, 2014), 230.

[195] Thompson, *William Morris*, 790.

from a workable or practical political strategy: "Morris wanted to improve the world, to make it simpler, more enjoyable, beautiful, fulfilling, and just. His socialist utopia educates our aspirations; it gives us a glimpse of a better world. We should be grateful, but our gratitude need not blind us to either his purism or the importance of political action."[196] I think Bevir is *mostly* right here: Morris's antipathy to parliamentary representation was aesthetic if we take that to mean that his experience with aesthetics helped him to understand a political situation in a particular and, I would argue, a particularly clear way. For Morris, the problem with Parliament wasn't that it was impure or ugly (although he certainly thought it both); the problem, as I have tried to demonstrate, was that the logic of political representation created conditions under which it was impossible to be anything other than shoddy, shabby, or dishonest.

His commitment to the ornamental part of life, which is to say the nonrepresentational part of life, wasn't, in that case, simply a purist's privileged aesthetic retreat from the hard-knock realities of politics and the political fight; it was, on the contrary, the reasonable and tactical result of an analysis of the logic of political representation that had been informed by but was not limited to his work as a poet, designer, and artist. What Morris saw was that both parliamentary representation and a vote that was its most concentrated form created or exacerbated problems essential to the experience and expression of individual and social desire. While the vote could make things happen, it often made them happen at the expense of the ability of people – and especially working people – to say or even to know what they really wanted from life. If Morris's solutions to that real problem either weren't workable or if he just couldn't manage to make them work, that's not reason to dismiss his analysis of political representation and its consequences. Morris's problem wasn't that he was a starry-eyed purist; it was, rather, that he managed, as few others have, to identify and describe a real, difficult, essential, and essentially human problem for which – despite all his efforts, all his ideas, and all his art – he had no simple or single solution. That, it seems to me, is what it means or, maybe, what it ought to mean to be political.

Come On!

Although they were very different, Carroll and Morris represent two divergent but related responses to the same set of historical problems. At

---

[196] Bevir, *Making of British Socialism*, 105.

first glance, their differences seem rightly to overpower any possible sympathy. Where the strange, shy, retiring Carroll burrowed more and more deeply and minutely into the logical viscera of political representation, the gregarious and *sometimes* unsubtle Morris loudly decried Parliament as an especially rotten index of an especially immoral system; and, where the conservative Carroll made increasingly elaborate rules precisely *because* he couldn't really believe in them, Morris's paradoxically sentimental nostalgia for the future led him right up to the edge of political violence. For all of that, however, both were responding to the same situation: a moment at which the contradictions of and the limits to the logic of parliamentary representation made it harder to suspend one's disbelief and to act *as if* the fictions necessarily underwriting Parliament were real. For Carroll the crisis led to what we might call a conservative *autonomization* of procedure. That is, when faced with the breakdown or the decay of "organic" institutions he saw as necessary or meaningful – the family, the college, the church, government – he opted not to abandon those institutions but rather to invest and to overinvest in their rules *qua* rules; both in Carroll's writing on politics and in Wonderland, rules that had before served institutions break away from those institutions to take on a new life, weight, and intensity. It is partly this autonomization or, to use another, related language, this *hypercathexis* of the rule that leads Carroll to the related modes of personification and allegory. What, after all, is Wonderland if not a world where the seemingly arbitrary rules that sometimes structure and sometimes terrorize childhood – when and what to eat, where to sit, when to sleep, how and when to speak, and when simply, as the Gryphon says, to "Come on!" – are brought to life as creatures equally powerful, capricious, absurd, and somehow lovable. "'Everybody says "come on!" here,' thought Alice as she went slowly after it: 'I never was so ordered about before, in all my life, never!'" Faced with the historical wane of different kinds of institutional legitimacy, Carroll retreated back into the procedural utopia of paradoxes, processes, and rules, a retreat that, as we shall see, had unexpected and profound consequences for a pronounced twentieth-century commitment in democratic theory to the axiom, the algorithm, and the model.

It is striking that Morris, whose politics and investments were so different, arrived at so similar a destination, arrived, that is, at the workaday, procedural utopia of Nowhere. On the face of it, Morris's procedures are quite unlike Carroll's. As opposed to the gamester's autonomization of the rule, Morris was focused on craft for its own sake, on an investment in knowing the best or the truest way to do things: to dye fabric, hang wallpaper, print a book, or, at last, remake a world. There is, of course, too much to say about all the ways in which the polymathic Morris dedicated himself to the details of knowing *how-to*. What is important here is to see that his dedication led, via a very different path, to another kind of procedural utopia. The residents of Nowhere think less about what things mean and more about how to do things – how to work, play, and live. As a result, although it is neither capricious nor cruel, Nowhere looks a lot like Wonderland insofar as it is a place where people talk incessantly and almost exclusively about what they're doing while they're doing it. On the one hand, this resonance is important because it helps us better to see a possible relation between the rise of speculative fiction in Britain and what we might call the autumnal phase of parliamentary representation. It can, after all, be no coincidence that More's *Utopia* (1516), Harrington's *The Commonwealth of Oceana* (1656), Swift's *Gulliver's Travels* (1726), Carroll's *Alice's Adventures in Wonderland*, and Morris's *News from Nowhere* were all written against the backdrop of and with more and less apparent reference to specific, procedural parliamentary controversies. On the other hand, and more importantly here, the unexpectedly deep resonance between Carroll and Morris will allow us to better see and understand a strain of radical, critical, or left thinking that runs alongside and sometimes within the conservative, proceduralist, or formalist turn that Carroll helped to initiate. Is Nowhere in Wonderland, or is Wonderland nowhere? Thinking about the real consequence of that nonsense question will, as we shall see in Chapter 4, help us to appreciate the imaginative nature, the political history, the practical consequence, and, as it were, the *feel* of some kinds of modern electoral theory.

The Impossibilists
Ralph Ellison and Kenneth Arrow

The ability to make consistent decisions is one of the symptoms of an integrated personality.
—Kenneth Arrow, *Social Choice and Individual Values* (1951)

Not like an arrow, but a boomerang.
—Ralph Ellison, *Invisible Man* (1952)

Looking back from the beginning of the twentieth century, H. M. Hyndman remembered his old rival William Morris as a sort of "impossibilist": "As to the impossibilists," he wrote in 1903, "they are many of them at bottom anarchists, who honestly believe that all political action is harmful. They are justified in holding that opinion, if they so believe; but they are certainly out of place in a political Socialist policy."[1] In a lighter style, G. B. Shaw wrote in 1895 to his friend, Janet Achurch – then performing in New York – that her husband, Charles Charrington, "seemed in excellent spirits, the day being pleasant. He is going to lecture – bless his heart, as you would say – at the Hackney Radical Club and at the Hammersmith Socialist Society; and this I think a good thing on the whole, as he ought to make an above-the-average public speaker, although among the Fabians he will probably be an Impossibilist of the Impossibilists."[2] And, in a 1910 account of an election in Yorkshire, an American journalist reflected on the logistical pressure that "socialist impossibilism" – combined with "three cornered fights" between "Liberals, Labors, and Tories" – could put on the will of working people: "In a scrutiny of the vote, the only evidence of lack of co-operation was, on one side, 20 ballots marked 'socialism,' and thereby 'spoiled,' indicating

---

[1] H. M. Hyndman, "Laborism, Impossibilism, and Socialism," *The International Socialist Review: A Monthly Journal of International Socialist Thought, Volume III* (Chicago: Charles H. Kerr & Co., 1903), 654.
[2] Bernard Shaw, *Collected Letters, 1874–1897*, ed. Dan H. Laurence (London: Max Reinhardt, 1965), 534.

socialist impossibilism, and a falling of the Labor candidate behind the Liberal by about 400 votes, indicating Liberal whiggism."[3] Impossibilism, in that case, not only named a critical attitude toward the very idea of elections but, in an unsettled period of tightening competition between Liberal and Labour candidates, could also emerge as a decisive factor within elections. Although the impossibilist was often imagined as impractical, utopian, or naïve, even a small handful of dreamy or distracted spoilers could make a large difference in a period of increasingly close and hard-fought elections.

The term "impossibilism" is thus peculiar not only for its finicky or infelicitously sibilant sound; rather, applied to someone like Morris, it somehow meant two things at once. On the one hand, it referred, as I have said, to the ostensibly utopian or impossible expectations that Morris and others brought to their political commitments at century's end. Imagining that real social change could and should happen without compromise, without coalitions, and without the apparatus of a modern political party, this version of the impossibilist simply believed in and hoped for the impossible, hoped for a social change that could emerge from within the working classes suddenly, organically, and without strategic oversight. Morris and his ilk, the term seems to suggest, were waiting for the impossible and, thus, they would wait in vain. On the other hand, the term seems also – if unintentionally – to index something like Morris's more critical attitude toward the possibility of meaningful elections. Instead of a naïve or ingenuous belief in the possibility of the impossible, the term could instead name one's lack of belief in the efficacy – in the *possibility* – of a political strategy that could claim to be both socialist (opposed to the existence of private property) and parliamentary (bound to protect the existence of private property). What's impossible in this case isn't necessarily what Morris believed about the future; what was impossible was, rather, what others believed about a present political strategy based, as he thought, on an essential and essentially disastrous contradiction between socialist principle and capitalist practice. For a true socialist, *Parliament* was impossible. Applied, in other words, to someone like Morris, the term could mean either that the impossible was really possible and thus worth waiting for, or that what was really and tactically impossible was an authentically socialist MP.

---

[3] L. F. P., "The Parliamentary Elections and the British Electoral System," *The Public* (February 4, 1910), 102.

These two senses of "impossibilist" follow a broader Victorian shift in the definition and ordinary use of the word "impossible." Where the word had long referred simply to what could not be, the *OED* tells us that the word began in the second half of the nineteenth century also to mean something softer, more contextual, and maybe closer to awkwardness, unsuitability, or excess. Its examples, starting with Carlyle in 1858, refer to the feeling of being put in an "impossible position," to a "dear old ugly lady ... in the speckly dress and impossible bonnet," and to an "impossible girl" who "said things that no other girl would have said." Insofar as it refers to what cannot happen, the impossible is simply what is *not* possible; insofar, however, as it refers to what can happen even or especially when it shouldn't, the impossible is, instead, that which is *excessively possible*. If, in that case, the first, utopian sense of Morris's "impossibilism" corresponds with the older and more absolute or binary sense of the term, his grittier feelings about the unhappily possible impossibility of a Socialist MP is the more jaded and more modern. One can imagine him deploying, while also deploring, Samuel Johnson's old and outré misogynist joke: a Socialist MP would be something "like a dog's walking on his hinder legs. It is not done well; but you are surprised to find it done at all."[4]

I want, in this chapter, to consider some other, later but related versions of the electoral impossible. I've had opportunity on a few occasions to refer to Kenneth Arrow's "impossibility theorem," the concept that set the terms for much thinking about the nature and efficacy of elections since the 1951 publication of *Social Choice and Individual Values*. Recalling Condorcet's paradoxically cyclical elections, Arrow argued that it was impossible to design an election that could *always* avoid paradox or contradiction while also observing a few minimal and "common-sense" conditions. It was, writes Prasanta K. Pattanaik, "one of those rare intellectual contributions that virtually transform entire disciplines or subdisciplines."[5] Amartya K. Sen writes that the theorem "is a result of breathtaking elegance and power, which showed that even some very mild conditions of reasonableness could not be simultaneously satisfied by any social choice procedure, within a very wide family."[6] Although Arrow is rarely discussed in works of cultural history or literary criticism, his writing

---

[4] James Boswell, *Life of Johnson* (Oxford: Oxford University Press, 2008), 327.
[5] Prasanta K. Pattanaik, "Introduction," in *The Arrow Impossibility Theorem*, ed. Eric Maskin and Amartya Sen (New York: Columbia University Press, 2014), 2.
[6] Amartya Sen, *Collective Choice and Social Welfare: An Expanded Edition* (Cambridge, MA: Harvard University Press, 2017), 4.

on choice, preference, and elections is enormously important. How we all think *ordinarily* about the meaning of votes, the design of elections, the legibility of preference, and the nature of democracy owes a surprising amount to Arrow and the fields he inspired. I'll have a lot more to say about the origins, nature, and outcomes of Arrow's impossibility theorem. For now, I want again to acknowledge the complex rhetorical pull of the word "impossibility."

As I mentioned in Chapter 3, the Scottish political theorist Duncan Black had arrived at conclusions almost identical to Arrow's at almost the same time. Where, however, Arrow would eventually win a Nobel Prize, Black toiled in near obscurity at the edges of the academy. Although there are several reasons why we might remember Arrow over Black – better institutional affiliations, a crisper prose style, a social and political milieu primed for both the intended and the unintended consequences of his result – some of Arrow's success must have come from the aesthetic immediacy and existential *frisson* of that phrase, "impossibility theorem." As was the case with other bleakly seductive concepts emerging from the Cold War scrum of think tanks and defense intellectuals – Mutually Assured Destruction, the Escalation Ladder, Thinking the Unthinkable, the Prisoner's Dilemma, and so on – "impossibility theorem" denotes a discrete and technically specific concept, while connoting a heady atmosphere of risk, anxiety, and dread. Impossibility, should you choose to accept it, is pretty exciting. Although, as we shall see, the details of Arrow's theorem are important, some part of its enduring appeal must be a function of what's dangerous and alluring about the very idea of impossibility.

Indeed, although almost everyone refers to it as "Arrow's impossibility theorem," its name in *Social Choice and Individual Values* was initially the "General Possibility Theorem," suggesting that some of the pessimism associated with Arrow's idea may have been cultivated after the fact. In a 2014 symposium on the theorem, Sen referred to and approved of its earlier and "rather cheerful name," taking it as proof of Arrow's "sunny temperament."[7] Arrow, however, begged to differ: Sen, he said,

> notes that I called the result a possibility theorem and attributes this to my sunny disposition. The facts are a little different. I have always regarded myself rather as a gloomy realist – but perhaps I am wrong. Instead, someone else, Tjalling Koopmans, insisted on using the word possibility.

[7] Amartya Sen, "Arrow and the Impossibility Theorem," in *The Arrow Impossibility Theorem*, ed. Eric Maskin and Amartya Sen (New York: Columbia University Press, 2014), 30.

He was upset by the term impossibility. Now, I cannot say that Tjalling had an extraordinarily sunny disposition, either. He was not necessarily a lively or a cheerful person, nor was he really an optimist. But he did dislike the feeling that things could not happen or change. And given that the dissertation was originally posed as a Cowles Commission monograph, I felt that to please Tjalling, I would call it a "possibility theorem." It was not, however, my idea at all.[8]

There's a lot to think about here: the institutional history of ideas and of entities like the Cowles Commission and the RAND Corporation; the relation between concepts, feelings, and dispositions (whether sunny or gloomy); and implicitly narrative investments in the likelihood of things happening or not happening, things changing or not changing. For now, I want to note the remarkable fact that, for all its vaunted precision, Arrow's idea could apparently have been called either a *possibility* theorem or an *impossibility* theorem and that the difference didn't matter enough to him to insist on one or the other. What does it mean that Arrow's idea can simultaneously index both possibility and impossibility? What historical, political, and conceptual conditions need to obtain in order to say "possibility is impossibility" or "impossibility is possibility" without falling headlong into nonsense? What, for Arrow, his readers, and the theory of elections should impossibility really mean? As with the doubled sense of Morris's impossibilism – it referred both to *my* desire for the impossible and to *my* belief that *your* belief about *my* belief was impossible – the history of Arrow's idea points to a contradiction or a paradox within *another idea* that underwrites the history, theory, practice, and aesthetics of elections.

In what follows I want to think about what impossibility meant in a few different but related contexts. First, I'll have more to say about Arrow's impossibility theorem. As I suggested above in my brief discussion of Lewis Carroll and William Riker, the pessimism, fatalism, or the *impossibility* of the impossibility theorem has worked powerfully on the modern political imagination, both for some conservatives, libertarians, and other democratic skeptics who look to Arrow for proof that elections can't really work, and for some left and progressive critics who take the impossibility theorem as evidence of the bad faith of democratic theory's economic turn.[9] I'll

---

[8] Kenneth J. Arrow, "Commentary," in *The Arrow Impossibility Theorem*, ed. Eric Maskin and Amartya Sen (New York: Columbia University Press, 2014), 58.

[9] Gerry Mackie observes that, "Just as the Condorcet paradox is used to shock at the elementary level of study, the Arrow possibility theorem is used to shock at a more advanced level." Mackie, *Democracy Defended* (Cambridge: Cambridge University Press, 2003), 82.

begin by looking both at the substance of Arrow's idea and at its history in order to suggest that both approaches fail to register the complexity and, as it were, the *meaning* of impossibility. In order to think this through, I'll want to consider Arrow in relation to three things: first, an unexpectedly Victorian genealogy of thinking about utility, individuality, and welfare; second, institutional, intellectual, and literary associations that belie the restricted perspective of his more vocal followers and critics; and, third, a more nuanced account of Arrow's place within the intellectual and political history of the Cold War. Where, that is, both supporters and critics have sometimes read Arrow's impossibility theorem as a product of a bluntly conceived East-West confrontation between communism and capitalist democracy, I'll argue not only that Arrow's politics are more nuanced but also that he was influenced by some of the same controversies – the Moscow show trials, the death of Trotsky, the Molotov-Ribbentrop Pact – that animated and defined the political and aesthetic investments of the anti-Stalinist left. Reading impossibility within the thickened historical context of City College, the Popular Front, and Cold War Kremlinology will give us a better sense of why the theorem can be understood – impossibly – as an argument both for and against both possibility and impossibility.

And, second, if impossibility emerges at midcentury as a way to think abstractly about th elections, it emerges also alongside another, different but related kind of impossibility: the *practically* impossible conditions that Black voters faced in the Jim Crow South and, more generally, in America before and after the passage of the Voting Rights Act of 1965. On the face of it, the abstract *jeux d'esprit impossibles* that occupied analysts at RAND can seem – and with good reason – tone-deaf, frivolous, or even obscene when considered next to Black voters' experience of a real and wholly manufactured electoral impossibility. That said, although Arrow's abstract sense of the meaning of electoral impossibility and the practical experience of Black voters faced with poll taxes, literacy tests, social terror, and physical violence are very different, they are not wholly unrelated. After Reconstruction, racist efforts to limit, to undercount, or to falsify Black votes relied on an increasingly baroque set of techniques to bend federal electoral law without breaking it. As a result, some of Arrow's more abstruse musings about the torsions of social choice seemed to find material expression in the logical contradictions, paradoxes, and double binds that were characteristic of electoral law under Jim Crow. As the techniques have become increasingly refined, recent efforts at voter suppression in communities of color have tended only to draw more on the calculated perversion of an analytical tradition that begins with Arrow.

Although there is no shortage of accounts to consider, I'll focus mostly on Ralph Ellison's essays and his *Invisible Man* for two reasons. First, Ellison's acute sense of the relation between race, agency, history, invisibility, and impossibility in American democracy finds sharpened expression in places in his writing where electoral procedures are represented or come – often absurdly – into play. For instance, the Invisible Man's several encounters with the otherwise transparent machinery of political representation (votes, caucuses, committees, and the rules of order) reveal that machinery as rigged, rickety, and deadly. Second, as we track Ellison's thinking about elections and democracy alongside his own development from a committed communist to a jaundiced fellow traveler and, finally to a complicated kind of liberal humanist, we will see not only that Ellison's thinking puts materialist and historical pressure on some of the abstractions of the impossibility theorem but also that his intellectual trajectory runs parallel to Arrow's in ways that demand a reconsideration of some of our stories about the course and character of politics, elections, race, and democracy in America at and after midcentury.

Late Victorians

With this chapter's move from Victorian voting, Victorian electoral reform, and Victorian fiction to American politics and American political culture at midcentury, it might seem that I've made my own leap into the dark. There is, however, less of a break at work here than it might seem. First, the intellectual history of electoral theory is itself strangely and significantly discontinuous. As I have already suggested, one of the curious things about Condorcet's paradox is its lost-and-found quality: an individual would stumble across the phenomenon or arrive at the idea, the idea would be straightaway misunderstood, ignored, or forgotten, and then, at some later date, another individual would have the same idea again. For instance, before Carroll rediscovered the paradox in the 1860s (without, as Black demonstrated, having read either Condorcet or Borda), that aspect of Condorcet's work had fallen, forgotten, into mathematical disrepute. Referring to the *Essai sur l'application de l'analyse à la probabilité des decisions rendues à la pluralitié des voix* (1785), Isaac Todhunter, one of the few Victorian mathematicians or historians to refer to the work at all, wrote that, "the obscurity and self-contradiction are without any parallel, so far as our experience of mathematical works extends . . . no amount of examples can convey an adequate impression of the evils."[10] And, although Carroll thought and wrote extensively about the theory of elections, his work was also almost entirely forgotten until Duncan Black rediscovered it in the 1940s. As Arrow acknowledges, it wasn't until he read Black that he realized fully that something like the impossibility theorem could even have a history: "I must confess," he admitted in 1963, "to a certain want of diligence in tracking down the historical origins of the theories of social choice."[11] Similarly, Robin Farquharson, an Oxford undergraduate "interested in the voting in the US Senate on the League of Nations Covenant ... discovered for himself Condorcet's voting paradox."[12] It was only after sharing his discovery with his tutor, Norman Leyland, that Farquharson went on to read Arrow, Black, Condorcet, and Carroll. Soon afterward, Farquharson, "dropped out," dropped acid, and reappeared briefly as a sort of counterculture guru, writing a short and unhinged book called *Drop Out!* Even there Carroll and his rules for counting held sway:

> Having written this chapter and, as I've said, feeling all to hell pleased about it, especially the complex sustained metaphor, instructions came through to destroy it. I argued, of course, but the instructions reiterated themselves and went on reiterating, and, as they say, "What I tell you three times is true" (L. Carroll, C. Dodgson?).[13]

In some cases, periods of punctuated rediscovery would remain more or less freestanding, as with Carroll and Arrow; and in others, it would lead, as it did with the punctilious Black, to sustained efforts at genealogical reconstruction. The point here is that, where it might appear that I've made a leap, I am rather on a circuitous and punctuated path that follows the broken trajectory of the idea itself.

It makes sense, in that case, that Arrow and Black, one writing in America and the other in Scotland, but both writing after World War II, are, as it were, peculiarly Victorian in some of their assumptions, investments, and references. I have, of course, already written at length about Black's increasingly deep engagement with the life, thinking, and writing of Lewis Carroll. Similarly, as Arrow writes his way through *Social Choice and Individual Values*, he draws on a range of very Victorian references:

[10] Quoted in Keith Michael Baker, *Condorcet: From Natural Philosophy to Social Mathematics* (Chicago: University of Chicago Press, 1975), 227.
[11] Kenneth J. Arrow, *Social Choice and Individual Values* (New Haven, CT: Yale University Press, 2012), 93.
[12] Michael Dummett, "The Work and Life of Robin Farquharson," *Social Choice and Welfare* 25 (2005), 475.
[13] Robin Farquharson, *Drop Out!* (London: Penguin Books, 1968), 67.

E. J. Nanson and F. Y. Edgeworth, Jeremy Bentham, W. S. Jevons, and T. H. Green; in other places, he refers to Shaw, Arthur Conan Doyle, Thomas Hardy, and Robert Browning (not to mention Dostoevsky and Edgar Allan Poe). (The depth and duration of Ellison's critical engagement with the whole history of the novel is, of course, well known.) On the one hand, Arrow's more than passing reference to the literature of the Victorian period is the result of his engagement with a tradition that begins with Bentham, the effort, that is, to think about individual and aggregate social goods in terms of theoretically calculable utilities. As we have seen and will see more, the question of what it would mean to measure and to compare preferences is at the conceptual and political center of Arrow's work; although the impossibility theorem looks like a rejection of Bentham's theory of individual and group welfare, its terms and its provenance put it in a direct line of descent not only from the nearly forgotten Carroll but also from the more familiar concerns of Bentham, Mill, Jevons, Marshall, Webb, and others. On the other hand, although Arrow's arguments can seem abstract, recondite, or cold, they are fundamentally about that most Victorian of problems: the social, political, and ethical relation between the individual and the group. Contrary to the pronounced libertarian drift of some of his most vocal followers, Arrow's work remained focused on the balance between individual and the community: "the demands of society and the needs of the individual, expressed only within that society, require that he be for others as well as for himself and that the others appear as ends to him as well as means."[14] How, in other words, can we both be ourselves and yet also manage to live together? In more than one place, Arrow invokes Rabbi Hillel: "If I am not for myself, then who is for me? And if I am not for others, then who am I? And if not now, when?"[15]

I want to make three related points here. First, seen as the subject of intellectual history or, to use an even older phrase – the history of ideas – electoral theory and social choice theory represent a conceptually continuous but temporally discontinuous field. Because, as I argued in Chapter 2, otherwise tacit electoral procedures tend to become visible only at moments of failure or crisis, the extant record of thinking and writing about elections will look considerably more broken or spasmodic than the phenomenon itself. So, where the history of elections would need to consider many points in between, the history of *electoral theory* must make

---

[14] Kenneth J. Arrow, *The Limits of Organization* (New York: W. W. Norton & Company, 1974), 15.
[15] Arrow, *Limits of Organization*, 15.

some strange jumps, like the one that takes us from Condorcet to Kenneth Arrow or from Lewis Carroll to Duncan Black. Second, this extended, maybe even attenuated sense of the Victorian as a mode or a problematic as opposed to a distinct and closed period follows some recent efforts within Victorian Studies to explore some generative tensions immanent to the practice of literary history. For instance, in her book on Victorian fiction and British psychoanalysis, Alicia Mireles Christoff writes about "how productive it can be to picture thoughts that are generated in the relation of two distinct historical moments."[16] Imagining, if only as a thought experiment, the *Partisan Review*, the RAND Corporation, or *Invisible Man* as somehow Victorian maybe won't (but then again it might) have much to tell us about the Corn Laws, the Cold War, or Jim Crow. What it might do, however, is to help us to trace and maybe to catch at forms of historical belief or historical desire that would otherwise go missing. Third, although the difference between times, places, ideas, and investments should not be underrated or ignored, I do want finally to argue for the existence of a longer and coherent period in which the expectations and assumptions that I've been tracking make sense, a timespan maybe longer than the period but shorter than the *longue durée*. Part of what connects George Eliot and Ralph Ellison, Anthony Trollope and Kenneth Arrow, William Morris and Whittaker Chambers is a shared experience of the horizons and limits – if not the value – of sincerity, democratic representation, and the willing suspensions of disbelief that both sincerity and democratic representation entail. Indeed, as Ellison famously argued in "The World and the Jug," his work as a Black novelist demands to be read both within the fraught and violent confines of its moment and also within a longer and less distinct field of literary and cultural reference; it demands that the reader read across levels of political and historical abstraction: "history," he writes, "is history; cultural contacts ever mysterious, and taste exasperatingly personal."[17] In whatever way we might want to characterize that timespan, that field, distribution, or that reading-across, I believe that something like it existed, and, as I will show both here and in Chapter 5 on Nixon and the silent majority, it couldn't and didn't last forever. To imagine any of these figures as "Late Victorians" isn't, in that case, to argue for the centrality, priority, or influence of a single time or place; it is rather to acknowledge, faced with the necessary failure of that or of any term, the

---

[16] Alicia Mireles Christoff, *Novel Relations: Victorian Fiction and British Psychoanalysis* (Princeton, NJ: Princeton University Press, 2019), 16.
[17] Ralph Ellison, "The World and the Jug," *Shadow and Act*, 118.

difficult existence of historical and conceptual continuities that are both entirely real and really resistant.

4.1   A CAUTIOUS CASE FOR KENNETH ARROW

Spy vs. Spy

What is the impossibility theorem, anyway? For Arrow, thinking about impossibility began, as I have begun to suggest, with a broader question about the relation between individuals and groups. Thinking back to the start of his project, Arrow later recalled its peculiarly and yet somehow appropriately affable start. On leave from the Cowles Commission in Chicago, Arrow took a summer job at the RAND Corporation in 1948:

> I remember one day at coffee. We had coffee regularly, and this philosopher, Olaf Helmer, whom I may have mentioned before, the man who translated [Alfred] Tarski's book, was there. Helmer said, "I don't understand something. We're trying to apply game theory to the Soviet Union and the United States, but this theory is applied to people, individuals. What do you mean by the United States? It's a collective of many people. They've got different views."[18]

In 1948, game theory was still *the done thing* at RAND, and thinking about the simmering contest between the US and the Soviet Union as a zero-sum game between two players made morphological sense.[19] For game theory, as imagined by John von Neumann, Oskar Morgenstern, and others at RAND, "a 'game' is a conflict situation where one must make a choice knowing that others are making choices too, and the outcome of the conflict will be determined in some prescribed way by all the choices made."[20] Because the strategic standoff between the Soviet Union and the United States could look or, maybe more, *feel* like just such a game – like a game of chess, poker, chicken, or roshambo – there seemed to be an intuitive fit

---

[18] Kenneth J. Arrow, *On Ethics and Economics: Conversations with Kenneth J. Arrow*, ed. Kristen Renwick Monroe and Nicholas Monroe Lampros (London: Routledge, 2017), 33.

[19] Arrow on game theory: "Of course one of the new ideas was game theory, which was spreading. John von Neumann and Oskar Morgenstern had written a book in 1944, I guess. It's one of the few things I read when I was in the army. It's a very long book and it's got all sorts of things in it; it's rather weird but it's clearly one of the important new ideas." Arrow, *On Ethics and Economics*, 32–33.

[20] William Poundstone, *Prisoner's Dilemma* (New York: Anchor Books, 1993), 6.

between it and the austere constraints of game-theoretical models like the prisoner's dilemma, cake-cutting, or counting pennies.[21]

The problem, as Helmer intuited and as Arrow demonstrated, was that, even though one might believe that or act *as if* there were only two players in this game (and, of course, that fiction was everywhere belied by the complex and interwoven realities of domestic conflict, colonial expropriation, nonalignment, decolonization, and proxy war), it was much harder to imagine these players as *rational* in any operable sense. To make choices "knowing that others are making choices too," one needs to assume that both players are acting rationally, that is, that they are acting coherently and in the service of definable interests. "Rational choice theorists," write Green and Shapiro, "generally agree on an instrumental conception of individual rationality, by reference to which people are thought to maximize their expected utilities in formally predictable ways."[22] This account of strategic rationality is, of course, limited in any case. For some, the shallow and, as it were, distorting horizons of rational choice present the researcher with an acknowledged and acceptable cost. Although the methodological reduction of human agency to so thin a model will occlude much that is real about life, what little it can tell us is valuable even if – or rather precisely because – it knows not to try and tell us everything. For others, however, the costs of this reduction are too high because what it leaves out is any reckoning with the kinds of agency, interest, and desire that make us both historical and human. A view of people so starkly attenuated can produce only false accounts of what people do and how they understand and live with one another. The model wins its limited coherence at the large expense of truth.

Helmer and Arrow, however, were working on a different problem. Even if one accepts the costs and benefits of game theory's methodological reduction, how should one apply its account of *individual* rationality to the behavior of groups, communities, or states? What would it mean to say that entities as big, as complex, as internally riven as the United States or the Soviet Union wanted something? If it can mean something definite or at least legible for me to say that I want a donut, it can't mean the same thing to say that a whole country wants open borders, lower taxes, social justice, or a fight to the death over pure prestige. There is, it seems clear,

---

[21] For more on the feel or the style of RAND thinking, see my essay, "RAND Narratology," *Representations* 149(1) (Winter 2020), 31–72.

[22] Donald Green and Ian Shapiro, *Pathologies of Rational Choice Theory: A Critique of Applications in Political Science* (New Haven, CT: Yale University Press, 1994), 17.

some metaphorical or metonymic relation between these two uses of "want," some way of relating, either conceptually or practically, the motives of the individual and the motives of the group. It seems, however, equally clear that those different but related uses are not finally the same: want≠want. This is what Arrow sought to demonstrate: how we might talk about groups or states as rational actors in a way that was more than like how we talk about individuals as rational actors.

The question of what Arrow was really doing for Helmer is a telling one. Joe Oppenheimer writes that Arrow

> was asked to figure out the best placement of submarines in the Pacific Ocean, given the increasing hostilities between the United States and the USSR. To calculate how each party might place its submarines rationally, Arrow needed to know what the national interests of both the Soviets and the Americans. [sic] He found the notion of national interest puzzling. He could conceptualize the USSR's interest as that of Stalin. But how was he to conceptualize the aggregate interest of the people of the United States?[23]

S. M. Amadae writes, on the contrary, that Arrow "was assigned the task of formulating a utility function for the entire Soviet Union in order to anchor a game theoretic calculation."[24] In these two overlapping but opposed accounts it was *either* the United States *or* the Soviet Union that posed a particular and, as it were, characterological problem for Helmer, Arrow, and game theory. Both accounts seem plausible for different reasons. On the one hand, the presence of Stalin as dictator would not only allow the analyst to take the state as an unwieldy proxy for the man but also would come tacitly to underwrite one of Arrow's four fundamental criteria: the condition of nondictatorship. It could make sense, in that case, to follow Oppenheimer and see that it was the pluralist fecundity, the Whitmanian multiplicity of America that could not be managed by something as sterile as the zero-sum game. On the other hand, the

---

[23] Joe Oppenheimer, *Principles of Politics* (Cambridge: Cambridge University Press, 2012), 198.

[24] S. M. Amadae, "Arrow's Impossibility Theorem and the National Security State," *Studies in History and Philosophy of Science* 36(4) (2005): 736. Alex Abella seems to follow Amadae's lead in his *Soldiers of Reason*: "This much we know: arriving at RAND as a summer intern in 1948, after studying statistics at Columbia University and working for the reform-oriented Cowles Commission, Arrow received a confidential-level security clearance with the task of establishing a collective 'utility function' for the Soviet Union." Since neither Oppenheimer nor Amadae and Abella offer any citations to support this part of their account, I still don't know how it is that "this much we know." Abella, *Soldiers of Reason: The RAND Corporation and the Rise of the American Empire* (Boston: Mariner Books, 2009), 49–50. Also see Amadae, *Rationalizing Capitalist Democracy: The Cold War Origins of Rational Choice Liberalism* (Chicago: University of Chicago Press, 2003), 102–103; and John McCumber, *The Philosophy Scare: The Politics of Reason in the Early Cold War* (Chicago: University of Chicago Press, 2016), 91–93.

RAND Corporation did spend a lot time in early days trying to *understand* a Soviet Union that was cast as strange, secretive, and ethnographically other:

> Judging it difficult to gauge Soviet intentions from official sources of information, RAND made an almost fantastic effort to get inside the Soviet mind. RAND instituted a hermeneutic study of the writings of Lenin and Stalin (*The Operational Code of the Politburo*) in the hope that this would assist American diplomats in dealing with their Soviet colleagues. They commissioned no less a figure than Margaret Mead to do a study on Soviet attitudes toward authority. One of the most amazing of the Soviet studies was the creation of a doppelgänger Soviet Ministry of Economics in Santa Monica.[25]

According to Amadae, the problem for choice was not America's unresolvable tension between agential sovereignty and democratic pluralism, but rather a more existential and overdetermined encounter with an Eastern and inscrutable other.

In truth, I haven't been able to find a place where Arrow really says the one thing or the other, so my guess is that he and Helmer were finally more interested in the general methodological problem of moving from individuals to groups, and that the question really didn't have much to do with the putative character of either the US or the Soviet Union. Writing in 1991, Arrow said as much: Helmer, he recalled, "was troubled about the application of game theory when the players were interpreted as nations. The meaning of utility or preference for an individual was clear enough, but what was meant by that for a collectivity of individuals?"[26] He said on another occasion that, "one of the questions that came up was: 'Well, what do we mean by the United States' interests?' The United States is an abstraction. The country is composed of a lot of people, with different interests, just as the Soviet Union is."[27] In any case, even if Arrow began with an especially Cold War problem, he moved quickly into less obviously fraught territory as he turned his attention, as many economists had before him, to collective decision-making as it occurs within the more contained context of the firm. That said, the tendency to read Arrow and the impossibility theorem wholly within the overdetermined explanatory matrix of the Cold War seems significant in itself; the tacit and binary

[25] Poundstone, *Prisoner's Dilemma*, 94.
[26] Kenneth J. Arrow, "The Origins of the Impossibility Theorem," reprinted in *The Arrow Impossibility Theorem*, ed. Eric Maskin and Amartya Sen (New York: Columbia University Press, 2014), 147.
[27] Arrow, *On Ethics and Economics*, 90.

assumption that Arrow must have been worried *either* about the Soviets *or* about the Americans reduces – ironically enough – an otherwise thickly historical question to yet another a zero-sum game. It's not a history *of* game theory; it's history *as* game theory.

Really Flat and Indefinitely Wide

As it was, Arrow took up Helmer's suggestion and set to work under-standing how to compare and then aggregate several individual preferences or utilities into the single preference or utility of a group. Preference, in this case, refers really to a *preference schedule*, a coherent and transitive ordering of preferences as those preferences appear related to a particular question, choice, or state of affairs. Writes Arrow:

> We assume that there is a basic set of alternatives which could conceivably be presented to the chooser. In the theory of consumer's choice, each alternative would be a commodity bundle, in the theory of the firm, each alternative would be a complete decision on all inputs and outputs; in welfare economics, each alternative would be a distribution of commodities and labor requirements.[28]

Following Jevons, Pareto, and others, Arrow assumed "that the behavior of each individual can be expressed by saying that, given any set of alternative actions, he chooses one or the ones which he prefers to all others in that set."[29] In practice, then, a preference schedule is an individual's real or imagined list of choices presented in ranked order of preference. If some-one likes chocolate (**A**) more than vanilla (**B**), and vanilla more than strawberry (**C**), the schedule would look like this: **A>B>C**. There are a few things to add about the logic of the preference schedule. First, as we've already seen in relation to the ordering of preferences in *Phineas Finn*, the schedule is taken as a purely *ordinal* arrangement: while it tells us that someone prefers **A** to **B** and **B** to **C**, it does not tell us *how much* or *why* they prefer them. To represent preferences as comparable, the schedule must ignore any *cardinal* information about those preferences; ignore, that is, those qualities that would make one person's preference for chocolate different from another person's preference for chocolate. Where you (an ice cream obsessive) love vanilla but *really* love chocolate, I (who, because I am no fun, dislike all flavors of ice cream) hate chocolate, but hate vanilla

---

[28] Arrow, *Social Choice and Individual Values*, 11.
[29] Kenneth J. Arrow, "The Possibility of a Universal Social Welfare Function," RAND P-41 (September 26, 1948), 3.

even more; although these positions are entirely different from a cardinal point of view, they are ordinally identical: **A>B**.

Second, although writers tend to present preference schedules as some succinct and thus immediately legible choice between **A**, **B**, and **C**, in practice one needs to imagine schedules as indefinitely, maybe even impossibly long: "Arrow took *individual* preferences to be complete orderings of the states of affairs."[30] When, for instance, I choose to buy a bicycle, I am choosing the bicycle not only instead of a unicycle but also instead of *every other thing* within the ostensibly defined but indefinitely large set of things I could also have bought, all of which must – according to the scheme – stand in one or another expressed or tacit relation of preference to the bicycle. Although we wouldn't, for instance, imagine the sequence *bicycle>unicycle>parrot* as meaningful, that sequence – although nonsensical or willfully surreal from the perspective of *cardinal* values – makes just as much *ordinal* sense as any other sequence. As a result, it becomes possible, indeed, necessary to imagine if not actually to describe a preference schedule the hypothetical length of which will approach a dizzying limit. Indeed, if the characters imagined by social choice theory are not deep, they are at least very, very wide; if, in other words, literary critics tend to think about the realistic representation of character in terms of an alterity or psychological depth that resembles the qualitative or metaphoric force of what Kant called the dynamic sublime, the always flat but indefinitely wide complexity of an ordinal preference schedule approaches the quantitative or metonymic density of the mathematical sublime and, perhaps, a point at which ordinal quantity might seem to tip over into cardinal or psychological quality.

Seen in these terms, the preference schedule can emerge, depending on how you see it, either as a theory of character or as a powerful but self-consciously limited means of representing something about character. The difference between a *theory* and a *means* follows, of course, from whether, on the one hand, we want the account to be a sufficient ontological claim, meant to tell us what people really are or whether, on the other, we want the account to be a limited heuristic, meant to tell us something *but not everything* about some people some of the time. Although both Arrow's supporters and his critics have sometimes taken him as offering an ontology of character, it's clear from his writing that his reliance on ordinal rankings of preferences as a limited representation of character is, rather, a particular means to a particular end; if a preference schedule can get you to

---

[30] Sen, *Collective Choice and Social Welfare*, 5.

a more robust set of decisions within the context of the firm, it can't get you to *Hamlet* – and Arrow also likes *Hamlet*.[31] That said, even if we take the preference schedule as a particular and limited means to a particular and limited representational end – a group's decision, a committee's choice, an election – it is or it implies a way of thinking about the complex relation between real people and how we choose to represent them.

I've suggested before that one of the difficult things about votes is that they can be taken *to mean* different things in different ways. Is a vote a representation of a preference or of a ranked relation between preferences? Is it an interest or a wish, a belief or a hope, a secret or even a lie? Is it a fact, a symptom, or maybe even a kind of dream? Is the vote the originating index of an essential truth about who I am and always have been, or is it, rather, a late and conditional trace of a deliberative process that could, under other conditions, have gone another way? Does a vote allow me to say what I really want to say, or does it rather shape in advance what it is even possible for me to say? Does a vote represent what I really think, what I only think I think, what I want others to think I think, or what I want others to think I only think I think? In whatever way you think about it, the vote is tied up with questions about the relation between people and representations of people. This is one reason why it's easy and right to feel that there must be some deeper historical relation between these questions and the proliferation of literary theories of character, between different economic models and ideas about flat or round characters (Forster), formal realism (Watt), the typical character (Lukács), and, of course, the Proper Name: the name, says Barthes, "is an instrument of exchange: it allows the substitution of a nominal unit for a collection of characteristics by establishing an equivalent relationship between sign and sum: it is a bookkeeping method in which, the price being equal, condensed merchandise is preferable to voluminous merchandise."[32] I'll want, however, to make a more particular case here. That is, while we might see Arrow as a slight variation on this theme, I want to argue instead that his implicit theory of character – of the possibility and impossibility of character – is shaped by a more specific historical context, one that makes for more definite links between the parallel development of electoral theory and literary value at midcentury.

---

[31] Arrow cryptically entitled a short biographical essay "I Know a Hawk from a Handsaw," in *Eminent Economists: Their Life Philosophies*, ed. Michael Szenberg (Cambridge: Cambridge University Press, 1992), 42–51.
[32] Roland Barthes, *S/Z: An Essay*, trans. Richard Miller (New York: Hill and Wang, 1974), 95.

Weak Criteria

Arrow's question was thus how to aggregate many or few really flat and indefinitely long preference schedules into the single preference schedule of a group. Is there an obvious or a best or even a good-enough system, device, or rule that would allow us to do that? And how, at last, would we know if it were good enough? What norms or expectations would allow us to test different methods and to distinguish the good from the bad and the better from the best? As we've seen, this is an old problem that reveals itself in both theory and practice. Looking all the way back to Chapter 1, we saw that this or something like it was at the heart of Rousseau's project in *The Social Contract*. "We ought," he writes, "to scrutinize the act by which people become *a* people, for that act, being necessarily antecedent to the other, is the real foundation of society."[33] What is that act, and what are its rules? How do we get from the one of the *individual*, to the many of the *people*, and then both forward and back to the one of the *general will*? And, as we saw with Carroll's work on decision-making in the context of committees, the same vote will produce very different and yet internally coherent results depending on the rules of the game. Counting the same votes according to a plurality rule or a simple-majority rule can result in two different winners, begging the question: how does one decide which rule to follow? When choosing a rule amounts to choosing a winner, on what good grounds can members of a committee make that quietly definitive choice-before-the-choice?

With this problem in mind, Arrow sought to identify "weak" criteria – which is to say uncontroversial expectations – against which to measure or to test the efficacy of different devices for making social choices. He came up with four of them, and, while they are all norms – values, not facts – they are indeed weak. The first is *Condition U* or *unrestricted domain*; the second is *Condition P* or the *Pareto principle*; the third is *Condition I* or *the independence of irrelevant alternatives*; and the fourth is *Condition D* or *nondictatorship*.[34] *U* says simply that a good or rational system should recognize – not restrict – every logically possible preference schedule. "Given the definition of a social welfare function, this condition amounts," says Prasanta Pattanaik, "to the requirement that, for every logically possible profile of individual orderings, the social welfare function should

---

[33] Jean-Jacques Rousseau, *The Social Contract*, trans. Maurice Cranston (London: Penguin, 1968), 59.
[34] Although the conditions are Arrow's, the now-standard nomenclature comes from Amartya Sen, who systematized Arrow's findings. See Amartya Sen, *Collective Choice and Social Welfare*.

specify a unique social ordering."[35] If, in other words, a given statement of preference is *possible* within the logical limits of a given set of choices, an individual should not be prevented from stating that preference; the rules of an election should not determine in advance what, within the constraints of that election, it is possible to prefer.[36] P "requires," writes Alfred MacKay, "that when every individual without exception prefers X to Y, the device [or rule] must rank X above Y in its social ordering. That is, whatever else it may do, an acceptable device must honor unanimity."[37] I, which we discussed at length in Chapter 2 (remember Morgenbesser's blueberry pie), says that the ordering of a social preference between **A** and **B** (**A>B**) should not be affected by the introduction of an irrelevant third alternative. Where, that is, the addition of **C** to an already stated preference for **A** over **B** can reasonably result in **C>A>B**, **A>C>B**, or **A>B>C**, it shouldn't – if the device is rational – be able to result in **B>A>C**, **B>C>A**, or **C>B>A.** And, finally, D says that if every person but X chooses **A>B**, then a rule or system that would result in **B>A** because X and only X chose it cannot be rational; or, rather, such a system cannot be *both* rational *and* democratic.

The strong force of these four weak conditions derives, paradoxically, from their very weakness. Who, Arrow seems implicitly to ask, would or could argue against conditions as reasonable, as mild as these, even if they are, in the end, asserted norms and not observable facts? They were meant, argues Amadae, to be "so minimally demanding as to serve as the basis of an uncontested consensus."[38] If a preference is possible and it's also yours, you should be able to say so, right? If *everyone* agrees that something is a good idea, then that's what we should do, right? You can't have a dictator in a democracy, can you? As, however, Arrow began to do the math and to test different aggregation systems against these four very minimal, "very reasonable" conditions, he discovered that there wasn't a single system that could meet all four conditions without even leading to the kinds of failure or paradox we've already seen at work in Carroll: "Under certain very reasonable restrictions," wrote Arrow in 1948, "there is no method of aggregating individual preferences which leads to a consistent social preferences scale, apart from certain trivial methods which violate democratic

---

[35] Pattanaik, "Introduction," *Arrow Impossibility Theorem*, 5.

[36] Imagine saying to someone, "We have chocolate, vanilla, and strawberry. But you can't have strawberry. Why? Because you can't."

[37] Alfred F. MacKay, *Arrow's Theorem: The Paradox of Social Choice* (New Haven, CT: Yale University Press, 1980), 8.

[38] S. M. Amadae, *Rationalizing Capitalist Democracy*, 114.

principles."[39] There was, in other words, no foolproof way to structure or to select a decision process or electoral procedure when three or more people were choosing between three or more alternatives that would *always* avoid paradox or contradiction while also observing these four restrictions. And, because one cannot design an election that would *always* produce both reasonable and noncontradictory results (that would observe at least these four minimally rational conditions and that would also never dead-lock in one or another form of logical paradox), settling definitively on a best form of democratic election is, according to Arrow's theorem, impossible.

That's Impossible!

Arrow's result can seem pretty dire. Putatively democratic elections were, it seemed to suggest, irrational, paradoxical, haphazard. Various democratic skeptics – William Riker (whom I discussed in relation to Carroll), James Buchanan, Mancur Olson, Garret Hardin, and others – argued not only that individual interests and collective action were antithetical but also that the very idea of collective action was either an enabling fiction or an outright lie. As Annie McClanahan writes in a brief but outstanding account of the coincident rise of microeconomics and the modern novel, methodological individualism (MI) "refuted both the intellectual claims of historical materialism and the politics or ideology of collectivism – indeed, it sought to debunk the idea that there was any such thing as a 'social totality.'"[40] In another bracing account of MI, Daniel Rogers writes,

> Strapped to the "impossibility theorem" that Kenneth Arrow had posited years earlier to explain why under certain conditions different preference rankings could not be unambiguously aggregated, voting produced no majority will. Majoritarianism yielded, to the contrary, only "a fundamental and inescapable arbitrariness," as Riker put it, an endless, chaotic play of logrolling and vote cycling as factions won and lost control of the agenda.[41]

Fueled, first, by the agendas of neoliberalism and the libertarian right ("there is," said Margaret Thatcher, "no such thing as society ... "), second, by the raw professional ambition of Riker and others, and, third,

---

[39] Arrow, "The Possibility of a Universal Social Welfare Function," 3.

[40] Annie McClanahan, "Methodological Individualism and the Novel in the Age of Microeconomics, 1871 to the Present," in *Timelines of American Literature*, ed. Cody Marrs and Christopher Hager (Baltimore: Johns Hopkins University Press, 2019), 268.

[41] Daniel T. Rogers, *Age of Fracture* (Cambridge, MA: Harvard University Press, 2012), 86–87.

by impossibility's dank rhetorical and maybe reactionary appeal, this especially gloomy take on Arrow has cast, as Gerry Mackie puts it, "a long, dark shadow over democratic politics":

> Although democratization is the main trend in the world today, the main intellectual trend in American political science is the view that democracy is chaotic, arbitrary, meaningless, and impossible. This trend originated with economist Kenneth Arrow's impossibility theorem, which was applied to politics by the late William Riker, political scientist at the University of Rochester. The earlier attack on democracy by Mosca, Michels, and Pareto was revived with fashionable new methods. Riker had great organizational resources and used them to promulgate a particular interpretation of Arrow's theorem ... and to recruit and place his students far and wide.[42]

Impossibility, it turns out, had legs.

If, however, this interpretation of Arrow succeeded largely because of Riker's institutional savvy and personal grit, its continuing appeal must owe something less placeable but maybe more powerful to the *feeling* of impossibility, to that little rush that comes with showing other people that what they take as a virtue is, in fact, exactly the opposite. It feels good somehow to show other people that they have felt good about something that should have made them feel bad. Recycling isn't really good; it's bad! Tofu isn't really good; it's bad! Almond milk isn't really good; it's bad! Exercise isn't really good; it's bad! Democracy isn't really good; it's bad! An all-too-familiar trollish indulgence, this is yet another version of A. O. Hirschman's "perversity thesis" from *The Rhetoric of Reaction*: "The perverse effect is a special and extreme case of the unintended consequence. Here the failure of foresight of ordinary human actors is well-nigh total as their actions are shown to produce precisely the opposite of what was intended; the social scientists analyzing the perverse effect, on the other hand, experience a great feeling of superiority – and revel in it."[43] Making the normies see that democracy wasn't just flawed but *impossible* felt good.

---

[42] Gerry Mackie, *Democracy Defended* (Cambridge: Cambridge University Press, 2003), 2–3. For more on Riker as institution builder, see Amadae and de Mesquita: "Riker's ambitious platform for reorienting political science may have gone little further than his personal biography had he not tirelessly and deftly built up a graduate program specifically geared toward generating theorists ultimately capable of transforming the entire discipline of political science. A unique constellation of circumstances provided Riker with the resources and institutional infrastructure requisite to carry out his program for reform." S. M. Amadae and Bruce Bueno de Mesquita, "The Rochester School: The Origins of Positive Political Theory," *Annual Review of Political Science* 2 (1999): 278–279.

[43] Albert O. Hirschman, *The Rhetoric of Reaction: Perversity, Futility, Jeopardy* (Cambridge, MA: Harvard University Press, 1991), 36.

The problem, however, with Riker's bleak take on Arrow is that it is based on a misreading or, rather, a misapplication of the idea of impossibility. While it might be exciting to think or to say that the impossibility theorem shows that democracy is impossible, Arrow's methodological aim was in fact far more limited; what the impossibility theorem shows to be impossible isn't democracy itself but, rather, the development of a foolproof evaluative or a normative procedure that would allow us to say once and for all that a given rule or device is the best rule or device for aggregating individual preferences. What is impossible is the establishment of a consistent or a universal norm against which we could test the rationality of democratic elections. What is impossible is demonstrating that any given rule or device would or could work in every possible case.[44] What *isn't* impossible according to Arrow is democracy as such. Elections happen all the time, and they often work. It is, however, difficult to say with certainty, first, if a given election or rule will work in a particular case and, second, why another election or rule wouldn't have worked better. "Social choice theory," says Arrow, "offers only a limited criticism of democratic procedures."[45] If, in other words, Arrow's result is profound, it is not profoundly undemocratic. It is a skeptical result but not a hopeless result.

While Arrow's real usefulness to the libertarian right has been thus overstated or misconstrued, some criticisms of his ideas as mere ideological artifacts of the culture of the Cold War or as intellectual apologies for acquisitive bourgeois individualism have also missed what's most interesting about Arrow. In her otherwise meticulous discussion of methodological individualism, McClanahan lumps Arrow in with other "midcentury microeconomists" who took "the individual as the relevant unit of economic analysis even when the object in question was far larger than a given individual."[46] Bruce Kucklick, sensing something more sinister at work in Arrow, writes that he "did not applaud democratic deliberation in order to let a thousand flowers bloom. Democracy could only produce a good society if it inculcated similar attitudes toward alternatives – a certain

---

[44] "Behind Professor Arrow's discussion of various election rules and their characterizing properties, I see a fundamental issue: is there one election scheme which should be employed in all cases, that is, independent of the contents of the underlying alternatives?" Wulf Gaertner, "Discussion of Arrow's Paper," in *Social Choice Re-examined*, ed. Kenneth J. Arrow, Amartya Sen, and Kotaro Suzumura (London: Palgrave Macmillan, 1996), 1:11.

[45] Kenneth J. Arrow, "The Functions of Social Choice Theory," in *Social Choice Re-examined*, ed. Kenneth J. Arrow, Amartya Sen, and Kotaro Suzumura (London: Palgrave Macmillan, 1996), 1:5.

[46] Annie McClanahan, "Methodological Individualism and the Novel," 267.

cultural homogeneity – that mimicked the unified will of a dictatorial society."[47] Similarly, Amadae argues that the otherwise inexplicable success of Arrow's theorem is the result of the ideological comfort it offered to the consolidation of a specifically capitalist democracy during the Cold War. Amadae argues: first, that Arrow's argument managed to put a formalist, definitive, and somehow comforting end to debates around questions about social welfare and the interpersonal comparison of utilities that had roiled professional economics in the 1930s and 1940s; second, that Arrow managed successfully to pit the humble, pragmatic, apple-pie empiricism of American economic theory against both "the philosophical idealism of Rousseau, Kant, and Marx" and the conceptual brutality of Soviet totalitarianism; and third, that Arrow endorsed an ego-syntonic (my term) "assumption of a thoroughgoing individualism that leaves it entirely up to the individual to decide what suits him, whether that individual acts as a Veblenesque conspicuous consumer or not."[48] For Amadae, in other words, Arrow's impossibility theorem thrived during the Cold War because it set the salience of the individual-as-consumer over and against what was cast as the decadent fiction of the socialist or communist collective: *Social Choice and Individual Values* "achieves its status as a classic economics text of the twentieth century by facing the challenges to American freedom as posed by Joseph Schumpeter, Karl Popper, and Friedrich Hayek, and by the visceral threat of the palpable social alternative offered by Soviet Russia."[49] This is a compelling kind of cultural analysis. It is historically grounded, it motivates both the production and the reception of Arrow's work, and it proposes a thick relation between context, ideology, and ideas that belies the minimalist investments of rational choice theories; it is thus not only a way of reading the capitalist democratic drift of Arrow's work but also a way of offering an implicit and critical answer to it.

The problem here is that the Cold War can't tell us everything about impossibility. (We saw something similar at work with the zero-sum assumption that, because he was writing during the Cold War, Arrow had to have been really saying something significant about *either* the Soviet Union *or* the United States when, it seems, neither was strictly the case.) First, Amadae suggests that Arrow "was a consummate defense intellectual

---

[47] Bruce Kucklick, *Blind Oracles: Intellectuals and War from Kennan to Kissinger* (Princeton, NJ: Princeton University Press, 2007), 29
[48] Amadae, *Rationalizing Capitalist Democracy*, 113, 107.
[49] Amadae, *Rationalizing Capitalist Democracy*, 125.

whose career as a key contributor to the neoclassical synthesis in economics is inseparable from his Cold War policy role."[50] At first blush, this seems reasonable enough, given the both the reality and the reputation of the RAND Corporation, where Arrow first came up with his theorem. That said, Arrow's comparatively intermittent affiliation with RAND (although he remained a titular consultant at RAND, he in fact left to join Stanford's Department of Economics shortly after writing up his impossibility result) makes it harder simply to cast him as a Cold Warrior, especially considering the fact that very little of his published work – early or late – deals explicitly with military matters.[51] Amadae tries to address this disparity by pointing to the fact that "most of the documentary evidence for this period in Arrow's life remains unavailable, either because it is covered by the secrecy blanket of secured information or because Arrow's personal papers are available only selectively from Duke University's archive of the work of twentieth-century economists."[52] The argument here seems to be that an absence of evidence is somehow really the best evidence of Arrow's top secret bona fides. That might be appealing from a narrative perspective, but it doesn't change the fact that, in this case, the absence of evidence isn't really evidence of anything or, at least, it isn't yet. That's not, however, to say that there isn't a relation between Arrow and his Cold War context. On the contrary, I'll argue in a moment that we need to resist thinking of the Cold War as a single, static, zero-sum game and to dig more and not less deeply into the political and cultural texture of those years.

Second, both Amadae and Kucklick seem to suggest that there is in Arrow's work some resistance or even antipathy to the democratic heterogeneity of the collectivity. For Amadae, this appears, first, in Arrow's

---

[50] Amadae, *Rationalizing Capitalist Democracy*, 85.

[51] The obvious exception is his 1955 paper, "Economic Aspects of Military Research and Development," but, even there, he uses the occasion for thinking about the military mostly to reflect broadly on the question of how civilian firms, which he sees as almost identical to military organizations, should understand investment in research over time. He has little very to say about the military as such. Other papers from the period on "cost-performance," "input-output projections," and related topics are legible within the larger turn at RAND from game theory to operations and systems analysis but, while they are of that milieu, it's hard to see them as the work of a dedicated defense intellectual. Arrow did write one paper during his World War II service, but as a meteorologist and not a military strategist. He published "On the Use of Winds in Flight Planning" in the *Journal of Meteorology* in 1949. Compare this record with the RAND publications of Albert Wohlstetter ("Selection and Use of Strategic Air Bases," "The Delicate Balance of Terror," etc.) or Thomas Schelling ("The Reciprocal Fear of Surprise Attack," "Nuclear Weapons and Limited War," etc.), and the difference between his work and the work of a really "consummate defense intellectual" becomes clear.

[52] Amadae, *Rationalizing Capitalist Democracy*, 85.

formative arguments with the assumptions of the welfarists and, second, in his resistance to the ideal collectivities of Rousseau, Kant, and Marx. (Kucklick, for his part, manages the frankly bizarre suggestion that Arrow's methodological individualism was not really an answer to Stalin but instead a way to achieve a homegrown and anti-pluralistic dictatorship *by other means*.) It seems to me, however, that Arrow's critical engagement with welfare economics as well as with Rousseau, Kant, and Marx was meant not to deny the idea or the possibility or the virtue of a shared sense of social welfare; indeed, his writings are often proof of an intense and anxious commitment to the importance, trouble, and reward of a life lived with others. Here's how he opens *The Limits of Organization*:

> The intricacies and paradoxes in relations between the individual and his actions in the social context have been put very well by the great sage, Rabbi Hillel: "If I am not for myself, then who is for me? And if I am not for others, then who am I? And if not now, when?" Here we have, in three successive sentences, the essence of a tension that we all feel between the claims of individual self-fulfillment and those of social conscience and action. It is the necessity of every individual to express in some matters his intrinsic values. But the demands of society and the needs of the individual, expressed only within that society, require that he be for others as well as for himself and that the others appears as ends to him as well as means. With two such questions with such different implications, it is no wonder we get to the third question: How can I behave urgently and with conviction when there are so many doubtful variables to contend with?[53]

What's more, in almost all accounts of his life and intellectual development Arrow maintains not only that he had been, like so many others, a socialist in his youth but also that his career ought to be understood as a long and admittedly cautious effort not to reject but rather to sustain, to modulate, and to extend that youthful commitment. "Raised in modest circumstances in New York City during the Depression," notes Tim Rogan, "Arrow had embraced socialism in his youth, and leaned left throughout his life."[54] "Economic theory," Arrow observed, "had two roles: as the needed basis for empirical inquiry using the tools of theoretical statistics and as the basis for a better economic world, possibly embodied in a democratic socialist system."[55]

---

[53] Arrow, *Limits of Organization*, 15.
[54] Tim Rogan, *The Moral Economists: R. H. Tawney, Karl Polanyi, E. P. Thompson, and the Critique of Capitalism* (Princeton, NJ: Princeton University Press, 2018), 193.
[55] Arrow, "I Know a Hawk from a Handsaw," 45.

In "A Cautious Case for Socialism," Arrow takes special care to distinguish himself both from the conservative gadfly Irving Kristol, whose career offered sardonic proof that "a Marxist background" appears to be "an essential prerequisite for the development of a neoconservative thinker" and, more significantly, from Friedrich von Hayek: "we certainly," he says, "need not fear that gradual moves toward increasing government intervention and other forms of social experimentation will lead to an irreversible slide to 'serfdom.'"[56] (One might also consider his sympathetic and surprisingly well-informed discussion of Althusser, Western Marxism, and Michael Harrington's *The Twilight of Capitalism* in the *Partisan Review*.)[57] As opposed to some accounts, Arrow's methodological break with the welfare economics needs, in that case, to be understood not as a blanket or neoconservative rejection of the social, of the collective, or even of *socialism*, but rather as a technical argument about the logical supposition that one could meaningfully compare or, for that matter, really know the preferences of others. One can, of course, believe both that we have to live with other people and that we can't know for sure what other people want or think. That's not an argument against the existence of the social; it's, rather, an acknowledgement that living life with others isn't easy. There is too such a thing as society, and it's really hard!

Which brings us to the third point: Arrow's individualism. As I have said, Amadae and others stress Arrow's reliance on the methodological priority of the individual at the expense of the social. One can find a similar argument in John McCumber's *The Philosophy Scare*:

> Social choices are thus entirely determined from individual preferences and take effect only insofar as they affect those preferences. Arrow asserts that this captures the individualism of the "classical liberal creed" as stated by F. H. Knight: "Liberalism takes the individual as given, and views the social problem as one of right relations between given individuals."[58]

---

[56] Kenneth J. Arrow, "A Cautious Case for Socialism," *Dissent* 25 (Fall 1978), 472.

[57] Kenneth J. Arrow, "The Economy and the Economist," *Partisan Review* 46(1) (Winter 1979): 113–116.

[58] McCumber goes on to offer a number of "extensions" that he sees as latent in Arrow: for instance, that "Arrow's findings on social choice must be extended from the locus of his empirical warrants – mainly, Western capitalist democracies – to societies the world over"; and that "reason is merely the ability to rank one's own preferences, and freedom is merely the ability to choose what one most prefers." It's good that McCumber acknowledges that neither of these "extensions" is actually "made in" or "even considered by" Arrow in *Social Choice and Individual Values* because these ideas are not in fact Arrow's; they seem, rather, to be more or less coherent ideas that McCumber has had about the Cold War that he wants subsequently to "discover" at work in Arrow's book. And discover them he does! McCumber, *The Philosophy Scare*, 81.

The problem here is that this position confuses methodological individualism with ontological individualism. If, in other words, Arrow were saying that people were really like the individual as imagined by rational choice theory – isolated, wholly self-interested, incapable of change, unaffected by history, ordinal and not cardinal – we would be right to recoil. When we really look, however, at the passage that McCumber cites, it is clear that Arrow is saying that in order to think *here and now* about this technical aspect of social choice, we need to act *as if* this is what people are like even when we of course know that they are not really like that at all; "we will," writes Arrow, "also *assume* in the present study that individual values are taken as data and are not capable of being altered by the nature of the decision process itself . . . though *the unreality of this assumption* has been asserted by such writers as Veblen, Professor J. M. Clark, and Knight . . . " (my emphasis).[59] Arrow is, in other words, clear that his individualism is an expedient heuristic or a methodological fiction as opposed to a hard ontological claim.

What's more, when Arrow speaks more directly about what people are really like and why we ought not to build social systems based simply on the interpersonal comparison of preferences, he talks in terms not of rationality or utility but rather of history and mystery. In terms of *mystery*:

> Respect for others is, to me, based on a certain degree of mystery about them. Others are different in ways that are not completely reducible to our understanding. Of course, there is a large degree of mutual comprehension; otherwise no genuine society would be possible. All I mean is that there will always be a degree of incomprehensibility, of unpredictability, that is an intrinsic element of individual autonomy.[60]

Or, as he writes elsewhere, "the values of others must always retain an element of mystery. The equal but different emotionally based axiological drives of others can never be fully communicated."[61] It makes sense, in that case, that when Arrow had occasion to write about the literature he loved, he neglected the transactional exemplarity of *Robinson Crusoe* in favor of the darkling uncertainties of Milton, Hardy, Proust, Joyce, Kafka, and Poe. And, in terms of *history*: "In some ideal sense, life philosophies, like economies, may be refined by successive adjustments through reflection, experience, and intellectual interaction with the past and the present

---

[59] Arrow, *Social Choice and Individual Values*, 7–8.
[60] Arrow, "I Know a Hawk from a Handsaw," 45.   [61] Arrow, "Cautious Case for Socialism," 472.

until they come into equilibrium independent of initial conditions. In fact, neither is ever independent of history."[62]

As opposed, in other words, to a view of individuals that would treat them as isolated, autonomous, and – at least in terms of their preferences – uncomplicated, Arrow's system relies instead on what we might think of as an especially novelistic or, to use Georg Lukács's phrase, a *problematic* view of character, on a view that assumes a dissonance between the inner and the outer life, a dissonance between a character's aims and the realization of those aims, a dissonance between the individual and the social world. Says Lukács:

> In the biographical form the unfulfillable, sentimental striving both for the immediate unity of life and for a completely rounded architecture of the system is balanced and brought to rest: it is transformed into being. The central character of a biography is significant only by his relationship to a world of ideals that stands above him: but this world, in turn, is realized only through its existence within that individual and his lived experience. Thus in the biographical form the balance of both spheres which are unrealized and unrealizable in isolation produces a new and autonomous life that is, however paradoxically, complete in itself and immanently meaningful: the life of the problematic individual.[63]

On the one hand, we can – if we squint just a little – see that the inadequate but necessary structure of the vote (as preference, interest, wish, belief, and so on) shares more than a little with its close bourgeois neighbor, the novel. Just as the novel exists for Lukács and others as both a representation and a symptom of a fallen or alienated world, a world far removed from the mythic immediacy of Greek life, so is the vote, as it functions within a modern representative democracy, both compensation for and an index of our distance from the ostensibly direct democracy of fourth-century Athens.[64] I've already written about how we might think of the fictions of electoral representation alongside "the novel and other discourses of suspended disbelief"; this is yet another way to think about that discursive relation. There is, on the other hand, a related but even closer connection to make between Arrow's implicit view of the historical character of the vote and the history of the novel. In *The Limits of Organization*, Arrow writes about a synthetic urge that he takes as broadly characteristic of contemporary politics:

---

[62] Arrow, "I Know a Hawk from a Handsaw," 43.

[63] Georg Lukács, *The Theory of the Novel: A Historico-Philosophical Essay on the Forms of Great Epic* (Cambridge: Massachusetts Institute of Technology Press, 1974), 77.

[64] Of course, the directness of Athenian democracy is itself something of a myth. See, for instance, Hélène Landemore, *Open Democracy: Reinventing Popular Rule for the Twenty-First Century* (Princeton, NJ: Princeton University Press, 2020).

The tension between society and the individual is inevitable. Their claims compete within the individual conscience as well as in the arena of social conflict. There is no sense in which anybody lecturing or writing a huge book can come to a final resolution of these competing claims. All I try to insist here is that some sense of rational balancing of ends and means must be understood to play a major role in our understanding of ourselves and our social role. Let me illustrate by presenting or, more precisely caricaturing some thought tendencies. We have one, loosely called "the new Left thought," not so new perhaps; some of us who have read a little bit of history of thought have heard of anarcho-syndicalism before. Bakunin and Sorel had spoken to the same point many years ago. But it is a real one. There is a demand for what might be termed sincerity, for a complete unity between the individual and the social roles, the notion that somehow in an ideal society there would be no conflict between one's demand on oneself and one's responses to the demands of society. It is true, of course, if you go back to Sorel, you would find mixed in with doctrines of this type the notion that these are also myths. This suggests that the resolution of conflict requires a certain restriction of our field of attention.[65]

After characterizing "the New Right, in its libertarian representatives," in similar terms, Arrow goes on to acknowledge that, "a truly rational discussion of collective action in general or in specific contexts is necessarily complex, and what is even worse, it is necessary incomplete and unresolved. Rationality, after all, has to do with means and ends and their relation. It does not specify what the ends are. It only tries to make us aware of the congruence or dissonance between the two."[66] Arrow ends up, in other words, in a position similar to what Lukács called irony: recognizing that the resolution of inner life and outer life, of the individual and the group, of personal interest and collective action is impossible – at least for us – both Arrow and Lukács take dissonance itself as an occasion for thinking, writing, and living. It is when someone wants simply to wish the dissonance away that we have problems.

This relation becomes more interesting when we consider the fact that Arrow gave the lectures on which *The Limits of Organization* is based only a year or so after Lionel Trilling gave the lectures that would, in turn, make up his last book, *Sincerity and Authenticity*. Although Trilling was older than Arrow, there are interesting points of overlap in their careers. As young men, both lived and worked in a New York intellectual atmosphere defined in part by the breakup of the American left and the argumentative style of the *Partisan Review*; Trilling's *The Liberal Imagination* appeared in

---

[65] Arrow, *Limits of Organization*, 15–16. [66] Arrow, *Limits of Organization*, 17.

1950, just one year before *Social Choice and Individual Values*; Arrow gave his Fels Lectures at Penn a year after Trilling's Norton Lectures at Harvard; and, after Trilling's death, Arrow gave his 1978 talk, "A Cautious Case for Socialism," as part of the Lionel Trilling Seminar at Columbia. In terms that anticipate Arrow's, Trilling defines sincerity – as opposed to authenticity – as something like a knowingly impossible aspiration toward what Arrow saw as "a complete unity between the individual and the social roles." Says Trilling:

> If sincerity is the avoidance of being false to any man through being true to one's own self, we can see that this state of personal existence is not to be attained without the most arduous effort. And yet at a certain point in history certain men and classes of men conceived that *the making of this effort* was of supreme importance in the moral life, and the value they attached to the enterprise of sincerity became a salient, perhaps a definitive, characteristic of Western culture for some four hundred years. (my emphasis)[67]

For Trilling, this sense of both the impossibility and the possibility of sincerity, a concept that remains somehow suspended between synthesis and dissonance, sits at the crossroads of literature, politics, and history; although outdated, the concept served for a time as a way to balance the need for meaning and "the death of God." I want, in what follows, to argue that a similar and similarly if unexpectedly *problematic* play between the individual and the group, between saying and meaning, between personal interest and collective action, between possibility and impossibility is at work in Kenneth Arrow.

Pessimism of the Intellect

For reasons having thus to do with politics, history, and rhetoric, both Arrow's most assiduous critics and some of his most ardent followers have tended to agree that his was a singularly pessimistic result. "Nihilism," writes Rogan, "was one possible (if misconceived) response to Arrow's proof that if economists' assumptions about individual behavior and expectations of rationality were to be upheld, then genuine social choice was impossible. There were certainly some in the American academy who took this view."[68] If, however, it is possible to read impossibility in negative terms, that reading fails, I think, to register the wider import

---

[67] Lionel Trilling, *Sincerity and Authenticity* (Cambridge, MA: Harvard University Press, 1973), 5–6.
[68] Rogan, *Moral Economists*, 194.

and the wider context of Arrow's result. "Unfortunately," writes Sen, "the pessimism generated by Arrow's impossibility result also tended to undermine his immensely important constructive programme of developing a systemic social choice theory that would succeed in characterizing particular ways of making participatory decisions that are possible for a society to have."[69] Sen, almost certainly Arrow's most thorough and generous reader, makes the case here and elsewhere that, while others have often seen the impossibility theorem as the end of the line, Arrow's conditions (U, P, I, and D) should instead be taken as pointed opportunities for thinking about how we might adjust our ideas about people and groups in order to get past or to overcome the logical impasses that would seem to make social life impossible. Says Sen:

> It should be clear that a full axiomatic determination of a particular method of making social choice must inescapably lie next door to an impossibility – indeed just short of it. . . . It is, therefore, to be expected that constructive paths in social choice theory, derived from axiomatic reasoning, would tend to be paved on one side by impossibility results.[70]

For Sen, impossibility isn't the end of the road; it is, rather, how one can recognize an adjacent possibility when one sees it: "The real issue is not, therefore, the ubiquity of impossibility . . . but the reach and reasonableness of the axioms to be used. We have to get on with the basic task of obtaining workable rules that satisfy reasonable requirements, rather than throwing up our arms in despair. . ."[71] This, to get back to the beginning, is yet another form of skepticism without despair.

Reckoning fully with the constructive possibilities raised by Arrow's impossibility result would require more space than I can give it. I'll point just briefly to some ways in which Arrow and Sen imagine what might come next. As we have seen, much of Arrow's early system turns on the assumption that interpersonal comparisons of preferences are not possible: "The viewpoint will be taken here that interpersonal comparison of utilities has no meaning and, in fact, that there is no meaning relevant to welfare comparisons in the measurability of individual utilities."[72] As Amadae has shown, this assumption is, among other things, a late expression of an argument against the logic of utilitarianism that had occupied economics for decades. In an influential 1938 note on "Interpersonal Comparisons of Utility" cited by Arrow, Lionel Robbins suggested that,

[69] Sen, *Collective Choice and Social Welfare*, 6.
[70] Amartya Sen, *Rationality and Freedom* (Cambridge, MA: Harvard University Press, 2004), 74.
[71] Sen, *Collective Choice and Social Welfare*, 9.   [72] Arrow, *Social Choice and Individual Values*, 9.

while he had come to economics as a committed utilitarian and thus as someone who would confidently measure the happiness of the one against the happiness of another, the more he thought about it, the less convincing those hedonic calculations seemed. If economics was to be an empirical study of facts and not an ethical assertion of values, it could not claim to know what could not be known:

> The assumptions of the propositions which did not involve interpersonal comparison of utility were assumptions which had been verified by observation or introspection, or, at least, were capable of such verification. The assumptions involving interpersonal comparison were certainly not of this order. "I see no means," Jevons had said, "whereby such comparison can be accomplished. Every mind is inscrutable to every other mind and no common denominator of feeling is possible."[73]

From the perspective of comparison and aggregation, other people had to be treated as if they were informationally poor even if that's not what they actually were. Indeed, they had to be treated that way precisely because that's *not* what they were. Neither Robbins nor Arrow argued that people were themselves creatures of pure, attenuated interest. It was rather because they were so full of so much other stuff that one had to embrace a deliberate and strategic form of methodological reduction in order to say anything limited but true about them.

Even so, Sen proposes a slight but crucial adjustment. If, with Robbins and the early Arrow, we understand other people and their preferences primarily in terms of *mental states*, it makes sense to resist the urge to compare them; if, however, one situates other people and their preferences within a world of politics, social class, and history, it becomes possible to broaden the informational basis of comparison without trading facts entirely for values. That is, even if we can't ever really know what another person thinks and feels, the fact that we can *observe* the similar effects of poverty, hunger, income inequality, systemic racism, etc. on whole groups of people means that we can thicken the informational basis for comparisons between persons in a way that might better balance the empirical status of observable fact and the identification of social welfare as a motivation and a value: "the use of such partial comparability can make a major difference to the informational basis of reasoned social judgments."[74] Once we see other people not simply as the external expressions

---

[73] Lionel Robbins, "Interpersonal Comparisons of Utility: A Comment," *The Economic Journal*, 48 (192) (December 1938), 637.
[74] Sen, *Rationality and Freedom*, 84.

of inner lives but rather as complex and, as it were, distributed and interrelated historical facts, it becomes possible to rethink both the meaning and the methods of social choice. "There are," writes Sen, "important ethical grounds for not concentrating too much on mental-state comparisons or utilities – seen as pleasures or desires – in comparing how different persons are respectively doing."[75] The question, in that case, is whether Arrow's system, because it assumes the inaccessibility of mental states as bases for comparison, would also insist necessarily on the inaccessibility of other, less internal kinds of information. What about history, culture, society?

If this takes us far from the monadic agent of rational choice theory or from the rigors of methodological individualism, that is because, contrary to many readings of Arrow's work, he does not simply assert the political or methodological sovereignty of the individual subject. On the contrary, he begins his thinking with the explanatory *failure* of the individual taken as an ontological given:

> The failure of purely individualistic assumptions to lead to a well-defined social welfare function means, in effect, that there must be a divergence between social and private benefits if we are to be able to discuss a social optimum. Part of each individual's value system must be a scheme of socio-ethical norms, the realization of which cannot, by their nature, be achieved through atomistic market behavior.[76]

Writing in 1950, Arrow seems already to have registered that what's missing from the available systems of aggregation is an account of the force of "socio-ethical norms," which is, perhaps, also to say an account of culture and history. As opposed to seeing Arrow's as an argument for the impossibility of democracy or the unreality of society, we should instead see it as what it seems in fact to be: a recognition that both democracy and society are hard, and we'll need better tools and better ideas if we're ever to make them happen. This is, I recognize, a very different Arrow than the one imagined in much writing about the intellectual culture of the Cold War. As opposed to a "consummate defense intellectual," committed to a streamlined and specifically capitalist democracy, this Arrow is less certain, more anxious, more humane; the meaning of other people isn't given, and society not only exists but also stands as the aspirational motivation behind his whole project. He's a cautious socialist and a lover of difficult poetry

[75] Sen, *Collective Choice and Social Welfare*, 23–24.
[76] Kenneth J. Arrow, "A Difficulty in the Concept of Social Welfare," *Journal of Political Economy* 58 (4) (August 1950), 343.

and fiction; and his work assumes as it aspires to a necessary but still inchoate account of the importance of culture and history to the possibility of a better or best way to realize a meaningful life with other people. Where does this Arrow come from, and, if in fact he exists, why do otherwise scrupulous researchers miss him?

In the next section I want to return to the Cold War as a context for the development of Arrow's impossibility theorem. Instead, however, of looking at the period as a settled and determinate two-person, zero-sum matrix in which all things must fall into one or another camp, I want to think about the texture of those years and, more to the point, about Arrow's repeated invocation of a particular historical event: the Moscow show trials. Whenever Arrow writes about his experience of the Cold War, he refers explicitly to the formative, the "traumatic" impression produced by the trials and not really either to McCarthy or to Mutually Assured Destruction. I want to do two things with this. First, I want to argue that seeing Arrow less as a "Cold War intellectual" and more as someone shaped by the situated and social experience of a particular set of historical events will give us a better and more detailed sense of some of the political and philosophical investments that underwrite the impossibility theorem and, thus, electoral theory after Arrow. Second, insofar as the contested interpretation of the trials was formative not only for Arrow but also for much of the American left, the trials give us a deeper context in which to understand the meaning of impossibility at midcentury. Because, in other words, the trials and their aftermath meant much to Richard Wright and to Philip Rahv, to Frida Kahlo and to Arthur Koestler, to John Dewey and to Dwight Macdonald, to Kenneth Arrow and to Ralph Ellison, they give us a chance to think about how *impossibility* sat with excessive significance at the intersection of leftist politics and democratic theory, anti-Stalinism and aesthetic value, social choice and racial justice during and after the Cold War.

Darkness at Noon

In Arrow's several published accounts of his intellectual development, he returns regularly and somewhat unexpectedly to the fate of the "Old Bolsheviks:"

> For me, the Moscow trials of 1935–36 were a dramatic, even traumatic turning point. It was clear that the Old Bolsheviks were unjustly convicted, and their confessions only increased the horror, since it spoke of barbaric

pressures. I reflected, too, that in the improbable event that the charges of treason were true, the Stalin regime was equally condemned; for what could induce those who had risked all under the Czars to create this new world to turn against it save a deep sense of its evil?[77]

In a 1992 reflection, "I Know a Hawk from a Handsaw," he writes:

> The trial of the Old Bolsheviks (Bukharin, Radek, and others) in 1935–6 was decisive for me, as it was for many other socialist sympathizers, such as John Dewey and Sidney Hook; it was inconceivable that the charges were true, and if it were true that the Old Bolsheviks would betray the Revolution when it was successful, it must be very rotten indeed. Having taken an anti-Stalinist position early, I was spared the necessity felt by those disillusioned later for accepting McCarthyism.[78]

In 2011, he recalled:

> I had been left-wing and a socialist but it was as a high school student that I felt that the show trials in Russia were wrong. These histories won't mean a thing to you but they were a big feature among intellectuals then. When I was a high school student or a college student, Stalin started putting the Old Bolsheviks on trial, people who had played a bigger role in the revolution than Stalin did. The revolutionaries of 1917 were now put on trial as traitors and conspirers or fascists and so forth. It obviously was all incredible.[79]

Incredible, decisive, dramatic, traumatic: in a way that demands comment, Arrow insists again and again on the importance of the trials to his intellectual development, a fact that at least suggests some possible link between them and his own great idea, the impossibility theorem.

The three Moscow trials, which resulted directly in dozens if not hundreds of executions and served as the start of the Great Purge, focused on the Old Bolsheviks, most notably Grigory Zinoviev, Karl Radek, and Nikolai Bukharin. Running from 1936 to 1938, they were remarkable both for the ludicrous enormity of the various charges – treason, conspiracy, attempts on Stalin's life, attempts on *Lenin's* life, collaboration with the Nazis, the planned restoration of state capitalism, etc. – and, maybe even more, for the abject style in which the accused ultimately made their public confessions. Take, for example, Ivan Kotolynov: "I request no mercy, I demand with great joy … the harshest punishment. Why? Because I will die not as a counterrevolutionary, but as a revolutionary

---

[77] Arrow, "Cautious Case for Socialism," 475.   [78] Arrow, "I Know a Hawk from a Handsaw," 44.
[79] Arrow, *On Ethics and Economics*, 42.

who, gathering all his courage, repented, and completely disarmed himself, ideologically and politically."[80] There is, of course, an enormous literature on the trials, which were, as Alan Wald writes, "a decisive event that simultaneously consolidated the [American] anti-Stalinist left while setting the stage for its disintegration."[81] On the one hand, there are many accounts of the trials themselves, many efforts to understand: first, their place within Soviet history and the context of Stalin's consolidation of power; second, their status as the expression of a topsy-turvy logic which was taken by some as a cynical break from Leninist theory or by others as the inevitable realization of it; and, third, as a case study in the coercive, obsessive, systemic, and brutally effective application of state pressure on bodies and minds. It is clear, suggests Robert Conquest,

> that the principle of confession in all cases, even from ordinary victims tried in secret, was insisted on. In fact, the major effort of the whole vast police organization throughout the country went into obtaining such confessions. When we read, in cases of no particular importance, and ones never to be made public, of the use of the "conveyor" system tying down team after team of police investigators for days on end, the impression one gets is not simply of vicious cruelty, but of insane preoccupation with a pointless formality.[82]

Even beginning to think through the significance of those accounts is, of course, well beyond the scope of this chapter. The grotesque logic of confession that emerged in contemporary accounts of the trials raises important questions about the relation between saying and meaning that, I will suggest, may have informed or at least affected some of Arrow's thinking about social choice and individual values.

On the other hand, there is the question of how the trials were seen and interpreted elsewhere, particularly in the context of the international and the American left. As we can see from Arrow's persistent reference to the trials, they were experienced both as a signal event and as a crisis of interpretation, of historical understanding, of political strategy, and of ethical commitment. The trials, as is well known, opened bitter and enduring fissures between members of the official Communist Party and the new anti-Stalinist left, which prepared the way, first, for odd and oddly influential points of Cold War contact between disaffected members of

---

[80] Quoted in Matthew E. Lenoe, *The Kirov Murder and Soviet History* (New Haven, CT: Yale University Press, 2010), [PAGE].

[81] Alan M. Wald, *The New York Intellectuals: The Rise and Decline of the Anti-Stalinist Left from the 1930s to the 1980s* (Durham: University of North Carolina Press, 2017), 128.

[82] Robert Conquest, *The Great Terror: A Reassessment* (Oxford: Oxford University Press, 2008), 130.

Old Left, the rising tide of the neoconservative right, the proliferation of neoliberal, public-policy think tanks, and, of course, the CIA; second, for lasting generational, ideological, and, as it were, characterological differences between the Old Left and the New Left that, even at a distance, continue to inform and, perhaps, to limit our political horizons; and, third, for the felt but inchoate urgency of lingering questions about history and science, theory and practice, strategy and tactics, thinking and belief.

Of course, it makes good biographical sense that Kenneth Arrow would have remembered the trials as formative and even "traumatic." Born in 1921 and coming from a Jewish immigrant family that had hit hard times during the Great Depression, a precocious, fifteen-year-old Arrow ended up at City College in New York, where he became interested in Marx and Freud, C. K. Ogden and I. A. Richards, logical positivism and psychological behaviorism, Wittgenstein and "the International style of modernist architecture."[83] Although less overtly political than some of his peers at City College, Arrow seems nonetheless to have hovered at the edges of the famous Alcove No. 1, where young Trotskyites like Irving Howe, Daniel Bell, Irving Kristol, Seymour Martin Lipset, Nathan Glazer, and others met to argue, discuss, and plan (the Stalinists met next door in Alcove No. 2).[84] The importance of the Moscow trials at this moment and to this group cannot be overstated. In the short term, different responses to and interpretations of the meaning of the trials – particularly the trials of Bukharin and of Trotsky *in absentia* – produced definitive intellectual and social fissures within the left and, more to the point, between members of the Communist Party and the burgeoning, largely Trotskyite New York Intellectuals. These differences produced striking incidences of conflict, argument, affiliation, improvisation, betrayal, and, in some cases, excommunication. They also produced some new and influential anti-Stalinist associations. There was the Trotsky Defense Committee, which included notables like Edmund Wilson, Sidney Hook, John Dos Passos, and Mary McCarthy, and which led, in turn, to a remarkable week of hearings attended by Trotsky, overseen by John Dewey, and held in the home of Frida Kahlo and Diego Rivera in Mexico in 1937. Similarly, the trials had galvanizing, specific, and lasting effects on the *Partisan Review* and its editors William Philips and Philip Rahv: "The most important cultural impact of the Moscow trials," writes Wald, "involved the evolution of the

---

[83] Arrow, "I Know a Hawk from a Handsaw," 43.
[84] See Alexander Bloom, *Prodigal Sons: The New York Intellectuals and Their World* (Oxford: Oxford University Press, 1986), 39–42.

Partisan Review in the late 1930s."[85] Rahv's pronounced stance on the trials – captured, for instance, in his "Trials of the Mind" – allowed the journal to assert its intellectual independence from the Stalinists, to signal their sympathy for Trotsky's internationalism as well as his commitment to "revolutionary ideas in art," and, maybe most importantly, to use these events and ideas to attempt a distinctly American synthesis of revolutionary politics and modernist aesthetics. And, given the fact that the *Partisan Review* was more-than-required reading at City College at the time, it makes sense to imagine that a take as powerful, idiosyncratic, and available as Rahv's might have an at least ambient effect on the similarly disposed Arrow.

As its title suggests, "Trials of the Mind" frames the Moscow trials not only as a political scandal but also as an existential crisis for intellectuals and the imagination:

> the trials are also performances, plays, dramatic fictions. If literature reflects life, then their reality or unreality as literature ought to affect our judgment. It might be useful to examine them from the point of view of literary criticism. Are they tragedies or comedies? What perceptions, what psychological insights do they contain? What do they make of human nature? Considered as closed imaginative wholes, what is their inner consistency, – what coherence obtains in them between act, motive, and character?[86]

The question of character, as a psychological fact, political problem, and literary or novelistic thing, runs throughout Rahv's essay; ground down by the process, the once-great, once-round Old Bolsheviks have been squashed flat and are now barely characters at all. The trials were thus not only a moral catastrophe but bad art, featuring characters or, rather, caricatures of the very weakest sort: "they are completely lacking in individuation; the psychology of each is the psychology of all the others."[87] Neither round in Forster's sense nor typical in Lukács's, the Old Bolsheviks had been forced to trade subtlety, irony, or depth for the leveling, nonfigural, and bathetic sincerity of the show confession; indeed, for the confession *qua* confession to work, a difference or tension between saying and meaning on which the novel depends is flattened, suspended, or stunned. The logical and aesthetic difference between character as shaped or leveled by the trials and character as richly and problematically imagined by literary fiction is important here.

---

[85] Wald, *New York Intellectuals*, 139.
[86] Philip Rahv, "Trials of the Mind," *Partisan Review* 4(5) (April 1938), 8.
[87] Rahv, "Trials of the Mind," 8.

On the one hand, it helps to account for the urgency of Rahv's own commitment – filtered through Trotsky's aesthetics – to a mode of literary representation that could be both politically radical and aesthetically difficult, both historically grounded and psychologically deep, both a little bit Marx and a little bit Freud. "What," writes Wald, "helped to distinguish the Trotskyist-influenced critics, especially those who would rally around the reorganized *Partisan Review*, and what exacerbated their relations with the Communists, was their willingness to openly blend Marxism with an aggressive sympathy for the modernist themes and techniques of the 1920s, exemplified by T. S. Eliot."[88] On the other hand, it helps motivate what, from our perspective, must seem like the strange and largely forgotten literary prestige of a number of confessional essays, memoirs, and novels written by former communists. One thinks first of Whittaker Chamber's *Witness*, a conservative favorite written in a hectic, sclerotic style that somehow manages to be both self-pitying and smug; *Witness*, the jacket copy informs us, "is a harrowing account of espionage, treason, terror, and faith ... told in a compellingly eloquent, deeply moving voice of Dostoyevskian power."[89] One thinks also of the considerably more interesting essays (by Arthur Koestler, Richard Wright, André Gide, Stephen Spender, and others) included in 1950s *The God that Failed: Six Studies in Communism*, a book that *Time* magazine still should not have cast as a "Canterbury Tales of the Twentieth Century."

One also thinks of what is probably the most important and, in its way, the best of this series, Koestler's *Darkness at Noon*, which tells the story of Rubashov, an Old Bolshevik and rough stand-in for Bukharin, who is arrested, interrogated, offers an obviously false confession, and is, at last, executed. Although no longer much read, *Darkness at Noon* was for years a staple of high school and college curricula, and it was, as recently as 1994, included on an American Academy of Arts and Sciences list of "the 100 books which have been most influential in the West since 1945"

---

[88] Wald, *New York Intellectuals*, 94.

[89] In his 1952 review of *Witness*, Rahv also takes up the Dostoyevsky comparison, but not as a compliment. Chambers's debt to the great writer, while real and recognizable, is, at last, adolescent: "It is ... a heady mixture of autobiography, politics, and apocalyptic prophecy; and it contains a good many of the characteristic elements of a production à la Dostoevsky, above all the atmosphere of scandal and monstrous imputation, the furtive meetings and the secret agents, the spies, informers, and policemen, desperate collisions, extreme ideas, suffering, pity, and remorse, the entire action moving inexorably toward the typical *dénouement* of a judicial trial, in the course of which heroes and victims alike are exposed as living prey to the crowds and all the secrets come tumbling out." Philip Rahv, "The Sense and Nonsense of Whittaker Chambers," *Partisan Review*, 19(4) (July–August 1952), 472.

(a list that, tellingly, also includes both *The God that Failed* and *Social Choice and Individual Values*).[90] What makes Koestler's novel work as something more than anti-communist propaganda is how it internalizes and motivates the tension that Rahv had also seen at work in the trials themselves; at the same time that the novel explores the brute up-is-down logic of the party and the trial ("they dreamed of power with the object of abolishing power; of ruling over the people to wean them from the habit of being ruled"), it also attends closely to the tics, habits, regrets, desires, and generally unruly inner life of its protagonist.[91] Rubashov dreams, thinks about sex, worries over a bad tooth, longs for a smoke, and compulsively "rubs his glasses on his sleeve."[92] Koestler takes care to represent Rubashov as a thick, rounded, and classically realist character in order both to render him as a believable person and to accentuate the ethical and aesthetic poverty of the party and its officials; "Gletkin," Rubashov's chief tormentor, "was a repellant creature, but he represented the new genera-tion; the old had to come to terms with it or be crushed; there was no other alternative."[93] For Koestler, the authentic Stalinist represents the failure not only of the revolution but also of humor, complexity, specific-ity, depth, and what Trilling would call sincerity; he represents an account of history and character that would have rendered the novel impossible.

What it would also render impossible is the necessary and necessarily problematic relation between social choices and individual values that underwrites Arrow's impossibility theorem. As I've already said, where some readers – both followers and critics – have been quick to see Arrow as offering a simple and singular methodological emphasis on the individ-ual at the expense of the social, a closer reading of both his 1951 text and

[90] "The Hundred Most Influential Books Since the War," *Bulletin of the American Academy of Arts and Sciences* 49(8) (May 1996), 12–18.

[91] Arthur Koestler, *Darkness at Noon*, trans. Daphne Hardy (New York: Scribner, 1941), 60.

[92] Koestler, *Darkness at Noon*, 17, 29, 250.

[93] Koestler, *Darkness at Noon*, 188. In his autobiographical essay for *The God that Failed*, Koestler represents himself as an especially novelistic or even a Dickensian figure. Just for instance, he writes about how his father, a down-at-heel eccentric, "embarked on a number of ventures which became the more fantastic the more he lost self-confidence in a changed world. He opened a factory for radioactive soap; he backed several crank-inventions (everlasting electric bulbs, self-heating bed bricks and the like) . . . " He continues, "Thus sensitized by a personal conflict, I was ripe for the shock of learning that wheat was burned, fruit artificially spoiled, and pigs were drowned in the depression years to keep prices up and enable fat capitalists to chant to the sound of harps, while Europe trembled under torn boots of hunger marchers and my father hid his frayed cuffs under the table." Arthur Koestler in *The God that Failed*, ed. Richard Crossman (New York: Columbia University Press, 2001), 17–18.

many pieces that followed reveal a more complicated picture, a theory based not on the individual alone but rather in the complex interplay between the mystery of selves and the ethical demands of life with other people. Part of what makes that misreading both possible and persuasive is, as I have said, a tendency to see Arrow simply as a Cold War intellectual, a figure whose thinking is legible only within the framework of an imaginary two-person zero-sum between the United States and the Soviet Union. What, among other things, that account misses is precisely the varied historical texture of the Cold War. As we have seen, the events that Arrow took as definitive came not from the paranoid, red-baiting period of the late 1940s and 1950s, but rather from an earlier, more confusing and earnest moment; what mattered to Arrow, what he recalled years later as traumatic, were the Moscow trials, an occasion that resulted not – or at least not immediately – in the blanket refusal of socialism and communism, but rather in a far more complicated set of political, cultural, and aesthetic distinctions amongst different aspects of and commitments to the left.[94] And, given Arrow's lifelong interest in a "cautious" form of socialism, his surprising familiarity with and interest in the details of Marxist theory, and, above all, his sustained commitment to a workable and characterologically rich answer to welfarism, it makes sense to see him more as a product of the fraught intellectual context of the late 1930s than simply as a "consummate defense intellectual." More to the point, seeing Arrow not merely as an ideological echo of the RAND Corporation but rather and more historically as someone who was shaped by the Moscow trials, someone who grew up on the *Partisan Review*, someone who spoke in Stanford seminars alongside René Girard and Ian Watt, and someone who continued – however cautiously – to make a case for socialism must encourage us at least to think differently about the relation between cultural history and electoral theory and to see that the real traffic between literature, economics, and political theory can be thicker, more complicated, and less certain than we sometimes think.[95] This is to take Kenneth Arrow – for good or for ill – as another evocative, situated, and uncertain case of the electoral imagination at work.

---

[94] Arrow, "I Know a Hawk from a Handsaw," 44.

[95] See Arrow's contributions, "The Economics of *Nineteen Eighty-Four*" and "The Economy as Order and Disorder," in *On Nineteen Eighty-Four*, ed. Peter Stansky (Stanford, CA: Stanford Alumni Association, 1983) and *Disorder and Order*, ed. Paisley Livingston (Saratoga, CA: Anma Libri, 1984), where his work appears alongside essays by Ian Watt, René Girard, Cornelius Castoriadis, Anne Mellor, and many others.

4.2   RALPH ELLISON'S NEWS FROM NOWHERE

On Impossibility in America

Of course, just as Arrow was at RAND, thinking through the logical possibility or impossibility of social choice, there was another, more immediate, egregious, and violent kind of electoral impossibility at work in America. While Arrow was abstractly considering the impossibility of aggregating the various preferences of the many into the one will-of-all, it had become calculatedly and concretely impossible for millions of Black Americans, particularly those living in the Jim Crow South, to cast a vote and to have that vote counted. In a 1941 essay on "The Negro in the Political Life of the United States," Ralph Bunche writes that, "The three most salient features of the internal Southern political scene are: the looseness and casual corruption in Southern politics; the disenfranchisement of virtually all black and large numbers of 'poor white' citizens; and the employment of the Negro issue as a political red herring."[96] What Bunch describes here is another version of what, so many pages ago, I called the "myth of rigging": In order to secure an unfair structural advantage, southern politicians again and again invoked the fabricated and phantasmatic threat of illegitimate Black votes. They stoked false, racially motivated fears and fantasies about rigging in order *really* to rig elections. With the end of Reconstruction in 1877, Democratic Party leaders "moved to reorder southern politics," disenfranchising Black voters and thus securing an advantage that would define the electoral character of the "Solid South" for decades.[97] Following the passage of the 1890 Mississippi Constitution, the first but not the last of its kind, states across the former Confederacy adopted "a dizzying array of poll taxes, literacy tests, understanding clauses, newfangled voter registration rules, and 'good character' clauses – all intentionally racially discriminatory but dressed up in the genteel garb of bringing 'integrity' to the voting booth."[98] This effort to game the vote against Black Americans continued – with more rules, more amendments, more tricks – right up to and, as we will see, well beyond the passage of the Voting Rights Act of 1965.

---

[96] Ralph J. Bunche, "The Negro in the Political Life of the United States," *Journal of Negro Education* 10(3) (July 1941), 567.
[97] Michael Waldman, *The Fight to Vote* (New York: Simon & Schuster, 2016), 84.
[98] Carol Anderson, *One Person, No Vote: How Voter Suppression Is Destroying Our Democracy* (New York: Bloomsbury, 2019), 3.

On the one hand, this brute version of electoral impossibility needs to be thought of in terms quite different – politically, ethically, socially, historically – from the abstract concerns that drove Arrow's thinking in *Social Choice and Individual Values*. Where, in other words, Arrow or, really, some of his followers would assume that the experience of impossibility was the experience of a logical and, thus, an apparently universal or natural contradiction, the forms of electoral impossibility that confronted Black Americans were avowedly contingent artifacts of a racist history that exposed a political contradiction at the heart of American democracy. "The entire constitutional history of the nation has reflected," says Bunche, "this compromise in the quixotic tendency to sanctify its democratic creeds while stubbornly retaining its racial bigotries."[99] A similarly taut reckoning with the conceptual impossibility of this political contradiction appears again and again in Ralph Ellison's writing: "Believing truly in democracy on one side of their minds, they act on the other in violation of its most sacred principles; holding that all men are created equal, they treat thirteen million Americans as though they were not."[100] "I need only," he writes elsewhere, "remind you that the contradiction between these noble ideals and the actualities of our conduct generated a guilt, an unease of spirit, from the very beginning, and that the American novel at its best has always been concerned with this basic moral predicament."[101] America is a democracy, and America is not a democracy; A is A and A is not A. That, says Ellison's narrator, "might sound like a hoax, or a contradiction, but that (by contradiction, I mean) is how the world moves: Not like an arrow, but a boomerang."[102] It would, thus, make sense either to see these two versions of impossibility as simply different in kind or, perhaps, to see the one as offering ideological cover for the other: what, the think tanks seemed to ask, if the problem with voting in 1951 or 1952 was *not* the systematic disenfranchisement of millions of Black Americans but, rather, an unhappily unavoidable problem internal to logic itself? That might be bad, but at least it wouldn't be *evil*.

On the other hand, there are ways in which thinking about these forms of impossibility together can be instructive. First, as we have already begun

[99] Bunche, "The Negro in the Political Life of the United States," 567.

[100] Ralph Ellison, "Beating that Boy," in *The Collected Essays of Ralph Ellison*, ed. John F. Callahan (New York: The Modern Library, 2003), 148.

[101] Ralph Ellison, "Hidden Name and Complex Face," in *The Collected Essays of Ralph Ellison*, ed. John F. Callahan (New York: The Modern Library, 2003), 206.

[102] Ralph Ellison, *Invisible Man* (New York: Vintage Books, 1995), 6. Hereafter abbreviated *IM* and cited parenthetically.

to see, racial disenfranchisement after Reconstruction often took the form of forced contradictions and bureaucratic absurdities as Black voters were forced to live out paradoxes that existed otherwise only in theory; it was often as if the trials, nightmares, or paradoxes of the mind had been brought awfully to life.[103] Writes Michael Perman:

> One by one over a period of two decades, each state in the former Confederacy set in motion complicated and hazardous electoral movements aimed at removing large numbers of its eligible voters. These ruthless acts of political surgery preoccupied the region's citizenry and dominated its political life as constitutional conventions were summoned into existence and constitutional amendments were formulated and then ratified.[104]

Instead, in that case, of seeing one version of impossibility as logical or abstract and another version as political or concrete, thinking through the reciprocal and, as it were, imaginative relation between the two can give us a chance to understand how those apparently opposed versions – latent and manifest – can in fact work together as a single conceptual system as an effective political machine. Indeed, much of Ellison's writing explores exactly this space – this dreamwork, as it were – between the two sides of segregated democracy, between *imaginative* racism as a morbid, outlandish, and yet formative condition of the American mind and, as it were, a *practical* racism that found expression not only in the arrangement of segregated buses and movie theaters but also in baroque procedural mechanisms that governed and undermined putatively democratic elections. "These circumstances," wrote Ellison, "have . . . all the elements of a social nightmare."[105]

Second, both versions of impossibility are especially resonant within the context of the Cold War and, more to the point, within the complex zone of contact that stood between the Civil Rights Movement, international communism, and the anti-Stalinist left. I've already described how Arrow's idea of impossibility is enlivened when seen in relation to a more complex,

---

[103] Quoting Cedric Robinson's *Black Marxism*, Vaughn Rasberry makes the persuasive case that a thematic and stylistic resonance between "an emergent European literature" that included Sartre, Lukács, Koestler, and others and the work of Richard Wright might be better understood if we see continuities between European totalitarianism and racial totalitarianism in America: "Wright," he says, "has not experienced a concentration camp, but he has survived Jim Crow." I want to argue here that the calculated logical impossibilities of Black voter registration in the Jim Crow South are a less spectacular but still vitally important aspect of that totalitarian experience.

[104] Michael Perman, *Struggle for Mastery: Disfranchisement in the South, 1888–1908* (Durham: University of North Carolina Press, 2001), 1.

[105] Ralph Ellison, "Tell It Like It Is, Baby," in *The Collected Essays of Ralph Ellison*, ed. John F. Callahan (New York: The Modern Library, 2003), 32.

more varied historical account of the Cold War and especially its early years; the possibility or impossibility of saying what you mean and having what you say, in turn mean something more (whether it be a vote or a confession), is itself all the more urgent when seen in relation to what Arrow recalled as the trauma of the Moscow trials. Similarly – and as Vaughn Rasberry, Mary Dudziak, Carol Anderson, Christine Hong, and others have shown – the hot days of Cold War blurred whatever lines had stood theoretically between the American racism and international relations: "the onset of the Cold War," writes Rasberry, "witnessed the contemporaneous rise of the Third World and the non-alignment movement, with onlookers from Asia and Africa paying close attention to discrimination against black Americans while adjudicating competing appeals from the communist and democratic spheres."[106] Insofar as the impossibility theorem answered a question about how difference survives in a democracy, it was always already about something more than the abstractions of set theory; and, insofar as Jim Crow had become not only a domestic but also a diplomatic scandal, the possibility or impossibility of casting a vote at home emerged as a matter of increasing geopolitical urgency. Both forms of impossibility were, in other words, related by and especially resonant within an international context structured by real and imaginary differences between totalitarianism and democracy.

Third, in the same way that one can and, I think, should see Arrow as sharing an unsettled and uncertain political cultural context that linked Lionel Trilling and Leon Trotsky, Irving Kristol and Mary McCarthy, Meyer Schapiro and Whittaker Chambers, so should we consider what electoral impossibility at midcentury meant not only for Black voters but also for Black writers. If, as I have argued throughout, the conceptual problems and suppositional risks of political representation both put pressure on and responded to the possibilities and limits of literary representation, how does that relation develop or change in the context of

---

[106] Vaughn Rasberry, *Race and the Totalitarian Century: Geopolitics in the Black Literary Imagination* (Cambridge, MA: Harvard University Press, 2016), 63. See also, Carol Anderson, *Bourgeois Radicals: The NAACP and the Struggle for Colonial Liberation, 1941–1960* (Cambridge: Cambridge University Press, 2015); Mary L. Dudziak, *Cold War Civil Rights: Race and the Image of American Democracy* (Princeton, NJ: Princeton University Press, 2000); Christine Hong, *A Violent Peace: Race, US Militarism, and Cultures of Decolonization in Cold War Asia and the Pacific* (Stanford, CA: Stanford University Press, 2020).

disenfranchisement and racial terror in America? I will focus here on Ellison for a few reasons. For one, Ellison's trajectory as a writer, as a political thinker, and as a public intellectual connects him in interesting and knowing ways with Arrow's early milieu: they lived in the same city, knew some of the same people, read some of the same magazines; they published their most important works within a year of each other and had similar stories to tell about an early belief in and subsequent fall away from communism. This association will give me the chance to work comparatively with electoral impossibility and possibility as they move between these contexts. What's more, in his fiction and in his essays, Ellison returned again and again to the *idea* of American democracy, sometimes in the form of a "political collectivity of individuals" and sometimes in the form of a cultural "collectivity of styles, tastes, and traditions"; sometimes in the form of "the rock upon which we toil" and sometimes in the form of a "little man at Chehaw Station"; sometimes as an answer to and sometimes as a symptom of an essentially American racism; but always as something uneasy, conflicted, and problematic: always – he said – as an "art of the impossible."[107] "So frequently," says Ellison, "does this conflict erupt into physical violence that one sometimes wonders if there is any other viable possibility for co-existing in so abstract and futuristic a nation as this."[108] As a result, the question of what it means not only to live with other people but also to say what you mean and to mean what you say *within a segregated democracy* is fundamental not only to Arrow's theorem but also to *Invisible Man:* "Who knows," he famously concludes, "but that, on the lower frequencies, I speak for you?" (*IM*, 581). Taken along with several of Ellison's essays, *Invisible Man* offers another account of the relation between individual choice and social values when those concepts – "the mysteries and pathologies of the democratic process" – are seen operating within the logically absurd and ethically grotesque confines of a society that worked consciously and explicitly to translate the hectic fantasies of white supremacy into the putatively minor, concrete details of electoral procedure.[109]

---

[107] Ralph Ellison, "The Little Man at Chehaw Station: The American Artist and His Audience," in *The Collected Essays of Ralph Ellison*, ed. John F. Callahan (New York: The Modern Library, 2003), 504, 506, 507. William Safire's Political Dictionary includes an entry on the "Art of the Possible": "Political figures, under fire for falling short of attaining lofty goals promised in campaigns, often fall back on the phrase, 'the art of the possible,' as a useful defense. It emphasizes the practical nature of political rule, with its built-in checks and balances." Safire, *Safire's Political Dictionary* (New York: Random House, 1978), 26.

[108] Ellison, "Little Man at Chehaw Station," 504.

[109] Ellison, "Little Man at Chehaw Station," 507.

Write Right from the Left

Although outright violence, organized terror, and brute voter intimidation were the *extralegal* norm under Jim Crow, southern state legislatures committed to creating *legal* justifications for disenfranchising Black voters could not do so as directly.[110] With the passage of the Fifteenth Amendment in 1870, the voting rights of Black men had been technically secured at a national level; in order, then, to circumvent federal law while also avoiding federal oversight, southern state lawmakers – first in Mississippi and then across the South – sought to create intricate electoral rules and voting procedures that could appear race-neutral while in fact targeting and disqualifying Black voters. Instead of focusing on the casting or the counting of votes, new "registration laws shifted disenfranchisement from the point of voting to the point of registration, erasing, not just restricting the black franchise."[111] The raft of new rules written over the next several decades were miscellaneous, procedurally elaborate, and terribly effective. In his 1941 essay, Bunche offers a compressed view of the latticework of legal, pseudo-legal, and extra-legal methods used to make Black votes impossible under Jim Crow:

> There are many variations of the more or less subtle devices employed in the South to prohibit or discourage Negro voting. No uniformity of practice as between Southern states is found. Some of the more important measures in current usage are the following: exclusion from the Democratic or "white" primary; requiring one or more (usually two) white character witnesses; strict enforcement of the literacy tests against Negro applicants; putting unreasonable questions to Negro applicants in constitutional understanding or interpretation tests; severe application of property qualifications and requiring only Negro applicants to show property tax receipts; basing rejection of Negro registrants on alleged technical mistakes in filling out registration blanks; evasion, by informing Negro applicants that registration cards have "run out," that all members of the registration board are not present, that it is "closing time," or that the applicant "will be notified in due course"; requiring Negro applicants to suffer long waits before the officials attend them; requiring Negro applicants to fill out their own blanks though those of white applicants are filled out for them by officials;

---

[110] See, Darryl Pinckney, *Blackballed: The Black Vote and U.S. Democracy* (New York: New York Review of Books, 2020): "White violence against blacks had gone unpunished for the most part during Reconstruction, when black candidates, black voting officials, and black voters were beaten or killed by gangs of hooded vigilantes" (3).

[111] Allan J. Lichtman, *The Embattled Vote in America* (Cambridge, MA: Harvard University Press, 2018), 137.

deliberate insults or threats by officials and/or hangers-on; discarding only
Negro applications for conviction of misdemeanors; requiring enrollment
in Democratic clubs, from which Negroes are barred; severe application of
the cumulative poll tax to Negro voters only; loss of jobs or threat of loss of
jobs; intimidation by physical violence or the threat of it.[112]

As Bunche represents it, the southern legal strategy for keeping Black
voters away from the ballot box after Reconstruction was a fecund network
of redundant and intentionally broken systems, a "vast, interlocked," and
overlapping set of illogical and degrading rules designed to realize racial
discrimination as a form of bureaucratic repression that was both terror-
izing and banal.[113] In a recent roundtable discussion, Carol Anderson
notes that voter suppression laws work best – both then and now – when
they are in fact miscellaneous and intersecting:

> [Y]ou know, it wasn't just the literacy test; it wasn't just the poll tax; it
> wasn't just the grandfather clause. . . . If they couldn't catch you this way,
> they'd get you this way; if they couldn't catch you, oh, they'd get you this
> way; if they couldn't do it, they'd get you this way. And so by having to
> jump over all of these obstacles, it therefore made it doubly difficult for
> African Americans to be able to vote, and that's what we're seeing today.[114]

It wasn't just the individual rule that disenfranchised Black voters; rather,
it was the systematic and yet improvised, excessive, and bewildering play
between many rules that turned the attempt to vote into a waking
nightmare. "By means of such legerdemain," writes Richard Valelly,
"the rules of the electoral game gradually changed throughout the
region."[115]

   As terrible as both these rules and the relations between them were, they
were also striking for their almost insouciant reliance on an absurd mix of
ordinariness, contradiction, and deliberate administrative ineptitude. They
were the banal institutional realization of what Ellison once referred to as
the "strange ways of segregated democracy."[116] "The disenfranchisers

---

[112] Bunche, "The Negro in the Political Life of the United States," 569–570.
[113] Richard M. Valelly, *The Two Reconstructions: The Struggle for Black Enfranchisement* (Chicago:
University of Chicago Press, 2004), 125.
[114] Stacey Abrams, Carol Anderson, Kevin M. Kruse, Heather Cox Richardson, and Heather Ann
Thompson, "Roundtable," in *Voter Suppression in US Elections*, ed. Jim Downs (Athens: University
of Georgia Press, 2020), 24.
[115] Valelly, *Two Reconstructions*, 125.
[116] Ralph Ellison, "On Being the Target of Discrimination," in *The Collected Essays of Ralph Ellison*,
ed. John F. Callahan (New York: The Modern Library, 2003), 827.

were," writes J. Morgan Kousser, "forced to contrive devious means to accomplish their purposes."[117] By focusing on the "point of registration" instead of the "point of voting," the new laws gave enormous power to county clerks and petty officials, a situation that mixed state terror, official malaise, and parochial cruelty in ways significantly reminiscent of scenes administrative violence in Kafka, Conrad, Dickens, and Coetzee. "The registrars' pleasure," writes R. Volney Riser, "was the fulcrum in this enterprise, and disfavored men simply could not tilt things their way – no matter how many correct answers they did or did not give."[118] Unwittingly aping the fallen logic of Dostoevsky's Grand Inquisitor, an Alabama politician, "when asked whether Christ could register under the good character clause," replied that it "would depend entirely on which way he was going to vote."[119]

The poll tax worked not only because it was expensive and because one had to pay it but also because the system made it difficult to pay even when one had the money; there were, writes Anderson, "arcane rules about when and where even to pay the tax."[120] The rules, observes C. Vann Woodward, were in fact "artfully devised to discourage payment."[121] As written into law, versions of the poll tax thus said both that you had to pay and that you could not pay. Shaped by this cleft imperative, the law was thus designed to end in paradox. It was designed *as* paradox. Similarly, Woodward notes that the adoption of a primary system meant "to democratize nominations and party control" ended up instead as "another of the fateful paradoxes" that characterized southern electoral law. Because, that is, primaries were overseen by political parties and not the state, lawmakers could both exclude Black voters and "avoid adverse court decisions."[122] The white primary, wrote W. E. B. Du Bois in *Black Reconstruction in America* (1935), "was made by law and public pressure the real voting arena in practically all southern states."[123] While Black voters could vote in

---

[117] J. Morgan Kousser, *The Shaping of Southern Politics: Suffrage Restriction and the Establishment of the One-Party South, 1880–1910* (New Haven, CT: Yale University Press, 1974), 46.

[118] R. Volney Riser, *Defying Disfranchisement: Black Voting Rights Activism in the Jim Crow South, 1890–1908* (Baton Rouge: Louisiana State University Press, 2010), 75.

[119] Kousser, *Shaping of Southern Politics,* 59.   [120] Anderson, *One Person, No Vote,* 32.

[121] C. Vann Woodward, *The Strange Career of Jim Crow* (Oxford: Oxford University Press, 2002), 84.

[122] Woodward, *Strange Career of Jim Crow,* 84.

[123] W. E. B. Du Bois, *Black Reconstruction in America,* ed. Henry Louis Gates, Jr. (Oxford: Oxford University Press, 2007), 620. Du Bois adds that as a result of the white primaries and other electoral novelties, "The disfranchisement of Negroes in the South became nearly complete. In no other civilized and modern land has so great a group of people, most of whom were able to read and write, been allowed so small a voice in their own government. Every promise of eventual recognition of the intelligent Negro voter has been broken. In the former slave states, from Virginia

the general election (assuming they had been able to register), they often could not vote in the primary. As a result, they could vote only for someone for whom they had not voted. Voting under these conditions was both possible and impossible. Florida and South Carolina also adopted so-called eight-box laws that turned voting into a kind of diabolical shell game:

> Under eight-box laws, separate ballots for president, congressman, governor, state senator, etc., were supposed to be deposited in the proper boxes; if the ballots were distributed otherwise, they were not counted. Boxes were constantly shifted to prevent a literate voter from arranging the tickets of an uneducated friend in the correct order before he entered the voting place.[124]

As egregious were the many literacy tests and understanding clauses used to stymie Black registrants. Where some were asked to read and to interpret long tracts of legalese taken from the state or federal constitution, others were asked questions that were difficult only because they were nonsensical, obtuse, or idiotic.[125] One registrar in Louisiana "disqualified applicants who did not correctly list their age in years, months, and days." A registrar in Mississippi asked, "How many bubbles in a bar of soap?"[126] And, in a riddling style that seemed to come straight from a Mad Hatter's racist tea party, one Louisiana literacy test reportedly asked voters to, "Write right from the left to the right as you see it spelled here."[127]

The spread of bogus literacy tests rested partly on another, more venerable but, in this context, equally paradoxical innovation: the secret ballot. In Chapter 2, I discussed the transimperial movement of the secret ballot from Australia to Britain. Although Chartists and other reformers had agitated for secret voting for decades, two factors facilitated its ultimate adoption in 1872. First, there had been a palpable shift in the rhetoric around the meaning of secrecy. Where early advocates like George Grote

---

to Texas, excepting Missouri, there are no Negro state officials; no Negro members of legislatures; no judges on the bench; and usually no jurors. There are no colored county officials of any sort. In the towns and cities, there are no colored administrative officers, no members of the city councils, no magistrates, no constables and very seldom even a policeman. In this way, at least eight million Negroes are left without effective voice in government, naked to the worst elements of the community."

[124] Kousser, *Shaping of Southern Politics*, 50.
[125] For examples of the different kinds of passages given to and the very different standards applied to Black and white voters, see US Civil Rights Commission, "Registration in Forrest County, Mississippi," in *American Party Politics: Essays and Readings*, ed. Donald G. Herzberg and Gerald M. Pomper (New York: Holt, Rinehart, and Winston, Inc., 1966), 395–398.
[126] Anderson, *One Person, No Vote*, 7.
[127] Quoted in Kevin J. Fandl, *Law and Public Policy* (London: Routledge, 2019), 51.

had seen electoral secrecy as a way of *protecting voters* from the sway of politicians, landlords, and bosses, in the 1860s the secret ballot was reimagined as a way of *protecting elections* from the voters themselves. Seen as a check not on the real influence of the powerful but rather on the imagined duplicity of fraudulent voters, the secret ballot emerged as an answer to status quo anxieties about the expansion of the franchise. Second, by 1872 members of Parliament could point to a successful working model: a secret ballot that had been used with success in Australia since 1856, a circumstance that formed the basis for much practical discussion leading up to the passage of the Ballot Act.

Beginning in 1888, American states began to follow Britain's lead, first in Louisville, Kentucky and then almost everywhere else: "By 1891 thirty-two of the forty-two states had passed secret ballot laws."[128] On the one hand, the Australian Ballot was celebrated as a means of rationalizing the voting process. As opposed to the many, brightly colored, straight-ticket ballots produced and circulated by various parties and coalitions and the raucous and sometimes violent carnival atmosphere of open election days, a standardized secret ballot, printed and overseen by state governments, would bring order to the process and would also discourage the buying and selling of votes associated with the political machines. An enthusiastic supporter in Massachusetts observed in 1888 that:

> Quiet, order, and cleanliness reign in the polling-places. I have visited precincts where, under the old system, coats were torn off the backs of voters, where ballots of one kind have been snatched from voters' hands and others put in their places, with threats against using any but the substituted ballots; and under the new system all was orderly and peaceable. Indeed, the self-respect in voting under the new system is alone worth all the extra expense to the state.[129]

---

[128] Julian Go, "Empire, Democracy, and Discipline: The Transimperial History of The Secret Ballot," in *Crossing Empires: Taking US History into Transimperial Terrain*, ed. Kristin L. Hoganson and Jay Sexton (Durham, NC: Duke University Press, 2020), 99. Other historians have written about the relation between the Australian ballot and the history of political parties in America. Daniel Schlozman notes that the introduction of official ballots gave the two major parties an opportunity to shut out third-party opposition: taking away their ability to make competing ballots, "these laws ripped from third parties in a first-past-the post system their best opportunity to cobble together different voter blocs into majorities." Schlozman, *When Movements Anchor Parties: Electoral Alignments in American History* (Princeton, NJ: Princeton University Press, 2015), 158. For a detailed look at the effects of and forces at work within American ballot reform, see Alan Ware, *The American Direct Primary: Party Institutionalization and Transformation in the North* (Cambridge: Cambridge University Press, 2002), particularly Chapter 2, "The Catalytic Effect of Ballot Reform."

[129] Eldon Cobb Evans, *A History of the Australian Ballot System in the United States* (Chicago: University of Chicago Press, 1917), 23.

On the other hand, insofar as the Australian ballot system put the design of physical ballots into the hands of state legislatures, the secret vote could be easily turned against voters in places where a single party had outsized influence, as was the case across the former Confederacy. First, the ability centrally to print and to distribute ballots was a powerful form of agenda-setting. How, where, and even *if* candidates appeared on a ballot of course had measurable impacts on the outcomes of elections. If order isn't everything in elections, it is, as we have already seen, a whole lot. Second, control over the physical design of the ballot could amount to a *de facto* form of disenfranchisement:

> The Australian ballot was . . . an obstacle to participation by many illiterate foreign-born voters in the North, as well as uneducated black voters in the South. In some states, this problem was remedied by expressly permitting illiterate voters to be assisted or by attaching party emblems to the names of candidates; in others, it was compounded by complex ballot configurations that easily could stymie the illiterate.[130]

"Complex written instructions were also imposed," writes Julian Go, "such as the instruction to mark a line across the candidates' name only three-quarters the length exactly. If not done properly, the validity of the ballot could be challenged."[131] "Florida," for instance, "totally abolished party designations on its ballot [and] voters in one Virginia congressional district in 1894 confronted a ballot printed in the German Fraktur script."[132] Third, because it was necessary to *read* an Australian Ballot, its adoption gave southern state legislators an additional excuse to impose bogus literacy tests on voters at the point of registration.

As was often the case with these laws, the racist intent behind the adoption of the secret ballot was no secret. In Arkansas, the success of the secret ballot was measured explicitly and openly by the effect it had on Black voters; the editor of the *Pine Bluff Press-Eagle* wrote with approval that,

> In this city it was interesting to note the operation of the new election law . . . crowds of negroes gathered outside the ropes and discussed the situation, and many left for their homes without attempting to vote . . . when those who could not read were told to go to the polls and vote the

---

[130] Alexander Keyssar, *The Right to Vote: The Contested History of Democracy in the United States* (New York: Basic Books, 2009), 115.

[131] Go, "Transimperial History of The Secret Ballot," 101.

[132] Kousser, *Shaping of Southern Politics,* 52.

majority of them declined, some being distrustful of the judges and others not daring to expose their inability to make out their tickets unassisted.[133]

The numbers bore this out. "The year after Arkansas passed its Australian-ballot law, the percentage of black men who managed to vote dropped from seventy-one to thirty-eight."[134] In 1902, Virginia state senator Carter Glass boasted that his proposed state constitution would "not necessarily deprive a single white man of the ballot, but will inevitably cut from the existing electorate four-fifths of the Negro voters."[135] "Virginia Governor J. Hoge Tyler stated that 'thousands of defective or improperly marked ballots have been thrown out in every election since the [secret ballot] law was enacted – in many instances as many as one-third or one-half of the ballots deposited.'"[136] And, if there was any doubt about the real significance of the new ballot, the *Arkansas Gazette* went ahead and set segregated democracy to music: "The Australian ballot works like a charm, / It makes them think and scratch, / And when a negro gets a ballot / He has certainly got his match."[137] Where, in other words, the secret ballot began its life as a way to protect voters from the influence and retribution of the powerful, it had become yet "another of the fateful paradoxes" of segregated democracy; under the barely sustained guise of making it more possible to vote one's real interest or conscience, the southern adoption of the Australian Ballot made voting impossible for many.

Totalitarian Democracy

Although these many willfully paradoxical and yet also wholly effective electoral rules represent only one aspect of the larger social violence of Jim Crow, they are important for a few reasons. For starters, they represent, as should be clear, one outlandish and malicious realization of a phenomenon I've been talking about all along. I've written in previous chapters about the *suppositional* or *utopian* intensity that Jeremy Bentham and George Grote, Lewis Carroll and William Morris, Duncan Black and Kenneth Arrow brought to the logistical problems of casting votes, counting votes, and understanding what votes meant. The many boxes, ballots, rules,

---

[133] Quoted in Fon Louise Gordon, *Caste & Class, The Black Experience in Arkansas, 1880–1920* (Athens: University of Georgia Press, 2007), 29.
[134] Jill Lepore, "Rock, Paper, Scissors: How We Used to Vote," *New Yorker*, October 6, 2008, www .newyorker.com/magazine/2008/10/13/rock-paper-scissors.
[135] Quoted in Michael Waldman, *Fight to Vote*, 84.   [136] Kousser, *Shaping of Southern Politics*, 54.
[137] Quoted in Gordon, *Caste & Class*, 29.

procedures, devices, and schemes that these different figures imagined in
the forms of both of public policy and literary art often spoke to a real hope
that electoral systems could or should work better, that votes could,
perhaps, say better what individuals and groups really thought, wanted,
or believed. If, however, the imagination can be put to work making or at
least thinking about a better and more humane life, so can it be put to
work inventing new forms of cruelty; and, indeed, the considerable ingenuity that went into the byzantine and repellant structure of Jim Crow
electoral law is proof that, just because people *can* imagine something
better, it doesn't mean they will. "Wherever there has been popular
confusion between the essentials and the non-essentials of ballot reform,"
noted Philip Loring Allen in 1910, "politicians have taken advantage of
that confusion to pass laws granting the shadow and not the substance."[138]
As a result, accounts of Black Americans confronting these systems often
read, again, like waking nightmares; for Ellison, trying to navigate the
paradoxical systems of segregated democracy was like the feeling of "some
dreamer seeking to function responsibly in an environment which at its
most normal took on some of the mixed character of nightmare and
dream."[139] "For years," he remembers in "Hidden Name and Complex
Fate," "I kept a card warning Negroes away from the polls, which had been
dropped by the thousands from a plane which circled over the Negro
community."[140] "One 'is' literally," he writes in "Harlem Is Nowhere,"
"but one is nowhere; one wanders dazed in a ghetto maze, a 'displaced
person' of American democracy."[141] In some cases, the experience is the
record of being forced to live a logical contradiction: you have to pay the
tax, but you can't pay the tax; you can register to vote, but you can't
register to vote; you can vote, but you can't vote; it is possible, but it is not
possible; one "is," but one is *nowhere*. "Indeed," he writes, "Negroes are
not unaware that the conditions of their lives demand new definitions of
terms like *primitive* and *modern, ethical* and *unethical, moral* and *immoral,
patriotism* and *treason, tragedy* and *comedy, sanity* and *insanity*."[142] It is as if
Condorcet's Paradox, a recursive and crazy loop from which one cannot

---

[138] Philip Loring Allen, "The Multifarious Australian Ballot," *North American Review* 191(654) (May 1910), 605.

[139] Ralph Ellison, introduction to *Shadow and Act,* in *The Collected Essays of Ralph Ellison,* ed. John F. Callahan (New York: The Modern Library, 2003), 51.

[140] Ralph Ellison, "Hidden Name and Complex Fate," in *The Collected Essays of Ralph Ellison,* ed. John F. Callahan (New York: The Modern Library, 2003), 200.

[141] Ralph Ellison, "Harlem Is Nowhere," in *The Collected Essays of Ralph Ellison,* ed. John F. Callahan (New York: The Modern Library, 2003), 325.

[142] Ellison, "Harlem Is Nowhere," 322.

escape, were transformed from an abstract idea into a concrete thing, as if its weird geometry were a figment prosaically and yet sadistically realized as a maze, a treadmill, or a trap. In other cases, the accounts read, again, as if the extraordinary conceptual aggressivity of *Alice's Adventures in Wonderland* had been let practically loose on ordinary people's lives: "Spell backwards, forwards," demanded one literacy test.[143]

If such real and fictional accounts of lived paradox, waking nightmare, and bureaucratic obduracy seem wholly specific to the damaged and perverse proceduralism of the Jim Crow South, seen from another, wider and more geopolitical perspective, they are of a piece with what Vaughn Rasberry sees as the broader "literature of the totalitarian experience" both in their affective outlines and – more to the point here – in their evocation of a minutely, officiously, and cruelly administered society.[144] Taken in these terms, the "totalitarian experience" names both a distinct historical and political phenomenon and, more broadly, an inchoate but no less real way of thinking or feeling characteristic of certain types of social organization. Rasberry quotes the diplomat George Kennan:

> When I try to picture totalitarianism ... as a general phenomenon, what comes into my mind most prominently is ... the fictional and symbolic images created by such people as Orwell or Kafka or Koestler or the early Soviet satirists. The purest expression of the phenomenon, in other words, seems to me to have been rendered not in its physical reality but in its power as a dream, or a nightmare.[145]

Building on Cedric Robinson's *Black Marxism*, Rasberry goes on to make the persuasive case that a thematic and stylistic resonance between the work of Richard Wright, on the one hand, and "an emergent European literature" that would include Kafka, Orwell, Sartre, Camus, Solzhenitsyn, Malraux, and Koestler, on the other, might be better understood if we also recognize continuities between European totalitarianism and America's homegrown racial totalitarianism: "Wright," he observes, "has not experienced a concentration camp, but he has survived Jim Crow."[146] Once, in

---

[143] Quoted in Fandl, *Law and Public Policy*, 51.
[144] Rasberry, *Race and the Totalitarian Century*, 85.
[145] Rasberry, *Race and the Totalitarian Century*, 93.
[146] Rasberry, *Race and the Totalitarian Century*, 87. Louis Menand extends the list of works informed by totalitarianism in a recent discussion of Orwell's writing: "*Nineteen Eighty-Four* belongs to the midcentury literature on totalitarianism, a powerful agent in shaping postwar thought. Some of these books were based on personal experience: Victor Kravchenko's *I Chose Freedom* (1946), Margarete Buber-Neumann's *Under Two Dictators* (1948), Czeslaw Milosz's *The Captive Mind* (1953). Some were philosophical, such as Karl Popper's *The Open Society and Its Enemies* (1945) or academic, like Carl Friedrich and Zbigniew Brzezinski's *Totalitarian Dictatorship and Autocracy*

other words, one acknowledges that there is "evidence of a totalitarian impulse at the heart of US racial democracy," the thematic and stylistic overlap between the European "literature of the totalitarian experience" and the writing of Wright, Ellison, and others comes more intensely into view.[147]

What's more, if we think of the "literature of the totalitarian experience" in more particular and self-consciously limited terms, that is, in relation to its emphasis on the deadening, byzantine, and somehow adamant violence of being called before committees, filling out forms, waiting in lines, and speaking with petty officials, that overlap can help, I think, to motivate a novel like *Invisible Man* in relation not only to "the totalitarian century" but also to what I have been calling the *electoral imagination*.[148] I want to argue here that the calculated logical impossibilities of Black voter registration in the Jim Crow South are an aspect of that totalitarian experience. Insofar as these accounts put another kind of conceptual pressure on a Cold War explanatory matrix that imagined ideas, practices, procedures as democratic *or* totalitarian, they offer a way for us not only to imagine another point of ideological contact between the abstractions of electoral theory and the reality of segregated democracy at midcentury but also better to see how Ellison motivated scenes of bureaucratic process and social choice in order to show how the putative neutrality or transparency of electoral procedures could give way to the pointed reality of politics, history, and the nightmare logic of white supremacy.

Caucuses and Committees

As I've already observed, Ellison wrote variously and, as his career progressed, increasingly about the tension between the ideal potential and the real material contradictions of democracy in America. For instance, in his

---

(1956), a standard text in academic political science. Many were polemical: Friedrich Hayek's *The Road to Serfdom* (1944), Arthur Schlesinger, Jr.'s, *The Vital Center* (1949), Raymond Aron's *The Opium of the Intellectuals* (1955). And a few, including Arthur Koestler's *Darkness at Noon* (1940) (an influence on *Nineteen Eighty-Four*: Koestler and Orwell were friends) and Ray Bradbury's *Fahrenheit 451* (1953), were fictional." Menand, *The Free World: Art and Thought in the Cold War* (New York: Farrar, Straus, & Giroux, 2021), 36.

[147] Rasberry, *Race and the Totalitarian Century*, 93.

[148] It's worth noting that the semantic overlap between bureaucratic overreach and the "byzantine" seems to be an artifact of the totalitarian imaginary. William Safire notes that, "Arthur Koestler was fond of using this word to describe intricate political workings" and that, in the wake of the Cold War, the "Koestler use" had become a new norm: "the 1972 supplement to the *OED* defines the word as 'the spirit of Byzantine politics. Hence, intricate, complicated; inflexible, rigid, unyielding.'" Safire, *Safire's Political Dictionary*, 89.

wryly Jamesian preface to the 1981 edition of *Invisible Man*, Ellison makes a germinal link between the novel and American democracy explicit:

> Here it would seem that the interests of art and democracy converge, the development of conscious, articulate citizens being an established goal of this democratic society, and the creation of conscious, articulate characters being indispensable to the creation of resonant compositional centers through which an organic consistency can be achieved in the fashioning of fictional forms. ... Which suggested to me that a novel could be fashioned as a raft of hope, perception, and entertainment that might help keep us afloat as we tried to negotiate the snags and whirlpools that mark our nation's vacillating course toward and away from the democratic ideal. (*IM*, xx–xxi)

Ellison's analogy is suggestive. Sharing James's sense that an intelligent, watchful consciousness – in his case, the nervy and loquacious narrator – must stand as the necessary and form-giving center of a novel, Ellison extends the figure to reach after a similar kind of formal reciprocity between the individual and the group; just as the intelligent, reflective character brings the novel into order and into life, so, he suggests, can the "conscious, articulate" citizen shape and enliven and help direct the ship of state. Although only hinted at, this characterological account of the difficult but necessary relation between social choice and individual values connects Ellison not only with Arrow but also with Rousseau and everyone in between. Ellison came, in other words, to see the novel as a means of negotiating some relation between the limited and necessarily isolated perspective of the individual and the group understood as an aspirational, penultimate, and ideal whole; and, indeed, his novel's difficult mix of epic, tragic, ironic, and realist modes makes the problem of finding a place – a standpoint – from which to see and to understand the unfinished signif-icance of a society and, more particularly, a *segregated* society into a matter of acute and embodied urgency: "A hibernation," says the narrator from his brightly-lit sanctuary beneath the city, "is a covert preparation for a more overt action." In a way that recalls the title of Arrow's 1951 volume, the narrator thus imagines the isolated individual's choice as an expression of as-yet unrealized social values. By 1981 – thirty years after the first appearance of *Invisible Man* – Ellison had adopted and refined a compli-cated but finally optimistic set of arguments about the relation between generality and particularity, ideality and history, hope and violence in what was and remains still a segregated democracy.

As, however, a number of critics have argued, that Ellison cast this network of ideas not as one important and developing *effect* of his novel and its success but rather as its background and *cause* can obscure some of what's difficult about both his book and his earlier political investments: about the depth of his early commitment to communism, his political opposition to American involvement in World War II, and his formative but strained relationship – both personal and political – with Richard Wright.[149] As Barbara Foley writes in *Wrestling with the Left*, "*Invisible Man* is read as testimony to Ellison's maturation; the novel's repudiation of leftist authoritarianism and scientism and its embrace of democratic pluralism and epistemological ambivalence exhibit not just its protagonist's development from ranter to writer, but the increasing sophistication of the text's creator as well."[150] As she argues, that story of linear development belies both Ellison's early commitment to and his subsequent struggle with communism and the American left. Although, writes Alan Wald, "Ellison ... produced a work that proved serviceable to the post hoc construction of the Cold War liberal narrative in the novel," it was not "intended to be anti-Communist, let alone anti-Marxist" at its inception.[151] Although there's a great deal to say about all of that, I want to focus on another, more minor but, in this context, signally important difference. Alongside Ellison's many big ideas about aesthetics, politics, pluralism, and democratic possibility, one can also see a striking and often overlooked interest in the nature, effects, and technical details of electoral, parliamentary, and bureaucratic procedure. Where, in other words, the novel is often rightly cast as a big book about big ideas, the nature and future of democratic pluralism being one of the biggest, it is also a book about the many small ways that seemingly neutral procedures, processes, and rules of order both support and in some cases enact the violence of white supremacy. I'll offer a few examples.

Soon after being recruited by Brother Jack into the Brotherhood, the narrator gives a rousing speech on racial dispossession: "I am a new citizen of the country of your vision, a native of your fraternal land. I feel that here tonight, in this old arena, the new is being born and the vital old revived. In each of you, in me, in us all" (*IM*, 346). At first, the speech seems like a success: "The applause struck like a clap of thunder. I stood, transfixed, unable to see, my body quivering with the roar" (*IM*, 346). When, however, an enthusiastic Brother Jack asks the other members what

---

[149] See, Barbara Foley, *Wrestling with the Left: The Making of Ralph Ellison's* Invisible Man (Durham, NC: Duke University Press, 2010); Hong, *A Violent Peace*; and Alan M. Wald, *American Night: The Literary Left in the Era of the Cold War* (Durham: University of North Carolina Press, 2012).
[150] Foley, *Wrestling with the Left*, 4–5.   [151] Wald, *American Night*, 151.

they thought of it, they express a doctrinaire disapproval: "'It was a most unsatisfactory beginning,' [one member] said quietly, punctuating the 'unsatisfactory' with a stab of his pipe" (*IM*, 348). Unable to believe what he's hearing, Jack becomes angry and sarcastic:

> "Soooo," Brother Jack said, looking from face to face, "there's been a caucus and decisions have been made. Did you take minutes, Brother Chairman? Have you recorded your wise disputations?"
>
> "There was no caucus and the opinion still holds," the brother with the pipe said.
>
> "No meeting, but just the same there has been a caucus and decisions have been reached before the event is finished."
>
> "But, Brother," someone tried to intervene.
>
> "A most brilliant, operation," Brother Jack went on, smiling now. "A consummate example of skilled theoretical Nijinskys leaping ahead of history. But come down. Brothers, come down or you'll land on your dialectics; the stage of history hasn't built that far. The month after next, perhaps, but not yet." (*IM*, 349)

It's a curious moment, one that recalls some of what I talked about in relation to Carroll's invocation of the caucus as something ridiculous in Chapter 3. Brother Jack is disgusted that the other members can't see what he sees, can't see why – even if it diverged from the party line – the narrator's speech is maybe ideologically imprecise but practically effective; it has, in ways that will become clear only at the novel's end, already begun to unleash and to harness energies necessary to Jack's plan to foment racial strife in Harlem and, thus as it were, to *heighten the contradiction*. Why, though, does Jack use the image of a *caucus* as an insult? Why should a *caucus* challenge the other members and make them seem ridiculous?

There are, I think, a few reasons. First, invoking the idea of a caucus, along with the phrases "Brother Chairman" and "taking minutes," serves to diminish the other members, reducing their arguments to the water-cooler chatter of pencil-pushers, technocrats, or drones. Jack thus exploits an anxiety always lurking in political and especially clandestine movements, the worry that what feels like a vital and real kind of engagement, is maybe just an elaborate and inconsequential game. What's more, he opposes the imaginative sterility of the committee to what he understands as the intensity, immediacy, and racially overdetermined *authenticity* of the Harlem crowd. To Jack's crassly instrumental mind, the crowd appears spontaneous and real in a way that maybe the Brotherhood can't. Second, Brother Jack suggests that, because a caucus decides *before* the decision and votes on the outcome of a vote *before* a vote occurs, it should represent a kind of historical error or misprision. Referring to the other members as a caucus suggests that they've reversed cause and effect thus don't really understand the laws of history. Because they have, in other words, chosen to ignore history and its iron laws, they're the ones who are backward and reactionary. Third, by referring to them as a caucus, Jack manages to associate the other members with the local, fat-cat depravities of the political machine *and* to infer something even more damaging from a party perspective: as opposed to standing as a scientific criticism of the speaker's unreconstructed humanism, their resistance to the speech is rather proof of their own unconscious reliance on the values of competitive bourgeois individualism. Knowingly comparing his comrades with the *wrong* Russian – they're Nijinsky and not Lenin – Jack suggests that they're making imaginative leaps where they should be making logical links, that they have fallen into the cardinal error of mistaking aesthetic desire or individual pique for objective scientific analysis.

Later in the novel, after a series of organizing successes in Harlem and the appearance of a flattering magazine profile, the narrator is called before a committee where he is accused of being an "opportunist" and a "petty individualist" (*IM*, 401). The committee, made up of the local leaders of the Brotherhood, consider the question as what *Robert's Rules* would call an expedited motion: "since," says Brother Jack, "this is an emergency the committee asks that you leave the room while we read and discuss the questioned interview" (*IM*, 403). Once again, the moment is characterized by a tension between its apparent procedural order and its exaggerated, almost comic animus. His accuser

> struck the conference table with his fist, his eyes showing small and round in his taut face. I wanted to punch that face. It no longer seemed real, but a mask behind which the real face was probably laughing, both at me and at the others. For he couldn't believe what he had said. It just wasn't possible. *He* was the plotter and from the serious looks on the committee's faces he was getting away with it. Now several brothers started to speak at once, and Brother Jack knocked for order. (*IM*, 401)

As with the caucus, this scene is striking partly for the way it deals with the odd but somehow inevitable combination of bureaucratic infighting, procedural maneuvering, and revolutionary commitment. Like a face incongruously grinning, laughing, or screaming behind a stoic mask, there is a bad fit between the unofficial content of the scene – its anger, its jealousy, its excess – and its official, routine, humdrum form: "Brother Jack knocked for order."

The confrontation is reminiscent of experiences that Ellison's friend Wright had described in 1944. After being elected executive secretary by one faction within a John Reed Club (the writers) in order to alienate another, more racist faction within that same club (the painters), Wright becomes the object of a series of unfounded intraparty attacks: "I was termed a 'bastard intellectual,' and 'incipient Trotskyite'; it was claimed that I possessed an 'anti-leadership attitude' and that I was manifesting 'seraphim tendencies,' a phrase meaning that one has withdrawn from the struggle of life and considers oneself infallible."[152] Both Wright's and Ellison's stories are based in the idea that the same officious tactics that had led to the bad confessions in the Moscow trials had been exported – albeit in a dimmed, degraded, and bathetic way – into the small-town, sectarian disputes between American Stalinists and anti-Stalinists after the trials, the Molotov-Ribbentrop Pact, and – following Stalin's subsequent strategic *volte-face* – the Party's principal commitment to World War II as an anti-fascist as opposed to an imperial conflict. Although, as Ellison saw, Moscow Rules betray a kind of shabby gentility when seen in the context of John Reed Clubs, local meeting halls, and seedy bars, the relation does say something interesting about the diffuse reach of totalitarianism at midcentury. While both Ellison and Wright came in time to see communism as an existential crisis, what's most striking in these scenes is the related authoritarian pressure that apparently mild procedures can exert. The rules are not only a way to facilitate oppression; at key moments, the rules *are* the oppression. The rules that exist to set agendas, to nominate and to elect representatives, to lodge or to recognize complaints, or to expel or to punish errant actors are not neutral; "rules," writes Austin Ranney, "are never neutral."[153] On the contrary, their ostensible neutrality is precisely what allows one person or group to mobilize them against another.

And, in fact, after a second confrontation with Jack's committee, the narrator decides to adopt the recursive apparatus of forms, rules, programs, and ballots to turn the tables and take his revenge:

> They were blind, bat blind, moving only by the echoed sounds of their own voices. And because they were blind they would destroy themselves and I'd help them. I laughed. Here I had thought they accepted me because they felt that color made no difference, when in reality it made no difference because they didn't see either color or men ... For all they were concerned, we were so many names scribbled on fake ballots, to be used at their

[152] Richard Wright, in *The God that Failed*, ed. Richard Crossman (New York: Columbia University Press, 2001), 140–141.
[153] Austin Ranney, "Farewell to Reform – Almost," in *Elections in America*, ed. Kay Lehman Schlozman (Boston: Allen & Unwin, Inc., 1987), 89.

> convenience and when not needed to be filed away. It was a joke, an absurd joke. . . . I went to the apartment and fell across the bed in my clothes. It was hot and the fan did little more than stir the heat in heavy leaden waves, beneath which I lay twirling the dark glasses and watching the hypnotic flickering of the lenses as I tried to make plans. I would hide my anger and lull them to sleep; assure them that the community was in full agreement with their program. And as proof I would falsify the attendance records by filling out membership cards with fictitious names – all unemployed, of course, so as to avoid any question of dues. (*IM*, 510)

Fake ballots, falsified records, bogus forms of assent: for a brief period, Ellison's protagonist uses the tools of empty, insincere procedure to give the party apparatchiks a taste of their own medicine. The dark glasses that he twirls, however, pull the sense of the scene in different directions. On the one hand, they're part of his Rinehart disguise. Realizing a little earlier that he's a dead ringer for a local conman, pimp, and preacher named Rinehart, the narrator decides to embrace the fraudulent absurdity of his situation; if everything – the ballots, Bledsoe, the Brotherhood – is fake, then all is permitted. In the land of the blind, a conman can be king. On the other hand, as much as they represent a canny, streetwise freedom from illusion, the dark glasses are also a figure for yet another kind of blindness. If, that is, the conman has shed a lot of illusions, he needs, at last, to hold and to hold tenaciously onto one last lie: after everything, the conman needs still to believe in other people's beliefs. His insincerity is, as it were, unusually sincere; his enabling belief in the beliefs of others is the last, best illusion. What happens, though, when even that attenuated form of sincerity hits a wall? Although the narrator's Rinehartian game seems to work for a while, suggesting that the world really is made entirely of pliable phonies, the plan, the Brotherhood, and the novel all reach a hard limit as Harlem explodes into a phantasmagoric race riot at the novel's end. In some sense, the riot represents a late, cultural failure of the rules *qua* rules, as the fragile and often abused sincerity of ballots, forms, speeches, and parades gives way to the spectacle of riot, fire, and racial violence.

Machines Inside the Machine

The idea of seeing the rules as a fragile, susceptible, and especially palpable expression of a broader cultural logic of sincerity is important here. I wrote above about Arrow's and Trilling's related efforts to think about sincerity in relation to a willingness to act *as if* we could really and infallibly say what we mean when, after all, we know that we really can't. As opposed, that is, to seeing it as an ideal synthesis of meaning and saying, of intention and action, of private and public, Trilling took sincerity as something more modest and more difficult, as a socially necessary and socially willed suspension of disbelief. Informed by a tradition that connects Diderot, Rousseau, Dostoevsky, and – crucially – Freud, Trilling's citizen is the citizen as subject of psychoanalysis, a social being defined by a constitutive difference between ego and id, latent and manifest, saying and meaning, intention and act. Because you can never quite say what you mean, and because living with others in a complex and pluralist society demands that you to act nonetheless *as if* you could, sincerity emerges not only as an impossible but cherished goal – it is what makes modern subjects *interesting* – but also as one blanket term for the many fictive discourses that, as we have seen, Catherine Gallagher has cast as characteristic of and as necessary to modern life. Although this disposition is formative in many areas – e.g., the discourses of credit, contract, character, and the novel – procedural and parliamentary rules offer an especially palpable example of our fragile reliance on some forms of sincerity: the rules *qua* rules seem both to demand and to refuse interpretation.

Consider, for instance, *Robert's Rules of Order*, as those rules were framed by Henry Martyn Robert in the preface to the first edition of 1876:

> The object of Rules of Order is to assist an assembly to accomplish the work for which it was designed, in the best possible manner. To do this it is necessary to restrain the individual somewhat, as the right of an individual, in any community, to do what he pleases, is incompatible with the interests of the whole. Where there is no law, but every man does what is right in his own eyes, there is the least of real liberty. Experience has shown the importance of definiteness in the law; and in this country, where customs are so slightly established and the published manuals of parliamentary practice so conflicting, no society should attempt to conduct business without having adopted some work upon the subject, as the authority in all cases not covered by their own special rules.
>
> It has been well said by one of the greatest of English writers on parliamentary law: "Whether these forms be in all cases the most rational or not is really not of so great importance. It is much more material that there should be a rule to go by, than what that rule is, that there may be a uniformity of proceeding in business, not subject to the caprice of the chairman, or captiousness of the members, it is very material that order, decency and regularity be presaged in a dignified public body."[154]

---

[154] Henry Martyn Robert, *Robert's Rules of Order*, ed. Rachel Vixman (New York: Jove Books, 1967), 17–18.

There's a lot that's striking here, especially given the terrific and yet almost dumb ubiquity of *Robert's Rules*. Indeed, given its indisputable place in texture of social and professional life, it's hard to think of *Robert's Rules* as book written by *somebody* with a history, interests, and ideas all his own. It feels more like a natural object, something found, like a rock in the woods or on a beach, rather than something that someone made. It is surprising, in that case, to find Robert so animated about his sense of the book's social consequence; not just a useful set of rules for ordering deliberation and decision-making at meetings, the *Rules of Order* had, as he understood it, a particular role to play in a fragile and as-yet indefinite American democracy. It offered, at the level of the individual rule, a way to manage what I've been talking about all along, the effort to resolve the desires and dignity of the individual with the needs and welfare of the group.

Rachel Vixman, a professional parliamentarian who added a "modern guide and commentary" to a 1967 pocket edition of the *Rules*, expands on Robert's founding claim:

> There is a great need for more democratic policies on organization, communal and national levels. Since millions of men and women are banded together in hundreds of thousands of organizations – athletic, business, civic, cooperative, cultural, educational, fraternal, labor, philanthropic, political, professional, recreational, religious, scientific, social, etc., etc. – the faithful observance of democratic principles would become a major and impressive influence in shaping a stronger American democracy.[155]

Like Robert, Vixman takes democracy less as an autonomous ideal and more as an accretive (indeed, an alphabetic) entity, a social and cultural whole that is reliant on but greater than the listed sum of the many associations and rules that give form and impetus to its many conflicting preferences, interests, hopes, and wishes. This is even more striking given Robert's frank sense that his rules matter not because they are more rational or more true than other rules; his rules matter because, when there are no obvious or given rules, we must act as if some rules were obvious and given nonetheless. The rule – neither rational nor true – is a fiction; it is, however, a fiction on which democratic institutions rely. And, because it is a necessary fiction, the rule is, as we have seen, also susceptible to both systematic abuse and a kind of institutional decay.

The most explicit confrontation with the rules of order occurs early in Ellison's novel. After getting expelled from college, moving to New York,

---

[155] Rachel Vixman, "Guide and Commentary," in *Robert's Rules of Order*, by Henry Martyn Robert, ed. Rachel Vixman (New York: Jove Books, 1967), 130.

and learning that the letters of introduction provided by the college president, Dr. Bledsoe, recommended *against* giving him a job, the narrator ends up at Liberty Paints. Talking his way into a job, he starts off mixing ten drops – no more, no less – of a paradoxically whitening "dead black" liquid into cans of the company's signature "Optic White" paint (*IM*, 199). After that goes bad, he ends up working in a basement, "three levels underground," as an assistant to Lucius Brockway, the old man who oversees and operates the boilers, mixers, and other machines that, while hidden away, really keep the plant running: "They got,' he says, "all this machinery, but that ain't everything; *we are the machines inside the machine*" (*IM*, 217). At lunchtime, the narrator goes to fetch his "cold pork chop sandwich" from the locker room and wanders into the midst of a union meeting: "Upon opening the door I thought I had made a mistake. Men dressed in splattered painters' caps and overalls sat about on benches, listening to a thin tubercular-looking man who was addressing them in a nasal voice. Everyone looked at me and I was starting out when the thin man called, 'There's plenty of seats for late comers. Come in, brother . . . .'" (*IM*, 219).

When, however, he informs them that his foreman is the decidedly anti-union Brockway, the room reacts, and insults and accusations start to fly: "Get him the hell out of here!" "Throw him out! Throw him out!" "He looks like a dirty fink to me. A first-class enameled fink!" "Throw the lousy bastard out!" When the question of his joining the union comes up, "a fat man with shaggy gray hair leaped to his feet":

> "I'm against it! Brothers, this fellow could be a fink, even if he was hired right this minute! Not that I aim to be unfair to anybody, either. Maybe he ain't a fink," he cried passionately, "but brothers, I want to remind you that nobody knows it; and it seems to me that anybody that would work under that sonofabitching, double-crossing Brockway for more than fifteen minutes is just as apt as not to be naturally fink-minded! Please, brothers!" he cried, waving his arms for quiet. "As some of you brothers have learned, to the sorrow of your wives and babies, a fink don't have to know about trade unionism to be a fink! Finkism? Hell, I've made a study of finkism! Finkism is born into some guys. It's born into some guys, just like a good eye for color is born into other guys. That's right, that's the honest, scientific truth! A fink don't even have to have heard of a union before," he cried in a frenzy of words. "All you have to do is bring him around the neighborhood of a union and next thing you know, why, zip! He's finking his finking ass off!" (*IM*, 221)

Pressed by the chairman to remember that, "We're a democratic union here, following democratic . . . procedures," another man does what one does in a procedural democracy. He makes a motion:

"I want to put this brother's remarks in the form of a motion: I move that
we determine through a thorough investigation whether the new worker is a
fink or no; and if he is a fink, let us discover who he's finking for! And this,
brother members, would give the worker time, if he ain't a fink, to become
acquainted with the work of the union and its aims. After all, brothers, we
don't want to forget that workers like him aren't so highly developed as
some of us who've been in the labor movement for a long time. So I says,
let's give him time to see what we've done to improve the condition of the
workers, and then, if he ain't a fink, we can decide in a democratic way
whether we want to accept this brother into the union. Brother union
members, I thank you!" (*IM*, 222)

"'All right, brothers. We'll take a vote,' the chairman shouted. 'All in favor
of the motion, signify by saying "Aye" ... ' The ayes drowned him out.
'The ayes carried it'" (*IM*, 222). Over the course of a few pages, we thus see
a process unfold where the undisciplined and miscellaneous anger of a
crowd is focused first into the incoherent rant of an individual and then
into a formal motion and then into a vote and then – finally – into the
official expression of the will-of-all: the ayes carry it.

From one perspective, the meeting is a model of good parliamentary
order. The surprise appearance of the narrator raises an unexpected and
urgent question. Although expressed, first, as a series of disconnected and
rabid insults from the crowd, then as a marginally coherent rant about
"finkism," the idea is finally repurposed into what Robert would call a
"privileged motion" or a "privileged question" on a "question of privilege."
"Questions of Privilege," says Robert, "must not be confused with
Privileged Questions." A privileged motion or question is one that takes
"precedence of all other questions whatever, and on account of this very
privilege they are undebatable"; a question of privilege is one "relating to
the rights and privileges of the assembly, or any of its members."[156] What's
more, the motion to table the question until all parties can learn more is
also by-the-book: "It is not necessary that the assembly take final action
upon the question of privilege when it is raised – it may be referred to a
committee, or laid on the table."[157] Seen in action, the rules of order are a
powerfully constitutive discursive system. "Parliamentary law," says
Robert, "comprises the rules and customs governing deliberative assemblies. Its objects are to enable an assembly, with the least possible friction,
to deliberate upon questions in which it is interested, and to ascertain and

---

[156] Henry Martyn Robert, *Parliamentary Law* (New York: D. Appleton-Century Company, 1923),
126; Robert, *Robert's Rules of Order*, 32, 35.
[157] Robert, *Robert's Rules of Order*, 32, 35.

express its deliberate sense or will on these questions."[158] Faced, on the one hand, with the intensity and inevitability of social conflict and, on the other, with the difficulty of seeing in advance how opinions, arguments, and events will unfold, the rules are intended as a ready-made form that can manage and shape any content, a prefabricated discourse that could structure any story. They are meant to anticipate animus, conflict, and event and to give order to a complexity that would otherwise overwhelm the group. The rules shape potential antagonism into actual deliberation. And, insofar as the rules manage to transform the racial and political antipathy of the union members into the official coherence of a vote, all seems as it should be.

Taken on its own, however, that reading would obscure the scene's considerable and undeniable violence. Entering a roomful of white strangers just weeks after leaving the South, the narrator is grilled, insulted, shouted down, threatened, called a "fink"; even those more sympathetic to him back him into a corner, assuming that he should *want* to join the union when he knows nothing about it. It reads, in other words, like a refigured return to the "battle royal." And, rather than offering an escape from or an alternative to that violence, the right rules of procedure instead sharpen it, lending it legitimacy, consequence, direction, and official force. As the scene moves from shouted curses to an insulting speech and, then, to a formal motion and vote, what we see is not a move *away* from racial terror; it is rather a process by which violence, as it is given institutional shape, is made indisputable. Unable or unwilling to overcome their antipathies, they slap on a coat of procedural paint, and, as the sign says, "If It's Optic White, It's the Right White" (*IM*, 217).

The narrator, in other words, finds himself suddenly and unexpectedly taken up into a nightmare version of what, in Chapter 2, I referred to as the machinery of representation. Where, however, in Mill, Hare, and Carroll, the machinery of representation seemed good because perfectible, in Ellison the machine is dangerous, weaponized, rickety, or rigged. One procedural step leads to another with an irresistibility that evokes the complex, hazardous, totalizing machinery in Brockway's basement: "we are," he said, "the machines inside the machine." This sense of the electoral or political machine less as a tool and more as a trap becomes all the clearer when, after the meeting, Brockway sabotages his own miscellaneous machine, rigging it to explode in order to do away with the narrator. "It was a fall into space that seemed not a fall but a

[158] Robert, *Parliamentary Law*, 3.

suspension. Then a great weight landed upon me and I seemed to sprawl in an interval of clarity beneath a pile of broken machinery, my head pressed back against a huge wheel, my body splattered with a stinking goo" (*IM*, 230).[159] The distorting violence of the machine returns when, after the explosion, he wakes up within the guts of yet another strange machine. "A flash of cold-edged heat enclosed me. I was pounded between crushing electrical pressures; pumped between live electrodes like an accordion between a player's hands. My lungs were compressed like a bellows and each time my breath returned I yelled, punctuating the rhythmical action of the nodes" (*IM*, 232).[160] It turns out this "machine will produce the results of a prefrontal lobotomy without the negative effects of the knife"; it will, in other words, take a unique feeling, an angry thought, an imaginative act, and it will force it through a mechanistic and flattening process until it emerges as something fungible, something transitive, something ordinal like a motion, a preference schedule, or maybe even a vote (*IM*, 236).

Questions of Privilege

If it seems that these are two different ways of looking at the thing that is *Robert's Rules of Order* – as a tool and as a trap – the story is even more complicated. Although, as I said before, the flat, Gideon's Bible ubiquity of *Robert's Rules* makes it easy to treat it as something inevitable or even natural, the book's origins and afterlife are, in fact, mixed up with the history of segregated democracy in America in unexpectedly deep ways. Henry Martyn Robert was born in 1837 near Robertville, South Carolina. His father, Joseph Thomas Robert, was a Baptist clergyman and a member of a slaveholding family that made its money growing rice and indigo. As time went on, Robert found himself increasingly opposed to slavery, a fact that kept him and his wife Adeline constantly on the move between South Carolina, Kentucky, Ohio, Iowa, and Georgia. With the onset of the Civil War, tensions between Joseph and Adeline became acute:

---

[159] In his *Political Dictionary*, Safire offers this machine-minded pastiche: "*Geared* to press the *panic button* at the first *feedback* from *machine* politicos, government planners *mesh* their thinking to get *traction* for their programs to *spark* action, *engineering* their budgets so as to ignore *start-up* costs, and *mechanically* warn those *automatons* and *cogs* whose *machinations* might throw *monkey wrenches* into the *works* that *counterproductive* people usually get the *shaft*." Safire, *Safire's Political Dictionary*, 393.

[160] Both machines both anticipate and recall the destructive "speeding machine," associated with Ras the Destroyer, about which he dreams in the novel's Prologue (*IM*, 12).

"when," write R. Frank Saunders and George Rogers with unnecessary bathos, "the war came ... Joseph Robert would experience ... a personal civil war in his own household."[161] Where his opposition to slavery and thus to the Confederacy became more pronounced, Adeline "retained strong southern sympathies" and, even more, felt distraught at her separation from her slaveholding father and brothers. This conflict was made all the more acute because Henry, who had entered West Point at sixteen, decided to remain an engineer serving in the Union Army: "The idea," she wrote, "that young Henry and one of my brothers might be brought in actual contact on opposite sides pursued me like a ghost."[162] She tried and failed to convince him to switch sides and to fight for the Confederacy.

Soon after the war's end, Adeline died and Joseph moved to Augusta and then Atlanta, Georgia where he would become the first president of Morehouse College. Just as the war's aftermath led Joseph to one of America's first historically Black colleges, Henry's experience of social conflict must have fed into his effort, begun in 1863 and first finished in 1876, to imagine rules that might prevent social conflict from again sliding into catastrophe. He wrote in 1923:

> Where there is radical difference of opinion in an organization, one side must yield. The great lesson for democracies to learn is for the majority to give to the minority a full, free opportunity to present their side of the case, and then for the minority, having failed to win a majority to their views, gracefully to submit and to recognize the action as that of the entire organization, and cheerfully to assist in carrying it out, until they can secure its repeal.[163]

Although abstracted to the point of nearly pure form, *Robert's Rules* has to be seen at least in part as a product of the Civil War and the arguments about slavery that roiled both the nation and his own family. Indeed, as Benjamin Brawley writes in his history of Morehouse College, the Roberts's stories came together "during the year 1877–8, [when] Major H. M. Robert, of the U . Engineer Corps, presented one thousand copies of his Parliamentary Guide to be at the disposal of the President for the benefit of the Institute."[164] Although such a gift must be seen – especially

---

[161] R. Frank Saunders, Jr. and George A. Rogers, "Joseph Thomas Robert and the Wages of Conscience," *Georgia Historical Quarterly* 88(1) (Spring 2004), 10.
[162] Quoted in Saunders and Rogers, "Wages of Conscience," 11.
[163] Robert, *Parliamentary Law*, 4.
[164] Benjamin Brawley, *History of Morehouse College* (Atlanta: Morehouse College, 1917), 26.

Seen in relation to Ellison's bitter and sardonic depiction of his narrator's college days – as an expression of gross condescension, it does represent another moment when the rules revealed themselves not as neutral or transparent but rather as palpable, if obscure, indices of a real and violent history.

This relation between race and *Robert's Rules* returned with a vengeance a few years later. In 1939, Henry's daughter-in-law, Sarah Corbin Robert, was a parliamentarian, a "trustee" of *Robert's Rules of Order* – which she would edit and thoroughly revise in 1970 – and the president-general of the ultraconservative Daughters of the American Revolution. In January of that year, Charles Cohen, chairman of Howard University's concert series, contacted the DAR and sought to reserve Constitution Hall in Washington, DC for an Easter Sunday concert by Marian Anderson, the famous contralto singer. By 1939, Anderson had worked with Toscanini, Sibelius, and had performed to great acclaim throughout the United States and Europe for over a decade. Referring, however, to a "white artists only" clause that they had inserted into their standard contract in 1932, the DAR refused to allow Anderson to perform; although they claimed that such a clause was usual to Washington venues, it was, in fact, "not at all compelled by local custom. The exclusion of black performers was an extreme measure for the city of Washington."[165] Following a number of protests, which would culminate with Eleanor Roosevelt's public resignation from and condemnation of the group, Robert "convened the [DAR] Board of Management, persuaded them ... that no exception could be made for Anderson as far as the 'white artists only' clause was concerned, and won a victory of 39 to 1."[166] With the committee behind her, Robert wrote to Anderson in terms that were both morally grotesque and procedurally precise: "The artistic and musical standing of Miss Marian Anderson is not involved in any way. In view of the existence of provisions in prevailing agreements with other organizations and concert bureaus, and the policy which has been adopted in the past, an exception cannot be made in this instance."[167] "In light of the DAR's history throughout the 1920s and most of the 1930s," writes Allan Keiler, "these explanations on the part of the president-general seem like high comedy." He continues:

> Here was an organization that was portraying itself as helplessly restricted by prevailing policy, swallowed up by social and political forces over which they could hardly be expected to have any control or impact. Yet here was

[165] Allan Keiler, *Marian Anderson: A Singer's Journey* (Urbana: University of Illinois Press, 2002), 188.
[166] Keiler, *Marian Anderson*, 197.   [167] Keiler, *Marian Anderson*, 197.

an organization whose leadership had for years circulated a blacklist of all those who opposed the DAR's views, that had testified before congressional committees in support of anti-liberal legislation, that had summarily expelled members who disagreed openly with DAR policy. Can there be much doubt that the DAR banned Anderson because she was black, and what's more because her concert was sponsored by the prestigious black Howard University, and because she was defended by officials of the NAACP, an organization that had been included in the infamous blacklist?[168]

Anderson would, of course, perform in Washington that Easter, singing on the steps of the Lincoln Memorial for a crowd of 75,000 and for millions more over the radio. There's a lot more to say about this event and its significance. Here, though, I want to highlight the simple but resonant fact that the history and the existence of *Robert's Rules of Order* is anything but neutral. On the one hand, we need to see the *Rules* as an historical artifact, as a system that emerged at least partly out of a traumatic encounter with the fact of slavery and the experience of Civil War. On the other hand, we need also to see that, because all rules are historical, no rule can ever be neutral. As we've seen throughout, while defined rules, devices, procedures are necessary to any electoral or democratic process, the fact that they are always necessary does not guarantee that they will always do good. So, when the Invisible Man finds himself unrelieved by the rules of order – motion, second-the-motion, vote – he is not alone.

History/Mystery

The cleft nature of elections, electoral rules, and democracy itself is a persistent theme running through Ellison's work. On the one hand, his writing is everywhere characterized by a sharp sense of the lived texture of segregated democracy, how Black life within American culture is often defined and, in fact, often driven mad by rules, institutions, practices, and expectations that are violent and capricious, trivial and determinate, mundane and yet matters of life and death. Drive here, but not there; say this, but not that; check the gauge every fifteen minutes, but don't ask why; exactly ten drops, but don't ask why; give a speech, don't give a speech, but don't ask why. In Ellison, this capricious and unmotivated network of rules, traps, expectations, and impediments often takes, as I have said, on the character of a dream or a nightmare, an illogical space in which one is

---

[168] Keiler, *Marian Anderson*, 198.

forced to expend enormous imaginative energy on projects that, because they are both malignant and meaningless, must come to nothing: "For this is a world in which the major energy of the imagination goes not into creating works of art, but to overcome the frustrations of social discrimination."[169] And if, on the other hand, Ellison gave form to the impossible nightmare particulars of a segregated democracy, he was also committed – albeit warily – to the idea of American democracy as big, pluralistic, complex ambiguous, violent, often hypocritical, and – in the end – *possible*. He writes in a 1964 essay, that:

> In order to orient myself I also began to learn that the American novel had long concerned itself with the puzzle of the one-and-the-many; the mystery of how each of us, despite his origin in diverse regions, with our diverse racial, cultural, religious backgrounds, speaking his own diverse idiom of the American in his own accent, is, nevertheless, American. And with this concern with the implicit pluralism of the country and with the composite nature of the ideal character called "the American," there goes a concern with gauging the health of the American promise, with depicting the extent to which it was being achieved and made manifest in our daily conduct.[170]

Years later, in a eulogy for Romare Bearden, he casts America as a "collage of a nation, and a nation that is ever shifting about and grousing as we seek to achieve the promised design of democracy." "Therefore," he continues, "one of the reasons that we revere Romie is for his discovery that one of the ways for getting at many of the complex matters which we experience, but seldom find recorded in official history, is through art. Art is the mystery which gets left out of history."[171] As is often the case in Ellison's later writings, the political problem of segregated democracy is recast here – partially and cautiously – as a kind of aesthetic opportunity; he writes, in other words, as if a clear and present social *impossibility* ought to be understood not as an end but rather as an imaginative impetus toward an as-yet unrealized and mysterious *possibility*.

Critics sometimes – and not without reason – write about this doubleness in Ellison as a betrayal of earlier and clearer political commitments. Barbara Foley, to take the most thorough example, understands Ellison's later embrace of artistic experimentalism and political pluralism as part of a revisionist and increasingly conservative effort to downplay or even to erase

---

[169] Ellison, "Harlem Is Nowhere," 322.   [170] Ellison, "Hidden Name and Complex Face," 207.
[171] Ralph Ellison, "Bearden," in *The Collected Essays of Ralph Ellison*, ed. John F. Callahan (New York: The Modern Library, 2003), 840.

his early political commitments, a process that finds its starkest expression in the intricate textual history of *Invisible Man*:

> The examination of Ellison's many cuts and substitutions from early versions of *Invisible Man* conveys the cost of anti-communism, that is, what is sacrificed when a leftist vision is expunged. For just as the ultimate target of the McCarthy-era witch hunts was, arguably, not so much Communists themselves as the millions who might heed their message, what is lost from *Invisible Man* through Ellison's revisions is a full and rich sense of the potential for conscious and radical historical engagement on the part of Harlem's working class.[172]

This is a compelling argument, and, as we saw with the case of Arrow, understanding the Cold War and the history of the American left in the vulgar terms of a game of spy vs. spy distorts not only the nature of the many hard decisions and compromises that individual actors had to make at the time but also the variegated texture of a history marked by many, often conflicting interpretations and events. I want, however, to gesture toward something less definite but equally important in Ellison, a style of thought that cuts, I think, across versions of his work. What connects his early commitment to dialectical materialism and his later embrace of democratic pluralism, is an imaginative effort to think impossibility and possibility at the same time, to see them not as a debilitating and dead-end opposition but rather as competing aspects of historical experience.[173] The urge to see in the apparent impossibility of the present a demand for future possibilities is, after all, a style of thinking that, for all their differences, cuts across Ellison's early and late phases; in these terms, what Marxism and democratic pluralism share — even if they can share little else — is a resistance to what Ellison called a "final and unrelieved despair."

Impossible Possibility

We have seen that Arrow's impossibility theorem did not claim that elections are impossible; what it said rather was that settling on a single procedure that would work in relation to any kind of election, with any possible outcome, at any moment in time was impossible. I think this

---

[172] Foley, *Wrestling with the Left*, 22.
[173] "Ellison," writes Darryl Pinckney, "opposed the notion of black life as a 'metaphysical condition' of 'irremediable agony' because that made it seem as though it either took place in a vacuum or had only one theme." Pinckney, *Blackballed: The Black Vote and US Democracy* (New York: New York Review Books, 2020), 100.

means a few things. First, it means that the rules matter. Having identified and accepted a few reasonable constraints, Arrow went on to test different aggregation models against them. What he found was not that elections don't produce results but rather that different rules can produce different results out of the same raw materials. As Carroll had done before him, Arrow realized that the same set of votes on a question will produce different winners depending on how you count those votes: a plurality winner will not always be the majority winner. As a result, he saw that, because there is no rule that will work in every situation, it is crucial in every situation to know how our rules work or don't work. Second, it means that the rules are historical. Because different rules will lead to different results in the same election, it becomes necessary to compare those rules not only at any given moment but also across time. It is necessary to ask not only will a rule work but also will a rule work *for us*, given the shifting and unfinished values, norms, and constraints that characterize things "now and around here." The attentive reader will recall that phrase from my discussion of Bernard Williams, who argued that the meaning and value of different political systems and rules is a fundamentally *historical* problem: what "makes sense" (MS) as a political rule "is a category of historical understanding – which we can call, if we like, a hermeneutical category. There are many difficulties of interpretation associated with it, for example whether there are not some historical constellations of belief which altogether fail to MS. ... But when we get to our own case, the notion 'MS' does become normative, because what (most) MS to us is a structure of authority which we think we should accept."[174] To think, in that case, about what rules work *for us* cannot be managed in the abstract; we need to consider not only the meaning and utility of a given rule or system but also the tacit assumptions, values, and norms that define things "now and around here." We need, in other words, to think hard about the meaning of "us." That means that when a rule fails, sometimes we need to change the rule and other times we need to change everything else. It also means, as we saw with Ellison, that rules which work for *some of* us do not always work for everyone; indeed, the history of voting in America shows us how seemingly neutral electoral rules and procedures have often been used *against* Black voters with brutal efficiency. Which leads me to a third meaning of the impossibility theorem: it means that one has to try. The historicity or the limits of a rule or a system isn't

---

[174] Bernard Williams, *In the Beginning Was the Deed: Realism and Moralism in Political Argument* (Princeton, NJ: Princeton University Press, 2005), 11.

necessarily reason to abandon it; on the contrary, it means that one must think all the harder about what rules work for us and for others, for how things are, and for how they should be. For Arrow, impossibility wasn't a terminal point or cause for libertarian gloom; it was rather a limit against which the nature and value of possibility could be empirically measured. And, for Ellison, both early and late, the complex and dialectical negoti-ation between the possibilities and impossibilities of segregated democracy wasn't a source of "unrelieved despair"; it was, rather, a way and a reason really to see and, perhaps, to overcome contradictions that were the necessary result of a procedural democracy caught still in the two-fisted grip of bad faith and white supremacy.

Conclusion
A Silent Majority

Great care has gone into the construction of the shadow which declares itself to be Richard Nixon.

—Murray Kempton, 1956

Whereof one cannot speak thereof one must be silent.

—Ludwig Wittgenstein, 1922

Despite their evident and sometimes pronounced differences in logic, rhetoric, strategy, and style, all the figures I discuss in this book rely on a few shared and underlying assumptions. While they can and do disagree about its shape, meaning, value, and future, they tend all to accept that modern social and political life is and has been defined by the question of how to manage a difficult negotiation between the ideas, preferences, and desires of individuals and the ideas, preferences, and desires of the group. Whether it be Jean-Jacques Rousseau or Jeremy Bentham, George Eliot or George Grote, William Morris or William Riker, Ralph Ellison or Kenneth Arrow, the writers and thinkers I've addressed take it as a fraught and incomplete given that the periodic crises and the essential complexity of modern life make it necessary not only to imagine new models of the group but also to identify practical methods and schemes that would allow one at least to act *as if* there were a significant and even organic way of recognizing what the people really think and want. Although some were enthusiasts, some were skeptics, and some were cynics, all of them recognize the importance of the problem established in Rousseau's *Social Contract*: "How to find a form of association which will defend the person and goods of each member with the collective force of all, and under which each individual, while uniting himself with the others, obeys no one but himself, and remains as free as before."[1] Of course, for Rousseau, it was not enough simply to assert, announce, or even dream the existence of the

---

[1] Jean-Jacques Rousseau, *The Social Contract*, trans. Maurice Cranston (London: Penguin, 1968), 60.

general will; one needed also to imagine the mechanism, the process, the model of association or aggregation that would allow individuals to come together as something significantly more than the sum of their respective parts. Although the questions raised by Rousseau's text are themselves legion, I have in this book focused on problems and paradoxes raised specifically by the nature and the machinery of aggregative political representation. Although Rousseau mostly hated the idea – perhaps because it was an idea from which he could not escape – others tend to accept that his imagined and fundamental "form of association" must amount to one or another model of representative as opposed to direct democracy; what gets you to something even remotely like the general will in large, pluralist societies will probably take the form an election whereby some individuals are somehow selected by other individuals somehow to represent the will of all.

As Edmund Morgan argues, this idea – that elected individuals or groups could somehow really represent the preference, will, or well-being of a whole people – is a fiction. He writes:

> It was widely acknowledged that the people could not speak for themselves – there were too many of them. And the question of who could speak for them was complicated by the perceived alienation of the majority of the population from those who were most eager to speak, most eager to affirm the sovereignty of the people. ... The problem of reconciling the wishes and needs and rights of actual people with the overriding will of a fictional sovereign people was not temporary. It was, indeed, inherent in the new fictions.[2]

Because one person can't really or reliably represent the will of another person – never mind represent the aggregated wills of a million other persons – representation must be a fiction; because, however, it is hard if not impossible to imagine another way effectively to manage large, pluralist societies, representation is a *necessary* fiction. It is or at least it has been necessary for people willingly to suspend their disbelief and to act as if there really were such a thing as the general will; as if a parliament really were an accurate reflection of a people; as if what is wanted by only slightly more than half of everyone really is or at least ought to be what everyone else wants, too. For Morgan, these fictions, while false, are not pernicious: they are not lies. On the contrary, "because fictions are necessary, because we cannot live without them, we often take pains to prevent their collapse by moving the facts to fit the fiction, by making our world conform more

---

[2] Edmund S. Morgan, *Inventing the People: The Rise of Popular Sovereignty in England and America* (New York: W. W. Norton & Company, 1989), 82.

closely to what we want it to be. We sometimes call it, quite appropriately, reform or reformation, when the fiction takes command and reshapes reality."[3] A good fiction is not only good for itself; if *not disbelieved*, a good fiction can make the world different, perhaps better and perhaps worse. It can imaginatively reform the world into something new. Fictions are, thus, not essentially lies, first, because they are the result of a *willing* suspension of disbelief and, second, because, as instruments of the imagination, they can sometimes remake the world in their image and can become true where once they were not.

As I argued at the beginning of this book, this mix of fictionality and actuality, imagination and empiricism, wishing and working aligns the electoral logic of political representation with what Catherine Gallagher identifies as "the novel and other discourses of suspended disbelief." "Modernity," she writes, "is fiction-friendly because it encourages disbelief, speculation, and credit."[4] She continues:

> Indeed, almost all of the developments we associate with modernity – from greater religious toleration to scientific discovery – required the kind of cognitive provisionality one practices in reading fiction, a competence in investing contingent and temporary credit. One telling acknowledgment of the benefits of such mental states was the increasing use of the word *fiction* to mean, "a supposition known to be at variance with fact, but conventionally accepted for some reason of practical convenience, conformity with traditional usage, decorum, or the like," as in "legal fiction."[5]

Although Gallagher doesn't explicitly mention the many necessary fictions that underwrite representative governments in general and electoral procedures in particular, it should be clear by this point that part of what allows those governments and procedures to work – part of what makes them seem or feel *legitimate* – is precisely our willingness to act together as if we believed in them; and, if and when enough people decide that they will no longer act as if they believe in governments or in electoral procedures, those governments and procedures will lose their legitimacy, and they will fail. This is one reason why Bernard Williams says that "for there to be legitimate government, there must be a legitimation story."[6]

---

[3] Morgan, *Inventing the People*, 14.
[4] Catherine Gallagher, "The Rise of Fictionality," in *The Novel, Volume I: History, Geography, and Culture*, ed. Franco Moretti (Princeton, NJ: Princeton University Press, 2006), 345.
[5] Gallagher, "Rise of Fictionality," 347.
[6] Bernard Williams, "From Freedom to Liberty," in *In the Beginning Was the Deed: Realism and Moralism in Political Argument*, ed. Geoffrey Hawthorne (Princeton, NJ: Princeton University Press, 2005), 94–95.

Part of what's important here is the fact that, as opposed to legitimation in the abstract, a *legitimation story* reveals legitimacy as historical; because, in other words, stories and fictions are made – because they are, in one sense and as I have said, always rigged – they will make sense in some places, at some times, and for some people but not in, at, and for others. As we know from Henry James, Georg Lukács, and other theorists of the novel, fictions derive their form and their meaning from the shaping relation between what gets included and what gets excluded: "Really, universally, relations stop nowhere, and the exquisite problem of the artist is eternally but to draw, by a geometry of his own, the circle within which they shall happily *appear* to do so."[7] The political history of more or less democratic elections – from Athens to the Estates-General, from the Levellers to the Chartists, from the secret ballot to women's suffrage and civil rights – can thus be understood as an ongoing effort to rewrite the plot and, even more, to reimagine the *form* of the legitimation stories that underwrite political representation at any given time. Who gets to appear in the story and who doesn't, who narrates and who is narrated, how does the story handle focalization, character, description, closure, order, tempo, and plot: these are questions that can be meaningfully asked about the novel as well as about the stories that both authorize and limit the nature and scope of elections and electoral procedures as they exist "now and around here."[8]

And, if it makes sense at the level of representative government to think in the large terms of the *logic* of fictionality, it might make sense at the level of the election and, even more, at the more granular level of the individual vote to think in terms of what we might call the *grammar* of figurality. As I've argued throughout, given both the basic difficulty of saying what one really means and the larger problem of saying it in a way that can inform or add to what everyone else is trying to say, the vote and other forms of political expression are, perhaps, best understood as figures of speech, as attempts to find one or another stable and communicable form with which to convey the resistant and protean stuff of preference, interest, analysis, desire, hope, or whatever else we might imagine. A vote is, in other words, not only an action; it is a representation, a way of figuring or giving shape to a preference, interest, wish, hope, or belief. Of course, it is hard and maybe impossible to say which of these things (preference, interest, wish,

---

[7] Henry James, *Roderick Hudson* (New York: Macmillan & Co., 1921), x.

[8] Bernard Williams, "Realism and Moralism," in *In the Beginning Was the Deed: Realism and Moralism in Political Argument*, ed. Geoffrey Hawthorne (Princeton, NJ: Princeton University Press, 2005), 8.

etc.) the vote represents because, of course, some or all of these different motives will always be present – and sometimes inconsistently so – at the site of a decision. As Richard Wollheim points out, faced with a choice between A and B, an individual can want A but also think that B ought to be the case: "We may well have a desire and a moral belief that runs counter to that desire."[9] A vote, in that case, must stand in not only either for the desire for A or for the belief in B but also for a nervous and unstable relation between the two, for inclination's seduction of evaluation or for evaluation's executive power over inclination.[10] As a sign, symbol, or index, the vote not only has to represent a lot of different things but also sometimes to represent a lot of different and even incommensurate things all at once. If the preference, interest, wish, or whatever else is the tenor, the vote is the vehicle; and, if love is a red, red rose, what you or I really and idiosyncratically want and believe and think and want people to think we want, believe, and think is a vote. Neither claim really makes much sense, but we are often ready to act nonetheless as if both claims do. Fictionality and figurality: as I've argued throughout, part of what makes thinking and talking about elections amenable to the methods of literary analysis is the fact that they have historically relied on some of the same flexible but fragile structures and assumptions that make the novel modern and modernity novelistic.

As I said at the start, the figures I've considered thus far were variously *of* this system; whatever they wanted ultimately to do with it, they all seemed to accept some version of this fictional and figural relation between the individual and the group as a definitive and fundamental aspect of or problem for modern life. How, to say it once again, can we get from the feelings, desires, and ideas of the one to the feelings, desires, and ideas of the group? With the help of what discipline, procedure, method, or delusion could we identify and pursue what is good and true not for only some of us but rather for all of us? Even if the "all of us" was always a fiction, it was nonetheless a legitimating fiction; it was a way for members of these large, pluralist societies to make some sense of and even to believe in a set of systems that are both necessary and necessarily flawed. In what remains, I want to turn briefly and finally to a text that represents a more recent and dispiriting alternative to the kinds of fiction that I've been describing. It's not the only alternative, and it's for sure not

[9] Richard Wollheim, "A Paradox in the Theory of Democracy," in *Philosophy, Politics, and Society, Second Series*, ed. Peter Laslett and W. G. Runciman (Oxford: Basil Blackwell, 1964), 77.
[10] See my reading of Lydgate's bind in Chapter 2.

the best. It is, however, one that continues to put a profound and delegitimizing pressure on the fragile and flawed norms that underwrite modern democratic systems. I want, in other words, to turn to a televised speech that Richard Nixon delivered on November 3, 1969, the "Silent Majority" speech. In ways that continue to shape and distort our politics, Nixon's use of that phrase not only effectively harnessed white ressentiment in the service of securing political power but also altered the ordinary meaning of the word "majority" in fundamental and lasting ways. While Nixon's speech was no fiction, it was in many ways a lie. Understanding the essential difference between a necessary fiction and a big lie will, I hope, offer us a way both to reflect on the historical contours of my story and to consider, however briefly, what moral it might offer (Figure 5.1).

A Do-It-Yourself People

Although Nixon's speech is often remembered as the "Silent Majority" speech, the phrase and its argument or its appeal aren't really central to the speech as a whole. The words appear only once and, even then, they appear only at the end of a thirty-two-minute Oval Office speech. Nixon was, of course, fixated on antiwar protests and domestic discord in late 1969. That said, his carefully constructed speech wasn't really (or at least wasn't evidently) about conflict at home; he offered, rather, an apparently scrupulous and performatively logical account of (1) the history of America's involvement in Vietnam, (2) the differences between Johnson's and Nixon's strategies, (3) the sorry state of diplomatic play between Hanoi, the US, and the USSR, (4) what choices "we have if we are to end the war," and (5) "the prospects for peace." The speech was, in other words, primarily an articulation of the "Nixon Doctrine," the policy of "Vietnamization" that, Nixon claimed, would allow the US more effectively to train the South Vietnamese army, to draw down American combat troops, and to slow and eventually cease bombing in the North. "We Americans," said Nixon in what must stand as history's most mawkish defense of colonial violence, "are a do-it-yourself people. We are an impatient people. Instead of teaching someone else to do a job, we like to do it ourselves. And this trait has been carried over into our foreign policy." He later recasts this bit of disingenuous corn into the more recognizably oratorical form of rhetorical antithesis: "In the previous administration, we Americanized the war in Vietnam. In this administration, we are Vietnamizing the search for peace."

Figure 5.1 " ... to you, the great silent majority of my fellow Americans ... "

If, however, the speech was about Vietnam at the level of its ostensibly rigorous logic, as a rhetorical performance it belongs almost entirely to the silent majority. Looking over Nixon's earlier speeches, it becomes clear that he had been looking for the phrase for a lot longer than he had been thinking about Vietnam. He had referred previously and almost haphazardly to "the quiet Americans," "the forgotten Americans," "the nonshouters," "the new majority," and "the silent center" before landing at last on a phrase that would bring these elements together and would come to shape the imaginary contours of American electoral politics for decades. When Nixon arrives finally at that phrase – after thirty characteristically Nixonian minutes of policy leavened with bathos – he looks directly to camera as it slowly tracks in for a final close-up, and he smiles slightly; you can see that this is the moment for which he has been waiting and he knows that it's going to land perfectly: "And so tonight – to you, the great silent majority of my fellow Americans – I ask for your support." In the wake of the speech, as he celebrated good reviews and a significant polling bump, the phrase became a kind of rhetorical and conceptual benchmark. On the day after the speech, H. R. Haldeman crowed to his diary that "almost all" of the responses were favorable and "about 43 referred to 'quiet majority.'" "Forever more," writes Rick Pearlstein, Nixon "would point his speechwriters to 'the November 3 speech' as what they should be aiming for."[11] More important, the phrase took on increased weight as a kind of suppositional reality, as way to remake or to reform a lot of different people into a single political power. Where before there was an inchoate and protean mass, now there was the silent majority. On January 12, 1970, Haldeman writes that, after looking at the polls, Nixon was "especially interested in the strength of the Silent Majority"; on February 4, he writes that we "have to mobilize the Silent Majority and get our own fires burning"; on May 21, he writes that Nixon "thinks we're still too timid on mobilizing the Silent Majority."[12] What had been a phrase had become a basis for making political policy; what had been a figure of speech had become a way practically to invent and to mobilize an electorate.

All of this was contained in the complex rhetorical structure of Nixon's plea: "to *you*, the great silent majority." More than just a phrase, his second-person invocation of the silent majority is an unexpectedly precise

---

[11] Rick Pearlstein, *Nixonland: The Rise of a President and the Fracturing of America* (New York: Scribner, 2009), 435.

[12] H. R. Haldeman, *The Haldeman Diaries: Inside the Nixon White House* (New York: Berkley Books, 1995), 144, 151, 202.

example of what Paul de Man identifies as the figure of prosopopoeia: "the fiction of an apostrophe to an absent, deceased, or voiceless entity, which posits the possibility of the latter's reply and confers upon it the power of speech."[13] For de Man, prosopopoeia is both ubiquitous and powerful. It is *ubiquitous* because the figure reproduces and, as it were, purifies the performative and "specular" structure of all language; character and identity in language cannot exist outside of a relation with some real or imagined other. As a result, linguistic being – we might as well say human being – is predicated on the invocation or the invention of an imaginary other. It is *powerful* because, even though we will always rely on some kind of imaginary other, the particular forms we choose will go far not only to describe but also to make our world, to identify and to shape the norms, values, and qualities in relation to which we define ourselves as living and *not* dead, self and *not* other, me and *not* you, us and *not* them. So, at the moment that he simultaneously invents and invokes the "voiceless entity" that is the silent majority, Nixon is doing more than contrasting the stoic virtues of "ordinary" Americans with the excesses of a "fervent" and irrationally "vocal" minority; he is, rather, exploiting a rhetorical, a value-laden, a "specular" as opposed to a merely quantitative or aggregative opposition between a majority and a minority in order to imagine, initiate, and to solidify a political realignment.[14] Put simply, he is redefining what a majority is and what a majority is for.

The Real Majority

Although historians argue about the precise nature of that realignment – as being about a southern strategy or the suburban Sunbelt, about values voters or "middle" Americans, about white flight or "law and order" – it meant a lot for the meaning of the majority in the late sixties and early seventies. Two books are worth mentioning. The first is Kevin Phillips's *The Emerging Republican Majority* (1969). Phillips, who worked as an adviser to Nixon's 1968 campaign, argued on the basis of that election

---

[13] Paul de Man, "Autobiography as De-Facement," in *The Rhetoric of Romanticism* (New York: Columbia University Press, 1984), 75–76.

[14] For more on the ideology and subsequent history of this realignment, see Corey Robin: "Nixon, Reagan, and Bush achieved their upward redistribution of rights and privileges by mobilizing a majority of the electorate based on some combination of muted racism, militaristic and/or Christian nationalism, and market populism." Robin, *The Reactionary Mind: Conservatism from Edmund Burke to Donald Trump* (Oxford: Oxford University Press, 2018), 268.

and new statistical methods that "elections were won by focusing people's resentments" and that, in 1968, those resentments were mostly cultural:

> The New Deal coalition rose by directing people's resentment of economic elites, Phillips argued. But the new hated elite...was *cultural* – the "toryhood of change," condescending and self-serving liberals "who make their money out of plans, ideas, communication, social upheaval, happenings, excitement," at the psychic expense of "the great, ordinary, Lawrence Welkish mass of Americans from Maine to Hawaii."[15]

Phillips put the case more succinctly when he told Garry Wills that "the whole secret of politics [is] knowing who hates who."[16] It was, in other words, that purity of resentment – both cultural and racial – that helped to explain George Wallace's relatively strong and wholly appalling showing in the 1968 election and that predicted what form that this new majority would eventually take:

> The emerging Republican majority spoke clearly in 1968 for a shift away from the sociological jurisprudence, moral permissiveness, experimental residential, welfare, and educational programming and massive federal spending by which the Liberal (mostly Democratic) Establishment sought to propagate liberal institutions and ideology – and all the while reaping growing economic benefits.[17]

After reading Phillips's data, Nixon told Haldeman, "Go for Poles, Italians, Irish, must learn to understand Silent Majority ... don't go for Jews and Blacks."[18] The second book is Richard Scammon and Ben Wattenberg's *The Real Majority*, in which they also argue for the arrival of socially as opposed to economically driven voting and for the consolidation of a solid voting majority that was, as they put it, "unyoung, unpoor, and unblack." For Scammon and Wattenberg, this realignment meant that winning candidates and coalitions would have to move increasingly and with paradoxical vigor toward the moderate middle: "It can be said that the

---

[15] Pearlstein, *Nixonland*, 277. See also Robert Mason, *Richard Nixon and the Quest for a New Majority* (Chapel Hill: University of North Carolina Press, 2004), 47–50.

[16] Garry Wills, *Nixon Agonistes: The Crisis of the Self-Made Man* (Boston: Mariner Books, 2002), 265.

[17] Kevin P. Phillips, *The Emerging Republican Majority* (Princeton, NJ: Princeton University Press, 2012), 552.

[18] Quoted in Jill Lepore, *If Then: How the Simulatics Corporation Invented the Future* (New York: W. W. Norton, 2020), 276. See Lepore for more on the early relation between Nixon, Phillips, predictive analytics, and data-driven approaches to shaping electorates that managed to anticipate "the machine in which humanity would in the early twenty-first century find itself trapped, a machine that applies the science of psychological warfare to the affairs of ordinary life, a machine that manipulates opinion, exploits attention, commodifies information, divides voters, fractures communities, alienates individuals, and undermines democracy" (324).

only extreme that is attractive to the large majority of American voters is the extreme center."[19] While Phillips took his results as proof that the Republican party would endure if it continued to stoke and to harness white cultural resentment, and Scammon and Wattenberg instead argued that *any* successful political movement would have to move to and activate the middle, both books were committed – as Nixon was committed – to reimagining the meaning of the majority.

This redefinition was demanded by a set of institutional developments that meant it was no longer possible to think about a real or an emerging or a silent majority simply numerical terms. First, although Nixon seemed comfortable and even pleased to refer to his great silent majority just one year after his election, he, in fact, did not win that election with anything like a majority. With Wallace's American Independent Party siphoning off votes everywhere but especially in the deep south, Nixon won his election with only 43.4 percent of the popular vote, with, in other words, fewer votes than any candidate since Woodrow Wilson's four-way split with Roosevelt, Taft, and Debs in 1912. The Nixon majority was not a majority. Second, if the majority was not a majority, neither was its silence all that silent. As I've already shown, the southern part of this new coalition had long been characterized by its violence and its blatant, byzantine, and, as it were, *loud* efforts to stymie the Black vote; and, in the wake of the violent "hardhat riot" against antiwar protesters in New York on May 8, 1970, the *National Observer* noted that this month "will be remembered as the month when one segment of what President Nixon calls the Silent Majority ended its public 'silence' with a vengeance."[20] And, third, part of what drove the statistical and demographic arguments in Phillips and Scammon and Wattenberg was the development of a more instrumental or even cynical understanding of effective electoral majorities. Where we might imagine that "majority" would refer to a numerical majority of all Americans (that clearly is what Nixon was suggesting in his national address to the silent majority), these writers understood a "majority" to mean the majority of *voters* in a given election, even or especially when the character of those voters did not really reflect the whole character of the country: "For example," write Scammon and Wattenberg,

[19] Richard M. Scammon and Ben J. Wattenberg, *The Real Majority: An Extraordinary Examination of the American Electorate* (New York: Coward, McCann, & Geoghegan, Inc., 1970), 21.

[20] Quoted in David Paul Kuhn, *The Hardhat Riot: Nixon, New York City, and the Dawn of the White Working-Class Revolution* (Oxford: Oxford University Press, 2020), 242. See also Jefferson Cowie, *Stayin' Alive: The 1970s and the Last Days of the Working Class* (New York: The New Press, 2010), 135–140.

"while the advocates of the New Politics in 1968 were reminding one another that half of all Americans were under twenty-five (which is roughly true), the canny psephologist was carefully noting that the average age of all *voters* was forty-seven (which is also true, and far more relevant)."[21] After 1968 the difference between a majority of a people and a majority of the voters became even more pronounced as political primaries were reformed as the result of populist objections to the centrality of the parties' old nominating apparatuses. Although the reforms did significantly weaken the party's old guard (this was especially true for the Democrats after their convention debacle in Chicago in 1968), they did not lead necessarily to fairer or more broadly representative elections.

Imagine, for instance, that you have a primary in a one-party or heavily gerrymandered area. In that case, the winner of the primary will almost certainly be the winner of the election. So, if a majority in a general election is anything greater than 50 percent of those votes and the winner of the primary is anything greater than that 50 percent of *those* votes, it is possible that the "majority" in a given election could represent 25 percent of voters, which, if only half the people actually vote, could amount to little more than 10 percent of an area's real population. According to this logic, one in ten people could constitute a state's practical if not its numerical majority. While that might seem insane or wrong, that was exactly the new math that Phillips, Scammon, and Wattenberg saw as requisite to the successful electoral strategist. To succeed in politics in the age of increasingly bareknuckle primaries, you needed to see that a majority was not a majority, that A was, somehow, not A.

If these changes and events were the institutional occasion for a practical redefinition of the majority, their effect went far deeper into the logic of things and, more to the point, into and against the play of fictionality and figurality with which I began this conclusion. The thinkers and systems I've tried to describe over the course of this book relied on the production of majorities as a procedural means to a distinct political or ethical end: the identification of the will of all, the general will, the greatest good, or the preference of the group. Making that link between individuals and those different aggregates was always going to be a fiction. Nonetheless, that fiction meant that we had at least to pretend that everyone mattered, that the majority was significant because it allowed us at least to imagine a whole people or community. Elections were – at least ideally – a means to some other end. In Phillips, Scammon, Wattenberg, and Nixon, however,

---

[21] Scammon and Wattenberg, *The Real Majority*, 21.

the production of majorities within the limited and dishonest terms of a corrupt game was no longer a means to an end. It *was* the end and, as a result, it did away with the fiction of the general will or the whole people and thus the idea that everyone should or could count. Elections became the end. The majority is what gets you elected. That's that. Nothing else matters.

Abiit ad plures

I said before that Nixon's invocation of the silent majority was a nearly perfect instance of the rhetorical figure, prosopopoeia. Speaking directly to an imagined, absent, and silent *you*, Nixon took an inchoate and miscellaneous collection of potential voters – suburbanites, hardhats, southern whites, urban Catholics, "Rocky Mountain and Pacific Interior populists" – and figured them not only into an expedient voting bloc but also into an imaginary, singular, and intentional subject: the silent majority.[22] As an instrumental *act* of address, the call to the silent majority conferred "a mask or a face" and thus a demographic reality onto a political entity that hadn't existed until it had been hailed.[23] As a result, and as I have suggested, Nixon's rhetorical move depends upon the same specular – one might even say *rigged* – structure of identity and address on which de Man relies. As it turns out, however, the connection between de Man's argument and Nixon's performance goes even deeper than that. Where de Man acknowledges different kinds of prosopopoeia, he focuses on the *Essays upon Epitaphs* and Wordsworth's invocation of "the fiction of the voice-from-beyond-the-grave," on the figure's unsettling capacity to imagine and to embody the unimaginable: the listening or the speaking dead.[24] We might think that this is one of the many, many ways in which Nixon and Wordsworth differ; although the silent majority isn't a living thing for

---

[22] Phillips, *Emerging Republican Majority*, 552.

[23] Given more time, I'd want to say something about an even deeper connection between Nixon and the logic of prosopopoeia. Although you can see a lot of presidents out and about on Halloween, none is more closely associated with his own rubber mask than Richard Nixon. This is, as the *Washington Post* cartoonist Herblock well understood, partly a function of facial features – the ski-slope nose, the jowls, the insistent need for a shave – that seemed especially ready for caricature. More significant, though, is the widely held impression that the Nixon mask was not only a caricature but also the rude index of the enormous effort it took for a strange, insecure, and avowedly introverted man to appear in public always as *someone else*. As David Greenberg writes, "the Nixon mask is powerful because it's redundant – the mask of a man who seemed to be wearing a mask already." Greenberg, *Nixon's Shadow: The History of an Image* (New York: W. W. Norton, 2003), xvi.

[24] de Man, "Autobiography as De-Facement," 77.

Nixon, it's not exactly a dead thing either, so we should be careful not to go too far with the comparison. That caution would, however, prevent us from seeing some of what's at stake in the November 3 performance. Part of what's so striking about Nixon's phrase is that, while we tend to assume that he or one of his advisers coined it, it in fact has a much longer history, one tied until relatively recently to the explicit invocation of the dead.

The phrase appears first in Greek and Latin antiquity to refer somewhat laconically to the ever-expanding population of the underworld; versions of it appear in Homer, in Plautus, and, with characteristic cheek, in Petronius's *Satyricon*. After telling the cold weather to "go fuck" itself, the profane Selecus recalls with irony the death of the abstemious Chrysanthus: "And yet he had been on an extremely strict diet? For five days he didn't take a drop of water or a crumb of bread into his mouth. But he's gone to join the majority [*abiit ad plures*]. The doctors finished him – well, hard luck, more like."[25] Thomas Browne seems to allude explicitly to Petronius in the dedicatory epistle to his *Urn Burial* (1658):

> We present not these as any strange sight or spectacle unknown to your eyes, who have beheld the best of urns and noblest variety of ashes; who are yourself no slender master of antiquities, and can daily command the view of so many imperial faces; which raiseth your thoughts unto old things and consideration of times before you, when even living men were antiquities; when the living might exceed the dead, and to depart this world could not be properly said to go unto the greater number.[26]

He adds a footnote here: "*abiit ad plures*."[27] In Edward Young's *Revenge: A Tragedy* (1721), Don Alonzo says that "Life is the desert, life the solitude. / Death joins us to the great majority."[28] Hugh Blair's "The Grave" (1743) observes that, "'Tis long since death had the majority."[29] Thomas Carlyle ends his essay on Mirabeau: "This Mirabeau's work then is done. He sleeps with the primeval giants. He has gone over to the majority: *Abiit ad plures*."[30] Ebenezer Brewer's 1898 *Dictionary of Phrase*

---

[25] Petronius, *The Satyricon*, in *The Satyricon and The Apocolocyntosis*, ed. J. Sullivan (New York: Penguin Books, 2005).

[26] Sir Thomas Browne, *Hydriotaphia*, in *The Works of Sir Thomas Browne*, ed. Simon Wilkin (London: George Bell & Sons, 1889), 3:4.

[27] Browne, *Hydriotaphia*, 4.

[28] Edward Young, "The Revenge. A Tragedy," in *The Works of Edward Young* (London: J. Dodsley, 1798), 2:223.

[29] Hugh Blair, "The Grave," in *Select Poets of Great Britain*, ed. William Hazlitt (London: Thomas Davison, 1825), 357.

[30] Thomas Carlyle, "Memoirs of Mirabeau," in *Historical Essays*, ed. Chris Ramon Vanden Bossche and Murray Baumgarten (Berkeley: University of California Press, 2002), 216.

and Fable defines "majority" very simply: "*He has joined the majority.* He is dead."[31]

The phrase appears again with a different emphasis and with surprising frequency in American occasional writing after the Civil War. One notable example is Junius Henri Browne's "The Silent Majority," an 1874 essay in *Harper's New Monthly Magazine* on the world history of burial practices and rites. Although William Safire invokes Browne's example only to dismiss it – "previous usage of any famous phrase can be found" – the title was, I think, more significant than that.[32] Where, that is, Plautus or Petronius would have used the phrase simply to distinguish one population from another, in postbellum America the phrase frequently appears in official and military eulogies; in America, one invoked the silent majority in order to mourn. In an 1884 narrative of the Civil War, George F. Williams writes that, "Each man in the long line knows that if an advance is made some of them will not see the sun set, and he cannot shake off the feeling that perhaps his turn has come to join the silent majority."[33] "While we meet today in gladness to look in each other's faces," intoned Chief Mustering Officer, A. F. Spaulding in 1896, "and to grasp the hand of Comrades living, may we not forget our Comrades who have joined the silent majority on the other shore."[34] Writing about a Confederate soldier who had had to face and see his Union brother-in-law killed, James Longstreet uses the phrase in his *From Manassas to Appomattox: Memoirs of the Civil War in America* (1896): "He asked leave of absence shortly after this occurrence, and, gradually but hopelessly sinking, in a few months passed over to the silent majority to join his fallen kinsman."[35] Reporting on a "Confederate reunion recently held" in 1896, the *Richmond Dispatch* shares a story "familiar to all of those that still cherish the tenderest memories of the dead Confederacy."[36] Recalling the circumstances that led to a poem about and a painting of the wartime "burial of Latane," the

---

[31] Ebenezer Cobham Brewer, *Dictionary of Phrase and Fable* (London: Cassell, Ltd., 1898), 796.
[32] William Safire, *Safire's Political Dictionary* (New York: Random House, 1978), 650.
[33] George F. Williams, "Lights and Shadows of Army Life," *Century Magazine* 28(6) (October 1884), 819.
[34] A. F. Spaulding, "Report," in *Journal of Seventeenth Annual Session of the Department of Indiana Grand Army of the Republic* (Indianapolis, IN: Sentinel Publishing Co., 1896), 144–145.
[35] James Longstreet, *From Manassas to Appomattox: Memoirs of the Civil War in America* (Philadelphia: J. B. Lippincott Company, 1896), 262–263.
[36] R. C. S., "The Burial of Latane: A Touching Incident of the Civil War Recalled," in *Southern Historical Society Papers, Volume XXIV*, ed. R. A. Brock (Richmond: The Southern Historical Society, 1896), 192.

writer notes that "the rest of those present at the burial have themselves now gone to join the 'silent majority.'"[37] Although there are of course differences among these and other uses, the phrase often appears in cases where someone mourns the death of an individual soldier who *survived* the war, imagining that he will go now to join that greater number who died together *during* the war.

Given the number of references to it (these are just a few), it might be possible to link Nixon's political invocation of the silent majority directly to these earlier uses. Nixon was unusually well-read in both literature and history, so it wouldn't be a surprise to find that he had come across phrase in one or another of its classical or derivative forms. He once wrote that "Honoré de Balzac once wrote that politicians are 'monsters of self-possession.'"[38] And later: "One should not rule out great novels. You can learn more about the revolutionary force that convulsed Russia in the nineteenth century from Tolstoy and Dostoevsky than from the turgid scholarly histories of the period."[39] What's more, both as a veteran and as an assiduous if awkward gladhander, Nixon would have attended hundreds of military funerals, memorial services, and VFW dinners, where he may very well have heard some older man salute those who had gone on to join that great silent majority. Finally, the fact that the phrase seemed especially resonant in relation to the Civil War and, even more, in relation to mourning of the Confederate dead, makes it just possible to imagine the phrase as having an even thicker relation to the so-called Southern Strategy; it might seem like small beer compared to his more explicit racist appeals, but the connotation is undeniably there, and given what Ian Haney López identifies as Nixon's mastery of the "dark art" of dog-whistle politics, it would be at least hasty to ignore it.[40]

With all that said, I'm not sure it would be possible to make a *conclusive* case linking either the sense or the provenance of Nixon's phrase to this longer and more complicated story; it's also not exactly the argument I want to make. I'm interested instead in seeing how a phrase with this history and this rhetorical structure not only found its way into Nixon's signature speech on the war in Vietnam but also how that speech, which was about so much else, came to be known simply and, as it were,

[37] R. C. S., "Burial of Latane," 194.
[38] Richard M. Nixon, *Six Crises* (New York: Doubleday & Company, 1962), 215.
[39] Richard M. Nixon, *Into the Arena: A Memoir of Victory, Defeat, and Renewal* (New York: Simon & Schuster, 1990), 140.
[40] Ian Haney López, *Dog Whistle Politics: How Coded Racial Appeals Have Reinvented Racism & Wrecked the Middle Class* (Oxford: Oxford University Press, 2014), 24.

lopsidedly as the "Silent Majority" speech. Put differently, I want to argue that there is ample evidence *within* Nixon's language to reveal a powerful rhetorical and associative connection between death, politics, elections, shame, and the silent majority.

Future Vietnams

As Nixon moves toward his speech's big finish, he deploys a network of images, figures, and comparisons that, while apparently distinct, share a similar kind of rhetorical structure. The first and most obvious version is, of course, the already familiar comparison between the "silent majority" and the "vocal minority": "If," says Nixon, "a vocal minority, however fervent its cause, prevails over reason and the will of the majority, this nation has no future as a free society." It is, for starters, not at all obvious that a "free society" depends on safeguarding the power of the majority over a minority; indeed, as John Stuart Mill argued in *On Liberty*, it is precisely when the majority is allowed to tyrannize over the minority that a society's future is put at greatest risk: "The majority," he writes, "being satisfied with the ways of mankind as they now are (for it is they who make them what they are), cannot comprehend why those ways should not be good enough for everybody."[41] Because the present tends to suit the majority *as it is*, Mill thought that the future belonged to the minority: "it is," he adds, "important to give the freest scope possible to uncustomary things, in order that it may in time appear which of these are fit to be converted into customs."[42]

If, however, Nixon's argument is not convincing, it is rhetorically effective; there is, behind his speech's reassuring façade of logic and order, a powerful kind of obfuscation at work. While, in other words, we understand that the simple quantitative difference between a majority and a minority must be value-neutral (51 percent is *more* but not *better* than 49 percent), Nixon's quick semantic collapse of the "will" into the "reason" of the majority implies something about its essential goodness and rationality; although, as Mill saw, it doesn't follow that a thing is more reasonable because more people would like it to be so, Nixon's rapid sleight-of-hand manages to make that connection feel self-evident. What's more, because the quantitative difference between the majority

---

[41] John Stuart Mill, *On Liberty and the Subjection of Women*, ed. Alan Ryan (London: Penguin Books, 2006), 65.
[42] Mill, *On Liberty*, 76.

and the minority battens parasitically on a parallel and yet qualitative difference between the "silent" and the "vocal," Nixon's comparison assumes not only the fundamental irrationality of articulate dissent but also an inversely proportional relation between speech and sanity. Followed through, Nixon's apparently makeshift association of ideas (student protesters, minority voters, big talkers, young people, etc.) allows him to strike an avuncular pose while gathering together the raw materials that someone else – like Spiro Agnew did in Des Moines just a week later – could assemble as a weapon to use against the haters: the "ideological eunuchs," the "parasites of passion," "the troglodytic leftists who dominate Congress," the "effete corps of impudent snobs who *characterize* themselves as individuals," and "the nattering nabobs of negativism."[43] Although a minority is technically anything less than half of 100 percent, as the concept moves through Nixon's distorting field of association and reference, it becomes synonymous with violence, volume, and volubility; as the minority shrinks, it comes, somehow, to take up more and more space. Run through the works Nixon's rhetorical machine, a majority isn't just bigger than a minority: it is better. What's more, it is under threat.

Nixon sets up a similar relation between Vietnam and "future Vietnams." As I have already said, despite its subsequent reputation as the "Silent Majority" speech, the argumentative emphasis of Nixon's address falls squarely on his explanation of the "Nixon Doctrine" or "Vietnamization": "The defense of freedom is everybody's business – not just America's business. And it is particularly the responsibility of the people whose freedom is threatened. In the previous administration, we Americanized the war in Vietnam. In this administration, we are Vietnamizing the search for peace." I've already pointed to the aggressively rhetorical quality of this antithesis, to the fact that its considerable balance as a sentence seems to gesture toward a significance and a rightness that its thought cannot sustain. And, indeed, if the line seems on the verge of collapsing under the weight of its hackneyed equipoise, that's because, in essence, Nixon says that in order to have more peace, we must have more war: war is peace. What he says sounds, in other words, like nonsense. As, however, the speech continues, he offers a different, more subtle justification for this dangerous equivalence.

The reason, he says, that more war in Vietnam can be equal to more peace in Vietnam is that he is thinking not of one but rather of two

---

[43] Pearlstein, *Nixonland*, 432, 431, 524, 526. In a memo to Nixon, a young Pat Buchanan called Agnew "the Robespierre of the Great Silent Majority." Quoted in Cowie, *Stayin' Alive*, 129.

Vietnams: there is Vietnam (V_1) as it stands in relation to this war and there is Vietnam (V_2) as it stands in relation to other possible wars in other "future Vietnams." In other words, Nixon turns the problem of war in Vietnam into a set-theoretical problem that resembles the figural play between the vocal minority and the silent majority. Although more war for Vietnam must certainly mean more war for Vietnam (V_1), it can also mean *less* war for Vietnam (V_2) if we see "Vietnam" as, on the one hand, naming one unit within an indefinitely large set of "other Vietnams" (V_1) and, on the other, also naming that indefinitely large set (V_2). What means *more* war for the unit (V_1) might mean *less* war for the set (V_2). So, if we see – as Nixon implicitly asks us to see – the problem of Vietnam as one that works concurrently but differently at different levels of scale, it could be that more war means both more war and less war; it could be that both A=A and A≠A are true. If Vietnam is not or is not only Vietnam, then war can be peace and peace can be war. In other words, and as we already saw in the relation between the "vocal minority" and the "silent majority," Nixon mixes the arguably value-neutral structure of logic with the value-laden effects of rhetoric to make a lie look and feel like a fact.

A final example: during his late reflections on the difference between the vocal minority and the silent majority, Nixon offers one more comparison between larger and smaller numbers. Returning once again to the mawkish well, Nixon shares own "powerful personal reasons" for wanting to end the war. "This week," he says, "I will have to sign 83 letters to mothers, fathers, wives, and loved ones of men who have given their lives for America in Vietnam. It is very little satisfaction to me that this is only one-third as many letters as I signed my first week in office." Nixon walks a fine line here as he tries (1) to acknowledge and to mourn the 83 lives lost, (2) to take some credit for the reduction in those losses, (3) to claim that the reduction does not give satisfaction or rather that it does not give *a lot* of satisfaction, (4) to criticize his predecessor without naming his predecessor because, as we know, even flattering contrasts can foster unwelcome comparisons: "This was the only way to avoid allowing Johnson's war to become Nixon's war." What's striking here is how Nixon's thinking about the war dead reproduces the play between quantity and quality, logic and rhetoric that I've been describing. What, in other words, makes the idea of 83 dead satisfying-not-satisfying to Nixon is the simple fact that 83 is not 249, that, compared with the silent majority of soldiers who died before or who could have died in another, counterfectual Vietnam, 83 is a minority. What's more, it is a present minority that both authorizes and softens our feelings of relief and grief, satisfaction and guilt, anger and culpability for the loss of that other, absent majority.

This, it should be clear, is where the older, American, and elegiac sense of the silent majority makes its return. As I said before, many postbellum uses of the phrase marked the strange moment when, decades after a war, someone who had survived died at last and went to join the great silent majority of soldiers who hadn't survived. Although the difference between those who lived and those who died is always fraught, it was especially so in the case of the American Civil War, where the survivors had not only to live but also to live as losers amongst winners in what history cast rightly as a shameful war. The phrase "silent majority" was, in other words, a way to acknowledge and to manage survivor's guilt and, thus, to see death as an escape from the shame of simply having lived. Death was a release from the stigma of the living minority, and becoming part of the silent majority meant, most of all, that you no longer needed to feel bad about living with shame while others died with what seemed like honor.

This helps, I think, to account for the mix of pathos and bathos, guilt and satisfaction, aggression and self-pity that runs through Nixon's speech. What, after all, goes almost wholly unsaid in Nixon's speech is that fact that the Vietnam War's real silent majority far exceeded three times eighty-three; the real majority of war dead in Vietnam was, in fact, made up of the many, many thousands of Vietnamese, Cambodian, and Laotian civilians and soldiers who had been and were then being shot, bombed, displaced, starved, burnt, and poisoned.[44] Denied almost any acknowledgment or representation in Nixon's speech, those were the people who made up both the real majority of the dead and, given their complete rhetorical absence on November 3, the truly silent majority. "Nixon," writes Michael Rogin, "represented the silent partly because he presided over a war requiring political silence."[45] Sunny Xiang writes that "the very notion of numerical countability constitutes a form of nationalist self-reckoning

---

[44] Although Nixon took care to cast it as a hokey teach-a-man-to-fish opportunity for South Vietnam, the logic of "Vietnamization" was always to reduce the number of US troops and, thus, US casualties in a doomed war by shifting more and more of the cost over to the Vietnamese. "The success of Vietnamization," writes William Shawcross, "in this regard is shown most starkly in a year-by-year comparison of American and South Vietnamese causalities. The South Vietnamese official figures are not very reliable, but they give a broad impression. In 1969, 9,414 Americans and 21,833 Vietnamese died in combat; in 1970, the figures were 4,221 and 23,346; in 1971, 1,380 and 22,738. The 1972 offensive made that year the worst for the South Vietnamese. Almost 40,000 of them died, along with 300 Americans." Shawcross, *Sideshow: Kissinger, Nixon, and the Destruction of Cambodia* (New York: Cooper Square Press, 1979), 172.

[45] Michael Rogin, *Ronald Reagan, the Movie and Other Episodes in Political Demonology* (Berkeley: University of California Press, 1988), 102.

that is more ontological than quantitative: it is more about *who* is counted than *what* the count is."[46] This brings us to the grotesque and lasting genius of Nixon's speech. In 1969 he understood that a lot of Americans found it unpleasant or uncomfortable to have to claim culpability and to mourn the Vietnamese dead; however, rather than simply saying to them that, no, you don't need to mourn *that* silent majority, he took things a step further.[47] Not only, he suggested, do you not need to mourn that silent majority, but you yourselves are the *real* silent majority; you've been slighted, insulted, and made to feel bad about a lot of things. You should be mourned for being made to feel bad; you should be mourned for being told that you should have to mourn someone else. So, don't mourn those others; mourn yourselves. You deserve it. And while you're at it, my real, emerging, and silent majority, vote for me.

And the Results Are In

Although they can look a lot alike, a fiction is not the same thing as a lie. As I've argued throughout this book, the fictions of the electoral imagination ask us to suspend our disbelief *willingly* and to act *as if* the general will could be real, *as if* a parliament can really represent a people, *as if* my vote really counts, *as if* this electoral system is the best electoral system, *as if* ordinary people can really know enough to make good laws, *as if* the results of an election are legitimate even when the winning candidate is not my candidate, and *as if* regular, periodic, and open elections can be enough to prevent real, inevitable, and rational disagreements about the definition of a good life from devolving into internecine social conflict and physical violence. Recognizing these and other beliefs as fictions is, as I hope I have demonstrated, not to disparage or to dismiss them. As Edmund Morgan says, "I can only hope that readers who persevere to the end of the book will recognize that the fictional qualities of popular sovereignty sustain rather than threaten the human values associated with it."[48] Indeed, the

[46] Sunny Xiang, "The Ethnic Author Represents the Body Count," *PMLA* (2018), 133.24, 423. "What then are we to make of this mass of Vietnamese dead whose bodies cannot be located, identified, or remembered? What of that other body count, those Southern Vietnamese whose lives are disremembered by both Vietnam and the United States?" (426).

[47] "Americans," writes Viet Thanh Nguyen, "of all kinds are still haunted by the war, if not by the Vietnamese, haunted by the question of what to do with all those dead and missing people, the millions in whose name the war was ostensibly fought." Viet Thanh Nguyen, "Speak of the Dead, Speak of Viet Nam: The Ethics and Aesthetics of Minority Discourse," *CR: The New Centennial Review* (2006), 6.2, 23.

[48] Morgan, *Inventing the People*, 15.

possibility of fair and regular elections standing as a real and functional alternative to coercion, cruelty, and violence depends on our understanding and confronting their inevitable misuses, abuses, limits, flaws, and oversights with the mix of intelligence, imagination, irony, flexibility, historical perspective, and hope that is, I think, characteristic of a full, open, and critical engagement with the intellectual demands of literary fiction. I don't believe that we enjoy fictions because they lie to us about the world; I believe we enjoy fictions because, in showing us something different from but related to the world, they let us see the world as it really is while opening a space – however narrow, however provisional – to imagine how it might be otherwise. This is what I have meant by skepticism without despair, a phrase that can be applied equally to the willing suspension of disbelief and to the vigilant but open attitude that seems to me necessary to anyone living with other people in a democracy.

What Nixon said on November 3, 1969 – that a majority was not a majority – was not a fiction. It was a lie. It was a big lie. More than that, it was an effort to use a lie specifically to threaten and maybe to negate the old and necessary fiction that elections were a means to an end other than the end of winning elections, that we identify numerical majorities not simply to make winners but rather to make policies and laws and to cultivate conditions that aspire to be good for everyone. History shows us that this salutary fiction is rarely realized in practice; it is, however, better than the alternative. By redefining the majority not as a provisional, periodic, and necessarily incomplete representative of a whole people but rather as the minimum number of votes required to win an election and to amass power, Nixon helped to alter the meaning of democracy. Democracy and the making of a majority were no longer a means of discovering or inventing or aspiring toward an aspirational general will; they were no longer a way at least to imagine that anyone or everyone could count. They were, instead, a way to mix cultural and racial ressentiments with increasingly sophisticated and data-driven approaches to voter suppression, gerrymandering, demographic apportioning, and direct marketing in order to produce high-intensity coalitions that would win elections precisely because they did *not* represent everyone, because – having been made to feel aggrieved, slighted, and left behind – they were encouraged to see the vote as an activist refusal of wider representation, as a refusal of the significance and the meaning of other people. They were encouraged explicitly to stop acting *as if* democracy was for everyone; they were encouraged to give up on the old, necessary, and incomplete fictions of the electoral imagination. They were, to come back to my original terms, encouraged to believe that those fictions were rigged so that a new and increasingly sophisticated generation of strategists, schemers, plumbers, and ratfuckers might rig them for real. They were encouraged, in other words, to exchange a fiction for a lie. Anyone reading this book will know that we are living still in the time of the big lie, that the integrity of ballots, election officials, and individual voters is under constant threat, and that bad actors are questioning the legitimacy of legitimate elections so that they can rig those elections more effectively. I hope that what I've written not only helps to account for how we got here but also demonstrates that preserving and improving democracy will require, as it always has, a lot of work and more than a little imagination.

References

Abella, Alex. *Soldiers of Reason: The RAND Corporation and the Rise of the American Empire.* Boston: Mariner Books, 2009.

Abrams, Stacey. *Our Time Is Now: Power, Purpose, and the Fight for a Fair America.* New York: Henry Holt, 2020.

Abrams, Stacey, Carol Anderson, Kevin M. Kruse, Heather Cox Richardson, and Heather Ann Thompson. "Roundtable." In *Voter Suppression in U.S. Elections,* edited by Jim Downs, 15–90. Athens: University of Georgia Press, 2020.

Adorno, Theodor W. "Late Style in Beethoven." In *Essays on Music,* edited by Richard Leppert. Translated by Susan H. Gillespie, 564–568. Berkeley: University of California Press, 2002.

Ahmed, Amel. *Democracy and the Politics of Electoral System Choice: Engineering Electoral Dominance.* Cambridge: Cambridge University Press, 2013.

Aldous, Richard. *The Lion and the Unicorn: Gladstone vs. Disraeli.* New York: W. W. Norton, 2007.

Allen, Philip Loring. "The Multifarious Australian Ballot." *North American Review* 191(654) (May 1910): 602–611.

Althusser, Louis. *Politics and History: Montesquieu, Rousseau, Marx.* London: Verso, 2007.

Amadae, S. M. "Arrow's Impossibility Theorem and the National Security State." *Studies in History and Philosophy of Science* 36(4) (December 2005): 734–743.

Rationalizing Capitalist Democracy: The Cold War Origins of Rational Choice Liberalism. Chicago: University of Chicago Press, 2003.

Amadae, S. M., and Bruce Bueno de Mesquita. "The Rochester School: The Origins of Positive Political Theory." *Annual Review of Political Science* 2 (1999): 269–295.

Anderson, Amanda. *Bleak Liberalism.* Chicago: University of Chicago Press, 2016.

Anderson, Carol. *Bourgeois Radicals: The NAACP and the Struggle for Colonial Liberation, 1941–1960.* Cambridge: Cambridge University Press, 2015.

One Person, No Vote: How Voter Suppression Is Destroying Our Democracy. New York: Bloomsbury, 2019.

Aristotle. *The Art of Rhetoric*. Translated by Robin Waterfield. Oxford: Oxford University Press, 2018.

Arrow, Kenneth J. "A Cautious Case for Socialism." *Dissent* 25 (Fall 1978): 472–480.

"A Difficulty in the Concept of Social Welfare." *Journal of Political Economy* 58 (4) (August 1950): 328–346.

"The Economy and the Economist." *Partisan Review* 46(1) (Winter 1979): 113–126.

On Ethics and Economics: Conversations with Kenneth J. Arrow. Edited by Kristen Renwick Monroe and Nicholas Monroe Lampros. London: Routledge, 2017.

"The Functions of Social Choice Theory." In *Social Choice Re-examined*, Vol. 1, edited by Kenneth J. Arrow, Amartya Sen, and Kotaro Suzumura, 3–9. London: Palgrave Macmillan, 1997.

"I Know a Hawk from a Handsaw." In *Eminent Economists: Their Life Philosophies*, edited by Michael Szenberg, 42–50. Cambridge: Cambridge University Press, 1992.

The Limits of Organization. New York: W. W. Norton, 1974.

"The Possibility of a Universal Social Welfare Function." RAND P-41. September 26, 1948.

Social Choice and Individual Values. New Haven, CT: Yale University Press, 2012.

Astor, Maggie. "'A Perpetual Motion Machine': How Disinformation Drives Voting Laws." *The New York Times*, May 13, 2021. www.nytimes.com/2021/05/13/us/politics/disinformation-voting-laws.html.

Auerbach, Erich. *Mimesis: The Representation of Reality in Western Literature*. Princeton, NJ: Princeton University Press, 2013.

Baker, Keith Michael. *Condorcet: From Natural Philosophy to Social Mathematics*. Chicago: University of Chicago Press, 1975.

Bakunin, Mikhail. *Bakunin on Anarchism*, edited by Sam Dolgoff. Montreal: Black Rose Books, 1980.

Balinski, Michel, and Rida Laraki. "The Ballot Bill," *The Spectator*, February 18, 1837.

"Ballot-Voting," *The Spectator*, February 25, 1837.

Majority Judgment: Measuring, Ranking, and Electing. Cambridge: MIT Press, 2010.

Balzac, Honoré de, *Lost Illusions*. New York: Modern Library, 2001.

Père Goriot. Translated by A. J. Krailsheimer. Oxford: Oxford University Press, 1999.

Banerjee, Sukanya. "Transimperial." *Victorian Literature and Culture* 46(3–4) (Fall/Winter 2018): 925–928.

Bartels, Larry M. "Ethnic Antagonism Erodes Republicans' Commitment to Democracy." *Proceedings of the National Academy of the Sciences of the United States of America* 117(37) (September 15, 2020): 22752–22759. https://doi.org/10.1073/pnas.2007747117.

Bartels, Larry M., and Christopher H. Achen. *Democracy for Realists: Why Elections Do Not Produce Responsive Government*. Princeton, NJ: Princeton University Press, 2016.

Barthes, Roland. *Mythologies*. Translated by Annette Lavers. New York: Farrar, Straus, and Giroux, 1972.

S/Z: An Essay. Translated by Richard Miller. New York: Hill & Wang, 1974.

Bartholdi, J., III, C. A. Tovey, and M. A. Trick. "Voting Schemes for Which It Can Be Difficult to Tell Who Won the Election." *Social Choice and Welfare* 6(2), (1989): 157–165.

Bassetti, Victoria. "New Anxieties and Old Friends." In Alicia Yin Cheng, *This Is What Democracy Looked Like: A Visual History of the Printed Ballot*, 165–171. New York: Princeton Architectural Press, 2020.

Bax, E. Belfort. "The Will of the Majority." In *The Ethics of Socialism*, 120–128. London: Swan Sonnenschein, 1902.

Beaumont, Matthew. *Utopia Ltd.: Ideologies of Social Dreaming in England 1870–1900*. Chicago: Haymarket Books, 2009.

Beer, Gillian. *Alice in Space: The Sideways Victorian World of Lewis Carroll*. Chicago: University of Chicago Press, 2016.

Benoit, Kenneth. "Which Electoral Formula Is the Most Proportional? A New Look with New Evidence." *Political Analysis* 8(4), (2000): 381–388.

Bentham, Jeremy. *Bentham's Radical Reform Bill*. London: E. Wilson, 1819.

Essay on Political Tactics. In *The Works of Jeremy Bentham,* Vol. 2, edited by John Bowring, 299–373. London: Tait, 1843.

Bevir, Mark. *The Making of British Socialism*. Princeton, NJ: Princeton University Press, 2011.

Black, Duncan. *A Mathematical Approach to Proportional Representation: Duncan Black on Lewis Carroll*. Edited by Iain McLean and Alistair McMillan. New York: Springer, 1996.

The Theory of Committees and Elections. Cambridge: Cambridge University Press, 1958.

Blackstone, William. *Commentaries on the Laws of England*. Vol 1. Chicago: Callaghan & Company, 1884.

Blair, Hugh. "The Grave." In *Select Poets of Great Britain*, edited by William Hazlitt, 354–359. London: Thomas Davison, 1825.

Bloch, Ernst. *The Principle of Hope*. Translated by Neville Plaice, Stephen Plaice, and Paul Knight. Cambridge: Massachusetts Institute of Technology Press, 1986.

Bloom, Alexander. *Prodigal Sons: The New York Intellectuals and Their World*. Oxford: Oxford University Press, 1986.

Bogdanor, Vernon. *The People and the Party System: The Referendum and Electoral Reform in British Politics*. Cambridge: Cambridge University Press, 1981.

Borowitz, Andy. "Trump Signs Executive Order Banning Month of November." *New Yorker*, July 31, 2020. www.newyorker.com/humor/borowitz-report/trump-signs-executive-order-banning-month-of-november.

Boswell, James. *Life of Johnson*. Oxford: Oxford University Press, 2008.

Boyd, Richard. "Justice, Beneficence, and Boundaries: Rousseau and the Paradox of Generality." In *The General Will: The Evolution of a Concept*, edited by James Farr and David Lay Williams, 247–269. Cambridge: Cambridge University Press, 2015.

Božovič, Miran. "Introduction." In *The Panopticon Writings*, by Jeremy Bentham, 1–28. London: Verso, 1995.

Bradley, A. C. *Shakespearean Tragedy*. London: Penguin Books, 1991.

Brawley, Benjamin. *History of Morehouse College*. Atlanta: Morehouse College, 1917.

Brennan, Jason. *Against Democracy*. Princeton, NJ: Princeton University Press, 2017.

   The Ethics of Voting. Princeton, NJ: Princeton University Press, 2012.

Brent, Peter. "The Australian Ballot: Not the Secret Ballot." *Australian Journal of Political Science* 41(1) (March 2006), 39–50.

Brett, Judith. *From Secret Ballot to Democracy Sausage: How Australia Got Compulsory Voting*. Melbourne: Text Publishing, 2019.

Brewer, Ebenezer Cobham. *Dictionary of Phrase and Fable*. London: Cassell, Ltd., 1898.

Browne, Thomas. *Hydriotaphia*. In *The Works of Sir Thomas Browne*, Vol. 3, edited by Simon Wilkin, 1–49. London: George Bell & Sons, 1889.

Bulwer-Lytton, Edward. *My Novel, or Varieties of English Life*. Boston: Little, 1892.

Bump, Philip. "Trump Embraces the 'Reverse Racism' Feared by His Supporters in a New 'Squad' Attack." *Washington Post,* July 22, 2019. www .washingtonpost.com/politics/2019/07/22/trump-embraces-reverse-racism-feared-by-his-supporters-new-squad-attack/.

Bunche, Ralph J. "The Negro in the Political Life of the United States." *Journal of Negro Education* 10(3) (July 1941): 567–584.

Burdick, Eugene. "Political Theory and the Voting Studies." In *American Party Politics: Essays and Readings*, edited by Donald G. Herzberg and Gerald M. Pomper. New York: Holt, Rinehart, & Winston, Inc., 1966.

Caplan, Bryan. *The Myth of the Rational Voter: Why Democracies Choose Bad Policies*. Princeton, NJ: Princeton University Press, 2011.

Carlyle, Thomas. *Latter-Day Pamphlets*. London: Chapman, 1898.

   "Memoirs of Mirabeau." In Thomas Carlyle, *Historical Essays*, edited by Chris Ramon, Vanden Bossche, and Murray Baumgarten, 153–218. Berkeley: University of California Press, 2002.

   "Parliamentary Radicalism." In *Chartism and Past and Present*, 54–57. London: Chapman & Hall, 1870.

Carroll, Lewis. *Alice's Adventures in Wonderland and through the Looking-Glass*. Edited by Peter Hunt. Oxford: Oxford University Press, 2009.

   Notes by an Oxford Chiel. Oxford: James Parker and Co., 1865–1874.

   The Political Pamphlets and Letters of Charles Lutwidge Dodgson and Related Pieces: A Mathematical Approach. Edited by Francine F. Abeles. New York: The Lewis Carroll Society of North America, 2001.

Cassirer, Ernst. *Substance and Function and Einstein's Theory of Relativity.* Chicago: Open Court Publishing Company, 1923.

Chaudhuri, Nirad C. *Scholar Extraordinary: The Life of Professor the Rt. Hon. Friedrich Max Müller, P. C.* New York: Oxford University Press, 1974.

Cheeseman, Nic, and Brian Klass. *How to Rig an Election.* New Haven, CT: Yale University Press, 2018.

Chesney, Bobby, and Danielle Citron. "Deep Fakes: A Looming Challenge for Privacy, Democracy, and National Security." *California Law Review* 107(6) (December 2019), 1753–1820.

Chesterton G. K., "Both Sides of the Looking-Glass." *The Listener* (Nov. 29, 1933).

Childers, Hugh. *The Ballot in Australia: A Speech Delivered in the House of Commons.* London: James Ridgway, 1860.

Christoff, Alicia Mireles. *Novel Relations: Victorian Fiction and British Psychoanalysis.* Princeton, NJ: Princeton University Press, 2019.

Cohen, Joshua. *Rousseau: A Free Community of Equals.* Oxford: Oxford University Press, 2010.

Cohn, Nate. "Why Political Sectarianism Is a Growing Threat to American Democracy." *The New York Times,* April 19, 2021. www.nytimes.com/2021/04/19/us/democracy-gop-democrats-sectarianism.html.

Coleridge, Samuel Taylor. "Kubla Khan: Or, A Vision in a Dream." In *The Complete Poems,* edited by William Keach, 249–251. London: Penguin Books, 1997.

Condorcet. "On Elections." In *The Democracy Sourcebook,* edited by Robert A Dahl, Ian Shapiro, and José Antonio Cheibub, 315–316. Cambridge: Massachusetts Institute of Technology Press, 2003.

Conquest, Robert. *The Great Terror: A Reassessment.* Oxford: Oxford University Press, 2008.

Cowie, Jefferson. *Stayin' Alive: The 1970s and the Last Days of the Working Class.* New York: The New Press, 2010.

Crook, Malcom, and Tom Crook. "Ballot Papers and the Practice of Elections: Britain, France and the United States of America, c.1500–2000." *Historical Research* 88(241) (August 2015): 530–561.

"Reforming Voting Practices in a Global Age: The Making and Remaking of the Modern Secret Ballot in Britain, France and the United States, c. 1600–c. 1950." *Past & Present* 212 (August 2011): 199–237.

Crossman, Richard, ed. *The God that Failed.* New York: Columbia University Press, 2001.

Dahl, Robert A. *Democracy and Its Critics.* New Haven, CT: Yale University Press, 1989.

On Democracy. New Haven, CT: Yale University Press, 2008.

Davis, Benjamin J. *"Autobiography as De-Facement,"* in *The Rhetoric of Romanticism.* New York: Columbia Press, 1984.

"Why I Am a Communist." *Speech and Power* 1, edited by Gerald Early.

de Man, Paul. *Allegories of Reading: Figural Language in Rousseau,*

Nietzsche, Rilke, and Proust. New Haven, CT: Yale University Press, 1982.

Descartes, René. *Meditations on First Philosophy.* Edited by John Cottingham. Cambridge: Cambridge University Press, 2017.

Diamond, Larry, Lee Drutman, Tod Lindberg, Nathan P. Kalmoe, and Lilliana Mason. "Americans Increasingly Believe Violence Is Justified of the Other Side Wins." *Politico,* last modified October 9, 2020. www.politico.com/news/magazine/2020/10/01/political-violence-424157.

Douglas-Fairhurst, Robert. *The Story of Alice: Lewis Carroll and the Secret History of Wonderland* (Cambridge, MA: Harvard University Press, 2016).

Dowling, Linda. "Victorian Oxford and the Science of Language." *PMLA* 97(2) (March 1982), 160–178.

Downie, James. "Even Trump's Most Die-Hard Minions Struggle to Defend Him Anymore." *Washington Post,* August 16, 2020. www.washingtonpost.com/opinions/2020/08/16/even-trumps-most-die-hard-minions-struggle-defend-him-anymore/.

Downs, Anthony. *An Economic Theory of Democracy.* Boston: Addison Wesley, 1957.

Droop, H. R. "On Methods of Electing Representatives." *Journal of the Statistical Society* 44(2) (June, 1881): 141–202.

Du Bois, W. E. B. *Black Reconstruction in America.* Edited by Henry Louis Gates, Jr. Oxford: Oxford University Press, 2007.

Dudziak, Mary L. *Cold War Civil Rights: Race and the Image of American Democracy.* Princeton, NJ: Princeton University Press, 2000.

Duffy, A. E. P. "Differing Policies and Personal Rivalries in the Origin of the Independent Labour Party." *Victorian Studies* 6(1) (September 1962): 43–65.

Dummett, Michael. "The Work and Life of Robin Farquharson." *Social Choice and Welfare* 25 (2005), 475–483.

Dunn, John. *Democracy: A History.* New York: Atlantic Monthly Press, 2005.

During, Simon. *Modern Enchantments.* Cambridge, MA: Harvard University Press, 2002.

Eliot, George. *Middlemarch.* New York: W. W. Norton, 2000.

Elliott, Robert C. *The Shape of Utopia: Studies in a Literary Genre.* Chicago: University of Chicago Press, 1970.

Ellison, Ralph. *The Collected Essays of Ralph Ellison.* Edited by John F. Callahan. New York: The Modern Library, 2003.

Invisible Man. New York: Vintage, 1995.

Elster, Jon. *Explaining Social Behavior: More Nuts and Bolts for the Social Sciences.* Cambridge: Cambridge University Press, 2015.

Securities Against Misrule: Juries, Assemblies, Elections. Cambridge: Cambridge University Press, 2013.

Empson, William. *Some Versions of Pastoral.* New York: New Directions, 1950.

Estlund, David M. "Democracy Without Preference." *The Philosophical Review* 99(3) (July 1990): 397–423.

Evans, Eldon Cobb. *A History of the Australian Ballot System in the United States.* Chicago: The University of Chicago Press, 1917.

"The Fabian Society – Nationalizing Accumulated Wealth." *The Practical Socialist* 1(1) (January 1886).

Fandl, Kevin J. *Law and Public Policy.* London: Routledge, 2019.

Farrell, David M. *Electoral Systems: A Comparative Introduction.* London: Palgrave, 2011.

Farquharson, Robin. *Drop Out!* London: Penguin Books, 1968.

Fawcett, Henry. *Mr. Hare's Reform Bill Simplified and Explained.* London: James Ridgway, 1860.

Fiell, Charlotte, and Peter Fiell. *William Morris: A Life of Art.* Köln: Taschen Books, 2020.

Fish, Stanley. *Surprised by Sin: The Reader in Paradise Lost.* Cambridge, MA: Harvard University Press, 1967.

Fitzgerald, F. Scott. *The Crack-Up.* New York: New Directions, 1945.

Flaubert, Gustave. *Selected Letters.* Translated by Geoffrey Wall. London: Penguin Classics, 1998.

Foley, Barbara. *Wrestling with the Left: The Making of Ralph Ellison's Invisible Man.* Durham, NC: Duke University Press, 2010.

Foucault, Michel. *Discipline and Punish: The Birth of the Prison.* New York: Vintage, 1995.

Fraser, W. Hamish. *Scottish Popular Politics.* Edinburgh: Edinburgh University Press, 2001.

Freeden, Michael. "Political Realism: A Reality Check." In *Politics Recovered: Realist Thought in Theory and Practice,* edited by Matt Sleat, 344–368. New York: Columbia University Press, 2018.

Freedgood, Elaine. *The Ideas in Things: Fugitive Meaning in the Victorian Novel.* Chicago: University of Chicago Press, 2006.

Freeman, Edward A. "University Elections." *Contemporary Review* 43(1) (January 1883).

Fukuyama, Francis. *The End of History and the Last Man.* New York: Free Press, 2006.

Freud, Sigmund. "Family Romances." In *The Standard Edition of the Complete Psychological Works of Sigmund Freud, Volume IX (1906–1908): Jensen's 'Gradiva' and Other Works.*

Gaertner, Wulf. "Discussion of Arrow's Paper." In *Social Choice Re-examined,* Vol 1, edited by Kenneth J. Arrow, Amartya Sen, and Kotaro Suzumura, 10–14. London: Palgrave Macmillan, 1996.

Gallagher, Catherine. "The Rise of Fictionality." In *The Novel, Volume I: History, Geography, and Culture,* edited by Franco Moretti, 336–363. Princeton, NJ: Princeton University Press, 2006.

Gallagher, Catherine, and Stephen Greenblatt. *Practicing New Historicism.* Chicago: University of Chicago Press, 2001.

Garcha, Amanpal. "Choice." In *From Political Economy to Economics through Nineteenth-Century Literature: Reclaiming the Social,* edited by Elaine Hadley, Audrey Jaffe, and Sarah Winter, 197–218. London: Palgrave, 2019.

Gardiner, Martin, ed. *The Annotated Alice*. New York: W. W. Norton, 2015.

Gay, Peter. *The Dilemma of Democratic Socialism*. New York: Columbia University Press, 1962.

Gellman, Barton. "The Election That Could Break America." *The Atlantic*, November 2020. www.theatlantic.com/magazine/archive/2020/11/what-if-trump-refuses-concede/616424/.

Go, Julian. "Empire, Democracy, and Discipline: The Transimperial History of the Secret Ballot." In *Crossing Empires: Taking U.S. History into Transimperial Terrain*, edited by Kristin L. Hoganson and Jay Sexton, 93–111. Durham, NC: Duke University Press, 2020.

Goldman, Emma. *Anarchism and Other Essays*. New York: Mother Earth Publishing Association, 1911.

Gomme, George Laurence. *The Village Community, with Special Reference to the Origin and Form of Its Survivals in Britain*. London: Walter Scott, 1890.

Gordon, Fon Louise. *Caste & Class, The Black Experience in Arkansas, 1880–1920*. Athens: University of Georgia Press, 2007.

Gray, John. *Enlightenment's Wake: Politics and Culture at the Close of the Modern Age*. London: Taylor & Francis, 2007.

Green, Donald, and Ian Shapiro. *Pathologies of Rational Choice Theory: A Critique of Applications in Political Science*. New Haven, CT: Yale University Press, 1994.

Green, Jeffrey Edward. *The Eyes of the People: Democracy in an Age of Spectatorship*. Oxford: Oxford University Press, 2009.

Green, Roger Lancelyn. *Introduction to Alice's Adventures in Wonderland and Through the Looking-Glass*, by Lewis Carroll. Edited by Roger Lancelyn Green. Oxford: Oxford University Press, 1998.

Greenberg, David. *Nixon's Shadow: The History of an Image*. New York: W. W. Norton, 2003.

Grofman, Bernard, and Scott L. Feld. "Rousseau's General Will: A Condorcetian Perspective." *American Political Science Review* 82(2) (1988): 567–576.

Grote, George. *History of Greece*. Vol. 5. London: John Murray, 1851.

The Minor Works of George Grote. Edited by Alexander Bain. London: John Murray, 1873.

Grote, Harriet. *The Personal Life of George Grote: Compiled from Family Documents, Private Memoranda, and Original Letters to and from Various Friends*. London: John Murray, 1873.

Guess, Raymond. *Philosophy and Real Politics*. Princeton, NJ: Princeton University Press, 2008.

Hadley, Elaine. *Living Liberalism: Practical Citizenship in Mid-Victorian Britain*. Chicago: University of Chicago Press, 2010.

Hakim, Danny, and Maggie Haberman, "Kanye West's Perplexing Run as a Potential 2020 Spoiler." *The New York Times*, September 16, 2020. www.nytimes.com/2020/09/16/us/politics/kanye-west-president-2020.html.

Haldeman, H. R. *The Haldeman Diaries: Inside the Nixon White House*. New York: Berkley Books, 1995.

Hamilton, Alexander, James Madison, and John Jay. *The Federalist Papers.* Edited by Ian Shapiro. New Haven, CT: Yale University Press, 2009.

Hancher, Michael. *Hansard Parliamentary Debates,* 3rd series (1830–1891). https://hansard.parliament.uk/.

The Tenniel Illustrations to the "Alice" Books. Athens: Ohio University Press, 1985.

Harden, Edward J. *The Life of George M. Troup.* Savannah, GA: Purse, 1859.

Hare, Thomas. *The Machinery of Representation.* London: W. Maxwell, 1857.

"Suggestions for the Improvement of Our Representative System: The University Elections Act of Last Session." In *Macmillan's Magazine, Vol. V. November, 1861–April,* 1862, edited by David Masson, 295–301. Cambridge: Macmillan & Co., 1862.

A Treatise on the Election of Representatives, Parliamentary and Municipal. London: Longman, Brown, Green, Longmans, & Roberts, 1859.

Hart, Jenifer. *Proportional Representation: Critics of the British Electoral System, 1820–1945.* Oxford: Clarendon Press, 1992.

Hartman, Geoffrey. "Romanticism and Anti-Self-Consciousness." In *Romanticism and Consciousness: Essays in Criticism,* edited by Harold Bloom. New York: Norton, 1970.

Hasen, Richard L. *Election Meltdown: Dirty Tricks, Distrust, and the Threat to American Democracy.* New Haven, CT: Yale University Press, 2020.

"I've Never Been More Worried about American Democracy than I Am Right Now." *Slate,* September 23, 2020. https://slate.com/news-and-politics/2020/09/trump-plan-supreme-court-stop-election-vote-count.html.

"The Only Way to Save American Democracy Now." *Slate,* January 11, 2021. https://slate.com/news-and-politics/2021/01/biden-pelosi-schumer-john-lewis-save-democracy.html.

"Trump's Legal Farce Is Having Tragic Results." *The New York Times,* November 23, 2020. www.nytimes.com/2020/11/23/opinion/trump-election-courts.html?searchResultPosition=1.

The Voting Wars: From Florida 2000 to the Next Election Meltdown. New Haven, CT: Yale University Press, 2013.

"We Can't Let Our Elections Be This Vulnerable Again." *The Atlantic,* January 4, 2021. www.theatlantic.com/ideas/archive/2021/01/we-cant-let-our-elections-be-vulnerable-again/617542/.

Hegel, G. W. F. *Elements of the Philosophy of Right.* Translated by H. B. Nisbet. Cambridge: Cambridge University Press, 1991.

Hegel's Phenomenology of Spirit. Translated by A. V. Miller. Oxford: Oxford University Press, 1977.

Heidegger, Martin. *Poetry, Language, Thought.* New York: Harper Collins, 2001.

Hirschman, Albert O. *The Rhetoric of Reaction: Perversity, Futility, Jeopardy.* Cambridge, MA: Harvard University Press, 1991.

Hofstadter, Richard. *The Paranoid Style in American Politics.* New York: Knopf Doubleday, 2008.

Hong, Christine. *A Violent Peace: Race, US Militarism, and Cultures of Decolonization in Cold War Asia and the Pacific.* Stanford, CA: Stanford University Press, 2020.

Honig, Bonnie. *Emergency Politics: Paradox, Law, Democracy.* Princeton, NJ: Princeton University Press, 2009.

Public Things: Democracy in Disrepair. New York: Fordham University Press, 2017.

Hume, David. *Selected Essays.* Edited by Stephen Copley and Andrew Edgar. Oxford: Oxford University Press, 1998.

"The Hundred Most Influential Books Since the War." *Bulletin of the American Academy of Arts and Sciences* 49(8) (May 1996), 12–18.

Hyndman, H. M. "Laborism, Impossibilism, and Socialism." In *The International Socialist Review: A Monthly Journal of International Socialist Thought, Volume III*, 653–656. Chicago: Charles H. Kerr & Co., 1903.

Jakobson, Roman. "Linguistics and Poetics." In *Language in Literature*, edited by Krystyna Pomorska and Stephen Rudy. Cambridge, MA: Harvard University Press, 1987.

James, Henry. *Roderick Hudson.* New York: MacMillan and Co., 1921.

Selected Letters. Edited by Leon Edel. Cambridge: The Belknap Press, 1987.

Jenkins, Roy. *Gladstone: A Biography.* New York: Random House, 2002.

Jones, W. H. Morris. "In Defence of Apathy: Some Doubts on the Duty to Vote." *Political Studies* 2(1) (1954), 25–37.

Kapp, Yvonne. *Eleanor Marx.* Vol. 2. New York: Pantheon Books, 1976.

Kaufman, Robert. "Aura, Still." *October* 99 (Winter 2002), 45–80.

Keane, John. *Power and Humility: The Future of Monitory Democracy.* Cambridge: Cambridge University Press, 2018.

Keiler, Allan. *Marian Anderson: A Singer's Journey.* Urbana: University of Illinois Press, 2002.

Keyssar, Alexander. *The Right to Vote: The Contested History of Democracy in the United States.* New York: Basic Books, 2009.

Kinna, Ruth. "Anarchism, Individualism, and Communism: William Morris's Critique of Anarcho-Communism." In *Libertarian Socialism: Politics in Black and Red*, edited by Alex Prichard, Ruth Kinna, Saku Pinta, and David Berry, 35–56. London: Palgrave Macmillan, 2012.

"Kropotkin's Theory of Mutual Aid in Historical Context." *International Review of Social History* 40(2) (1995), 259–283.

Koestler, Arthur. *Darkness at Noon.* Translated by Daphne Hardy. New York: Scribner, 1941.

Kousser, J. Morgan. *The Shaping of Southern Politics: Suffrage Restriction and the Establishment of the One-Party South, 1880–1910.* New Haven, CT: Yale University Press, 1974.

Kucklick, Bruce. *Blind Oracles: Intellectuals and War from Kennan to Kissinger.* Princeton, NJ: Princeton University Press, 2007.

Kuhn, David Paul. *The Hardhat Riot: Nixon, New York City, and the Dawn of the White Working-Class Revolution.* Oxford: Oxford University Press, 2020.

Landemore, Hélène. *Democratic Reason: Politics, Collective Intelligence, and the Rule of the Many.* Princeton, NJ: Princeton University Press, 2017.

Open Democracy: Reinventing Popular Rule for the Twenty-First Century. Princeton, NJ: Princeton University Press, 2020.

LaPorte, Charles. "Morris's Compromises: On Victorian Editorial Theory and the Kelmscott Chaucer." In *Writing on the Image: Reading William Morris,* edited by David Latham, 209–220. Toronto: University of Toronto Press, 2007.

Larmore, Charles. *What Is Political Philosophy?* Princeton, NJ: Princeton University Press, 2020.

Lawton, George. *The American Caucus System: Its Origin, Purpose, and Utility.* New York: Putnam, 1885.

Leatham, E. A. *The Ballot – Technically Considered.* Manchester: National Reform Union, 1871.

Lenoe, Matthew E. *The Kirov Murder and Soviet History.* New Haven, CT: Yale University Press, 2010.

Lepore, Jill. *If Then: How the Simulmatics Corporation Invented the Future.* New York: W. W. Norton, 2020.

"Rock, Paper, Scissors: How We Used to Vote." *New Yorker,* October 6, 2008. www.newyorker.com/magazine/2008/10/13/rock-paper-scissors.

Lefort, Claude. *Democracy and Political Theory.* Minneapolis: University of Minnesota, 1988.

Levitsky, Steven, and Daniel Ziblatt. *How Democracies Die.* New York: Crown, 2018.

Levinson, Marjorie. *The Romantic Fragment Poem: A Critique of a Form.* Chapel Hill: University of North Carolina Press, 1986.

L. F. P. "The Parliamentary Elections and the British Electoral System." *The Public* (February 4, 1910), 101–105.

Lichtman, Allan J. *The Embattled Vote in America.* Cambridge, MA: Harvard University Press, 2018.

Lippman, Walter. *The Phantom Public.* New York: Transaction Publishers, 1993.

Lloyd's Register of British and Foreign Shipping: Rules & Regulations for the Construction and Classification of Steel Vessels. London: Lloyd's Register, 1898.

Longstreet, James. *From Manassas to Appomattox: Memoirs of the Civil War in America.* Philadelphia: J. B. Lippincott Company, 1896.

López, Ian Haney. *Dog Whistle Politics: How Coded Racial Appeals Have Reinvented Racism & Wrecked the Middle Class.* Oxford: Oxford University Press, 2014.

Lubbock, John. *Representation.* London: Swan Sonnenschein & Co., 1885.

Lukács, Georg. *History and Class Consciousness: Studies in Marxist Dialectics.* Cambridge: Massachusetts Institute of Technology Press, 1972.

The Historical Novel. Lincoln: University of Nebraska Press, 1983.

The Theory of the Novel: A Historico-Philosophical Essay on the Forms of Great Epic. Cambridge: Massachusetts Institute of Technology Press, 1974.

MacCarthy, Fiona. *William Morris: A Life for Our Time.* New York: Alfred A. Knopf, 1995.

Macdonald, Dwight. "Beat Me, Daddy." *Partisan Review* 12(2) (Spring 1945), 181–187.

MacKay, Alfred F. *Arrow's Theorem: The Paradox of Social Choice.* New Haven, CT: Yale University Press, 1980.

Mackie, Gerry. *Democracy Defended.* Cambridge: Cambridge University Press, 2003.

Magnus, Philip. *Gladstone: A Biography.* New York: E. P. Dutton & Co., 1954.

Mansbridge, Jane J. *Beyond Adversary Democracy.* Chicago: University of Chicago Press, 1983.

Martel, Michael. "Romancing the Folk Mote: William Morris, the Socialist League, and Local Direct Democracy." *Useful and Beautiful: Newsletter of the William Morris Society* (Summer 2018), 7–17.

Maskin, Eric, and Amartya Sen, eds. *The Arrow Impossibility Theorem.* New York: Columbia University Press, 2014.

Mason, Robert. *Richard Nixon and the Quest for a New Majority.* Chapel Hill: University of North Carolina Press, 2004.

Mazzei, Patricia. "How a Sham Candidate Helped Flip a Florida Election." *The New York Times*, March 19, 2021. www.nytimes.com/2021/03/19/us/florida-senate-race-fraud.html.

McCaskill, Nolan D. "After Trump's Loss and False Fraud Claims, GOP Eyes Voter Restrictions Across Nation." *Politico*, March 15, 2021. www.politico.com/news/2021/03/15/voting-restrictions-states-475732.

McClanahan, Annie. "Methodological Individualism and the Novel in the Age of Microeconomics, 1871 to the Present." In *Timelines of American Literature*, edited by Cody Marrs and Christopher Hager, 264–282. (Baltimore: Johns Hopkins University Press, 2019.

McClosky, Herbert. "Consensus and Ideology in American Politics." *American Political Science Review* 58(2) (June 1964): 361–382.

McCormick, John P. *Machiavellian Democracy.* Cambridge: Cambridge University Press, 2011.

McCumber, John. *The Philosophy Scare: The Politics of Reason in the Early Cold War.* Chicago: University of Chicago Press, 2016.

McLean, Iain, Alistair McMillan, and Burt L. Monroe. "Editor's Introduction." In *The Theory of Committees and Elections,* by Duncan Black. Edited by Iain McLean, Alistair McMillan, and Burt L. Monroe. New York: Springer Science & Business, 1998.

Menand, Louis. *The Free World: Art and Thought in the Cold War.* New York: Farrar, Straus, & Giroux, 2021.

Mencken, H. L. *Notes on Democracy.* New York: Dissident Books, 2008.

Mill, John Stuart. *Autobiography.* London: Penguin, 1990.

Considerations on Representative Government. Charleston, SC: BiblioBazaar, 2007.

On Liberty and The Subjection of Women. Edited by Alan Ryan. London: Penguin Books, 2006.

Personal Representation. Speech of John Stuart Mill, Esq., MP, Delivered in the House of Commons, May 29, 1867. London: Henderson, Rait, & Fenton, 1867.

"Recent Writers on Reform." In *Dissertations and Discussions: Political, Philosophical, and Historical.* Vol. 4, 51–100. New York: Henry Holt, 1874.

Thoughts on Parliamentary Reform. London: John W. Parker & Son, 1859.

Miller, David A. "Deliberative Democracy and Social Choice." In *Democracy*, edited by David Estlund, 289–307. Oxford: Blackwell, 2002.

Hidden Hitchcock. Chicago: University of Chicago Press, 2016.

The Novel and the Police. Berkeley: University of California Press, 1988.

Miller, J. Hillis. *The Ethics of Reading: Kant, de Man, Eliot, Trollope, James, and Benjamin.* New York: Columbia University Press, 1987.

Miller, James. *Can Democracy Work? A Short History of a Radical Idea, from Ancient Athens to Our World.* New York: Picador, 2019.

Minnite, Lorraine C. *The Myth of Voter Fraud.* Ithaca, NY: Cornell University Press, 2010.

Moore, Barrington, Jr. *The Social Origins of Dictatorship and Democracy: Lord and Peasant in the Making of the Modern World.* Boston: Beacon Press, 1993.

Monmouth University Polling Institute. "Biden Leads But Many Anticipate Secret Trump Vote." July 15, 2020. www.monmouth.edu/polling-insti tute/reports/monmouthpoll_pa_071520/.

Morgan, Edmund S. *Inventing the People: The Rise of Popular Sovereignty in England and America.* New York: W. W. Norton, 1989.

Morrell, Jennifer. "I Watched the GOP's Arizona Election Audit. It Was Worse than You Think." *Washington Post*, May 19, 2021. www.washingtonpost .com/outlook/2021/05/19/gop-arizona-election-audit/.

Morris, May. *Introduction to The Collected Works of William Morris*, Vol. 20. Edited by May Morris. Cambridge: Cambridge University Press, 1913.

Morris, William. *The Collected Letters of William Morris, Volume I: 1848–1880.* Edited by Norman Kelvin. Princeton, NJ: Princeton University Press, 2016.

The Collected Letters of William Morris, Volume II. Edited by Norman Kelvin. Princeton, NJ: Princeton University Press, 2014.

The Collected Works of William Morris. Edited by May Morris. 24 vols. London: Longmans, Green, & Company, 1910–1915.

For Whom Shall We Vote? London: Commonweal, November 1895.

How I Became a Socialist. Edited by Owen Hatherley and Owen Holland. London: Verso Books, 2020.

Journalism: Contributions to Commonweal, 1885–1890. Edited by Nicholas Salmon. Bristol: Thoemmes Press, 1996.

Political Writings: Contributions to Justice and Commonweal 1883–1890. Edited by Nicholas Salmon. Bristol: Thoemmes Press, 1994.

"Statement of Principles of the Hammersmith Socialist Society." In Oscar Lovell Triggs, *Chapters in the History of the Arts and Crafts Movement.* London: Industrial Art League, 1902.

"Whigs, Democrats, & Socialists." In *Signs of Change*, edited by May Morris. London: Longmans, Green, and Company, 1895.

William Morris's Socialist Diary. Edited by Florence Boos. London: The Journeyman Press, 1985.

Morris, William, and E. Belfort Bax. *Socialism: Its Growth & Outcome*. London: Swan Sonnenschein & Co., 1893.

Mouffe, Chantalle. *The Democratic Paradox*. London: Verso, 2009.

Muñoz, José. *Cruising Utopia: The Then and There of Queer Futurity*. New York: New York University Press, 2009.

Mutch, Deborah. "Re-Righting the Past: Socialist Historical Narrative and the Road to the New Life." *Literature & History* 18(1) (Spring 2009), 16–34.

Neale, R. S. "H. S. Chapman and the 'Victorian Ballot.'" *Australian Historical Studies* 12(48) (1967), 506–521.

New York Times Editorial Board. "Congress Needs to Defend Vote Counting, Not Just Vote Casting." *The New York Times,* June 4, 2021. www.nytimes .com/2021/06/04/opinion/voting-law-rights-congress.html?action=click& module=Opinion&pgtype=Homepage.

Nguyen, Viet Thanh "Speak of the Dead, Speak of Viet Nam: The Ethics and Aesthetics of Minority Discourse." *CR: The New Centennial Review* 6(2) (2006), 7–37.

Niebuhr, Reinhold. *Major Works on Religion and Politics*. New York: Library of America, 2015.

Nixon, Richard M. *Into the Arena: A Memoir of Victory, Defeat, and Renewal*. New York: Simon & Schuster, 1990.

Six Crises. New York: Doubleday & Company, 1962.

Norris, Pippa. *Strengthening Electoral Integrity*. Cambridge: Cambridge University Press, 2017.

Why Elections Fail. Cambridge: Cambridge University Press, 2015.

Notopoulos, James A. "Parataxis in Homer: A New Approach to Homeric Literary Criticism." *Transactions and Proceedings of the American Philological Association* 80 (1949), 1–23.

Ober, Josiah. "Review Article: The Nature of Athenian Democracy." *Classical Philology* 84(4) (October 1989), 322–334.

"Old Oligarch." *The Constitution of the Athenians Attributed to Xenophon*. Edited by J. L. Marr and P. J. Rhodes. Liverpool: Liverpool University Press, 2008.

Oppenheimer, Joe. *Principles of Politics*. Cambridge: Cambridge University Press, 2012.

Pareto, Vilfredo. "Summary of Some Chapters of a New Treatise on Pure Economics by Professor Pareto." *Giornale degli Economisti e Annali di Economia* 67(3) (December 2008), 453–504.

Pearlstein, Rick. *Nixonland: The Rise of a President and the Fracturing of America*. New York: Scribner, 2009.

Pepper, John Henry. *The Playbook of Metals: Including Personal Narratives of Visits to Coal, Lead, Copper, and Tin Mines; With A Large Number of Interesting Experiments*. London: George Routledge & Sons, 1869.

Perman, Michael. *Struggle for Mastery: Disfranchisement in the South, 1888–1908.* Durham: University of North Carolina Press, 2001.

Peters, Jeremy W. "'Hidden' Trump Voters Exist. But How Much Impact Will They Have?" *The New York Times,* August 16, 2020. www.nytimes.com/2020/08/16/us/politics/trump-polls.html.

Peterson, William S. *The Kelmscott Press: A History of William Morris's Typographical Adventure* Berkeley: University of California Press, 1991.

Petronius. *The Satyricon and The Apocolocyntosis.* Edited and translated by J. P. Sullivan. New York: Penguin Books, 2005.

Phillips, Amber. "Examining the Arguments against Voting by Mail: Does It Really Lead to Fraud or Benefit Only Democrats?" *Washington Post,* May 20, 2020. www.washingtonpost.com/politics/2020/05/20/what-are-arguments-against-voting-by-mail/.

Phillips, Kevin P. *The Emerging Republican Majority.* Princeton, NJ: Princeton University Press, 2012.

Pinckney, Darryl. *Blackballed: The Black Vote and US Democracy.* New York: New York Review of Books, 2020.

Plato. *Republic.* Translated by G. M. A. Grube. Hackett, 1992.

Plotz, John. *Semi-Detached: The Aesthetics of Virtual Experience since Dickens.* Princeton, NJ: Princeton University Press, 2017.

Poe, Edgar Allan. Selected Poetry and Tales. *Edited by James Hutchisson.* Guelph, ON: Broadview Press, 2012.

Polanyi, Michael. *The Tacit Dimension.* Chicago: University of Chicago Press, 2009.

Popper, Karl. *The Open Society and Its Enemies.* Princeton, NJ: Princeton University Press, 2013.

Posner, Eric A. *The Demagogue's Playbook: The Battle for American Democracy from the Founders to Trump.* New York: St. Martin's Publishing Group, 2020.

Poundstone, William. *Gaming the Vote.* New York: Hill & Wang, 2008.

Poundstone, William. *Prisoner's Dilemma.* New York: Anchor Books, 1993.

Przeworski, Adam. *Capitalism and Social Democracy.* Cambridge: Cambridge University Press, 1985.

    "Minimalist Conception of Democracy: A Defense." In *The Democracy Sourcebook,* edited by Ian Shapiro, José Antonio Cheibub, and Robert Dahl, 12–17. Cambridge: Massachusetts Institute of Technology Press, 2003.

    Why Bother With Elections? New York: Wiley, 2018.

    The Putney Debates. Edited by Philip Baker. London: Verso Books, 2007.

Rahv, Philip. "The Sense and Nonsense of Whittaker Chambers." *Partisan Review* 19(4) (July–August 1952), 472–482.

    "Trials of the Mind." *Partisan Review* 4(5) (April 1938), 3–11.

Ranney, Austin. *Curing the Mischiefs of Faction: Party Reform in America.* Berkeley: University of California Press, 1975.

    "Farewell to Reform – Almost." In *Elections in America,* edited by Kay Lehman Schlozman. Boston: Allen & Unwin, 1987.

Rasberry, Vaughn. *Race and the Totalitarian Century: Geopolitics in the Black Literary Imagination*. Cambridge, MA: Harvard University Press, 2016.

R. C. S. "The Burial of Latane: A Touching Incident of the Civil War Recalled." In *Southern Historical Society Papers, Volume XXIV*, edited by R. A. Brock, Richmond, VA: The Southern Historical Society, 1896.

Reynolds, Andrew, Ben Reilly, and Andrew Ellis. *Electoral System Design: The New International IDEA Handbook*. Stockholm: International Institute for Democracy and Electoral Assistance, 2005.

Riker, William. *Liberalism against Populism: A Confrontation between the Theory of Democracy and the Theory of Social Choice*. Long Grove, IL: Waveland Press, 1988.

Riser, R. Volney. *Defying Disfranchisement: Black Voting Rights Activism in the Jim Crow South, 1890–1908*. Baton Rouge: Louisiana State University Press, 2010.

Robbins, Alfred F. "'Caucus' in English Politics." *Notes and Queries* ser. 8-VI(147) (October 20, 1894), 309–310.

Robbins, Lionel. "Interpersonal Comparisons of Utility: A Comment." *The Economic Journal* 48(192) (December 1938), 635–641.

Robert, Henry Martyn. *Parliamentary Law*. New York: D. Appleton-Century Company, 1923.

Robert's Rules of Order. Edited by Sarah Corbin Robert. New York: Scott, Foresman, 1970.

Robert's Rules of Order. Edited by Rachel Vixman. New York: Jove Books, 1977.

Robin, Corey. *The Reactionary Mind: Conservatism from Edmund Burke to Donald Trump*. Oxford: Oxford University Press, 2018.

Rogan, Tim. *The Moral Economists: R. H. Tawney, Karl Polanyi, E. P. Thompson, and the Critique of Capitalism*. Princeton, NJ: Princeton University Press, 2017.

Rogers, Daniel T. *Age of Fracture*. Cambridge, MA: Harvard University Press, 2011.

Rogin, Michael. *Ronald Reagan, the Movie and Other Episodes in Political Demonology*. Berkeley: University of California Press, 1988.

Rousseau, Jean-Jacques. *Emile: Or, on Education*. Translated by Allan Bloom. New York: Basic Books, 1979.

The First and Second Discourses. Translated by Roger Masters and Judith Masters. New York: St. Martin's Press, 1964.

The Social Contract. Translated by Maurice Cranston. London: Penguin, 1968.

Runciman, David. *The Confidence Trap: A History of Democracy in Crisis from World War I to the Present*. Princeton, NJ: Princeton University Press, 2017.

Rushing, Ellie, Chris Brennan, and Jonathan Lai. "'Bad Things Happen in Philadelphia,' Trump Says at Debate, Renewing False Claim about Poll Watchers." *Philadelphia Inquirer*, September 29, 2020. www.inquirer.com/poli tics/election/trump-poll-watchers-philadelphia-early-voting-20200929.html.

Safire, William. *Safire's Political Dictionary*. New York: Random House, 1978.

Salib, Peter, and Guha Krishnamurthi. "Post-Election Litigation and the Paradox of Voting." *The University of Chicago Law Review Online*, March, 10, 2021. https://lawreviewblog.uchicago.edu/2021/03/10/salib-krishnamurthi-election/.

Sartre, Jean-Paul. "Elections: A Trap for Fools." *New Indicator* 6(4) (November 4–17, 1980): 1, 4.

Saunders, R. Frank, Jr., and George A. Rogers. "Joseph Thomas Robert and the Wages of Conscience." *Georgia Historical Quarterly* 88(1) (Spring 2004), 1–24.

Scammon, Richard M., and Ben J. Wattenberg. *The Real Majority: An Extraordinary Examination of the American Electorate*. New York: Coward, McCann, & Geoghegan, Inc., 1970.

Scarry, Elaine. *On Beauty and Being Just*. Princeton, NJ: Princeton University Press, 2001.

Dreaming by the Book. New York: Farrar, Straus, & Giroux, 1999.

Schmitt, Carl. *The Concept of the Political*. Translated by George Schwab. Chicago: University of Chicago Press, 1996.

The Crisis of Parliamentary Democracy. Translated by Ellen Kennedy. Cambridge: Massachusetts Institute of Technology Press, 1988.

Schor, Naomi. *Reading in Detail: Aesthetics and the Feminine*. London: Routledge, 2006.

Schumacher, E. F. *Small Is Beautiful: Economics as if People Mattered*. New York: Harper Perennial, 2010.

Schumpeter, Joseph. *Capitalism, Socialism, and Democracy*. New York: Harper Perennial, 2008.

Schwarz, Roberto. *Misplaced Ideas: Essays on Brazilian Culture*. Translated by John Gledson. London: Verso Books, 1992.

Scully, Richard. "The Lion and the Unicorn – William Gladstone and Benjamin Disraeli Through William Empson's Looking-Glass." *International Journal of Comic Art* 15(1) (Spring 2013), 323–337.

Sen, Amartya. *Collective Choice and Social Welfare: An Expanded Edition*. Cambridge, MA: Harvard University Press, 2017.

The Idea of Justice. Cambridge, MA: Harvard University Press, 2009.

Rationality and Freedom. Cambridge, MA: Harvard University Press, 2004.

Shapiro, Ian. *The Real World of Democratic Theory*. Princeton, NJ: Princeton University Press, 2010.

Shaw, Bernard. *Collected Letters, 1874–1897*. Edited by Dan H. Laurence. London: Max Reinhardt, 1965.

Shawcross, William. *Sideshow: Kissinger, Nixon, and the Destruction of Cambodia*. New York: Cooper Square Press, 1979.

Shell, Marc. *Stutter*. Cambridge, MA: Harvard University Press, 2009.

Shklar, Judith. *Men and Citizens: A Study of Rousseau's Social Theory*. Cambridge: Cambridge University Press, 1985.

Sidney, Sir Philip. *Sidney's "The Defence of Poesy" and Selected Renaissance Literary Criticism*. Edited by Gavin Alexander. London: Penguin, 2004.

Sieyès, Emmanuel Joseph. *Political Writings*. Translated by Michael Sonenscher. Indianapolis, IN: Hackett, 2003.

Sleat, Matt. "Introduction: Politics Recovered – On the Revival of Realism in Contemporary Political Theory." In *Politics Recovered: Realist Thought in Theory and Practice*, edited by Matt Sleat, 1–26. New York: Columbia University Press, 2018.

Sloterdijk, Peter. *Critique of Cynical Reason*. Translated by Andreas Huyssen. Minneapolis: University of Minnesota Press, 1987.

Smalley, Donald. *Anthony Trollope: The Critical Heritage*. London: Routledge, 1995.

Smith, George Barnett. *The Life of the Right Honourable William Ewart Gladstone: Popular Edition*. London: Cassell, Petter, Galpin, & Co., 1880.

Smith, Goldwin. *The Elections to the Hebdomadal Council: A Letter to the Rev. C. W. Sandford, M. A.* Oxford: James Parker & Co., 1866.

Smith, Sydney. *Ballot*. London: Longmans, Green, & Company, 1871.

Sneed, Tierney, and Matt Shuham. "How the Far-Right's Dream of Undermining Arizona's Mail Voting Turned into a Reality." *Talking Points Memo*, March 17, 2021. https://talkingpointsmemo.com/news/how-the-far-rights-dream-of-undermining-arizonas-mail-voting-turned-into-a-reality.

Somin, Ilya. *Democracy and Political Ignorance*. Stanford: Stanford University Press, 2016.

Spaulding, A. F. "Report." In *Journal of Seventeenth Annual Session of the Department of Indiana Grand Army of the Republic*. Indianapolis, IN: Sentinel Publishing Co., 1896.

Stahl, Jeremy. "Arizona's Republican-Run Election Audit Is Now Looking for Bamboo-Laced 'China Ballots.'" *Slate*, May 5, 2021. https://slate.com/news-and-politics/2021/05/arizona-republican-audit-bamboo-ballots-china.html.

"Statement of Concern: The Threats to American Democracy and the Need for National Voting and Election Administration Standards." *New America*, June 1, 2021. www.newamerica.org/political-reform/statements/statement-of-concern/.

Steinlight, Emily. *Populating the Novel*. Ithaca, NY: Cornell University Press, 2018.

Sterne, Simon. *On Representative Government and Personal Representation*. Philadelphia: J. B. Lippincott & Co., 1871.

Sutherland, Robert D. *Language and Lewis Carroll*. Ann Arbor: University of Michigan, 1970.

Tafuri, Manfredo. *The Sphere and the Labyrinth: Avant-Gardes and Architecture from Piranesi to the 1970s*. Translated by Pellegrino d'Acierno and Robert Connolly. Cambridge: Massachusetts Institute of Technology Press, 1990.

Taylor, Astra. *Democracy May Not Exist But We'll Miss It When It's Gone*. New York: Henry Holt, 2019.

Thompson, C. S. *An Essay on the Rise and Fall of the Congressional Caucus as a Machine for Nominating Candidates for the Presidency*. New Haven, CT: Yale University Press, 1902.

Thompson, Dorothy. *The Dignity of Chartism*. London: Verso Books, 2015.

Thompson, E. P. *Customs in Common*. New York: The New Press, 1993.

William Morris: Romantic to Revolutionary. Oakland, CA: PM Press, 2011.

Thompson, Paul. *The Work of William Morris*. New York: Viking Press, 1967.

Thompson, John W. "Coombs' Theory of Data." *Philosophy of Science* 33(4) (December 1966), 376–382.

Tocqueville, Alexis de. *Democracy in America*. Translated by Harvey C. Mansfield and Delba Winthrop. Chicago: University of Chicago Press, 2002.

Trilling, Lionel. *Sincerity and Authenticity*. Cambridge, MA: Harvard University Press, 1973.

Trollope, Anthony. *An Autobiography,* edited by Nicholas Shrimpton. Oxford: Oxford University Press, 1980.

Doctor Thorne. Edited by David Skilton. Oxford: Oxford University Press, 1980.

Phineas Finn. Edited by Simon Dentith. Oxford: Oxford University Press, 2011.

Victoria and Tasmania. London: Chapman and Hall, 1875.

U. S. Civil Rights Commission. "Registration in Forrest County, Mississippi." In *American Party Politics: Essays and Readings*, edited by Donald G. Herzberg and Gerald M. Pomper. New York: Holt, Rinehart, & Winston, Inc., 1966.

US Election Assistance Commission. *Election Management Guidelines*. Washington, DC: Election Assistance Commission, 2006.

Valelly, Richard M. *The Two Reconstructions: The Struggle for Black Enfranchisement*. Chicago: University of Chicago Press, 2004.

Van Reybrouck, David. *Against Elections*. Translated by Liz Waters. New York: Seven Stories Press, 2018.

Vernon, James. *Politics and the People: A Study in English Political Culture c.1815–1867*. Cambridge: Cambridge University Press, 1993.

Viebeck, Elise, and Robert Costa. "Trump's Assault on Election Integrity Forces Question: What Would Happen If He Refused to Accept a Loss?" *Washington Post*, July 22, 2020. www.washingtonpost.com/politics/trumps-assault-on-election-integrity-forces-question-what-would-happen-if-he-refused-to-accept-a-loss/2020/07/22/d2477150-caae-11ea-b0e3-d55bda07d66a_story.html.

Wald, Alan M. *American Night: The Literary Left in the Era of the Cold War*. Durham: University of North Carolina Press, 2012.

The New York Intellectuals: The Rise and Decline of the Anti-Stalinist Left from the 1930s to the 1980s. Durham: University of North Carolina Press, 2017.

Waldman, Michael. *The Fight to Vote*. New York: Simon & Schuster, 2016.

Ware, Alan. *The American Direct Primary: Party Institutionalization and Transformation in the North*. Cambridge: Cambridge University Press, 2002.

Watt, Ian. *The Rise of the Novel: Studies in Defoe, Richardson and Fielding*. Berkeley: University of California Press, 2001.

Weber, Max. *Economy and Society*. Translated by Keith Tribe. Cambridge, MA: Harvard University Press, 2019.

Weiner, Greg. "The Shallow Cynicism of 'Everything Is Rigged.'" *The New York Times,* August 25, 2019. www.nytimes.com/2019/08/25/opinion/trump-warren-sanders-corruption.html.

White, Hayden. *Metahistory: The Historical Imagination in Nineteenth-Century Europe.* Baltimore: Johns Hopkins University Press, 2014.

Whitman, Walt. *Democratic Vistas and Other Papers.* London: Walter Scott, 1888.

Williams, Bernard. *In the Beginning Was the Deed: Realism and Moralism in Political Argument.* Edited by Geoffrey Hawthorn. Princeton, NJ: Princeton University Press, 2009.

Williams, David Lay. "The Substantive Elements of Rousseau's General Will." In *The General Will: The Evolution of a Concept,* edited by David Lay Williams and James Farr, 219–246. Cambridge: Cambridge University Press, 2015.

Williams, George F. "Lights and Shadows of Army Life." *Century Magazine* 28(6) (October, 1884), 803–819.

Williamson, Kevin. "Why Not Fewer Voters?" *National Review,* April 6, 2021. www.nationalreview.com/2021/04/why-not-fewer-voters/.

Wills, Garry. *Nixon Agonistes: The Crisis of the Self-Made Man.* Boston: Mariner Books, 2002.

Wittgenstein, Ludwig. *Philosophical Investigations.* Translated by G. E. M. Anscombe. Oxford: Blackwell, 1958.

Wolf-Meyer, Matthew J. *Theory for the World to Come: Speculative Fiction and Apocalyptic Anthropology.* Minneapolis: University of Minnesota Press, 2019.

Wollheim, Richard. "A Paradox in the Theory of Democracy." In *Philosophy, Politics, and Society,* edited by Peter Laslett and W. G. Runciman. Oxford: Basil Blackwell, 1964.

Woloch, Alex. *The One vs. the Many: Minor Characters and the Space of the Protagonist in the Novel.* Princeton, NJ: Princeton University Press, 2003.

Or Orwell: Writing and Democratic Socialism. Cambridge, MA: Harvard University Press, 2016.

Woodward, C. Vann. *The Strange Career of Jim Crow.* Oxford: Oxford University Press, 2002.

Xiang, Sunny. "The Ethnic Author Represents the Body Count." *PMLA* 133(2) (2018), 420–427.

Young, Edward. "The Revenge. A Tragedy." In *The Works of Edward Young.* Vol. 2, 185–239. London: J. Dodsley, 1798.

Younis, Mohamed. "Most Americans Favor Voting by Mail as Option in November." *Gallup,* May 12, 2020. https://news.gallup.com/poll/310586/americans-favor-voting-mail-option-november.aspx.

Zaveri, Mihir, and Alan Yuhas. "Where Does All the Swag Go after Campaigns Fail? Everywhere." *The New York Times, last modified* March 5, 2020. www.nytimes.com/2020/02/25/us/politics/leftover-campaign-shirts-hats-mugs.html.

Zerilli, Linda M. G. *A Democratic Theory of Judgment*. Chicago: University of Chicago Press, 2016.

Ziblatt, Daniel. *Conservative Parties and the Birth of Democracy*. Cambridge: Cambridge University Press, 2017.

Index